ROOSEVELT'S SECOND ACT

PIVOTAL MOMENTS IN AMERICAN HISTORY

Series Editors

David Hackett Fischer
James M. McPherson
David Greenberg

James T. Patterson
Brown v. Board of Education:
A Civil Rights Milestone and Its
Troubled Legacy

Maury Klein
Rainbow's End: The Crash of 1929

James McPherson
Crossroads of Freedom: The Battle of
Antietam

Glenn C. Altschuler
All Shook Up: How Rock 'n' Roll
Changed America

David Hackett Fischer
Washington's Crossing

John Ferling
Adams vs. Jefferson: The Tumultuous
Election of 1800

Joel H. Silbey
Storm over Texas: The Annexation
Controversy and the Road
to Civil War

Raymond Arsenault
Freedom Riders: 1961 and the Struggle
for Racial Justice

Colin G. Calloway
The Scratch of a Pen: 1763 and the
Transformation of North America

Richard Labunski
James Madison and the Struggle for the
Bill of Rights

Sally McMillen
Seneca Falls and the Origins of the
Women's Rights Movement

Howard Jones
The Bay of Pigs

Elliott West
The Last Indian War:
The Nez Perce Story

Lynn Hudson Parsons
The Birth of Modern Politics: Andrew
Jackson, John Quincy Adams, and the
Election of 1828

Glenn C. Altschuler and
Stuart M. Blumin
The GI Bill: A New Deal for Veterans

Richard Archer
*As If an Enemy's Country: The British
Occupation of Boston and the Origins of
Revolution*

Thomas Kessner
*The Flight of the Century: Charles
Lindbergh and the Rise of American
Aviation*

Craig L. Symonds
The Battle of Midway

Also by Richard Moe

*The Last Full Measure: The Life and Death of
the First Minnesota Volunteers
Changing Places: Rebuilding Community in
the Age of Sprawl* (coauthor)

RICHARD MOE

ROOSEVELT'S SECOND ACT

The Election of 1940 and the Politics of War

OXFORD
UNIVERSITY PRESS

OXFORD

UNIVERSITY PRESS

Oxford University Press is a department of the University of Oxford.
It furthers the University's objective of excellence in research,
scholarship, and education by publishing worldwide.

Oxford   New York
Auckland   Cape Town   Dar es Salaam   Hong Kong   Karachi
Kuala Lumpur   Madrid   Melbourne   Mexico City   Nairobi
New Delhi   Shanghai   Taipei   Toronto

With offices in
Argentina   Austria   Brazil   Chile   Czech Republic   France   Greece
Guatemala   Hungary   Italy   Japan   Poland   Portugal   Singapore
South Korea   Switzerland   Thailand   Turkey   Ukraine   Vietnam

Oxford is a registered trademark of Oxford University Press
in the UK and certain other countries.

Published in the United States of America by
Oxford University Press
198 Madison Avenue, New York, NY 10016

Library of Congress Cataloging-in-Publication Data
Moe, Richard.
Roosevelt's second act : the election of 1940 and the
politics of war / Richard Moe.
pages   cm
Includes bibliographical references and index.
ISBN 978-0-19-998191-5
1. Presidents—United States—Election—1940.
2. Roosevelt, Franklin D. (Franklin Delano), 1882–1945.
3. United States—Politics and government—1933–1945.
4. United States—Foreign relations—1933–1945.
5. Presidents—Term of office—United States.
6. World War, 1939–1945—United States. I. Title.
E811.M58   2013
973.917092—dc23   2013004529

1 3 5 7 9 8 6 4 2

Printed in the United States of America
on acid-free paper

To Julia

That quality of simplicity which we delight to think marks the great and noble was not his. He was the most complicated human being I ever knew; and out of this complicated nature there sprang much of the drive which brought achievement, much of the sympathy which made him like, and liked by, such oddly different types of people, much of the detachment which enabled him to forget his problems in play or rest, and much of the apparent contradiction which so exasperated those associates of his who expected "crystal clear" and unwavering decisions. But this very complication of his nature made it possible for him to have insight and imagination into the most varied human experiences, and this he applied to the physical, social, geographical, economic and strategic circumstances thrust upon him as responsibilities of his time.

Frances Perkins

CONTENTS

EDITOR'S NOTE

For much of 1939 and 1940, Franklin Delano Roosevelt was thinking about two big decisions he had to make—two of the biggest decisions in all of American history. The first was whether to seek an unprecedented third term as president. The second was whether to go to war.

He knew his mind on the latter better than on the former.

Despite rampant isolationism on both the left and the right, Roosevelt firmly grasped that the United States couldn't sit idly by while Hitler and the Germans lay waste to Western Civilization. Indeed, ever since his waters-testing speech in October 1937 calling for a "quarantine of aggressor nations," and through his drive to revise the misguided Neutrality Acts of the mid-thirties, FDR had been readying the public to confront the eventual necessity of war. Yet the president had to move slowly and deliberately. If he were to outrun public opinion, he wouldn't be able to lead at all.

But if Roosevelt was cagey about his intentions in Europe, when it came to breaking with the presidential tradition of serving only two terms he was downright opaque. This issue provoked intense curiosity. Ever since George Washington and Thomas Jefferson foreswore any interest in continuing their tenures in office, the injunction that presidents should retire after eight years in the White House had become nearly inviolable. And Roosevelt, who had already been caricatured as a power-mad dictator by rightists hostile to his activism, was sensitive to overstepping boundaries.

Still, for month upon month as pundits kibitzed about his plans, FDR played his cards close to his vest—so close, in fact, that he seemed barely able to glimpse them himself. At the December 1939 Gridiron Club dinner, during which the press corps routinely roasted the president amid song and libation, members wheeled out an eight-foot-tall papier-mâché sphinx featuring Roosevelt's already iconic grinning mug and cigarette holder. Of the towering creature they asked: "Will you run? / Or are you done?"

In the audience that night, FDR laughed as hard as anyone. And the papier-mâché sphinx remains to this day on view at his presidential library in Hyde Park.

The riddle of how and when Roosevelt made up his mind to seek a third term perplexed not only the press corps at the time but also the president's closest confidants, and even his wife, Eleanor. It has also for decades bedeviled historians, who have tried to form judgments based on a fragmentary and unreliable documentary record.

It is but one achievement of Richard Moe, in his splendid account of these years, that he has offered the fullest and most patient analysis of all the relevant information on the elusive subject of Roosevelt's pivotal decision to seek a third term in 1940. Moe doesn't give us a single eureka moment in which the president suddenly makes up his mind. Rather, he recounts a continuous flow of events—the political and international narratives elegantly intertwined—in which FDR, genuinely unsure of what he wanted to do, tacks and gybes in order to keep his options open; then, as the Democratic convention nears, the president has, as if by sleight of hand, dispensed with all credible challengers. But even then Roosevelt is coy. With the nomination securely in hand, he is shown—in a strange, fascinating final twist—ready to forsake it all so as to get the vice president he wants, Henry A. Wallace.

The Franklin Roosevelt that Moe limns in this gripping volume is familiar insofar as he is shrewd, inconstant, mischievous, and deeply political. But it is also a well-rounded portrait that highlights the surprising depth of Roosevelt's convictions, including his growing confidence that the Democratic Party was best equipped to lead the nation in the coming world war and that he was best equipped in the four years ahead to lead the Democratic Party.

Indeed, Moe shows that the decision to gird for war with Nazi Germany and Imperial Japan and the choice to seek a third term cannot be understood in isolation from each other. The coming war helped confirm FDR in his decision to run, and, once he was renominated, it gave him the issue with which to defeat his Republican challenger, the hapless Wendell Willkie. "Franklin Roosevelt is not running against Wendell Willkie," remarks a Republican observer, in one of many telling details that Moe discerningly included. "He's running against Adolf Hitler." Having led the nation through Depression, Roosevelt would soon bring upon himself the burden of leading America through world war.

David Greenberg

PREFACE

With the exception of Abraham Lincoln, no American president has been subjected to more scrutiny than Franklin Delano Roosevelt. That's not surprising, given that FDR dominated the great events of his time as completely as Lincoln had those of his own. The difference is that Roosevelt had a direct role in shaping not only the country but the world that succeeded him. Just as there are with Lincoln, there are thousands of books on Roosevelt. Why do we need another one?

This book answers that question. Nearly everything written about the Roosevelt presidency has focused on the New Deal of his first two terms or his leadership during the world war of his third and fourth terms. Very little has been written about the period, and especially the election, that bridges these two epochal achievements. None has sought to uncover in detail what lay behind Roosevelt's decision to stand for an unprecedented third term or attempted to use FDR's momentous decision as its primary focus. There has been an inclination by many to conclude that the decision was inevitable, that he had decided long before July 1940 to break the two-term tradition established by Washington and Jefferson and regarded as inviolable for a century and a half. Several presidents, among them FDR's boyhood hero and distant cousin Theodore, had tried to breach the tradition, but none had succeeded. There was nothing inevitable about Franklin Roosevelt's decision. He made it as he made all of his major decisions—virtually alone and not before the last possible moment, which is to say not until he had to. In the end, this decision by this most complicated human being, as Frances Perkins put it, was shaped decisively by the circumstances—extraordinary circumstances—that had been thrust upon him.

By compressing the narrative into a short time span, mainly the years 1939–40, this book focuses heavily on the interplay of events and characters, with FDR always at center stage. It is meant to revive the ultimate political mystery, even as the outcome is known to all: what was going on in the president's head? This is no simple question to answer at any time, but it is much more difficult when the president leaves no written record. Unlike all of his successors with the exception of John F. Kennedy, Roosevelt did not live to write his memoirs. That fact, plus FDR's unwillingness to reveal his thought process even to his closest associates, makes it extremely challenging to explore how he approached the great questions he faced.

What we have are the written accounts of those closest to him, and our understanding of the historical context in which those decisions were made. The election of 1940 took place in the context of the outbreak of war in Europe and, as I will argue, was inextricably linked to it. With the New Deal having run its course, Roosevelt's focus shifted to an effort to save the democracies, and especially Great Britain, by getting them the assistance they needed to survive the onslaught of Adolf Hitler. Given the strength of isolationist sentiment in the United States, that effort required him to confront the question of whether he should run for a third term.

This book attempts to assemble the elements of these two inextricably linked moving parts into a narrative leading up to and beyond what can be argued was one of the most consequential presidential decisions of the twentieth century, which led to a pivotal moment in American history. Roosevelt's third term not only affected the course of the United States on the eve of the most horrific war in history but also affected how the world would be after it was over.

Most immediately, of course, it would place a supremely confident and gifted leader at the helm during the war that he believed, well before the 1940 election, was coming to America. Nonetheless, FDR couldn't have known the full extent to which his decision would change the longer trajectory of history. His determination to save Britain and defeat Hitler would result in replacing isolationism, which had characterized the country's foreign policy since its inception, with his own brand of internationalism. Thereafter the United States would remain enmeshed in the affairs of the world, in peacetime as well as in war. The decision would also change the nature of the presidency, as its authority would be hugely expanded by Roosevelt's assumption of extraordinary powers immediately before and after the 1940 election. And as a result of these developments, the American electorate came to view the presidency, and the qualifications established for its occupant, differently.

Roosevelt's decision to seek a third term, and then a fourth, the latter when he was clearly ill and visibly impaired, prompted the newly empowered Republicans to ensure after his death that such a thing would never happen again. Finally settling the issue that the Philadelphia Convention of 1787 had failed to resolve, the Congress and a sufficient number of state legislatures amended the Constitution of the United States to limit future presidents to two terms.

While FDR was approaching his decision about a third term, his essential duality came into play more clearly than at any other point in his presidency: the bold, perceptive, prescient, and moral statesman who set lofty and principled goals, and the cautious, ambitious, and sometimes arrogant and manipulative politician he could be in pursuit of those goals. Biographers and historians have struggled to understand and explain this duality—James MacGregor Burns famously called it "the lion and the fox"—and I don't claim to have succeeded where they did not. I have simply sought to set those two aspects of Roosevelt in bold relief so that the reader can perhaps determine what to make of this obsessively solitary and brilliantly social individual, and appreciate the nature of the huge decision that was his to make.

Knowing that the decision lay ahead kept his advisors, the press, the leaders of the Democratic Party, and much of the nation in a growing state of suspense from September 1939, when Hitler invaded Poland, until July 1940, when the Democratic National Convention convened in Chicago. Roosevelt kept everyone guessing. Reporters and political cartoonists took to depicting him as a "sphinx." During all that time the president essentially debated with himself. In the end, he would make the decision about his second act in his own way and according to his own script.

ROOSEVELT'S SECOND ACT

Introduction

History Repeating Itself

Franklin Delano Roosevelt was an unusually sound sleeper. At fifty-seven and well into the seventh year of his presidency, he had long since developed the habit of sleeping through the night apparently unencumbered by whatever concerns weighed on him during the day. In the early morning hours of Friday, September 1, 1939, Roosevelt was wakened by a White House operator, who said that William Bullitt, the U.S. ambassador to France, was calling from Paris.

Bullitt, an experienced diplomat and longtime advisor to the president, reported that he had just heard from his counterpart in Warsaw, who was unable to get through to Washington, that German troops and armored columns had crossed the border into Poland and were advancing rapidly. German aircraft were simultaneously bombing major Polish cities, including Warsaw. With Britain and France having pledged to defend Poland from precisely this kind of invasion, Roosevelt knew immediately that the event he most feared was about to occur—a major war in Europe, and perhaps beyond. "Well, Bill," he said, "it has come at last. God help us all."[1]

The president immediately called his secretary of state, Cordell Hull, and Hull's undersecretary, Sumner Welles, as well as the secretaries of war and the navy. He also alerted his acting press secretary, William Haslett, instructing him to break the news to the White House press corps. Few would be shocked on hearing of this latest development in the long-unfolding saga of Adolf Hitler's relentless pursuit of *Lebensraum,* or new living space, for the German people, and in the process abrogating the harsh terms imposed on Germany by the Treaty of Versailles following the Great War. His strategy of intimidating Germany's neighbors with his formidable armed forces had been highly effective, resulting in bloodless occupations of the Rhineland, Austria, the Sudetenland of Czechoslovakia, and finally the rest of that beleaguered nation.

But Poland was different. Poland was a sovereign nation much admired in the West for its history and culture. Once again the victim of its geography, it was the next logical target of Hitler's designs, and the Poles were determined to resist him with everything they had. The potential loss of Poland as a free nation was seen as too much even for the very elastic policy of appeasement to accommodate. In the spring of 1938 Britain had hastily and unilaterally promised to come to the aid of the Poles in the event of a German incursion into Polish territory. France, whose fortunes in Europe were inextricably linked to those of Britain, followed suit, leaving the fate of the two nations tied to that of Poland. Now the question was whether the Western powers would live up to their promise or, once again, accommodate Hitler's aggression.

As officials and journalists all over Washington raced to their offices through the early morning darkness, the president of the United States, knowing there was nothing more for him to do at the moment, went back to bed. His struggle to resume physical independence after suffering near-total paralysis from polio years before had taught him patience and discipline. He would approach this crisis as he had others. First, however, he would sleep.

He was awakened again at six-thirty with another call from Bullitt—the first had come just before three in the morning—who reported that French premier Edouard Daladier had just assured him that France would definitely abide by its pledge to Poland. Given France's recent track record on such commitments, this had been anything but certain, and even now some doubts may have persisted. Again Roosevelt returned to sleep, but after just a few minutes he was awakened once more with a call from Joseph P. Kennedy, the U.S. ambassador in London. Kennedy, who was close to Chamberlain's government and a supporter of its appeasement policy, had been arguing that Poland should make concessions to Germany to avoid armed conflict. With that armed conflict now a reality, he was convinced that Britain would declare war. This, the despondent ambassador told the president, meant "the end of the world, the end of everything."[2] Roosevelt, who knew Kennedy's moods and views well, wasn't buying into pessimism. He never had and wasn't about to start now.

By this point FDR was awake for good and made no attempt to return to sleep. He called his wife, Eleanor, at their home in Hyde Park, New York, with the news; she said later that her thoughts went back to the June visit of the king and queen of England "and the lump that had come into my throat as they stood on the back platform of their departing train. Now their people faced the final hour of decision."[3] The president sat up in bed and ate his breakfast while scanning the daily newspapers in a room that he had shaped to his liking. "Like every room in any Roosevelt house," Arthur Schlesinger had noted, "the presidential bedroom was hopelessly Victorian—old-fashioned and indiscriminate in its furnishings, cluttered in its décor, ugly and comfortable."[4] An assortment of nautical prints covered the walls, while an odd collection of pigs and family photographs decorated the mantle above the fireplace. He used a small table beside his narrow bed as a mini desk, and on it were paper, pencils, and two phones.

Finishing the newspapers, he called for Marguerite "Missy" LeHand, his confidential secretary, to begin the day's work. She didn't have far to come, living as she did on the third floor of the White House. She had been with FDR longer and was more devoted to him than nearly anyone else in his official family. Beginning in the 1920 vice presidential campaign and continuing through his long and difficult recovery from polio as well as his gubernatorial and presidential campaigns, Missy had become the central figure in FDR's workday; cabinet members and ambassadors courted her favor to gain access to the president or to glean a hint of his thinking.

She was the essence of loyalty and discretion, and her understanding of Roosevelt and her close relationship with him enabled her to be much more than a conventional secretary. She could anticipate nearly his every need as well as whom he would want to see, and she was not hesitant to speak her mind to him when she thought he was wrong. Missy was totally devoted to FDR; he was her entire life. When she arrived this morning he gave her orders and requests for information to be sent to officials throughout the government. It was the president's custom to begin his workday in bed, usually surrounded by staff and cabinet members tending to whatever happened to be on his mind that morning. On his mind this morning was the likelihood of a major war in Europe and what it would mean for the United States.

Soon the president called for his valet, Irvin McDuffie, an African American former barber whom he had met in Warm Springs, Georgia, and who also lived, with his wife, on the third floor. McDuffie helped Roosevelt get out of bed, snapped his heavy steel leg braces in place, and dressed him. When he was ready, an usher pushed his custom-built wheelchair to the elevator and then across Jefferson's colonnade to the West Wing, conceived and built by FDR's boyhood hero and fifth cousin, Theodore, as the principal offices of the president and his staff. Speechwriter Robert Sherwood often watched the crippled president on his way to work and saw him "as the people believed him to be—the chin up—and the air of irrepressible confidence that whatever problems the day might bring he would find a way to handle them."[5] And so it would be this day with a major war on the horizon.

After again greeting Missy, now stationed just outside his door, he entered the Oval Office to begin his official day by holding a regularly scheduled Friday press conference. The Oval Office hadn't always been oval, having seen several redesigns since his cousin Theodore's presidency, and FDR's attempt in 1933 to make it more distinguished, more accessible for his wheelchair, and more private was the most recent. Working with a staff architect—FDR loved playing architect himself—he added prominent Georgian details, such as pediments over the doorways, deep crown molding, and bookcases set into niches. A large medallion of the presidential seal was placed in the ceiling. He created the Oval Office essentially as it still exists, including the tradition of placing two high-backed chairs in front of the fireplace at the opposite end of the room from the desk for the president and visiting dignitaries to be pictured seated, a requirement for FDR since he could not stand unassisted. This morning, as always, he was seated at a wooden desk cluttered with ceramic donkeys, a ship's clock, and assorted other memorabilia that he had collected over time. The desk was flanked by the American and presidential flags, and in back of the seated president were three large windows draped in heavy red velvet opening on the South Lawn. His broad shoulders, thick neck, and large chest complemented his cheerful demeanor to convey a picture of vigor and robust health, the desk obscuring his withered legs.

The hall door opened, and a cadre of reporters hungry for news was ushered in, assembling by rank and seniority, with the wire services claiming the front row, the most prominent dailies standing behind them, and the rest scattered randomly around the back of the room. Roosevelt liked to engage in casual banter with the reporters while playing with the objects on his desk. He knew that they enjoyed these exchanges as much as he did, and the custom helped maintain a friendly and informal air in their relationship. He frequently called the reporters by their first names, as he did with others, conveying an easy familiarity that was of course flattering. Most important, he gave them what they wanted, access and news, and they gave him in return what he wanted, fair and balanced coverage. This symbiotic arrangement largely obviated the frosty if not quite hostile relationship FDR had with their publishers, most of whom had fervently opposed the New Deal. After Roosevelt quipped about how early they had all risen that morning, an usher announced, "All in!" before closing the door.

The president quickly assumed a more serious tone and said that regarding developments in Poland he didn't have any news that they didn't already have. He didn't yet know when Congress would be called into session or when a proclamation of neutrality would be issued, as required by law. Eventually he was asked the question "uppermost in the minds of the American people today," as one reporter phrased it: "Can we stay out?" Roosevelt had anticipated the question. "I not only sincerely hope so, but I believe we can," he said with deliberate care, and "every effort will be made by the Administration so to do." The governing rule in these sessions was that everything FDR said was off the record and intended only for background or guidance. He was not to be quoted directly unless he gave his permission. Asked if he could be quoted directly on this last statement, he said yes.[6]

At a cabinet meeting later in the day FDR recalled that when he received the early morning message from Bullitt he had an eerie sense of being back in his old post as assistant secretary of the navy during the First World War, when other urgent messages awakened him in the night. It was "like picking up again an interrupted routine," he said. "Unless some miracle beyond our present grasp changes the hearts of men the days ahead will be crowded days—crowded with the same problems, the same anxieties that filled to the brim those September days of 1914. For history does in fact repeat."[7]

The president underscored his point from the press conference—that the United States would do everything possible to avoid being drawn into the war. Urging the cabinet to appreciate the difference between preparing for war and preparing for problems related to war, Secretary of State Cordell Hull quoted him as saying, "Pay attention only to the latter, because we are not going to get into war."[8]

The atmosphere in the White House that day was hectic but orderly, according to Grace Tully, FDR's other principal secretary. Having been called into work at 7:00 a.m. by Missy LeHand to help out, Tully installed herself in the Lincoln Bedroom, down the hall from FDR's, to receive and organize the numerous messages pouring in from embassies abroad and from officials in Washington. The mood of the day, she recalled later, was "crisp and businesslike. Orders had to be given. People had to be summoned for consultation. Proclamations had to be issued." Tully attributed "this somewhat impersonal mood" to the fact that "we had been following the course of the gathering storm and knew in advance when and how it would break."[9]

Two days later Britain and France declared war on Germany. Chamberlain's decision to act had to be bolstered by loud hectoring from members of Parliament from all sides, who saw his appeasement policy crashing and burning in Poland. To the disappointment of many of them, he declined to resign. France, having failed, as expected, to receive a response from Berlin to its ultimatum, followed. History was indeed repeating itself.

―――――――

When Roosevelt wanted to explain his most important policies to the American people, he invariably did so through his "fireside chats." The president of the United States was able to command the airwaves of the nation for up to an hour to address millions of his fellow citizens by radio, although he seldom required that much time. It was a technique that he had begun using while governor of New York and had perfected as president. Roosevelt understood the power of direct communication that radio offered. No longer would his pronouncements have to appear solely on a printed page or be filtered through the words of others. However carefully prepared, these talks employed a conversational tone that was intended to make it seem as if he felt right at home in living rooms and kitchens all over America.

Roosevelt had the ability to make complex issues understandable to ordinary people without talking down to them. His skill in using this new form of communication was arguably the most effective tool in his political kit. "He was the first great American voice," David Halberstam noted. "For most Americans of this generation, their first memory of politics would be sitting by a radio and hearing that voice, strong, confident, totally at ease.... Most Americans in the previous 160 years had never even seen a President; now almost all of them were hearing him, in their own homes. It was literally and figuratively electrifying."[10]

The largest audiences were usually available on Sunday evenings, when entire families would huddle around the radio to listen to their favorite programs such as *The Chase and Sanborn Hour*, featuring the ventriloquist Edgar Bergen and his dummy, Charlie McCarthy. So it was Sunday evening that FDR preferred for his chats. He asked for airtime on September 3, for the fourteenth fireside chat of his presidency, to talk about the events then unfolding in Europe. He spoke only a few hours after the formal declarations of war had been issued in London and Paris.

"I have said not once, but many times," he began, "that I have seen war and that I hate war. I will say that again and again. I hope that the United

States will keep out of this war. I believe that it will. And I give you my assurance and reassurance that every effort of your Government will be directed toward that end." There were two other points that he made to help Americans understand the broader implications of the war. The first was that, as much as it might want to, the country could not ignore the war: "Passionately though we may desire detachment, we are forced to realize that every word that comes through the air, every ship that sails the sea, every battle that is fought, does affect the American future."

The other point was more indirect: that while America would "remain a neutral nation," the president could not also ask that every American remain neutral in "thought." Being neutral did not mean that citizens couldn't face facts and make their own determination as to what those facts meant.[11] Roosevelt was painting the larger picture for his listeners, reassuring them about the immediate while at the same time urging them to look beyond the immediate and informing them that a dangerous world lay beyond their shores, one that the nation could not ignore.

The address was that of a lifelong internationalist speaking to a nation that was largely isolationist. While acknowledging the country's wariness of foreign entanglements and pledging to keep it out of war, Roosevelt also signaled his sympathies for the victims in this new conflict. His ear was finely attuned to public opinion; polls would reveal shortly that while the overwhelming majority of Americans wanted the United States to stay out of the war, almost as many hoped that Britain and France would prevail. That was certainly Roosevelt's view.

While France had the larger army, the president looked primarily to Britain to thwart Hitler's advance, though he had little confidence that Chamberlain was up to the task. After the prime minister's appeasement policy failed in Poland, he was compelled to bring Winston Churchill into his cabinet as First Lord of the Admiralty, the same position he had held during World War I. Churchill had been the most prominent critic of Chamberlain's appeasement policy in the Conservative Party if not in the nation. Roosevelt had met Churchill for the first time in 1918, when FDR was assistant secretary of the navy; to Roosevelt's chagrin, Churchill later did not remember that occasion. "He acted like a stinker at a dinner I attended, lording it over all of us," the president told Joe Kennedy, speaking of that first meeting. Nonetheless, he saw "a strong possibility" that Churchill would soon be Chamberlain's successor, and he decided to open a private channel of communication with him.[12] "I shall at all times welcome it if you will keep me in touch personally with anything you want me to know about," Roosevelt wrote Churchill, inviting him to ignore formal bureaucratic channels and instead "send sealed letters through your [diplomatic] pouch or my pouch."[13] Thus began one of history's most important relationships.

Staying removed from foreign wars had become such a tenet of American thought that it was embodied in law. In 1935 Congress had passed and Roosevelt had signed, reluctantly, a revision of the Neutrality Act that prohibited, among other things, the sale of armaments to belligerents in foreign conflicts. The arms embargo made no distinction between those who committed aggression and those who were its victims, a provision that FDR strongly disliked and that he had since been urging Congress, unsuccessfully, to revise. Nonetheless, on September 5, two days after his chat, he invoked the embargo, as required by law, but soon thereafter called Congress into special session to ask for repeal of the embargo provisions, which he called "most vitally dangerous to American neutrality, American security and, above all, American peace."[14] Roosevelt believed that prospects for peace were best served by having the ability to sell weaponry to nonaggressor nations such as Britain and France, which he saw as America's first line of defense against Nazism's worldwide ambitions. Isolationists saw it very differently, believing that repeal of the arms embargo would mean in effect taking sides in the conflict and setting the country on a slippery slope toward war. The lines were very clearly drawn.

Isolationists at this time consisted of many disparate groups—Christian pacifists, Norman Thomas socialists, the German-American Bund, Communists, business leaders, and countless others, including many New Dealers who fervently believed that the country needed to concentrate on its own economic problems. The isolationist voice that surfaced first and most prominently in these new circumstances was that of an iconic American hero, Charles A. Lindbergh.

In 1927, at age twenty-five, Lindbergh had become the first person to fly alone across the Atlantic Ocean, a feat that many had thought impossible. He was widely acclaimed for his courage, stamina, and skill, all of which were undeniable, and the triumph earned him the nickname "Lucky Lindy." Now, in the fall of 1939, it was the old idea that America should not become entangled in the affairs of other nations that propelled Lindbergh once again into the American spotlight, this time as the chief spokesman for the millions of his fellow citizens who wanted desperately to stay out of the war. A product of the traditionally isolationist upper Midwest and the son of a Minnesota congressman who had opposed entry into World War I, he needed little persuasion to fill this role. Four days after FDR's fireside chat, Lindbergh decided, with the encouragement of conservative friends, to enter the fray. "I do not intend to stand by and see this country pushed into war if it is not absolutely essential to the future welfare of the nation. Much as I dislike taking part in politics and public life," he added in a statement no one could doubt, "I intend to do so if necessary to stop the trend which is now going on in this country." With the assistance of the conservative commentator Fulton Lewis Jr., he agreed to deliver a national radio address the following week.[15]

"Won't it be strange," Lindbergh's wife, Anne, wrote her mother-in-law, "if Charles will be fighting the same fight as his father, years ago!"[16] Thus it was on the evening of September 15, just twelve days after Roosevelt's address to the nation, that Lindbergh arrived at the Carlton Hotel in Washington, just two blocks from the White House across Lafayette Square, to speak to an audience as large as the president's had been.

Roosevelt had learned of Lindbergh's plan, and he didn't like it. As a result, the aviator was visited in his hotel room earlier that day by his old friend Truman Smith, who, as military attaché in Berlin, had guided him through three tours of German aircraft facilities to assess the strength and technical proficiency of the Luftwaffe. Smith, now a colonel, had been sent by Gen. H. H. "Hap" Arnold, chief of the U.S. Army Air Corps. Arnold's message, Smith reported, was that the president was prepared to offer Lindbergh a new "secretaryship for air" in the cabinet if he declined to deliver his address. It was a clumsy move on Roosevelt's part; Lindbergh said it did not surprise him. What did surprise him was that the president could believe that he might be tempted by such an offer.[17]

That evening, instead of directly addressing the question of repealing the arms embargo, Lindbergh sought to lift the debate to another plane. The national hero urged his countrymen to see the world situation with cold detachment, not allowing "our sentiment, our pity, or our personal feelings of sympathy, to obscure the issue, to affect our children's lives. We must be," as he put it, "as impersonal as a surgeon with his knife." He argued that America should never enter a war unless there was absolutely no other recourse, and he made the case forcefully that such was not the situation here. "We must either keep out of European wars entirely," he added, "or stay in European affairs permanently." Then Lindbergh embarked on a discourse that one biographer called "his synthesis of years of xenophobic thinking." America was not being threatened by an "Asiatic intruder," such as a Genghis Khan or a Xerxes. "This is not a question of banding together to defend the White race against foreign invasion. This is simply one more of those age old quarrels within our own family of nations—a quarrel arising from errors of the last war—from the failure of the victors of that war to follow a consistent policy of fairness or of force."[18] So long as America did not "decay from within," as he put it, there was no need to fear an invasion.[19] Thus the lines were drawn between the two best-known and most-admired people in America; while both said they wanted to keep the United States out of the war, they—and the country—were sharply divided on how to do so.

So the stage was set. War had been declared but, with the notable exception of Poland, there was as yet no armed conflict. No one believed that Hitler's ambitions would end there. His pattern had been to target one vulnerable country after another. Now that he had effectively divided up eastern Europe with Stalin, it was logical that he would turn his sights to the west. Thus Britain and France mobilized their forces behind the latter's supposedly impregnable Maginot Line, where they would await the inevitable attack.

In the United States Roosevelt was walking a very fine line. As a longtime internationalist who believed that the United States should be engaged with the rest of the world, he had followed developments in Europe closely, and in the last few years very closely. He loathed Hitler and the menace he represented to the continent and ultimately to the world; he was determined to do whatever he could to stop him, short of committing the United States to war. But his confidence in the ability of the political leadership in Britain and France to lead a successful effort against Hitler was slight, and he harbored equally serious doubts that their military forces could withstand the German juggernaut. Giving the Allies all assistance "short of war," as he had put it earlier, meant getting them the means of defeating Hitler. They would need additional tanks, aircraft, and other equipment from abroad, and there was only one country capable of providing that matériel. But America couldn't provide it without repealing the arms embargo of the Neutrality Act.

There were isolationists in both parties in Congress, and they were supported by large segments of the press as well as millions of people around the country. They were determined to keep the country out of this war, and there was a plausible case to be made that selling arms to belligerents brought the nation closer to it. In making the opposite case—that helping the Allies to prevail was more likely to keep the country out of war—FDR faced one of the greatest challenges of his presidency. There was no knowing who was right on this question. History provided little guidance.

Roosevelt walked this fine line with seeming confidence and vigor, but his political standing was at a low ebb. After his overwhelming reelection in 1936, he had pulled back on federal spending, and the country had slipped into the "Roosevelt recession" when two million more workers were laid off work. Then he suffered the most serious congressional defeat of his presidency in 1937 when he sought approval to "pack" the Supreme Court with new members to overcome the opposition of the current majority, which was thwarting major pieces of his New Deal program. In perhaps the most audacious act of his presidency, he sought, without consulting Congress or barely anyone else, to radically transform one of the bedrock institutions of American democracy; he was unceremoniously slapped down for what was widely seen as arrogance. The next year, the 1938 congressional elections had seen a record number of Democrats lose their seats, and the president received a good deal of the blame. Many who survived were bitter that he had tried to purge the Democratic Party of conservatives who had opposed his domestic program. There was a strong belief in Congress as well as in the country as a whole that the New Deal had effectively run its course. The heady enthusiasm generated by passage of program after program in the first term was gone, and many thought there was little that remained that could—or should—be done.

Therefore the president was playing a weak hand. Moreover, he had just over a year to serve in his second term, and at this point virtually everyone, himself included, assumed that he would be retiring to his home in Hyde Park when that time came. After George Washington had set the precedent, there was an almost sacrosanct rule in American presidential politics that a chief executive should serve no more than two terms. Roosevelt never openly took issue with that precedent, and he was actively planning for retirement. When he broke ground for his presidential library in Hyde Park that September, it was with the intention that it would be completed well before his departure from the presidency on January 20, 1941. It was here where he planned to spend most of his time after leaving the White House, organizing his papers, writing his memoirs, and playing the role of senior statesman. In the fall of 1939 he told his longtime speechwriter Sam Rosenman that he was considering a proposal to write an autobiography and he already had in hand a lucrative three-year contract to write regular articles for *Collier's* magazine. The president wanted Rosenman to come along to help. Harry Hopkins, his most trusted aide, planned to buy a house nearby. FDR had already designed and built Top Cottage, the modest but comfortable retreat at Hyde Park, remote from the Big House, where he could work on his papers and relax with his cherished stamp collection without fear of intrusion. (As a condition for allowing him to build it on property that she still owned, however, his mother, Sara, made him promise that he would not sleep overnight there as long as she was alive.)[20] Retirement was on Roosevelt's mind, and he enjoyed anticipating it.

Nonetheless, if he announced his intentions publicly, he would be increasingly seen as politically irrelevant, a lame duck president whom members of Congress and foreign leaders could ignore with impunity. He was at his core a man of *action*—to him the ability to act was the political equivalent of the ability to breathe—and there was no way that he would forgo that ability if he could help it. Therefore he would say nothing until events compelled him to break his silence.

After seven years in office Franklin Roosevelt had arrived at a place where no other president had quite been before—caught up in an international crisis fraught with dangers posed by both action and inaction, one that demanded maximum flexibility and freedom of action. There was no history to guide him; the experiences of such two-term presidents as Jefferson, Jackson, and Wilson offered no relevant lessons. At heart he wanted to help the democracies of Europe to survive, but without drawing his country into war, and he had precious little time to act. His chief adversary, Adolf Hitler, was well aware of the popular and congressional limitations on Roosevelt's ability to act. The decisions that FDR—and the country—would face in the next year would make 1940 one of the most fateful in history. Roosevelt, who had over the years developed a keen sense of the theatrical, sensed the level of the drama involved, as did the rest of the world.

It was only fitting that a playwright-turned-speechwriter, Robert Sherwood, best reflected this view when he wrote that the situation confronting the president represented "the greatest problem any President had faced at least since Lincoln made the determination against the urgent advice of all his Cabinet to send relief to Fort Sumter."[21] The parallels with Lincoln would continue throughout Roosevelt's presidency, but they would never be as salient as they would be in the coming year.

F. Scott Fitzgerald had famously observed a few years earlier that there were no second acts in American lives. In the case of Franklin Roosevelt, who saw himself as, among other things, an actor, he was wrong. The curtain was going up on the second act.

1

Shifting Gears

Franklin Roosevelt's first term as president had been consumed almost entirely by trying to lift the country out of the most serious economic crisis it had ever known. Essentially improvising, he used his first one hundred days in office in 1933, and then a second hundred days in 1935, to send program after program to Congress, programs that when enacted constituted the New Deal and represented an unprecedented effort to improve the lives of ordinary people. All this dramatically expanded the role of government, and it worked. After four years millions of unemployed Americans were back at work, and millions more had food and shelter to sustain them through the hard times. The Great Depression was by no means over, but for the first time since it began people had confidence that the government in Washington, and particularly the president leading it, was on their side. He gave them hope, and they gave him a second term in 1936 in a resounding vote of confidence.

Roosevelt's second term would see his attention move gradually toward events abroad. Even before his reelection, Roosevelt was compelled to acknowledge the dual threats coming from Germany and Italy. In early 1935 Hitler thumbed his nose at the Treaty of Versailles by announcing that his country intended to build a large army as well as an air force. Simultaneously Italy under Benito Mussolini reinforced its army in Italian East Africa with the clear intention of moving against adjacent Ethiopia. "These are without doubt the most hair-trigger times the world has gone through in your lifetime or mine," FDR told his ambassador in Rome. "I do not even exclude June and July 1914."[1] Convinced that the United States had to begin rebuilding its own meager armed forces, he proposed a record-breaking $1.1 billion defense budget.

The combination of these events caused students, New Dealers, and veterans, among others, to take to the streets in protest. Pacifist sentiment in the country was wide and deep, stemming as it did from a belief that desperate powers in Europe aided by greedy financiers and munitions makers at home had lured America into the tragically unnecessary First World War. Trading with the Allies during the early years of the war, it was argued, had led inevitably to U.S. involvement in the conflict, a mistake now compounded by the unpaid war loans to Britain and France. The lesson, therefore, was that it would be a fool's errand to go down that road again: the United States should be strictly neutral in any future conflict and barred from financial dealings with any belligerent, whether the aggressor or the victim of aggression. Even before Charles Lindbergh's 1939 speech supporting neutrality, public rallies and newspaper editorials echoed this view, which quickly found its voice in Congress.

Roosevelt read public and congressional opinion to mean that some form of neutrality legislation was likely if not inevitable, but he hoped to put it off so that it wouldn't interfere with his heavy domestic agenda, or at least to modify it to allow maximum presidential flexibility and discretion. After several weeks of jousting with congressional leaders, he finally capitulated to save his domestic program. The final bill, enacted in August 1935, placed a mandatory embargo on "arms, ammunition, or implements of war" to all belligerents; the only concession Roosevelt could wring from Congress was to limit the embargo provisions to six months. Although Roosevelt rationalized it as an acceptable compromise, he felt strongly enough about his chief objections to it that he emphasized them at the signing. "History is filled with unforeseeable situations that call for some flexibility of action," he said. He was concerned that the limitations would have an effect opposite to what they intended. "In other words, the inflexible provisions might drag us into a war instead of keeping us out."[2] Preserving the president's ability to conduct foreign policy was the key issue in FDR's mind, and he was neither the first president nor the last to fight to preserve that prerogative. Optimistic and confident of his own abilities as always, he believed that he could persuade Congress to change the provisions when they expired in six months.

In early 1936 Hitler made the first of his moves to reassert German sovereignty and to expand German territory. In violation of the Treaty of Versailles and the Locarno Pact of 1925, he ordered his military to reoccupy land on both sides of the Rhine River bordering France. The lessons of history had persuaded the French that the Rhineland should never again be home to German forces, which is what the Locarno Treaty, with Germany as a signatory, had promised. France was understandably alarmed by the unexpected move but, like Great Britain, had no appetite to do anything more than protest. It was the first of Hitler's successful efforts to intimidate the Western nations into acquiescence.

Although still preoccupied with his domestic program during his first term, Roosevelt spent increasing amounts of time following events abroad. He feared Hitler's long-range intentions in Europe, and his instincts told him that the United States could not ignore these developments and had to deal with them realistically. The seeds of that thinking had first been instilled in him during frequent travels as a child—he visited Europe eight times by age fourteen—and later as a student at Groton and Harvard, experiences that left him with the belief that engagement with the world was in the natural order of things. By far the greatest influence on his thinking, however, was his exposure to Woodrow Wilson's form of progressive internationalism when he served as assistant secretary of the navy for nearly eight years. The young Roosevelt especially absorbed the concepts of self-determination, with an emphasis on democracy, and collective security, but more than anything else the experience imbued in him a sense of idealism in dealing with world affairs. During the course of World War I Wilson became convinced that the United States was inextricably linked to the rest of the world and needed to shed its historic isolationism, and Roosevelt took the lesson to heart. His embrace of Wilson's vision of internationalism was almost certainly furthered by its postwar popularity, particularly within the Democratic Party, to whose leadership Roosevelt was already aspiring.

As an observer at the Versailles treaty negotiations in 1918 and especially after an intimate shipboard conversation with President Wilson returning from Europe, Roosevelt became a fervent supporter of America's entry into the League of Nations, the apotheosis of internationalism to that point in American history. When isolationism came back into the ascendancy in the 1920s, however, causing the Democratic Party to walk away from the League, so too did Roosevelt. As a candidate for president in 1932, when the Great Depression clearly overshadowed events abroad, he deeply disappointed internationalists when he succumbed to expediency and went so far as to repudiate the League. But at his core FDR remained an idealist when it came to world affairs, although his version of idealism over time came to be more nuanced and more pragmatic than Wilson's rigid approach.

A year into his second term FDR confronted what he saw as a dangerous situation abroad that neither he nor the country could any longer ignore. In a Chicago speech in October 1937 he rediscovered his internationalist impulses and gave them full voice. Citing examples of unprovoked aggression and the sinking of ships without cause or notice, he charged that an "epidemic of world lawlessness is spreading. When an epidemic of physical disease starts to spread, the community approves and joins in a quarantine of the patients in order to protect the health of the community against the spread of the disease."[3]

A crowd of a hundred thousand Chicagoans who had come to hear the president dedicate a Works Progress Administration (WPA) bridge roared its approval for what speechwriter Sam Rosenman called "Roosevelt's first direct appeal in behalf of collective security as distinguished from isolationism and from impartial, blind neutrality."[4] But immediately after the speech the president lunched with Chicago cardinal George Mundelein, the New Deal's strongest supporter in the Catholic hierarchy, and gave a more nuanced view of what he had meant. He was not proposing military action "against unjust aggressor nations," Cardinal Mundelein recorded, "nor does it involve 'sanctions' as generally understood, but rather a policy of isolation, severance of ordinary communications in a united manner by all the governments in the pact."[5]

The reaction to the speech beyond Chicago was "quick and violent— and nearly unanimous," Rosenman recalled. Many saw it as "warmonger- ing and saber-rattling." The press attacks were particularly harsh, charging that the speech was "more likely to promote war than peace." Isolationists and several Republican members of Congress called for the president's im- peachment for putting the country on the road toward war. Democrats in Congress—and even some in his own administration, such as Secretary of State Hull, the former senator from Tennessee, with whom he did not con- sult on the quarantine language—said nothing in the president's defense, which he naturally found galling. Rosenman would explain that Roosevelt had made a rare mistake in "trying to lead the people of the United States too quickly, and before they had been adequately informed of the facts or spiritually prepared for the event."[6]

FDR was unprepared for the strong response and the degree of hos- tility behind it. The Chicago speech was his first serious venture into the foreign policy arena, and as he quickly learned, the American people were still both totally preoccupied with hardships at home and content with their distance from events abroad. The president recognized his miscalculation immediately and backed off. Pressed at a news confer- ence the next day to define what he had meant, Roosevelt demurred. In fact, he concluded that he wasn't sure what he had meant, but he was sure now that this early plea for collective security with echoes of Wil- sonianism was too much for a nation that had resisted the concept for almost its entire history, most emphatically in rejecting Wilson's League of Nations. A British newspaper commented that the speech represent- ed more an attitude than a program. Rather than advocating a policy of sanctions, historian Robert Dallek observed, its real intent was "to give expression to his long-standing desire to find some new concept for pre- serving peace."[7]

"It's a terrible thing," the president told Rosenman afterward, "to look over your shoulder when you are trying to lead—and to find no one there."[8] FDR was determined that it would not happen again. The episode reinforced his innate caution in charging into foreign affairs without events to carry him. It also reinforced his belief that, much more than a president's words, only those events could significantly change public opinion. But some historians have concluded that FDR may have misread the reaction to what historian Kenneth Davis called his "flamboyant gesture toward internationalism." As fixated as Roosevelt was on isolationist sentiment in the country—probably too much so—and as fixated as the country was on domestic economic issues, there might nonetheless have existed, Davis concluded, "enough support for the collective security policy." Davis argues that FDR had lost momentum and perhaps even some nerve after the Court-packing debacle, and simply didn't have the resolve necessary to pull it off.[9] It raises a question that would recur during the next three years and right up to the election of 1940: could events on their own move public opinion, or could it be shaped by a political vision? FDR had likely concluded that the answer lay in their combination and that it would be a matter of timing.

Hitler was less patient and forced events to fit his vision. He asserted himself again in March 1938 when he effectively annexed Austria into the German Reich, again in violation of treaty provisions stemming from the end of the First World War. By this point he was convinced that he could ignore the Allies with impunity. He thought that they would be indecisive, uncoordinated in their response, and in the end gun-shy, and he was seldom disappointed in these expectations. France remained silent, Britain was passive, and the League of Nations did not even meet on the question. Seeking, as always, to maintain a balance of power in Europe as well as to defend the territorial integrity of their continental neighbors, France and Britain strongly protested these incursions, but to no avail. Unlike Hitler, the governments of Neville Chamberlain in London and Edouard Daladier in Paris were not prepared to go to war over the issue. The memory of the previous war, in which each nation lost nearly a generation of young men in the trenches of western Europe, was too fresh. Public opinion in their countries would not allow another war with Germany. They knew it and Hitler knew it, and he played it to full effect.

Hardly missing a beat since swallowing Austria, Hitler set his sights on the Sudetenland, where more than three million ethnic Germans lived in the section of Czechoslovakia created out of the wreckage of the First World War. Playing skillfully on the frustrations of those who had been separated from their homeland, the Führer contrived a crisis that threatened to break into armed conflict if the Czech government didn't cede the disputed territory. There was much hemming and hawing from the Allies but no unified or effective response that caused Hitler even to pause. With the Allies now erring "on the side of caution," one historian concluded, it "was a replay of August 1914 with the film running in reverse."[10]

Roosevelt's ambassadors in Europe urged him to take steps to negotiate a peaceful end to the crisis or to otherwise defuse it. He desired peace as much as the Europeans, but he was basically "a powerless witness, unable to influence events," as biographer Frank Freidel concluded.[11] As the leader of a nation preoccupied with its own economic recovery, possessing no credible military force and in any case divided as to what to do about the crisis, he declined the urgings of his ambassadors. In doing so, it has been argued, he abetted the prevailing policy of appeasement in Europe that he so loathed. "Unwilling to throw his weight into the balance," biographer James MacGregor Burns wrote, "the President was still confined to a policy of pinpricks and righteous protest."[12] The "pinpricks" included a telegram to Hitler on September 27, suggesting a conference of interested nations to resolve the current crisis, although Roosevelt was quick to add that the United States could not participate in such a gathering nor could it state its views on the merits of various positions.

The next day Hitler extended invitations to Mussolini of Italy, Daladier of France, and Chamberlain of Great Britain to join him in Munich to reach an agreement. When Chamberlain immediately accepted the invitation, Roosevelt wired him: "Good man."[13] The four principals gathered at noon on September 29 and worked into the early morning hours of the next day, when they agreed to cede the Sudetenland to Germany and to oversee the destruction of Czechoslovakia's fortifications. Chamberlain separately managed to get Hitler's signature on a document affirming the mutual "desire of our two peoples never to go to war with one another again." The prime minister returned to London waving the paper and declaring, famously—or infamously—"I believe it is peace in our time."[14] British aversion to armed intervention in Europe, born of the cost of the previous war, was no less powerful than the American variant. Chamberlain confidently declared that peace had been preserved through his policy of appeasement, and he was heartily applauded. At the time the word *appeasement* didn't carry the pejorative meaning it later acquired, especially in its connection to Munich. Rather, it was associated with keeping the peace, and was widely, though not universally, embraced in both Britain and France. Parliament rushed to approve a motion praising the policy "by which war was averted."

One of the few dissenters was Winston Churchill, just emerging from his "wilderness" years—out of power and out of government—who argued that this was "a total and unmitigated defeat." He warned Parliament that this was not the end of the matter. "This is only the first sip, the first foretaste of a bitter cup which will be proffered to us year by year," until and unless "we take our stand for freedom."[15]

At this point, war was inevitable, though few besides Churchill saw it at the time. Most didn't want to see it. The lingering pain of the First World War on both sides of the Atlantic prevented a clear view of that prospect, feeding as it did an inclination to be unrealistically hopeful. Roosevelt was not totally immune to these forces, and his congenital optimism was always a strong element of his thought, even though he was better positioned than most by virtue of his office to see the reality. He was realist enough to know that after the disasters of the Court-packing plan and the "Roosevelt recession"—as the newspapers delighted in calling it—his standing with the public and Congress had never been lower. Whatever he thought about the likelihood of a major war, he was still sobered by the reaction to his "quarantine" speech. FDR didn't believe he could get out ahead of the Europeans. Events would have to take their course.

Roosevelt decided that the best thing he could do to protect America was to help build a first line of defense—through Great Britain and France.

That would mean getting armaments and particularly aircraft to those countries so they could withstand and ultimately defeat the mighty German military machine. FDR was convinced, as were most observers who paid attention to such matters, that in 1938 Hitler's air force was already larger and more powerful than those of Britain, France, Czechoslovakia, and the Soviet Union combined. This "paralyzing fear" of the Luftwaffe, as one historian called it, dominated the strategic thinking of political leaders in the democracies.[16] They were rightly concerned, to be sure, though the estimates were inflated. The story of how this came about is an account of how an American hero became the unwitting instrument of a clever Nazi regime to mislead and intimidate the already timid Allied powers.

After a storybook wedding to socialite Anne Morrow and five years of celebrity, Charles A. Lindbergh's life took a tragically unlucky turn with the kidnapping of his baby, Charles junior, from a crib in his New Jersey home and his subsequent murder. Because of Lindbergh's notoriety it quickly became "the crime of the century" and a media sensation; the press relentlessly hounded Lindbergh and his family through the aftermath in a way that became intolerably painful. After the trial and conviction of Bruno Richard Hauptmann for the crime, they fled to Europe in 1935 to escape it all. They spent two years outside London, surfacing only to dine at Buckingham Palace and to socialize with the aristocracy. They then moved to a remote island off the coast of Brittany, largely so that Charles could spend time with a brilliant if controversial French scientist and biologist named Alexis Carrel, who was an admirer of Benito Mussolini and who in another context worried about the "salvation of the white races." "Eugenics is indispensable for the perpetuation of the strong," he wrote. "A great race must propagate its best elements." He and Lindbergh spent the better part of a summer discussing among other things "race betterment," paralleling discussions then under way in Germany.[17] These experiences opened Lindbergh's mind to new ideas, and many of them took hold.

In the spring of 1936, Major Truman Smith, the military attaché to the American embassy in Berlin, was frustrated in his inability to determine with any accuracy the strength and technical proficiency of the Luftwaffe.

He had the inspired idea of asking the Germans to invite Lindbergh to visit the country's factories and airfields, and perhaps even to test-fly new German aircraft. Hitler's Air Ministry enthusiastically embraced the idea, and within days a formal invitation from the minister himself, Hermann Goering, was on its way via Smith to Lindbergh. Although the visit was to be unpublicized, the Germans saw it as an opportunity to get the message to the democracies, through a famous and credible authority on airpower, that the Luftwaffe was the most powerful air force in the world and growing stronger every day. It fit perfectly into their larger strategy of intimidating those governments, a strategy that to date had worked so well.

Lindbergh was drawn to the patriotic nature of Smith's request and quickly agreed to the mission. On his arrival in July and on two subsequent trips the Germans feted the great aviation hero and threw open the gates of their military bases and production facilities for his inspection; some of them had never before been seen by an American. The numbers and technical sophistication of the aircraft he saw—and flew—surprised and impressed Lindbergh. One day Goering showed him photographs of seventy separate airfields. "I knew warplanes were being built to fill those fields," Lindbergh would write.[18] He got the message his hosts wanted him to get: Germany had the potential to dominate Europe through airpower and gave every sign of preparing for a major war.

According to Kenneth Davis, Lindbergh "was psychologically prepared to see what the Nazi leaders wanted him to see, and to draw from what he saw the conclusions his Nazi hosts wanted him to draw."[19] Smith's reports conveyed those conclusions to the War Department, where, he told Lindbergh, policy makers had finally woken up to realize the "imposing rearmament program in Germany."[20]

In a later letter to Truman Smith, Lindbergh revealed that it was not the German military alone that had impressed him: "While I have many reservations, I have come away with a feeling of great admiration for the German people." To a friend in New York he wrote that while Hitler showed signs of fanaticism, "he is undoubtedly a great man."[21]

Smith invited Lindbergh to return the following year for essentially the same purpose. Lindbergh readily agreed, and at the end of his tour he gave

Washington a detailed picture of the aircraft he had seen and an estimate of the size and strength of the entire Luftwaffe, of which he in fact had no specific knowledge.

The third visit, in 1938, was the most consequential, both for Lindbergh personally and for the information he conveyed to London, Paris, and Washington. The purpose of the tour was expanded to include an assessment of the air strength of Russia, Czechoslovakia, France, and Britain compared with that of Germany. Guy La Chambre, the French air minister, already despondent over the condition of his air force, was further shaken by what he heard from Lindbergh, who wrote later, "One is forced to the conclusion that the German air fleet is stronger than that of all the other European countries combined."[22]

Ambassador Bullitt sent Lindbergh's comparative figures to Washington, where officials found them alarming in the extreme. After meeting with the aviator in London, Ambassador Joseph Kennedy did the same with the aim of removing any doubts that appeasement was the proper course as Chamberlain headed for Munich and a showdown with Hitler. "Germany now has the means of destroying London, Paris, and Prague if she wishes to do so," Lindbergh wrote. "I am convinced that it is wiser to permit Germany's eastward expansion than to throw England and France, unprepared at this time, into a war at this time."[23] His conclusions met with little if any disagreement at Westminster.

One evening during this third tour, Goering presented the American with the Service Cross of the German Eagle with Star, Germany's second-highest medal, by "order of der Führer." Adorned with swastikas, it was accompanied by a proclamation on parchment signed by Hitler. Although Goering's remarks paid tribute to Lindbergh's crossing of the Atlantic, many would conclude that the medal was Germany's way of expressing appreciation for his help in spreading the message of its invincibility in the air. Lindbergh thought nothing of the incident at the time—he had received so many awards by this point in this life—and was surprised when a furor erupted over it in the United States. Without dissent from Roosevelt, Secretary of the Interior Harold Ickes said that Lindbergh "forfeits his right to be an American," feeding a rash of press criticism.

The golden image of Lindbergh had been tarnished during the years he had appeared to be so friendly with a Nazi regime that increasingly appeared to be brutal if not yet demonstrably evil. That evil would be revealed within weeks in the form of Kristallnacht, "Night of Broken Glass," when on a pretext Hitler ordered the burning and looting of thousands of Jewish properties, including nearly two hundred synagogues, and the indiscriminate murder and arrest of hundreds of Jews. The event uncovered the true face of the Nazi regime. Its proximity to Lindbergh's receipt of Hitler's medal was too much for many people. The aviator was increasingly seen as at best naive and over his head in international diplomacy. His reputation began to be compromised, yet he still managed to retain considerable pull in American public opinion.

Although Roosevelt had grown to dislike Lindbergh—Ickes's harsh remarks almost certainly reflected the president's own views, as they usually did—he, too, had been unwittingly affected by the aviator's inflated estimates of German air strength. And, like most Americans, he had been deeply affected by Kristallnacht, recalling the American ambassador from Berlin and telling a press conference, "I myself could scarcely believe that such things could occur in a twentieth century civilization."[24] These developments reinforced his belated misgivings over Munich and reenergized his efforts to build an effective line of defense through Britain and France. In his view this meant building enough industrial capacity to produce large numbers of warplanes, especially for France.

To bolster Britain, he sent a confidential message to Chamberlain. In the event of war with Germany, he assured the shaky prime minister, he would have "the industrial resources of the American nation behind him" to the extent that "he, the President, was able to achieve it." This message and its secret means of delivery—if Hitler didn't know of it, what was its deterrent value?—symbolized the argument that Roosevelt was then having with himself: he knew the democracies needed help and he wanted to help, but he couldn't do so openly or the isolationists in Congress and the public at large would have his hide, and then he wouldn't be able to do anything at all. At this point, stepping too far over a line with the isolationists meant that what remained of his presidency, and even the New Deal programs that were still in full force, could be crippled. It was of a piece with his decision at about the same time to authorize the sale of U.S.-manufactured warplanes of the latest design to France directly, with diplomat and businessman Jean Monnet working out the arrangements with Henry Morgenthau at Treasury. It, too, needed to be wrapped tightly in a cloak of secrecy.

The president may have been willing to use secrecy, but he preferred to move with the support of at least those within his administration. He convened a meeting in the Oval Office on November 14, 1938, of his top national security advisors with a sprinkling of others, such as Morgenthau and the WPA's Harry Hopkins, who was in the ascendancy as a broad-based counselor and confidant. Roosevelt began by hypothesizing that Hitler would not have dared to take the stand he did at Munich had the United States possessed 5,000 warplanes and an accelerated production capacity. The country faced a greater threat of attack from across the ocean than at any time since its earliest days, he argued, concluding that to protect itself it needed a fleet of 20,000 aircraft and the ability to produce up to 24,000 more annually. Since Congress was unlikely to appropriate funds for more than half those numbers, he would settle for 10,000 planes with 12,000 more each year.[25]

Roosevelt gave his advisors every impression of having carefully thought the plan through and having all but decided on it. He wasn't really inviting dissent, and he wasn't disappointed; the response for the most part was muted and noncommittal. He finally noticed Brigadier General George C. Marshall, the deputy chief of staff of the army, who was in charge of preparing the service's budget. Marshall, who was new to the position and who hoped to be named chief of staff when the incumbent retired, was a distinguished and courtly Virginian who in none of his professional relationships invited intimacy. "I think I've made a pretty good case for my program," the president said. "Don't you think so, George?" The room was absolutely silent before Marshall responded calmly but with an icy tone in his voice: "I am sorry, Mr. President, but I don't agree with that at all." Roosevelt was obviously shaken by the unexpected response; as Marshall's biographer described it, "his mobile countenance registered a dismaying realization that the general resented the use of his first name, evidently deeming it patronizing as well as deceitful in its implication of intimate acquaintance." The president quickly adjourned the meeting without seeking an elaboration from Marshall. As the advisors filed out of the Oval Office, Marshall recalled later, some of them "bade me goodbye and said that my tour in Washington was over." In fact, it had barely begun; Roosevelt came to see in Marshall the candid, intelligent, and incorruptible professional soldier he needed by his side. During more than six years working closely together, the president never again addressed him by his first name.[26] And whenever he later proposed a plan of action involving the military, he made sure it had Marshall's endorsement.

By the end of 1938 FDR had long since mastered domestic policy, but the importance of the New Deal was gradually receding as Hitler loomed ever larger on the horizon. So now Roosevelt was learning how to shift policy gears from domestic to foreign, much as he had learned how to shift gears on the hand-operated car that he had designed himself and which he used at Hyde Park. He was learning another part of his job, that of commander in chief, and he was determined to master it as well.

2

A Laying On of Hands

By 1939, retirement was very much on FDR's mind. He had already built a retreat that some were calling his "dream house," a term he intensely disliked, and he was busy overseeing virtually every aspect of what would soon become the nation's first presidential library. He needed to replenish the family finances—Sara was dipping into her capital to support Hyde Park—and to that end Harry Hopkins and Sam Rosenman had agreed to help him write his memoirs as well as pieces on current events.

But before he could retire there was the matter of who would succeed him as president. It mattered hugely to him, of course, because it would determine whether his legacy would survive his departure. Roosevelt's place in history was almost surely secured by his bold and decisive leadership during the calamitous economic crisis, but there was no guarantee that the New Deal—either its many component parts or its overarching premise, that government has an obligation to help those in need—would survive. Even though the New Deal by now had run its course, most Republicans still hated not just the specific programs but more generally what the New Deal represented, and there were signs that 1940 could well be a Republican year.

Even if Congress remained in Democratic hands, FDR's missteps in 1937 and 1938—first the Court-packing plan, and then his attempt during the off-year election to unseat congressional Democrats who had opposed his plans—had cost him a working majority, and that wasn't likely to change. Republicans and conservative Democrats had realized that by joining forces they could effectively thwart progressive initiatives. The notion that ideology trumped party would gain more currency in the years to come, but at the time the development had to remind FDR of something Woodrow Wilson had told him two decades earlier during one of their frequent conversations: "It is only once in a generation that a people can be lifted above material things. That is why conservative government is in the saddle two-thirds of the time."[1] America had already had its once-in-a-generation moment—created by economic disaster—and conservative government was now back in the congressional saddle. Moreover, a Republican president would have ways of effectively neutralizing if not eliminating New Deal programs by strangling them administratively or starving them financially.

Roosevelt owed it to the country as well as to himself, he believed, to prevent that from happening, and this meant finding someone who was a committed New Dealer and who also could be nominated and elected. That was a tall order. FDR had cast such a large shadow over the Democratic Party for so long that it was hard for anyone, including the president himself, to imagine someone else taking his place.

There was no logical or obvious successor in sight. John Nance Garner had enough public recognition as vice president to give him impressive support, but he and the New Deal—and he and FDR personally—were sufficiently out of sync to remove him from serious consideration. Moreover, he was seventy years old and determined to retire to his native Texas. Democratic Party chairman James A. Farley, who doubled as postmaster general, did have an interest in seeking the 1940 nomination, but since he was by no means a liberal and was unschooled in foreign affairs, few besides his loyalists in the party saw him as viable.

So if there was no apparent successor, FDR reasoned, he would have to create one. He would start with the man closest to him in the administration,

Harry L. Hopkins. On its face it may have appeared odd that Hopkins, the administrator of the Works Progress Administration, a purely domestic agency created to spend billions of federal dollars to support the economic recovery, was in the Oval Office meeting to discuss military preparedness. But in FDR's world there was nothing unusual about it, and none of the attendees was at all surprised that he was there. In recent years Hopkins had emerged as the single most important advisor to Roosevelt in the administration, and not just on matters related to the WPA. He had earned the unquestioned respect and affection of the president, and of Eleanor as well.

Hopkins was born in Sioux City, Iowa, in 1890, the son of a harness maker. After working his way through Grinnell College, where he was imbued with a powerful sense of social justice and civic responsibility, he found his way to the Lower East Side of New York City, where he saw slums and poverty unlike anything he had known in the Midwest. "This was his real birth as a crusader for reform," his friend and first biographer, Robert Sherwood, wrote. "The missionary impulse inherited from his mother became the most powerful force within him."[2] He threw himself relentlessly into social work and over the years earned a reputation as a brilliant innovator as well as an able administrator.

Hopkins first met Roosevelt during the latter's campaign for governor of New York State in 1928. Although he made no immediate impression on Roosevelt himself, people around him, such as FDR advisor Frances Perkins, took notice of Hopkins as someone to keep an eye on. As the Depression appeared and unemployment soared, he was enlisted to undertake the largest and most innovative relief program that any state had ever attempted. Now Hopkins caught the governor's attention: he was creative, he was fast, and he gave FDR and his political advisors little to trouble them.

President Roosevelt brought Hopkins to Washington early in his administration to do what he had done in Albany: get public money out the door quickly and efficiently to help those who were in need. Hopkins made it clear to all who would listen that the relief he was administering was not charity but rather a public obligation to those who needed assistance. He challenged past notions of social welfare, insisting it include not only food but also, in a radical departure, clothing, shelter, and medical care. Hopkins constantly improvised, always in an effort to get better results. He toured the country to see what was happening in the real world, and FDR and Eleanor devoured his findings, which he often presented in the form of human stories. For the first couple, Hopkins became the New Deal's eyes and ears.

Through his years of contending with the various alphabet agencies Roosevelt created—not just the WPA but also the Federal Emergency Relief Administration (FERA), Public Works Administration (PWA), and Civil Works Administration (CWA), among others—Hopkins oversaw the disbursement of more than $11 billion, the vast majority of it intended for direct relief and for job creation programs. He accomplished this astounding feat with a management style that belied his penchant for spending, operating with a bare-bones staff and working them relentlessly. But no one worked harder than he did. Roosevelt increasingly came to admire Hopkins's talents and to appreciate his loyalty, and as a result, he delegated ever-greater authority to him. FDR did not delegate readily or often; the main tenet of his management style was to keep ultimate authority in his own hands. To Hopkins, however, who not only was getting results but was unquestionably dedicated to the president and his agenda, he granted huge amounts of authority. Over time FDR came to feel closer to Hopkins than to anyone else in his official family, admiring what one historian called Hopkins's "cynical idealism," which in some ways paralleled the approach taken by Louis Howe, FDR's close friend and advisor for nearly twenty years, who had died in 1936.[3]

As popular as Hopkins was with the president, however, he was the administration's chief lightning rod for its critics. Sherwood, who both liked and admired Hopkins, wrote that he "came to be regarded as the Chief Apostle of the New Deal and the most cordially hated by its enemies. I think it may fairly be said that he earned this distinction."[4]

Although Hopkins gave every appearance of selflessly serving the president and his agenda, he was not immune to personal or political ambition. He frequently saw his name on the front pages of America's leading newspapers and his picture on the covers of weekly magazines, and an increasingly healthy ego caused him to entertain the notion of seeking elective office for himself. The thought may have occurred to him as early as 1935, but certainly by 1936 it was in his mind that he might be the Democratic candidate for president in 1940, when Roosevelt would complete his two terms. Before the idea could gain traction, however, a double tragedy struck. In the summer of 1937 his second wife died of cancer, and within weeks Hopkins himself was diagnosed with the same disease when surgeons removed a large part of his long-troubled stomach at the Mayo Clinic. Although the cover story was that Hopkins was treated for ulcers, the operation revealed a series of stomach disorders that would plague him for the rest of his life.

During the fall of 1937, while Hopkins was laid up, *Collier's* magazine had cited him prominently as a possible successor to FDR, and the rumor mill, with the president's encouragement, started buzzing. During the spring of 1938, after Hopkins's return, Roosevelt had a private conversation with his friend about the future. Hopkins made notes of the talk, which Sherwood, years later, faithfully reported in his biography. For his own part, the president said, he had a "personal disinclination" to run again and that Mrs. Roosevelt was "strongly opposed." Therefore, he concluded, he planned to retire to Hyde Park after the end of his term, to attend to the family estate and his own finances, both of which had suffered during his presidency. He didn't flatly close the door on running again, but he said the chance of that happening was very small; he suggested he would consider it only in the event of war. As for his successor, he wanted a "liberal" who was committed to the New Deal and who could be elected. He listed a number of possible candidates—Cordell Hull, Jim Farley, and Harold Ickes among them—and ruled most of them out as too conservative, unelectable, or both. He saw Farley, who he knew was already angling for the nomination, as "clearly the most dangerous" of the potential candidates, since he was cool to the New Deal and inexperienced in foreign affairs.

Then he turned to the man sitting opposite him and rendered his assessment of Harry Hopkins as a potential candidate. On the liability side, of course, was Hopkins's health, although FDR didn't think it politically fatal since the public had been told he was treated for ulcers. Nonetheless, he advised, Hopkins should consider the punishing toll a campaign and the presidency could take on him. Next was Hopkins's divorce from his first wife, but this, too, the president discounted because his second marriage had been a happy one and therefore he likely would be viewed as faultless in his first. He noted that Grover Cleveland had been elected even after it became known that he had fathered an illegitimate child.

More than offsetting these points, in FDR's view, was Hopkins's impressive record as an adroit and able administrator committed to the New Deal; moreover, he had come to understand the world of politics and he was electable. Roosevelt advised Hopkins to think through what a successful campaign would entail, including rehabilitating his image with moderate conservatives and especially with the business community. To that end, he said, he intended to nominate Hopkins to be secretary of commerce, where that task would be made easier. He urged Hopkins to carefully plan his campaign and avoid becoming too visible too soon so as not to attract the wrath of potential opponents. He concluded by offering Hopkins "hopes and assurances" and promising to help however he could.[5]

Roosevelt was as good as his word, taking Hopkins with him to public appearances, whether on the rear platform of a train or at a baseball game, and making sure the two were photographed together. Eleanor, who was equally fond of Hopkins, helped the cause by writing in her "My Day" newspaper column that Hopkins "is one of the few people in the world who gives me the feeling of being entirely absorbed in doing his job well . . . He seems to work because he has an inner conviction that his job needs to be done and that he must do it. I think he would be that way about *any job he undertook.*"[6]

The balance of 1938, however, was a bittersweet time for Hopkins. He had won the confidence and affection of both Roosevelts. Eleanor became the legal guardian as well as a surrogate mother for his daughter, Diana, and the White House became home to both of them for the next few years. Hopkins would increasingly make visits to Warm Springs, where just he and Missy LeHand were in residence with the president. In influence and intimacy, he was where only Louis Howe had been before. There had to have been times when his situation absolutely amazed him: here was the president of the United States, an aristocrat from the Hudson River Valley, suggesting that the son of a harness maker from Iowa might succeed him.

However much he may have savored the idea, it soon became unmistakably clear to Hopkins that his health would never withstand either the scrutiny or the rigors of a presidential campaign. While the cancer failed to reappear, other ailments related to his digestive system did, causing him great discomfort and even disabling him for long periods. During his first eighteen months at Commerce, he spent barely thirty days, intermittently, at his desk. As a result, his presidential campaign never got off the ground. His debilitating illness drained him not only of his strength but of his ambition as well. He gradually put aside any thoughts of a Hopkins presidency and instead refocused whatever energies he had on once again serving the president. It turned out to be a fortunate thing for the president: like FDR himself, Hopkins was to have a second act in public life.

Robert H. Jackson, FDR's assistant attorney general, may have been the first to receive presidential prodding toward the White House, earlier even than Hopkins. Although he possessed a modest title as the number three man at the Justice Department, Jackson became a Roosevelt favorite, with their common roots in upstate New York having much to do with it. He was also a superb lawyer with a reputation for decency and absolute integrity; the president valued his legal advice highly. Moreover, Jackson testified in the Senate on behalf of Roosevelt's politically motivated and ill-considered Court-packing plan, but his principled arguments adhered strictly to the law. FDR came to like Jackson so much that he became a regular, together with Hopkins, Harold Ickes, and Admiral Ross McIntire, the president's physician, in FDR's frequent poker games.

In the late fall of 1937 Jackson met with the president one morning to tell him that, for family and financial reasons, he would have to resign his position at Justice and return to the practice of law. FDR was sympathetic, but not very. "Bob, you can't leave now," he said. "You're in this thing. You can't quit. I want to talk with you about the New York situation. I think that you are the logical man to run for governor of New York." After what

Jackson later called "quite a long talk about the governorship," the president got to the real point: "If you can be elected Governor in '38, you would be in an excellent position for the Presidency in 1940. I don't intend to run. Every once in a while somebody suggests that I'm going to run, but I want to get up to Hyde Park." Jackson, whose fires of political ambition burned low if at all, demurred, saying he didn't find the governorship an attractive office because, among other things, it inevitably left its occupant broke. Nonetheless, he was moved enough toward the idea that he asked if he shouldn't talk with Jim Farley about it. It was a sensible question, since Farley's titles included that of chairman of the Democratic Party of New York, putting him effectively in the position to either veto the idea or to help make it happen. "No," Jackson reported that Roosevelt replied elliptically, "you don't need to talk to Jim. I think Jim and I have a very thorough understanding on the subject."[7]

That afternoon Ernest Cuneo, an associate general counsel at the Democratic National Committee (DNC), received a call from Jackson asking him to come immediately to his office at the Justice Department. On arriving, Cuneo was met by his friend Tom Corcoran, who, like Ben Cohen, Jim Rowe, and Cuneo himself, was an eager young political/policy operative reporting to the White House but housed elsewhere. On entering Jackson's office, Cuneo found an excited Corcoran: "It was a laying on of hands, Ernie," Corcoran told him, recalled Cuneo in his unpublished memoirs. "A laying on of hands! We've just seen the President, and he wants Bob to have the job. 'I want you to sit in this chair,' he said to Bob, 'I want you to carry on!' Bob nodded to me that that was what had happened, with a sort of gentle Believe-it-or-Not expression."[8]

Cuneo, who probably had Corcoran to thank for his job at the DNC, was a former journalist with a keen eye and a talent for capturing people and events. He was a full tier below Corcoran in the political pecking order and thus didn't have a personal relationship with FDR, but he was a player nonetheless, one whose loyalties ran close to the White House. Reacting to this surprising new development, Cuneo said it reminded him of a remark by his old boss Fiorello LaGuardia in a similar situation when he said he was running a candidate "in response to an enormous lack of demand." In this instance, Cuneo observed, the "demand would have to be created," and Cuneo was tasked to create it by managing Jackson's campaign for governor of New York. The episode is revealing for, among other things, the extent to which Roosevelt was willing to go—or not—to support those whom he encouraged.[9]

Jackson's gubernatorial campaign became plagued with tactical errors, the candidate's own reluctance, and Roosevelt's failure to clear the way for him in New York. FDR had told Jackson he needn't speak with Jim Farley, implying that the powerful chairman wouldn't be a problem, but in the end Roosevelt never made his wishes clear to Farley, who became a very big problem, indeed a decisive one. At a major Democratic dinner where Jackson was to speak, Cuneo spotted Farley, his nominal boss at the DNC, and decided to bell the cat. "Jim, I understand you discussed the governorship of New York with the President yesterday." Cuneo's memoirs record the exchange:

> "Yes," said Jim easily. "I certainly did."
>
> "And," I said, "the President mentioned Bob Jackson."
>
> "Why, yes, he did," said Jim. "He asked me what I thought about his chances. I told him Jackson wasn't well known enough in New York. I told the President that Bob could walk from the Battery to Buffalo and there wouldn't be ten people who could recognize him. That was all I said."

"We were sunk," Cuneo recalled thinking as he walked away. "Bob Jackson's candidacy was dead."[10]

Jackson emerged from the experience, as he put it, "infinitely more happy that it turned out just as it did," as well he should have, since he had neither the drive nor the temperament of a successful politician. He had, on the other hand, superb qualities as a lawyer. The president within the next few years would appoint him solicitor general, attorney general, and associate justice of the Supreme Court.[11]

Secretary of State Cordell Hull, a Tennessean from a hardscrabble background, was another of those who received the laying on of hands, or at least fingers. A liberal by southern standards as well as a longtime member of Congress and early supporter of FDR's bid for the presidency, he was first in rank not only among foreign policy advisors but in the cabinet as a whole. He was respected for his integrity and his principled positions on policy issues by virtually everyone who knew him. Tall, lean, and a bit shy for a successful politician, he conveyed a quiet dignity in enunciating his views; while he was not a great orator, his words nonetheless commanded attention. Roosevelt was among those who admired these qualities, and in selecting him he had noted that, as a highly regarded former member of Congress, Hull was the only member of the cabinet who brought to the administration a political strength that the president didn't already have. It was a notable comment for a man who didn't make many such admissions.

At a meeting with FDR in October 1938, Hull referred to a foreign policy issue that wouldn't be resolved for several years. "Why, that's fine," the president said. "At that time you'll be in my chair, if my efforts succeed, and you'll be in good position to deal with it." Hull wrote later that from that point until July 1940, "President Roosevelt expressed himself as definitely in favor of my being his successor in 1940."[12] He subsequently heard from a number of senators and other political leaders who had heard that same message directly from the president. Sumner Welles told his State Department colleague Adolf Berle in mid-November 1939, "The President has indicated that in the next campaign he will support Mr. Hull."[13] The refrain continued into the spring of 1940, when Mrs. Hull, seated next to the president at a cabinet dinner, mentioned that her husband didn't like to make speeches. "Well, tell him he had better get used to it," FDR said to her. "He'll have a lot more of it to do soon."

Throughout this period Hull disclaimed any interest in the presidency, citing the need to concentrate on the situation in Europe. "I believe the world is going straight to hell," he told the president after yet another conversation on the subject, "and I think I can be of greater service in the State Department." There is reason to believe he may have been more than a little interested in the presidency—he had, after all, held elective office for many years—but not enough to do anything about it. He adhered to his sincerely held belief that any political activity on his part would be inappropriate in his role as secretary of state.[14]

_____

As was so often the case, Roosevelt's motives weren't as clear at the time as they became in retrospect. He knew that when he officially announced his plans to retire, he would no longer have the leverage to name or perhaps even to influence the choice of the man who would become the Democratic nominee in 1940. The party regulars would see to that by seizing back control of the process, which FDR had effectively removed from their hands after his first election. The enormous popularity he achieved from a transformative presidency enabled him to dominate the party as no Democratic president before him had. But as much as the party bosses valued his vote-getting ability for the ticket, they nonetheless resented the political meddling of the most ardent New Dealers around him. If and when FDR said he wasn't running for another term, the party leaders would listen respectfully to any recommendation he may have had as to a successor, but in the end most of them would go their own way, which likely would be toward a much more moderate, pro-business candidate. Roosevelt was realistic enough to know this and crafted his strategy accordingly. Thus through most of 1938 and 1939 he chose to encourage a number of potential candidates to consider pursuing the nomination, trying in effect to let a thousand flowers bloom. FDR could only plant the seed—a brief laying on of hands—and it was up to the individual to see it come to blossom. He hoped that at least one of them would so that he could be assured of a liberal successor and a tranquil retirement.

Not unreasonably, most of the recipients of presidential encouragement took it as tantamount to an endorsement. Roosevelt had the intuitive ability to lead others, particularly in an intimate setting when he was at his most earnest, to believe they were hearing what they _wanted_ to hear, particularly because it was so undeniably flattering. This characteristic was a key element of his widely acclaimed charm. Such a conversation, however, was not an endorsement. It was simply an invitation to see if the chosen one could rise to the occasion or, as a later generation might put it, to demonstrate political viability.

Was Roosevelt, as some have claimed, using his refusal to state his intentions as a way of "freezing" the field and thereby making his own nomination inevitable? Was the laying on of hands simply designed to camouflage such a strategy and to make FDR appear even more attractive as a candidate by comparison? Perhaps, but if so, he likely did not see himself as being disingenuous. His way was to wait on events and to put off making a decision until he had to, and that is what he was doing now. He was waiting to see if there would be a war, one that affected America, because only such a war, he believed, would persuade the public that he was justified in seeking what no other president had achieved, a third term. But being justified in running didn't mean that he *would* run—that was a separate question.

Methods Short of War

As January 1939 arrived, Roosevelt found himself adrift, perhaps for the first time in his presidency, if not the first time in his life. He was deeply unsettled about where both he and the country were heading. By now the threat of a major war loomed in Europe, and there was growing fear in the United States of getting sucked into its vortex. While still determined to keep the country out of war, FDR saw the degree to which that would conflict with keeping the country safe, and therefore with the need to get help to the democracies that were standing between Hitler and the United States. He as yet saw no way of doing the latter without running totally afoul of the prevailing isolationist sentiment, the force of which, if aroused, could threaten his credibility to lead the nation both at home and abroad.

So it was that on January 4, in delivering his annual address to Congress, the president sounded an uncertain trumpet. After citing recent developments in Europe that had averted war, he turned to new "storms from abroad" that challenged a number of things Americans strongly believed in, including religion, democracy, and good faith. Furthermore, the situation in Europe "can find no place within it for the Prince of Peace." "The United States," he proclaimed, "rejects such an ordering, and retains its ancient faith." Sam Rosenman, who helped FDR craft the speech, wrote later that the president had personally dictated the passage. By putting religion first, Rosenman said, the president was revealing how strong he believed the connection to be between it and "all American ideals." He added that the president intended that it "show the falseness of the philosophy of some of our industrialists that 'we can do business with Hitler.'" Yes, the United States could do business with him, but in the process the country would lose everything it stood for. "That 'everything' was encompassed in 'religion, democracy and international good faith.'"[1]

Roosevelt did not often mention religion publicly, although he saw it as an integral part of his approach to public life. Moreover, Eleanor noted, "it had something to do with his confidence in himself.... It was a very simple religion. He believed in God and in His guidance." From there came the conclusion that human beings were placed on earth with certain tasks to perform and the ability and means to perform them. Religion was therefore not simply resigning oneself to God's will; rather, it involved seeing God's will as something one had the responsibility to enact. Therefore, Eleanor believed, her husband "could pray for help and guidance and have faith in his own judgment as a result."[2]

The president shared with Congress lessons he took from recent events abroad, and again invoked religion. "We have learned that God-fearing democracies of the world ... cannot safely be indifferent to international lawlessness anywhere." But what was to be done to thwart the lawlessness? "There are many methods short of war, but stronger and more effective than mere words, of bringing home to aggressor governments the aggregate sentiments of our own people." He didn't spell out what he meant by "methods short of war" beyond making yet another plea to Congress to revise the Neutrality Act. He continued his remarks on surer ground in arguing that America must rebuild its own defenses, citing "the old, old lesson that probability of attack is mightily decreased by the assurance of an ever ready defense." He offered no specifics as to what that meant, but noted that he would "send up" his ideas in due course.[3]

This was no clarion call for bold action to deter aggression. The speech was instead an unpersuasive effort to reconcile his desire to do something of consequence abroad with the political realities he faced at home; its temporizing message left predisposed listeners free to read into it what they wanted to hear, and it left others confused. His "methods short of war" formulation gave advocates of collective security some comfort, while the *New York Times* said his call for lifting the arms embargo was a turning point in his foreign policy.[4] Others saw the speech as a sure road to war. Robert A. Taft, the newly elected Republican senator from Ohio and already the self-anointed spokesman for conservatives, said one could only take from it that the United States was heading toward another war, with American troops "again sent across the ocean."[5]

Roosevelt concluded from the reaction that, if anything, the speech had been too bold; any stronger case he might make for the repeal of the arms embargo would likely only serve to divide his Democratic base while strengthening the Republicans. He was thus easily persuaded by Senator Key Pittman, the isolationist-leaning Nevadan who chaired the Senate Foreign Relations Committee, to withhold administration proposals for amending the Neutrality Act and to allow Pittman to work out a compromise. But the committee soon became intimidated by the politics of the issue and, with no strong leadership from Pittman, voted unanimously to postpone hearings.

FDR was determined nonetheless to get first-line aircraft to the threatened democracies, and especially, as we've seen, to France. Accomplishing that goal would necessarily build U.S. production capacity to meet American needs as well. In fact, Roosevelt had already authorized Treasury Secretary Morgenthau to oversee the transfer of aircraft to the democracies. The unusual assignment was a direct result of FDR's distrust of Henry Woodring, his isolationist-leaning secretary of war, whom he was interminably reluctant to move out of the cabinet, given that his presence allowed FDR the appearance of bowing to isolationist sentiment. This is what the president really meant by "methods short of war": getting armaments in the hands of those who would serve as a first line of defense for the United States.

FDR was now convinced that it had to be done with the utmost secrecy in order to prevent the public backlash that disclosure would surely bring. Roosevelt was leavening his longtime attraction to adroit manipulation with a heavy dose of secrecy, embracing the latter even though his insistence on it during the Court-packing plan had badly backfired. Now, dealing instead with foreign affairs, he seemed to see it as the only alternative to making a forceful and straightforward case for his policies, a case that at this point would not work. Even when meeting with his own advisors in November he led them to believe that his primary purpose in accelerating aircraft production was to build up the American air force when his real intention had been to get planes to France. Roosevelt was still uncomfortable with this level of subterfuge. He never had to do this with his domestic policies because he had had public opinion behind him from the beginning. But now he genuinely feared the isolationists' ability to whip up a public furor over steps they would see as leading to war and bring the effort—and his administration—to a halt. He was at this stage unwilling to test the notion of aid to the democracies in the public arena, but at the same time he was determined to act. He was at his core a man of action, and he would act secretly if he must, but he would act.

French premier Edouard Daladier authorized his purchasing team, headed by Jean Monnet, to place orders for up to one thousand U.S. aircraft if the specifications and timetables met French needs. On January 20, a little more than two weeks after the State of the Union address, two French air force colonels, wearing civilian clothes and speaking English to disguise their mission, arrived in California to inspect the bomber the French sought to purchase. On a test flight the aircraft spun out of control at a low altitude. The pilot was killed attempting to parachute, and the French officer accompanying him was severely injured when the plane crashed. As he was pulled from the craft before it caught fire, his fellow Frenchman, understandably upset, began speaking excitedly in his native tongue. Their cover was blown, and word quickly reached Washington, where it created precisely the kind of controversy the president was eager to avoid. Isolationists voiced outrage at a closed meeting of the Senate Military Affairs Committee a few days later when it became known that both the Treasury and War departments had approved the French plan.

The next day muddled news accounts of the hearing prompted a reporter to ask Roosevelt at his news conference whether the government had "taken any steps to assist or facilitate France in buying planes in this country." Carefully parsing his words, the president prevaricated: "As you put the question, no." He added that of course the French wanted to buy American aircraft and that the process of speeding up production to accommodate them would serve U.S. defense as well as economic goals. Thus "we told them it would be an excellent idea" for them to place orders quickly "before our larger program can be authorized and actually got under way."[6] Roosevelt didn't publicly seem to question that the "larger program" would be "authorized," but he knew well that it was not a given; in fact, the odds were stacked against it.

On the same day the Senate Military Affairs Committee heard Morgenthau and Woodring offer their explanations, which did little to quiet the firestorm that was building. Most damaging was Woodring's view that the French purchase could not be fulfilled by midyear, when U.S. production was scheduled to begin, and his comment that he had shared that view with Morgenthau.

Now the fat was in the fire. Here was the American government disclosing military secrets—in terms of production schedules and new technologies—to another nation as part of a secret plot to sell aircraft to that nation in a way that was calculated to get the United States involved in an armed conflict. It was the isolationists' worst fear, and they went on the warpath in editorials and speeches and of course in the halls of Congress. The outrage, however, did nothing to dissuade Roosevelt from his purpose. His innate caution only kicked in *before* he made a major decision; having made it, no matter the criticism, he dug in his heels. So it had been with the Court plan, and so it would be here. He told his cabinet that his plans to sell aircraft had not changed, and he instructed Morgenthau to sell the French whatever they wanted.

Nonetheless, the president also knew that he had to deal with the uproar in Congress, and he decided to rely on his charm and powers of persuasion to do it. He invited the full membership of the Senate Military Affairs Committee to a confidential briefing at the White House where he would candidly lay out his views on foreign policy. He began the session by saying he was not of "the school of thought that says we can draw a line of defense around this country and live completely and solely to ourselves," adding that it was the embargo legislation of the time that drew the nation into the War of 1812. He then emphasized the need for confidentiality in the matter he was about to reveal because, as he put it, they didn't "want to frighten the American people." Instead, as he put it, "we want them to gradually realize what is a potential danger." The senators should understand, however, that the danger was not potential; it was near and it was real. Not only Germany but also Italy and Japan, having formed "an offensive and defensive alliance," posed an actual threat to the United States that could not be ignored.

The question facing them all, Roosevelt said, was how best to deal with this very real threat. The country could once again seek refuge in isolation from the world, of course, and hope the threat would go away. It was far more sensible, he argued, to recognize the danger and meet it by creating a "first line of defense" in both the Pacific and the Atlantic. There were sixteen independent nations in Europe, he said, standing between Hitler and the Western Hemisphere. In reality, however, there were only two, Great Britain and France, because if they fell the others would be quickly consumed one by one; indeed, some were already gone. And then "Brother Hitler" would have a clear path to Africa because much of it had been divided into colonies under the British and the French, and thence to South and Central America and the doorstep of the United States.

This was not some fanciful theory that FDR concocted for the benefit of his audience. He believed that Nazi Germany, once it conquered western Europe, envisioned using the Azores and Dakar, Senegal, to leap across the Atlantic to the "bulge" in Brazil, from which it would foment uprisings in Argentina, Brazil, Uruguay, and perhaps even Mexico. He took it seriously enough that the administration war-gamed this possibility in 1938. He also attempted to use his very successful Good Neighbor Policy toward Latin America (a policy that had been shaped principally by Welles) as a bulwark against the Nazis.

It wasn't hard to see where this early version of a "domino theory" was heading: if the United States did nothing, the country would be surrounded by hostile nations and faced with the choice of submitting to intimidation or fighting on its native soil. Roosevelt told the assembled senators, including such fervent isolationists as Gerald Nye of North Dakota and Bennett Champ Clark of Missouri, that the answer was to pursue his policy of sending assistance to "any government which we know, on the doctrine of chances, will never be an enemy of ours."

This first-line-of-defense rationale led naturally to the sale of aircraft to France, which had started the whole furor. FDR told the senators such a sale could be accomplished without affecting plans to produce planes for American military use. His hope was that the French would purchase "the fastest pursuit planes we can turn out" as well as "the best heavy and medium bombers they can buy in this country." The same went for the British, who he believed planned to purchase up to four hundred planes. He stressed Germany's sobering capacity in this area. According to his estimates, the Germans would be capable of producing forty thousand planes a year. "I cannot overemphasize the seriousness of this situation," he gravely concluded.[7]

It was a quintessential Roosevelt performance. He spoke with authority about specific numbers and bolstered technical detail with the conviction that this was a matter of vital importance to the country. Earlier in his presidency such a grasp of the subject matter combined with the force of his personality likely would have left his audience either agreeing with him or persuaded that it was useless to disagree. That was not the case here. The senators around the room were being asked to buy into a theory of world domination that to many of them was implausible. More significant, FDR was no longer the indomitable figure he had been a few years before. Too much damage had been done to his credibility—first by the Court-packing scheme and then by his 1938 attempt to purge Democratic members of Congress who had opposed key elements of his program. The president had gone so far in this purge effort as to recruit liberal candidates to run against these recalcitrant conservatives in their state primaries. Almost all of the targeted legislators survived the unprecedented intrusion into traditionally local matters and had returned to Congress, understandably more than a little unhappy with their president. Now there was this French fiasco, which, combined with everything else, led most members of Congress to no longer stand in awe of him.

Questions from the senators underscored this new reality. The president was asked by the isolationist J. Hamilton Lewis of Illinois if he really meant that the United States had the "duty" to "maintain the independence of these nations you described . . . by whatever efforts may be necessary." FDR recoiled at the implication that the United States should be prepared to go to war to save the independent nations of Europe. "No, no!" he blurted out. But instead of clarifying what he had meant by calling for a "first line of defense" as a "method short of war," he began a rambling discourse on how much he detested war: "I probably saw more of the war in Europe than any other living person." His exaggerated response to Senator Lewis's legitimate question further hurt his credibility with the senators. It also revealed the dilemma inherent in the meeting itself: obviously the country could be drawn into a war in the grim scenario he had outlined, but he couldn't say so explicitly, as neither the public nor Congress was prepared to accept that fact. He also knew that it was highly likely that what he said in this meeting would appear in the next day's newspapers, despite his insistence on confidentiality. If he conceded even the possibility of the country fighting in a European war, his entire first-line-of-defense strategy, including the sale of aircraft to France, would crumble. It was even conceivable that impeachment proceedings could be initiated against him. He was thus caught up in a dilemma largely of his own making: he was determined to blunt the threat to America by arming its allies, but he believed he could accomplish that goal only through secret means.

The gist of the meeting, as he expected, was splashed across the front pages of the newspapers the following day. The *New York Times* reported that the president had said that the senators should "regard France as the actual frontier of America in an apparently inevitable showdown between democracies and dictatorships," while other news organizations claimed that he had placed that frontier "on the Rhine." While London and Paris received these reports enthusiastically, in the United States they only added fuel to the press firestorm that had begun with the crash of the bomber in California during its test flight for the French.[8] Roosevelt became angry and stubborn when confronted with this public debate, a debate he had been so eager to avoid, and, as he sometimes did when cornered, he dissembled.

Rather than using his press conference on February 3 to explain what he had meant in his meeting with the senators, he denied virtually the entire thrust of his original remarks. When asked if he would permit Germany, Japan, and Italy to acquire munitions on the same cash-on-the-barrelhead basis as France, he equivocated, although he had told the senators he would do "everything I possibly can" to prevent it. He lambasted the "frontier on the Rhine" characterization as "a deliberate lie," adding, "Some boob got that off." Pressed on whether the Rhine reference, if not literally accurate, nonetheless conveyed the gist of his remarks, he said it absolutely did not. Although he had attempted to impose complete confidentiality on the meeting's participants, he minimized the degree of secrecy he had requested. Asked finally whether he planned to clarify the "confusion" of his changing foreign policy to the American people anytime soon, he flatly denied there was any change.[9]

It was not FDR's finest moment. For members of Congress and others following world events closely, it confirmed their growing belief that he found bending the truth a too-convenient option when trying to extricate himself from a self-dug hole. Senator Hiram Johnson, a progressive isolationist Republican from California, lashed out at the president, who he said "seems to have gone perfectly mad because his policy in respect to the world situation is opposed." Roosevelt cared no more for what might happen to Americans in a war "than the man in the moon." This was, according to Johnson, the sign that the president "has developed a dictator complex."[10]

Ironically, there was more public support for what Roosevelt was trying to do than he had assumed. One Gallup poll during this period indicated that 65 percent of the American people favored selling aircraft to Britain and France. Another showed that if those two nations were attacked by Germany and Italy, 69 percent supported the United States doing "everything possible to help" short of going to war.[11] Public opinion on foreign policy was essentially where Roosevelt's own views were: shaped by events in Europe and slowly evolving, but clearly on the side of bolstering the ability of democratic nations to resist aggression and, in the process, provide that first line of defense for America.

Why, then, was FDR so determined to publicly dissemble on his real beliefs and intentions? Part of the answer lay in a predisposition to conceal the truth in order to prove his own cleverness. He had long since learned to exaggerate, hide things, and hedge, and he seldom passed up an opportunity to employ his skill at it. As the Democratic vice presidential candidate in 1920, for example, he claimed to have personally written a new constitution for Haiti, which was patently untrue, and he was called on it. His rationale for expanding the Supreme Court in 1937 was that its caseload was too heavy, a claim that also was proved false and which helped lead to the plan's demise. Even his successful efforts to portray himself as a man in robust good health were a deception—a justifiable one, perhaps, but a deception nonetheless. The quality had become embedded in his character.

A larger part of the answer lay in the uniquely American form of isolationism that had shaped the country's foreign policy from its beginning, and which was still alive and well in the late 1930s. It was the elephant in every room where foreign policy was discussed, and Roosevelt, to whom the concept was antithetical to the country's interests, especially in such dangerous times, never allowed himself to ignore it.

The War of Independence had been fought, of course, for just that—independence. The Founding Fathers and most other Americans took that to mean not just independence from Great Britain but also independence from the machinations and alliances of European powers, which seemed only to lead to endless wars. Rather, the United States should chart its own destiny, make its own decisions as to what was in its own best interests, and not become hostage to the will of other, more powerful nations. As it did in so many other ways, George Washington's presidency shaped this tenet of fundamental American belief in a way that would endure. "Europe has a set of primary interests which to us have none or a very remote relation," he said in his Farewell Address. Therefore, Americans should "steer clear of permanent alliances" and association "by artificial ties in the ordinary vicissitudes of her politics and the ordinary combinations and collisions of her friendships and enmities."[12] He knew well that if his young and still weak nation became an ally of a much greater one, its interests were likely to be ignored if not subsumed. He also believed, as did virtually all of his fellow citizens, that with a vast ocean between the United States and Europe, geography was the Americans' friend; it was a huge barrier to anyone with hostile designs on the country. The logical conclusion of this thinking was that independence from foreign entanglements left it free to base its foreign policy solely on its own interests as perceived at any given time.

Thomas Jefferson a few years later reaffirmed this notion when he said that the country's foreign policy should be premised on "peace, commerce and honest friendship with all nations, entangling alliances with none."[13] And of course it was further strengthened by the Monroe Doctrine, designed to keep European influence from the entire Western Hemisphere; to enforce it, successive administrations strove vigorously to maintain the independence of its Latin American neighbors. This newly created policy of independence in foreign affairs—it was not yet known as isolationism—would remain the basis of American foreign policy for the balance of the nineteenth century. It was not until the advent of Woodrow Wilson's presidency and the First World War that the policy was seen in a different light. The country's entry into war was a unilateral act, prompted primarily by outrage over the loss of American lives when Germany began a campaign of indiscriminately torpedoing merchant ships in the Atlantic Ocean. Nonetheless, it meant sending American boys to fight and die in what was essentially a European conflict.

Tragic as the war was for America and others, it was not until its conclusion and Wilson's heavy involvement in the treaty negotiations that he ran up squarely against the determination to maintain America's independence in the conduct of its foreign policy. When he became the chief advocate for adoption of the proposed League of Nations, first at Versailles with other heads of government and then back in the United States, he became the first president to challenge directly the assumptions underlying the policy. "The isolation of the United States is at an end," Wilson argued in 1919, "not because we chose to go into the politics of the world, but because by the sheer genius of this American people and the growth of our power we have become a determining factor in the history of mankind and after you have become a determining factor you cannot remain isolated, whether you want to or not."[14]

But when the United States Senate decisively rejected ratification of American membership in the League of Nations, it revealed what Wilson could not see or had not wanted to see: most of his countrymen had no desire to be "a determining factor" in world affairs and still had an aversion to "entangling alliances." The war had changed many things; it hadn't changed that.

As America settled into the 1920s determined to heal its war wounds and return to "normalcy," it conducted its foreign affairs much as it had before the war. Gradually, however, several prominent figures—Senator Gerald Nye of North Dakota would become the most vocal—propounded a revisionist theory of how America had come to be engaged in the war in the first place. It was the result, they argued in sum, of the beguiling propaganda of the Allies and the greed and machinations of American bankers and businessmen. There were enough receptive ears to give this theory traction, reinforced as it was by the perceived ingratitude of the European powers for America's huge sacrifice in lives and treasure and their failure to repay their war debts.

The cumulative effect of all this was growing acceptance of what some termed the "devil theory of war"—it wasn't really America's unilateral decision, based on its perceived self-interest, that took the country into war, but rather "the devil made us do it." In this case the devils were the bankers, financiers, and arms merchants who sought to make large profits from the conflict. The theory was given quasi-official credence when, in the early years of the Roosevelt administration, a special Senate committee concluded after two years of hearings and investigations that the charges were essentially justified. Chaired by Senator Nye, the committee report found "highly unethical" relationships between U.S. businesses and their German counterparts designed to create arms monopolies that constituted "a discredit to American business." It went on to condemn by implication the roles of such prominent bankers as J. P. Morgan and Thomas W. Lamont, as well as high officials of the Wilson administration for bending to the financiers' will when it lifted the ban on credits to belligerents in 1915.[15]

With few willing to attempt to refute these charges, the isolationism of the 1930s took on a new dimension: the independent and unilateral freedom to act in foreign affairs so historically prized by Americans became linked with the avoidance of war. With Germany, Italy, and Japan making increasingly hostile noises in all directions, the likelihood of war loomed over the world, and the vast majority of Americans decided they wanted no part of it. By 1936, polls showed, 95 percent of Americans opposed such a development.[16]

The breadth of isolationist feeling in the country transcended virtually every line of politics, ideology, and geography. Many liberals believed that serious engagement abroad would undercut the momentum of New Deal reforms; many conservatives worried that it would threaten the country's free enterprise system. Although historically the remote and rural Midwest had contained the deepest strain of isolationism, no region of the country was immune. Even in the East, traditional home to the country's establishment and internationalist way of thinking, strong isolationist sentiment could be found. Still, while isolationism dominated political thinking when it came to foreign affairs, it would be a mistake to underestimate the degree of public indifference on the subject; most Americans were simply absorbed in their *own* affairs.

Many moved with the tide of public opinion on the issue, among them the eminent historian Charles Beard. A believer in economic causation, Beard concluded that significant trade abroad would lead to greater entanglements of other kinds that would override in importance what little benefit trade offered domestically. Norman Thomas had a following that went far beyond the Socialist Party he had led for so long, and he was particularly popular among intellectuals. His deep-seated belief in pacifism persuaded many that war would undercut any hope of social and economic progress for America's poor. At the other end of the political spectrum, former president Herbert Hoover, in an attempt to restore his discredited political standing, argued that the Great Depression had come about as the result of too much contact with other nations; ignoring his own history as a long-time internationalist and especially his role in effectively distributing food to starving Europeans after the war, he moved decidedly in the direction of the isolationists.

Father Charles Coughlin, the so-called radio priest from Detroit, was harder to place on the political spectrum. Beginning in the twenties, he discovered he had a talent for communicating with large numbers of people via the newly popular broadcast medium, and he quickly gained a large following. At the peak of his popularity his broadcasts reached millions of listeners, and it was not unusual for him to receive up to eighty thousand approving letters a week. At first his efforts concentrated on countering anti-Catholicism, particularly from the Ku Klux Klan, but increasingly he wandered into the political arena. He was an early supporter of FDR's New Deal, but with the rise of fascism in Europe his allegiance shifted again. Despairing of Roosevelt's efforts to save the capitalist system, he became enamored of Hitler's and Mussolini's efforts to transform their societies, and fascism, racism, and anti-Semitism became his favored themes. His strong support of the isolationist tide then rising in the United States was a natural extension of these themes, based more on the desire to see the Axis powers prevail than on the desire to keep America out of a war.

Naturally, the isolationism advocated by all of these disparate voices was well represented in the halls of Congress. Since the Constitution gave the Senate particular powers in the foreign policy area, especially that of ratifying treaties, it was no surprise that the most vocal opponents of involvement in European affairs should come from that body. Chief among them was William E. Borah of Idaho, a crusty if principled Republican who first entered the Senate in 1907. In 1919, as the leader of a group known as the "irreconcilables," he helped doom prospects for ratification of the Treaty of Versailles and the charter for the League of Nations. Like the chief advocate of those measures, Woodrow Wilson, Borah toured the country, but in opposition; his speech on the Senate floor before the ratification vote was regarded as both eloquent and decisive. From 1925 to 1933 he chaired the Foreign Relations Committee, where he successfully led the case for ratification of the 1928 Pact of Paris prohibiting war "as an instrument of national policy," authored by U.S. secretary of state Frank B. Kellogg and his French counterpart, Aristide Briand.

When the Democrats took control of the Senate in 1932, Borah became the ranking minority member of the Foreign Relations Committee, but this did little to diminish his influence. By now the senior member of the Senate, his stature enhanced by his forceful personality and his leonine mane of hair, he was widely respected by all for his unquestioned integrity and his willingness to go against the political grain. Borah played an important role in the passage of the Neutrality Act in 1935. There were others in Congress who shared his views. However, until his death in 1940 at age seventy-five it would be Borah who stood unchallenged as Congress's leading proponent of protecting the country from the kind of foreign entanglements that could lead to war.

The president lacked a formal apparatus to help him shape strategy for dealing with events abroad. There was as yet no such thing as a National Security Council of administration principals, supported by a White House staff of foreign policy and defense experts. With no clear structure, the decision-making process in foreign policy paralleled that in other areas: the president simply solicited views from whichever cabinet members or others he wanted to hear from, either individually or collectively, and then made the final decisions. It was often a haphazard and even messy process, and reflected the nation's sometimes casual regard for foreign policy in the absence of a crisis. But it was a process that suited Roosevelt just fine. As a rule, FDR didn't believe in formal structure, at least where decision making was concerned. His favorite practice, according to Arthur Schlesinger Jr., was "to keep grants of authority incomplete, jurisdictions uncertain, charters overlapping." The result of "this competitive theory of administration" was frequently "confusion and exasperation on the operating level." Nonetheless, no other method, as Schlesinger put it, "could so reliably ensure that . . . the decisions, and the power to make them, would remain with the President."[17]

As secretary of state, Cordell Hull was of course Roosevelt's principal and most visible foreign policy advisor. Although he brought little foreign policy experience to the job, Hull had already distinguished himself by putting in place FDR's Good Neighbor Policy toward Latin America and by negotiating a number of free trade agreements. His stiff demeanor and sense of office led to a mostly formal relationship with the president, whose style was more relaxed. Roosevelt was sometimes careless in offending the only member of his cabinet who had an independent political constituency, and he had stumbled badly when he failed to consult Hull before delivering his ill-timed "quarantine" speech in 1937. Still, for the most part they worked well together, and Hull played a significant role in shaping an emerging American strategy to meet potential threats from abroad. He fully shared the president's worries about Hitler's expansive moves in Europe: Hull was a strong advocate of strengthening America's defenses, crafting a system of collective security, and using "methods short of war" to help the European democracies.

Sumner Welles, Hull's undersecretary and effectively the number two official in the State Department, could not have been more different. Hull had been born in a log cabin in middle Tennessee and worked his way from a hardscrabble early life to political distinction. Welles was the essence of urbanity whose distinguished East Coast family tree included Charles Sumner, the eminent Massachusetts senator and leading abolitionist of the Civil War, and Gideon Welles, Lincoln's secretary of the navy (the elegant family residence on Massachusetts Avenue in Washington, D.C., now serves as the Cosmos Club). He was even related distantly to the Roosevelts—he had served as a groomsman at Franklin and Eleanor's wedding—and from an early age FDR took a liking to him. Seeing in Welles the pedigree, temperament, and adroitness of a successful diplomat, Roosevelt counseled him to enter the foreign service and used his influence to facilitate the move.

The president elevated Welles to undersecretary in 1937 not only because he admired his talents but also because he genuinely enjoyed his company. Their common background yielded an easy familiarity between the two that was absent with the more fastidious Hull. Whereas the secretary could go on endlessly to make a point, usually boring the president in the process, Welles could demonstrate a quick and incisive intelligence that the president prized. Since FDR's practice of ignoring formal structures and protocols meant that he often met directly with Welles without going through Hull, this created obvious tensions in the State Department. Hull was frequently hurt when the president snubbed him or embarrassed him by undercutting his authority, though his stoic nature would not permit him to react openly. Instead he exercised seemingly endless patience and discretion, privately pained but publicly silent.

Although Roosevelt was comfortable with his foreign policy team, like other presidents before him, especially his heroes "Uncle Ted" and Woodrow Wilson, he had an instinctive distrust of the State Department's bureaucratic biases. That distrust reinforced his determination to establish his own sources of information and to keep all significant decision making in his own hands, becoming effectively his own secretary of state. He built an informal network of individuals to keep him current on events and personalities that could bear on critical issues around the world. This network was by no means limited to Americans. He made it a point to see foreign diplomats, businessmen, and old friends when they came to Washington, usually pumping them for new information or insights. And he encouraged many of them to write to him directly on important matters. This was a practice he particularly encouraged among his key ambassadors, whom he didn't want to feel stifled by the rigidities of formal channels; he wanted information and views unfiltered. Arguably it was a cumbersome process, but it was the process that worked for FDR. No one else had all of the information that he had, which meant that he was both well informed and in complete control.

If the first months of 1939 saw the shift of the president's attention toward foreign affairs, the events of March 15 accelerated it when Hitler arrived in Prague to announce that Czechoslovakia was henceforth under German protection. His troops poured into the country, in obvious violation of the pact that had been signed only recently in Munich, extinguishing freedoms and issuing anti-Semitic proclamations as they went. Even though Hitler's goal of dominating all of Europe was now laid bare, Neville Chamberlain clung to his faith in his appeasement policy, arguing that the world still wanted peace. But Hitler's blatant breach of his own pledge and flagrant violation of another nation's sovereignty outraged nearly everyone in Britain, including many of appeasement's most devoted acolytes. Chamberlain's closest parliamentary advisors persuaded him that his government would almost certainly fall unless he reversed course. It was clear to all, including the prime minister himself, that his policy was dead. He scrambled in the two weeks that followed to reformulate his government's position on German aggression, particularly toward Poland, which most observers agreed was likely to be Hitler's next target. On March 31 Chamberlain rose in Parliament to reveal his new policy to the world: if Poland was invaded, Britain and France would go to war.[18]

It was a momentous decision, hastily arrived at and dramatically unveiled to deal with the firestorm of protest following German occupation of Czechoslovakia. Europe's fate was now hostage to whatever steps Hitler might take toward Poland, the geography of which, combined with the relative weakness of British and French forces, would make it virtually impossible to defend. One member of Parliament who saw the consequences was Winston Churchill, so ardent a critic of appeasement that he was shunned by his own Conservative Party's leadership. "God helping, we can do no other," he told the House in support of the new policy.[19]

Roosevelt's chief aim coming out of the Czech affair was to use it as a catalyst to amend the Neutrality Act. After vigorous efforts by Hull to move the issue forward, Key Pittman, the chairman of the Senate Foreign Relations Committee, took a modest step forward to propose a bill. It was an unwise move: he was buffeted by both the isolationist and internationalist factions on his committee, causing him to take two steps back. He reneged on a commitment to allow his committee to act on the bill and, instead, convened a session on July 11 for the sole purpose of deferring consideration of the issue until 1940.

Effectively appealing the decision, Roosevelt convened a meeting of the bipartisan leadership of the Senate together with Vice President Garner and Hull. The purpose of the session was to overcome the steadfast opposition of William Borah, who led opposition to amending the Neutrality Act by his cowing of Pittman.

The evening of July 18 was hot and humid as the shirtsleeved conferees gathered in the Oval Study, upstairs in the residence portion of the White House (and not to be confused with the Oval Office in the West Wing). After helping themselves liberally to the liquor FDR had thoughtfully provided, they listened to him expound for nearly an hour on the case for amending the act—Hitler's aggressions, appeasement's failures, and the likelihood of an imminent world war. He stressed his own efforts to avert such a war but said they had been undercut by the Neutrality Act as it now stood. "I've fired my last shot," he concluded. "I think I ought to have another round in my belt." Hull, uncharacteristically emotional, continued with an even more dire assessment of the situation in Europe, arguing that war was all but inevitable unless the embargo was repealed; even with repeal, odds were at best even. Those opposing repeal were by their actions in fact encouraging, not preventing, a war that threatened American security and perhaps even America's survival. Hull looked to the president for support on this point, and FDR affirmed that the country's security was indeed at risk because of the unbending isolationism of opponents such as Senator Gerald Nye.

Borah saw his opening, telling the president that Senator Nye was not alone. He went on to state categorically that there would be no war in Europe, and that all the hysteria was "manufactured and artificial." The president saw that this claim was agitating Hull, and asked, "Cordell, what do you say to that?"

The secretary of state, who was indeed taking Borah's comments personally as well as an insult to the integrity of his department, attempted to control himself before responding. He invited Borah "to come to my office and look over the cables coming in. I feel satisfied he would modify his views."

Borah responded that he had his own sources of information, sources "more reliable than those of the State Department," and those assured him "that there is not going to be any war."

Hull, clearly beside himself with fury, became literally speechless. As the congressional participants stated their views, only one of the Republicans spoke out for repeal. Vice President Garner, who was enjoying this opportunity to see the president squirm, brought the issue to a head when he asked the majority leader, Alben Barkley, whether he had the votes to bring the bill to the floor. Barkley conceded he did not, and other senators confirmed the conclusion. "Well, Captain," the vice president told Roosevelt, reprising his similar role after the Court battle, "we might as well face the facts. You haven't got the votes and that's all there is to it." It was a telling sign—not lost on Roosevelt—that he said "you" and not "we"; by this point this relationship was in sharp decline.[20]

Three months earlier, on April 20, 1939, Lindbergh had arrived at the White House for a noon appointment with the president. It would be the one and only time these two men would meet face-to-face. They were almost certainly the two most famous men in America, both greatly admired although for very different reasons, and the meeting understandably stirred much public interest. On approaching the White House Lindbergh passed through a group of photographers and what he called "inane women" who were screeching at him. He thought it was disgraceful they would be allowed to do so right in front of the presidential mansion: "There would be more dignity and self-respect among African savages."[21]

The ostensible reason for this meeting was for Lindbergh to brief the president on his observations of the German Luftwaffe, although each was almost certainly eager to take the personal measure of the other. We have only Lindbergh's version of the fifteen-minute session, and from his account it was on the surface amiable. No surprise there, as it was deeply imbedded in FDR that he should be personally amiable to everyone, even those whom he disliked. The simple warmth of Roosevelt's greeting, Sam Rosenman remembered, could cause a visitor to believe "that nothing was so important to him that day as this particular visit, and that he had been waiting all day for this hour to arrive."[22]

The president asked about the aviator's wife, Anne, who had attended school with Roosevelt's daughter, Anna. Lindbergh noted later that the president was "an accomplished, suave, interesting conversationalist," and perhaps someone he "could get along well with."[23] But as the discussion progressed, Lindbergh began to have doubts. He thought there was something about the president that he didn't trust, "something a little too suave, too pleasant, too easy." Lindbergh believed that there was no reason for antagonism between them, despite their disagreements, but that they would probably not have much of a relationship.

"Roosevelt judges his man quickly and plays him cleverly. He is mostly politician, and I think we would never get along on many fundamentals," Lindbergh commented, though he seemed willing to try despite his reservations. "It is better to work together as long as we can; yet somehow I have a feeling that it may not be for long."[24] To Lindbergh, Roosevelt had the "gray look of an overworked businessman," and his voice carried the "even, routine tone that one seems to get when [the] mind is dulled by too much and too frequent conversation." Nonetheless, Lindbergh could see that the president, even though tired, gave the impression of having "enough energy to carry on for a long time."

4

Redefining Neutrality

The new flash point in Europe was the city of Danzig, a historically German port on the Baltic, and the thin corridor that connected it now with Poland. The Versailles Treaty had made Danzig—which the Poles called Gdansk—a free city with an economy closely aligned with Poland's. The fact that the corridor divided East Prussia from the rest of Germany had always rankled Hitler, and he was determined to reclaim his country's historical boundaries. Ironically, it was among the Führer's more legitimate claims. Nonetheless, the Poles, no doubt reassured by the British and French pledges of support, were having no part of it. There was no way now for the world to avoid war if Hitler was serious in his intentions. There was absolutely no reason to believe that he wasn't.

Thus on September 1, the Führer sent his dive bombers over Warsaw and his armored columns across the Polish border, causing Britain and France to honor their pledges to come to Poland's defense. Their declarations of war were unavailing as far as that beleaguered nation was concerned, for its fate was quickly sealed by German troops pouring in from the west and

Soviet troops from the east. It was the outcome that everyone had feared and that everyone had tried to avoid—everyone, that is, except Hitler.

Roosevelt was among those who had seen this coming, and the question is whether he could have done more to prevent it, and if so, given the power and ubiquity of isolationist sentiment, what. As we have seen, he made several attempts to publicly warn the American people of the ultimate danger they faced from Nazi aggression in Europe, beginning with his "quarantine" speech in the fall of 1937. The negative reaction to that speech, some of it fierce, surprised him, and he backed off. He thereafter followed a public path of caution on the matter and lacked a coherent strategy backed by a clear policy to thwart the aggression that he feared would eventually involve the United States. In early 1939, in his State of the Union speech, he had unveiled his "methods short of war" approach to helping the democracies, soon supplemented by his decision to build America's first line of defense through Britain and France. The only real hope he had of implementing such a policy, however, was by repealing the embargo provisions of the Neutrality Act, so that those two countries had the means to defend themselves. This he had failed to do, not because he didn't make his case forcefully to the lawmakers but because he wasn't convinced that making his case forcefully to the American people would sufficiently change public, and eventually congressional, opinion. Rather, he believed that only facts and events, not words, would move minds. He therefore tried to have it both ways: he sincerely wanted to help the Allies, but he preferred to do it behind closed doors, relying on the force of his personality—as Lindbergh among others had experienced—which had worked so well for the previous seven years. He had soon found that his powers of persuasion with senators weren't what they once had been, and when the secrecy unraveled, as it did when the Douglas bomber crashed in California, that strategy was doomed; he was seen, at least in Congress, as a duplicitous schemer.

The president had been perhaps too cautions. But the mood of isolationism in the country was, if not ubiquitous, at least palpable. In the view of most Americans, maintaining the peace meant staying neutral in any foreign conflict, and this was by far the single most important fact of political life for FDR, particularly since it was embraced by many ardent New Dealers such as Jerome Frank, Robert La Follette, and Rexford G. Tugwell.

Anyone who failed to recognize the pull of this force, Roosevelt believed, risked his own, and his party's, political future. More important, the president realized that he risked his own credibility and with it any chance of significantly affecting events, domestic or diplomatic.

By 1939 it was abundantly clear that there was little consistent about his approach to policy or straightforward about his manner of executing it. One of FDR's most eminent biographers, James MacGregor Burns, is harshly critical of Roosevelt's failure to shape public opinion in the run-up to war: "In the gravest international situation the nation had ever faced, where was the leadership of the man whose very name since 1933 had become the symbol of candor and courage?" Burns acknowledges the extent and the intensity of the opposition and concedes it would have been "disastrous" for Roosevelt to override it. Instead, he argues, the president's "real mission as a political leader was to modify and guide this opinion in a direction closer to American interests as he saw them."[1] Burns may be right. No doubt FDR could have been more skillful and persistent in this regard. Nonetheless, there are two additional factors that need to be considered. First, the "candor and courage" that Burns attributes to Roosevelt's early years as president were real, to be sure, but they were employed to fill a leadership vacuum created by Hoover's failure to acknowledge the Great Depression's impact, particularly on ordinary people. FDR didn't have any immediate answers, either, but he was willing to try anything that might work, and that, accompanied by his upbeat attitude, gave people hope. The situation was so desperate that nearly everyone—even those who saw him as a "traitor to his class"—was willing, at least temporarily, to support him.

None of this was true of the international situation FDR faced in his second term. Only a few saw the situation as desperate, or even as a serious threat for the United States; there was powerful opposition, both in the country and in Congress, to what he was trying to do, which was, very gradually, to prepare the country for war. This was new terrain for Roosevelt. As a result, he was often unsure of himself, and therefore sometimes he faltered. Yet in spite of the fact that he had few allies in the press or Congress, the internationalist in him was so strong that whatever the political repercussions—and given that he was near the end of his term as president, those were not clear—he felt had no real choice.

Given that removal of the arms embargo was the sine qua non to send aid to the Allies, Roosevelt faced a supremely practical decision: should he press for a record vote on repeal, he stood a very good chance of being defeated, and that would have huge consequences. The president focused most of his efforts on the Senate Foreign Relations Committee, on the premise that it would be the key to winning not only the full Senate's support but that of the House of Representatives as well. Because under William Borah the committee had become a bastion of hard-core isolationists from both parties, it had to be won over decisively if repeal of the embargo was to be viable. The fact was that the votes for repeal were never there—as Garner had pointed out—particularly after FDR lost two that he otherwise would have had, had he not tried, and failed, to purge them the year before. Nor is it likely that public proselytizing by the president would have changed votes on the committee. For the most part the members of the committee were philosophically committed to their isolationist doctrine, and they had committed constituencies at home backing them up. A few in the middle were waffling, such as committee chairman Key Pittman, but they were more influenced by strong personalities such as Borah and Nye than they were by Roosevelt.

A defeat on the merits of loosening the embargo, even in committee, would have signaled to many that the issue was dead for the foreseeable future, because positions would simply harden. And it would be a terrible blow to morale in the European democracies, which were counting on military assistance from the United States, thereby strengthening the hand of the appeasers. FDR of course knew all this, and his political instincts told him not to press the matter until events made success possible. In September 1939 that event occurred in the form of a declared war.

By mid-September Roosevelt was cautiously optimistic that he could win the votes to repeal the embargo, but he still wasn't taking any chances. He would be speaking to a special session of Congress only days after Charles Lindbergh's quasi-racist but emotionally effective address on September 15, in which he urged the nation to stay out of the war. That address, though it never mentioned the Neutrality Act, had elicited a huge response. Moreover, the president was aware that his own standing in Congress was still precarious, and that he needed to tend to more than a few bruised feelings and egos there. He understood that he couldn't state outright that his principal reason for repealing the embargo was to send aid to Britain and France; the rationale would have to be couched in less provocative terms, particularly now that Senator Borah and others were calling themselves the "peace bloc." Not least, the situation called for everyone, and especially the president, to seem to be above politics in the face of such grim tidings; setting an early bipartisan tone would be essential.

Working behind the scenes, the White House reached out to Governor Alf Landon of Kansas and Frank Knox of the *Chicago Daily News*, the Republican presidential and vice presidential nominees in 1936, together with Henry Stimson, Herbert Hoover's secretary of state, all of whom agreed to support repeal. Other respected opinion leaders such as President James B. Conant of Harvard and the well-known newspaper editor William Allen White joined in. Administration operatives went to work on individual congressmen of both parties and began to make progress in soliciting support. Representative Usher Burdick, a Republican from North Dakota, told the president he was "satisfied I was wrong" in previously supporting the embargo and pledged to change his vote.[2]

To cap off this activity, the president invited the bipartisan leadership of Congress, together with Landon and Knox, to the White House on the afternoon of September 20, the day before his scheduled address. The stated reason for the meeting was unclear, and at least some of the Republicans assumed that they would be given new information and asked to offer their views on policy. However, Roosevelt and Hull, badly burned by the meeting of the Senate Military Affairs Committee back in January and the public row that followed, had no intention of risking that sort of embarrassment again. As soon became evident to everyone, the real reason for the meeting was the meeting itself, not its conclusions, of which there were few.

Assembled in a semicircle around the president's desk in the Oval Office, the leaders listened as Roosevelt opened the two-hour session by repeating his determination to keep the country out of the war. He recounted the history of the Neutrality Act and the various proclamations he had already issued pursuant to it. He cited the parallels, and the absence thereof, to the

First World War, and otherwise reiterated points already well known to the conferees. At one point Joe Martin, the Republican leader in the House, leaned over to Landon and whispered, "I'd like to know what we're here for."[3] Both Landon and Knox showed signs of resenting being used as props on FDR's stage, but neither said anything.

Roosevelt made reference to the tentative understanding he had already reached with the congressional leadership: the present embargo provision would be repealed, and in its place Congress would insist that henceforth arms could only be sold to belligerents on a "cash-and-carry" basis. The latter meant that no credits would be provided for sales, as they had been in the previous war. This required, further, that the purchased goods must be transported in foreign vessels, not American ones. The reason for the cash-and-carry provision was simple, but to the members of Congress it was compelling. As one of the unidentified conferees put it bluntly to the president that afternoon, outright repeal would cause "the man of the street" to say, "Why, those fellows are repealing the neutrality law and . . . the next thing we know we will be in this war." On the other hand, if the gist was repeal of the embargo and implementation of cash-and-carry, "he has got no objection to it."[4]

Before the session adjourned, another conferee mentioned that he had recently supported repeal publicly because the real purpose, after all, was to get aid to the democracies. "I am darned glad you said something I couldn't say," FDR shrewdly offered, "and that is without question the overwhelming sentiment in this country is in favor of France and England winning the war."[5] It was the elephant not only in this room but in the entire debate: neither the president nor Congress could hold the United States out as a neutral nation if its official policy was designed to assist specific belligerents. Virtually everyone recognized it as a fiction, but a fiction that had to be maintained.

Missy LeHand had phoned Sam Rosenman the day before with the message that the president would like him to come down on the night of the twentieth to help him finalize the speech. This was not an unusual request, as FDR had relied on Rosenman, a former state legislator and now a trial judge in New York, for help on major speeches ever since his days as governor. Rosenman knew Roosevelt as well as anyone could; he was a skilled craftsman who had a gift for putting into the right words just what the president was trying to say. In 1932, for example, he drafted FDR's pledge of "a new deal for the American people," although neither he nor Roosevelt foresaw the lasting effect the term would assume. The most difficult challenge for any speechwriter when writing for an ambitious politician is to find his "voice." FDR, perhaps more than any president since Lincoln, cared deeply about how he phrased ideas and how to fit them into his own way of enunciating and dramatizing points. After more than a decade of working intimately with Roosevelt, Rosenman had long since found his principal's voice. And the president had found a modest and self-effacing man whom he valued as much for his judgment and loyalty as for his literary talents.

Arriving at the White House about five-thirty, while the session with the Senate leaders was still going on, Rosenman set up shop in the Cabinet Room with various drafts Missy LeHand gave him, including the most recent one that the president himself had dictated. When the meeting was finally adjourned at six o'clock and the senators had departed, he went next door to see FDR. Roosevelt expressed satisfaction with the meeting but feared that Republican leader Joe Martin might "play politics" with the repeal effort. Getting the president's latest thoughts on the speech with no indication that the recent meeting had affected them, Rosenman returned to work until it was time to join the president for a relaxed dinner with Missy and Grace Tully.

After dinner Hull arrived to weigh in with the State Department's most recent views and they worked together until eleven, when the president retired. Rosenman and Tully continued to work until two-thirty, and Rosenman was back at it at seven the next morning for two hours before taking the latest version of the speech—incorporating all of the previous day's conclusions—into FDR's bedroom. They spent the rest of the morning working on it. As Rosenman recalled, "He did his work sitting up in bed; and we sent the pages over one by one to Grace, who rapidly typed a reading copy. I talked with Hull by phone several times during the morning, reading him some new language and getting his suggestions."[6] The session reveals clearly how FDR organized his thoughts and set his script, reflecting a highly refined and usually very successful method of getting relevant views into the mix before taking it over and finally putting it into final form, typically at the last minute. FDR relied on the inherent drama of the process— the bringing together of different ideas in a tight time frame—not so much to make up his mind about something as to express it convincingly. The calmness of his demeanor amplified his ability to seem above events, and somehow in control of them. At half past noon on September 21, he signed off on the last page of the speech he was to deliver at two o'clock.

The fact that this was the first time in his presidency that Roosevelt had asked to appear before Congress in extraordinary session, combined with the outbreak of war in Europe, filled the House chamber with nervous anticipation. The floor of the huge room was packed with representatives and senators, seated separately, and the galleries couldn't accommodate all the private citizens who came to witness a great event. Finally the large central door to the chamber opened and through it came the sergeant at arms, who announced, "Mr. Speaker, the President of the United States." An unsmiling Roosevelt, his steel leg braces in place, followed on the arm of an aide as he slowly and arduously made his way to the podium to polite applause that he ignored. As always in these situations, his concentration was on the difficulty of each step he was taking. As he was walking to the podium at the 1936 Democratic convention one of his braces had snapped and he went tumbling, his fall broken only at the last moment by a Secret Service agent. After that incident he was angrier in public than anyone had ever seen him, not least because it had taken several minutes to rearrange the papers of his speech. He lived in fear that it could happen again.

When Roosevelt reached the podium after tortuously climbing several steps, he placed a reading copy of his speech on the lectern as the members gave their chief executive a respectful if unenthusiastic reception. Many in his own party were still smarting from the disagreements and slights of recent years. Roosevelt had been president for nearly two terms, and he carried the baggage of them. Nonetheless, he was undeterred in his goal, which was to make the case to this audience and the public at large for repealing the arms embargo. He would do this without explicitly stating the primary rationale for doing so, but rather by wrapping it in the compelling argument of maintaining America's traditional neutrality and appealing for bipartisanship at a time of crisis. "Regardless of party or section the mantle of peace and of patriotism is wide enough to cover us all," he said early on. "Let no group assume the exclusive label of the 'peace bloc'"—an obvious reference to Borah's claim of that name for the isolationists. "We all belong to it." He won some credibility when he admitted error, a rare occurrence. The error, however, was not solely his. Arguing that Congress had deviated from "the sound principle of neutrality, and peace through international law" when it enacted the "so-called Neutrality Act of 1935," he confessed, "I regret that the Congress passed that Act. I equally regret that I signed that Act."[7]

His principal point was that the embargo did not serve the cause of neutrality because it helped the aggressors and therefore made it more likely that the United States would be drawn into the war. Transporting "uncompleted implements of war" to belligerents in American ships created "a definite danger to our neutrality and peace." That danger would be greatly reduced, he argued, under the cash-and-carry provision, which would prohibit extending credits for purchases and require that they be carried in foreign vessels. Together with prohibiting American ships and citizens from traveling to war zones, he said, the new policy would afford "far greater safeguards than we now possess, or have ever possessed, to protect American lives and property from danger." This policy was, he added, calculated to keep the country out of war. To make sure no one missed the point, he concluded, "Our acts must be guided by one single hard-headed thought—keeping America out of this war."[8]

The speech had its intended effect. While the response of those in the chamber was more muted than that for earlier addresses, thousands of letters and telegrams descended on the White House. They usually did following a presidential address, but this time, officials said, there were too many to be counted. Poll numbers on the question climbed, with 60 percent of Americans now favoring repeal of the act, according to Gallup. The effect of the speech on Congress after the public reaction registered was also as intended, touching heavily as it did on the essential political themes of patriotism, bipartisanship, neutrality, and, most important, peace. There was little on its face to criticize, and with the president's strong plea building on the momentum already under way, the legislators moved toward action at last. Within a week, the Senate Foreign Relations Committee reported out the cash-and-carry bill by a vote of 16 to 7. Even two elusive targets of the 1938 purge attempt, Walter George and Guy Gillette, voted with the majority, coming full circle.

Although all the signs were positive, FDR saw the situation as still precarious and he didn't want anything to upset it. But that was precisely what happened when, two days after the speech, Alf Landon called on Roosevelt to publicly rule out running for a third term in 1940, ostensibly to keep the issue out of politics. It had the opposite effect—as Landon knew it would—politicizing the embargo issue by encouraging congressional Republicans to rally to their 1936 standard-bearer. Roosevelt was still far from ready to even mention a third term. If anything, he was expending political capital and placing the success of his campaign for repeal of the Neutrality Act on keeping the issue out of the conversation.

Despite the administration's best efforts to stay on message by obscuring the real intention of the repeal effort, not everyone was buying, certainly not William E. Borah. He opened the Senate debate on the vote by arguing that repeal of the embargo would be tantamount to intervention in the hostilities, given that its real purpose was to get aid to Britain and France. Borah's reaction was to be expected. Somewhat more surprising was the October 5 speech of Hoover's former secretary of state, Henry Stimson, effectively confirming Borah's point that repeal was designed to aid the democracies. The highly respected former secretary of state had concluded that a straightforward approach was not only more honest but also more effective. It was certainly more in keeping with Stimson's high standards of public rectitude. Because he had pledged to work with the administration on the issue, he called Cordell Hull the day after Borah's speech to inform him of his plans. Hull was worried that Stimson's frank admission could significantly change the dynamic of the debate and put repeal at risk by ceding this central issue to the opposition. He pleaded with his predecessor to omit what he saw as potentially explosive language, or at the very least to soften it. Stimson would do neither, and thus the issue became whether he would cancel the speech or deliver it as intended.

———————

Hull convened a meeting at the State Department to determine whether the fallout from convincing Stimson—who was a private citizen—to cancel the speech, which was to be delivered over a national radio network, would be worse than allowing it to go forward. They decided that it would indeed be worse to cancel it, given Stimson's reputation for integrity and the likelihood that the inevitable controversy following cancellation would overshadow the debate; Hull called Stimson to withdraw his reservations. In the event, Stimson's broadcast was so well received that William Allen White mailed tens of thousands of copies of it to journalists and other opinion leaders around the country. The theme was quickly picked up in the congressional debate, with members openly stating that Hitler had to be stopped and that only Britain and France could do it with U.S. help. Even Ohio's Robert A. Taft—next to Borah one of the most confirmed isolationists—announced that he would support repeal because the current law "favors the aggressor against the peaceful nation," which of course had been FDR's refrain for years.

On October 13, Lindbergh gave another speech, which he had predicted was "going to create more criticism than the last one," a month earlier. Nonetheless, he was convinced that he needed to "speak clearly" on "fundamental problems," and particularly on "this present issue of 'neutrality.'"[9] Once he began speaking, again to a national radio audience, it quickly became apparent that one of the "fundamental problems" he wanted to get people thinking about was race. Dismissing the war in Europe as a struggle over the balance of power on the continent, he developed his main theme: "Our bond with Europe is a bond of race and not of political ideology. . . . It is the European race we must preserve; political progress will follow." To Lindbergh "racial strength" was the real issue. Politics was "a luxury." "If the white race is ever seriously threatened, it may then be time for us to take our part for its protection, to fight side by side with the English, French and Germans. But not with one against the other for our mutual destruction."[10]

The effect was to mystify the audience. Racial purity was hardly "one single hard-headed thought," and as a result, this speech was even more disjointed than the one he had delivered in September. It had little impact on the debate involving repeal of the arms embargo; nonetheless, Lindbergh pressed ahead, expanding on the racial theme a few days later in an article that reached three million people in *Reader's Digest*. "It is time to turn from our quarrels and to build our White ramparts again," he wrote. Western civilization depends "on a united strength among ourselves . . . on a Western wall of race and arms which can hold back either a Genghis Khan or the infiltration of inferior blood; on an English fleet, a German air force, a French army, an American nation, standing together as guardians of our common heritage, sharing strength, dividing influence."[11]

Roosevelt was as befuddled by the speech as anyone but guessed that Lindbergh was seeking to promote a negotiated settlement in Europe, as he knew his own ambassador in London, Joe Kennedy, was then secretly trying to do. Such a settlement, the reasoning went, would then permit the "white race" to stand united against the much greater threat of the "yellow peril" of Asia and the Communists of the Soviet Union. The theory was strengthened by Lindbergh's assertions in the article that "men must be accorded rights equal to their ability" and that "no system of representation can succeed in which the voice of weakness is equal to the voice of strength."[12]

Roosevelt assumed—reasonably enough—that Lindbergh harbored political ambitions, perhaps presidential ones, and he saw Lindbergh's speech through that lens. However, there was something deeper that galled the president. He was convinced that the great American hero did not believe in the most basic American value—democracy. Whatever other posturing was involved in the debate over world affairs, this went to the foundation of Roosevelt's beliefs. "If I should die tomorrow," Roosevelt told Henry Morgenthau a few months later, "I want you to know this. I am absolutely convinced that Lindbergh is a Nazi."[13]

If Lindbergh's was the principal voice of isolationism outside official Washington, William Allen White's was widely seen as its counterpart on the other side of the debate. Both were Republicans, both were small-town midwesterners, both were household names in America. There the similarities stopped. White was the longtime editor of the *Emporia Gazette*, a Kansas newspaper whose homespun humor and plain common sense made him a respected and even beloved spokesman for the small-town values that most Americans embraced. In 1896, outraged by what the Populists were doing to stifle business in his state, he wrote a blistering editorial, "What's the Matter with Kansas?" attacking them and their presidential candidate that year, William Jennings Bryan. With that he burst onto the national scene, and thereafter his editorials, for which he won a Pulitzer Prize, were widely reprinted. His politics were consistently of the progressive Republican variety, and in 1912 he helped Theodore Roosevelt establish the Bull Moose Party. But he stayed with the Republicans even when they weren't progressive, supporting Herbert Hoover in both 1928 and 1932 (although he famously called the politically paralyzed president "the greatest innocent bystander in history"). He was ambivalent about the New Deal, favoring some of its programs and criticizing others, but he was drawn to Roosevelt's internationalist view of the world.

Seventy-two years old in the fall of 1939, White devoted his energies to repeal of the arms embargo. The president had called him earlier to help mobilize public opinion for the effort, and White had agreed to do so. He had announced on October 2, 1939—just before Lindbergh's speech—the formation of the awkwardly named Non-Partisan Committee for Peace Through Revision of the Neutrality Act, with White as its chairman. It inevitably became known as the White Committee, and during the fall it distributed volumes of pro-repeal material, such as Stimson's address. Because White was so respected for his integrity and his willingness to put country before party, his was probably the most influential voice for the cause of repeal besides Roosevelt's own. The president was well aware of that fact and worked assiduously to cultivate an even deeper relationship with him. For his part, the man known as the "Sage of Emporia" loved to kibitz with presidents, including Democratic presidents, and FDR was more than ready to oblige him. They kept up a lively correspondence, with White frequently enclosing his most recent editorial.

Roosevelt was determined to leave no stone unturned as the repeal effort approached its early November climax in Congress. He dispatched one of his most eager and talented young operatives, Tommy Corcoran, to Chicago to enlist the support of the ranking Catholic cleric, Bishop Bernard J. Sheil, who delivered an administration-friendly radio address heavily influenced by Corcoran. Even Al Smith, FDR's onetime friend but recent adversary, was enlisted to appeal in yet another radio address to Irish Catholics in an effort to overcome their anti-British bias.

Everything helped in this highly orchestrated campaign, but perhaps nothing helped more than events—as Roosevelt had suspected they would. For a month Americans had been bombarded with news of Hitler's ruthless and unprovoked assault on Poland, a nation much admired in the United States. The picture of the ruthless Nazi war machine terrified most Americans, and when it was accompanied by Soviet moves to intimidate its small and peaceful neighbor to the north, Finland, also warmly admired in the United States, it could be readily imagined where all this was leading. German and Russian treachery had caused Poland to virtually disappear, and now the two nations had obvious designs to divide up the rest of the continent. Perhaps America's first line of defense was indeed on the Rhine, but if so, it could only be maintained with U.S. arms in the hands of the French and British. That was certainly Roosevelt's view, and it was beginning to win more and more adherents.

To counter this line of thinking and to lull the democracies once again into believing that war could be avoided, Hitler began yet another peace offensive. With weeks of propaganda culminating in a major speech in the Reichstag on October 6, the Führer maintained that he had worked tirelessly for peace with France and Britain and that he was willing to make one more effort at yet one more international conference. Before Chamberlain could formulate a response—but after Daladier did so, equivocally—Hitler, in a move obviously unknown to anyone outside Germany, ordered his military chiefs to prepare plans for a major incursion into France through the Low Counties as soon as possible, possibly in the coming weeks.

Throughout this period pressure built on Roosevelt to negotiate a peace accord between Hitler and the Allies, with Joe Kennedy leading the effort. "The president can be the savior of the world," Kennedy said less than two weeks after the invasion of Poland. FDR demurred as to whether this was the role he should play. He deeply and genuinely detested Hitler and was determined not to lend the German's actions the slightest legitimacy. A few weeks later Kennedy feared "the complete collapse of everything we hope and live for" if Britain went down to defeat in renewed fighting. The ambassador, Roosevelt told Morgenthau, "always has been an appeaser and always will be an appeaser." Should Germany or Italy make an offer for peace, he said, "Joe would start working on the King and his friend, the Queen, and from there on down, to get everyone to accept it." He had had about enough of Kennedy. As he told Morgenthau, "He's just a pain in the neck to me."[14]

The ambassador's pattern of behavior in such a critical position, obviously at odds with the policies of the administration, begs the question of why the president kept him on. Although Kennedy was much more conservative than Roosevelt, he had given FDR significant financial help in the elections of 1932 and 1936 with the expectation of an important appointment, preferably in the cabinet. The president made him the first chairman of the newly established Securities and Exchange Commission (SEC) over many objections and despite the fact that Kennedy had accumulated wealth from questionable investment practices that would be prohibited years later by the very same SEC. ("Set a thief to catch a thief," FDR replied.) But the SEC didn't begin to satisfy the ambitious Kennedy, and he soon launched an all-out campaign for the London post. Roosevelt distrusted Kennedy and saw him as "a dangerous man" but reluctantly agreed to the appointment, largely to get him out of Washington; he also thought it would be amusing to have an Irishman deal with the Brits. However, perhaps predictably, Kennedy's views made him disliked and distrusted in both Washington and London. Roosevelt nonetheless felt he was stuck with him, and the reason was largely political: he was worried about offending the Irish Catholic community, of which Kennedy was a respected lay leader, and he was certain that Kennedy would create serious problems in the 1940 election, probably by launching his own candidacy, as FDR knew he had been considering. So he left him in place but ignored his advice.[15]

The apparent lessening of the likelihood of imminent fighting in Europe during October only slightly cut into public support for embargo repeal. Events in Poland and the outrage and fear they conveyed to so many

Americans, reinforced by Roosevelt's efforts and the work of the White Committee, had clearly firmed up solid support for the bill now working its way toward final passage. At last, on November 3, the Senate voted 63 to 30 and the House 243 to 172 to repeal the arms embargo and substitute in its place the policy of cash-and-carry. Conservative southern Democrats in both chambers voted overwhelmingly with Roosevelt, and progressive Republicans voted just as overwhelmingly against him. No one on either side of the debate doubted that "neutrality" had been redefined. What it now meant, at least as far as Roosevelt was concerned, was that the productive capacity of the United States would be available to help stave off a Hitler-dominated Europe and thereby prevent the war from coming to America.

Unspoken and yet seemingly everywhere during 1939 was the question, fed constantly by rumors, of whether FDR would seek a third term. Several of those closest to him did their best to promote the idea. Interior secretary Harold Ickes, who seldom missed an opportunity to talk politics and with whom FDR liked to lunch frequently for that reason, was probably the first to float the idea. On his honeymoon to Europe in the summer of 1938, during which he met with political leaders in Britain and France, Ickes was stunned by what he was told. "Everywhere I went, I heard the same thing: 'war is inevitable'—'war is imminent,'" he would tell Robert Sherwood later. "I thought hard about this war prospect and about the Presidential election in 1940. I considered in my mind the whole field of candidates and I came to the conclusion there was only one man big enough to handle the world situation: Roosevelt."

On his return, Ickes said later, he "came out for a third term" and raised it at every opportunity. "The President did not give me one word of encouragement on this. But he did not tell me to stop," Ickes recorded in his diary. He added that he thought he was then the only member of the cabinet to support the idea. "Most of the others were candidates themselves—Hopkins, Hull, Farley, Wallace, Garner—you couldn't throw a brick in any direction without hitting a candidate."[16]

Harry Hopkins, whom a year earlier FDR had encouraged to believe that he could be the Democratic nominee before he had been effectively eliminated from contention by his health, was the next member of the cabinet to urge a third term. With his own presidential ambitions shelved at least temporarily (some thought he retained an interest in the vice presidency), he focused solely on keeping FDR in the White House. He told a reporter in June 1939 that he would urge Roosevelt to seek the nomination again. When the reporter asked, "How is President Roosevelt going to get around the third term bugaboo?" Hopkins responded, "You have the answer when you say 'President Roosevelt.'"[17]

Franklin Delano Roosevelt, the 32nd president of the United States, as he appeared in mid-October 1940. Courtesy of the Franklin D. Roosevelt Presidential Library

President Roosevelt with Marguerite LeHand, his confidential secretary of twenty years, in the second-floor Oval Study, his favorite room in the White House. "Missy," as she was called, knew his wants, needs, and moods better than anyone around him.
Courtesy of the Franklin D. Roosevelt Presidential Library

FDR with Harry Hopkins, who earned the president's trust administering New Deal funds for relief and job creation. During 1940, under Roosevelt's tutelage, he became chief political adviser and began to study foreign policy. Library of Congress, Prints & Photographs Division, NYWT&S Collection

Secretary of State Cordell Hull helped Roosevelt shape the strategy for sending aid to Great Britain and France to resist Adolf Hitler's aggression. Library of Congress

FDR rides with Secretary of the Interior Harold Ickes (center) and Secretary of Agriculture Henry Wallace, two former Republicans who became ardent New Dealers and strong advocates for a third term. Library of Congress

Springwood, more commonly known as the "Big House," FDR's beloved home in Hyde Park, New York. Library of Congress

Vice President John Nance Garner, known as "Cactus Jack" for his Texas roots, had a difficult relationship with the president. Ultimately they would have a bitter falling-out over the third-term issue. Associated Press

FDR returns from a baseball game with Democratic Party chairman James A. Farley, who had successfully managed his earlier campaigns for governor and president. Farley too objected to a third term for the president and, like Garner, sought the 1940 nomination for himself. Associated Press

When Roosevelt refused to state whether he planned to retire or to seek another term during the winter and spring of 1940, cartoonists and journalists depicted him as a "Sphinx" who wouldn't reveal his secrets.
A 1938 Herblock Cartoon, © The Herb Block Foundation

Four days before the Republican convention FDR named two of the most prominent Republicans in the country, Henry L. Stimson (right) and Frank Knox, as secretaries of war and navy respectively. The move both strengthened his national security team and unsettled the GOP leadership then assembling in Philadelphia.
Library of Congress

Senators Robert A. Taft (left) and Arthur A. Vandenberg congratulate Wendell Willkie after his dramatic come-from-behind victory to defeat them for the Republican presidential nomination. Bentley Historical Library, University of Michigan

Supreme Court Justice Felix Frankfurter swears in Frank Knox as secretary of the navy on July 11, 1940. FDR asked Frankfurter to return that evening for a two-hour discussion on the third-term question. Library of Congress

The president requested Frankfurter and Librarian of Congress Archibald MacLeish (above) to draft confidential third-term memos for him just days before the Democratic convention convened in Chicago. Library of Congress

Delegates stage a demonstration on the floor of the Democratic convention urging that FDR be "drafted" for a third term. Associated Press

Eleanor Roosevelt makes a dramatic appearance at the convention to urge the delegates to approve her husband's choice of Henry Wallace to be the vice presidential nominee. Associated Press

Secretary of Labor Frances Perkins, the first woman to be appointed to a cabinet position, had known FDR for nearly thirty years. Politically savvy, she engineered Eleanor's critical appearance at the convention. Washingtoniana, District of Columbia Public Library

Speaking to the convention and a national radio audience on a hot and humid evening in the White House, Roosevelt formally accepts his party's presidential nomination for the third time, July 18, 1940.
Bettmann/CORBIS

Following the Democratic convention, the president rides with Missy LeHand and his ambassador to France, William C. Bullitt, from the railroad station in Hyde Park.
AP/CORBIS

On August 17, 1940, Wendell Willkie returns to his hometown of Elwood, Indiana, to formally accept the Republican nomination for president and to begin his general election campaign. Bettmann/CORBIS

American sailors turn over refitted World War I–era destroyers to their British counterparts in a deal that Roosevelt had made with Winston Churchill in return for long-term leases of British bases in the Western Hemisphere. Courtesy of the Franklin D. Roosevelt Presidential Library

Just days before the election, the president watches as the blindfolded secretary of the navy, Frank Knox, draws a number in the first peacetime draft in American history.
Library of Congress

Ambassador Joseph P. Kennedy, Roosevelt's envoy to London with whom he had an on-again, off-again relationship and whom he feared would support Willkie, delivers a national radio address one week before the election endorsing FDR.
Library of Congress

Yale students Kingman Brewster (left) and Richard M. Bissell flank Charles A. Lindbergh on October 30, when the aviation hero and isolationist spokesman came to New Haven to address a meeting of the Yale America First Committee. Library of Congress

FDR's touring car passes through Kingston, New York, on November 4, 1940, on its way to Hyde Park for Election Day. Associated Press

Franklin Roosevelt with his mother, Sara, and his wife, Eleanor, on their way to vote in Hyde Park, November 5, 1940. Courtesy of the Franklin D. Roosevelt Presidential Library

Chief Justice Charles Evans Hughes administers the oath of office to Franklin Delano Roosevelt for the third time on the East Portico of the Capitol on January 20, 1941. Library of Congress

■ FDR fishes off the USS *Tuscaloosa* on a post-election vacation during which he receives a desperate plea from Churchill for more aid; this causes him to conceive the idea of Lend-Lease. Courtesy of the Franklin D. Roosevelt Presidential Library

FDR signs the Lend-Lease Act on March 11, 1941, making the United States the "Arsenal of Democracy" and giving the president extraordinary powers to distribute assistance to allied powers around the world. Library of Congress

5

The Sphinx

John Nance Garner was a product of Uvalde County in rural south Texas, which he called home for his entire life, and of the United States Congress, where he had served for thirty years. He embodied the mores and culture of both places, which is to say he was conservative, blunt, and hard-driving, yet on the whole cautious about his political survival. His weathered face was reddened as much by drink as by the Texas sun. Winning his first election to the House of Representatives in 1902, he earned the respect and even affection of most of his colleagues, who in 1931 elected him Speaker when the Democrats took control of the Congress for the first time in a decade.

At the 1932 Democratic National Convention, when FDR had been about 100 delegate votes short of the two-thirds margin he needed to be nominated, Roosevelt authorized Jim Farley to offer the vice presidential nomination to Garner if he would release his pledged delegates in the Texas and California delegations on the fourth ballot. Garner did so with some reluctance—he was wary of giving up real power in the House for an office he would later famously call "not worth a pitcher of warm piss"—but Representative Sam Rayburn of Texas and others persuaded him that winning back the White House required party unity and a quick end to the balloting, which only Garner could ensure.

Garner settled comfortably into the traditional role of a vice president as presiding officer of the Senate. It was an undemanding job, and most afternoons, in keeping with the prevailing ways of the Congress, he would convene "the board of education" in his office, where the agenda was heavily laced with bourbon and political gossip; those in attendance were encouraged to "strike a blow for liberty" when the bottle was passed around. FDR invited Garner to attend cabinet meetings and sometimes consulted with him on congressional strategy, but otherwise the vice president remained happily ensconced at the other end of Pennsylvania Avenue. As the Constitution was generally understood at the time, his office was considered more a part of the legislative branch of government than of the executive. (Not until President Eisenhower brought Richard Nixon downtown did the vice president even have a presence in the White House complex, and not until President Carter installed Walter Mondale in the West Wing did he have an office in the White House itself.) Nonetheless, Roosevelt and Garner had a respectful if distant relationship, and the latter faithfully supported, or at least acquiesced in, the president's New Deal initiatives during the first term, helping get them through the Senate.

Early in the second term, however, relations between the two started to sour. The most proximate cause was the president's Court-packing plan and especially his failure to consult beforehand with congressional leaders, including the presiding officer of the Senate. When the clerk of the Senate read aloud the president's message urging that he be given authority to appoint a new Supreme Court justice for every sitting justice over the age of seventy, most senators were stunned by the audacity of what he was proposing; if enacted at that time, it would have given Roosevelt six new appointments. On hearing the provision, Garner visibly pinched his nose with the fingers of one hand while turning down the thumb of the other. The message was clear, and the vice president confirmed it shortly afterward when he abruptly left for a "vacation" in Uvalde in the middle of the Court fight. Democratic Party chairman Jim Farley believed Roosevelt never forgave him for that, particularly after the Senate delivered a resounding and embarrassing defeat to the president. Garner thereafter frequently undermined the administration's agenda in Congress, with the notable exception of revisions to the Neutrality Act, which he supported. With the halcyon days of the first term gone, Garner reverted to his more conservative and irascible self. Cabinet meetings took on a different tenor, with the vice president frequently reminding FDR that he had months before said something similar to what the president had just said, or gratuitously offering an "I told you so." On one occasion the president sent an oblique but unmistakable message that the vice president needn't attend a particular cabinet meeting, and on another, when Garner wasn't present, Roosevelt announced that everyone was therefore free to speak candidly.

The 1938 attempted purge of several senators and congressmen, mostly southerners, who had opposed the Court plan or other elements of FDR's program added to the breach. This effort was anathema to the vice president not only because it sought to "purify" the Democratic Party ideologically but also because it violated an unwritten rule, which FDR had heretofore faithfully observed, that the president should stay out of intraparty primary contests. Garner was strongly reinforced in both of these points by the Democratic legislators with whom he spent most of his time. "It is not the business of the President of the United States to choose Senators and Representatives in Congress," Garner told a friendly journalist off the record. "He won't succeed. The people of the states will regard it as Presidential arrogance."[1] Needless to say, the vice president felt completely vindicated by the purge's near-total failure.

The relationship between the two continued to deteriorate to the point of bitterness; whatever mutual trust had existed was all but gone. Jim Farley, who was among those in the administration closest to Garner, urged the president to see him one-on-one to find a way to repair the breach. Roosevelt did so, and reported to Farley in late December 1938, "I'm afraid we didn't get anywhere. Jack is very much opposed to the spending program; he's against the tax program, and he's against the relief program. He seems to be pretty much against everything and he hasn't got a single concrete idea to offer on any of these programs. It's one thing to criticize but something else to offer solutions." Farley then talked with Garner and concluded,

"While the visit was pleasant, the two did not get anywhere because they held decidedly different views."[2]

FDR had assured Garner after the 1937 inauguration that he would be returning to Hyde Park in 1941, and Garner was initially inclined to take him at his word. Not surprisingly, a Garner-for-president movement started in Texas and gained popular support. By early 1938 the Gallup poll showed the vice president as the heavy favorite of Democrats to succeed Roosevelt if he retired: Garner led with 40 percent, with Hull and Farley at 10 percent each and Hopkins and former Indiana governor Paul McNutt in single digits. While this news gave the vice president a good deal of satisfaction, it couldn't have given FDR any. It was impossible for him to imagine Garner succeeding him even if he could be elected, which Roosevelt doubted. He saw Garner as a throwback to another era, disloyal in the extreme, and unlikely to defend the critical gains represented by the New Deal. FDR had come to detest his vice president.

Garner claimed he didn't want to be president; he simply wanted to go back to Uvalde and work his ranch. In late 1939, however, he heard growing speculation about FDR running again—Garner and Farley talked about the subject frequently—and, knowing FDR's clever ways, he believed it and didn't like it. Very much a traditionalist in such matters, he saw the unwritten two-term rule as almost as sacrosanct as the Constitution itself. He and Farley were the cabinet members most adamantly opposed to a third term for Roosevelt, and Garner allowed efforts for his own candidacy to go forward, ostensibly as a vehicle to help derail what he saw as Roosevelt's wrongheaded ambitions. He had no hard evidence of FDR's intentions, nor did anyone else, but what he took to be well-founded rumors and his own political instincts persuaded him FDR wanted a third term. There was no question but that his personal animosity toward FDR played a role as well.

He may have discounted his chances for the nomination, but at the same time he was a seasoned politician and knew that anything could happen in politics; lightning could strike in unlikely places. What's more, he was enjoying the attention—and probably the discomfort the polls were giving the president. Committees were formed, publicity was generated, and soon it appeared that a full-blown candidacy was under way. In December 1939

Garner formally announced that he would be a candidate for the Democratic presidential nomination in 1940, but without saying a word about the third-term issue. The event prompted the president to remark caustically at the next cabinet meeting, "I see that the Vice President has thrown his bottle—I mean his hat—into the ring."[3]

A few days later Farley told the president what he thought of Garner's chances. "I don't think Jack wants to be president. I am convinced he made his announcement only because of his opposition to a third term." Roosevelt said he didn't understand Garner and recounted the story of a conversation the two of them had had in 1937. "Jack came over and patted me on the shoulder asking, 'Are you going back to Hyde Park after 1940?' I told him I was. Then Garner said he was glad because he was going back to Uvalde. Now in view of that, you'd think he'd understand I was telling him, in so many words, that I was not going to run. I have proceeded on the theory that he would not, in view of his words. I think he should have accepted my assurance, provided he was thinking clearly."[4]

And then there was Jim Farley himself. The always-smiling, glad-handing, semi-bald Irishman was the embodiment of the professional Democratic politician of his time, at least in New York, except that he was far more skilled in the political arts than most. In 1909 he was elected town chairman in his hometown, Stony Point, and two years later town clerk. Eager to work his way up the ladder, he became town supervisor and then, in what he called the "big time," was elected Democratic chairman of Rockland County, which put him directly into state politics. He ultimately became chairman of the state party and helped Roosevelt in both of his gubernatorial elections. FDR valued him for his ability to work the Democratic organizations and the back rooms, and thus in 1932 Farley teamed up with Louis Howe to lay the groundwork for Roosevelt's presidential campaign. Farley traveled the country meeting with party leaders, assuring them that Roosevelt was electable and, not incidentally, someone they could work with. He was effective because of his natural bonhomie and because he was one of them. He was equally effective as FDR's floor manager at the convention in Chicago that year, helping to keep wavering delegations in line through four ballots and successfully engineering (with Sam Rayburn) the Garner vice presidential nomination.

President Roosevelt rewarded him in the traditional way, by naming him postmaster general, whose duties included dispensing patronage. Since he simultaneously held the post of chairman of the Democratic National Committee, he was well positioned to recognize and reward those who had helped FDR get to the White House, especially those who were for him before the 1932 Chicago convention. It was in that capacity that Farley met regularly with the president, who had a keen interest not only in the personnel of his administration but also in the politics of patronage; it was a tool he used strategically, and sometimes ruthlessly, to get his way in Congress. The relationship between the two was cordial, businesslike, and even friendly, but it was never intimate, a fact that the very sensitive Farley came increasingly to resent.

During the campaign of 1936, after Farley had appeared on the rear platform of a train with FDR during a stop in Chicago and received several shout-outs from politicians in the crowd, a staffer told him that "they thought it best" that such joint appearances be discontinued. Farley was indignant and reasoned, no doubt correctly, that the directive came straight from Roosevelt. A few weeks later he received another sign of presidential displeasure when Basil O'Connor, FDR's former law partner, told him Roosevelt thought Farley was nurturing ambitions for the presidency. And at the same time Vice President Garner told Farley that whenever he commended him for something in Roosevelt's presence, the president averted his eyes and never said anything in response. There were still other tea leaves adding up to a gradual but unmistakable decline in the relationship: no more "morning bedside conferences," no more personal phone calls, fewer White House lunches and consultations on appointments. "At first this did not disturb me," he said later. "Strange as it may seem, the President never took me into the bosom of the family, although everyone agreed I was more responsible than any other single man for his being in the White House." Farley claimed that he was never invited to spend the night in the White House or on the presidential yacht. "Mrs. Eleanor Roosevelt once said, 'Franklin finds it hard to relax with people who aren't his social equals.' I took this remark to explain my being out of the infield."[5]

The growing rift with the president bothered Farley far more than he would admit, then or later. The attention he received from politicians around the country fed his already healthy ego, as did his invitation to sit at the cabinet table and discuss matters of high policy. His denials to the contrary notwithstanding, Farley craved the recognition and stature that he imagined could be his if elected to either the presidency or the vice presidency. He was increasingly mentioned in the press and in polls as a potential candidate in 1940, further nourishing his ambitions.

On November 19, 1937, during a routine meeting, FDR went into the complicated political situation in New York State, at the end of which he urged Farley to consider running for either governor or senator. He listed the support he could get in either case. Farley was unmoved. He said that he didn't want to live in Albany, his wife didn't want to live in either Albany or Washington, and he couldn't afford more public service. FDR asked him to think it over. Three days later Farley conveyed the gist of the conversation to Garner at one of their regular lunches, and the vice president's reaction was the same as Farley's: the president wanted to get him out of the way in 1940. "Quite frankly, I don't think the boss looks on me as a qualified candidate," Farley told him. "Not that I have any feeling in the matter."

"Well, I do," Garner responded, according to Farley. "I have acquired a high regard for you and know that you are big enough to be President."[6] Almost certainly they were both right: FDR didn't think Farley "qualified," yet still saw him as enough of a problem to want him out of the way.

In August 1938, nine months after this exchange, Farley attended a dinner at Hyde Park with Roosevelt and members of his family, after which the two of them repaired to the president's study. "Jim, why don't you run for Governor?" Farley later claimed the president had begun, not stopping to allow him an opportunity to interpose his objections. Farley said the president argued he could be elected and that it would be a stepping-stone. "A lot of people are interested in you for 1940, Jim; and I'm not sure whether as Postmaster General and Democratic National Chairman you have sufficient background to be nominated and elected President." There it was, as bluntly as FDR felt he could put it. Unstated but implicit in his remarks was that Farley had little interest in and even less knowledge of policy matters, particularly foreign policy matters, which were rapidly coming to the forefront. Also implicit was Farley's lack of a strong commitment to the New Deal; preserving Roosevelt's legacy programs would be an absolute prerequisite for the president's blessing of any candidate to replace him, as Farley must surely have known. What's more, FDR no longer trusted him because he had acquired an agenda of his own; for Roosevelt, as for most presidents, there was only one agenda, and it was his. Ending the conversation, Farley tried to put it to rest. "As much as I would like to be Governor," he said he told FDR, "I just can't do it. Let's forget it once and for all."[7]

Following the disastrous 1938 elections two months later, however, Farley got serious about his presidential ambitions and began soliciting support from party leaders around the country. He used his contacts in the press to generate favorable publicity, and by the end of the year the three names most prominently mentioned for the Democratic presidential nomination in 1940 were those of Hull, Garner, and Farley. Of the three, Farley said, against all the evidence, "I had reason to believe Roosevelt would have preferred to see me nominated." The three had several things in common: they were all original members of the Roosevelt administration, they all represented the moderate center of the Democratic Party, and they were all opposed to a third term for FDR. On the last point, according to Farley, Garner was the most outspoken and Hull the least. Farley reasoned that his best chance of winning a place on the 1940 ticket was through an arrangement with one or both of the others. He regularly consulted with Garner and Hull after the 1938 elections, exchanging gossip, ingratiating himself through flattery, and, most important, taking the political temperature of each as to his likely intentions. "There isn't any doubt in my mind that if I assist in bringing about Garner's or Hull's nomination," he wrote confidently, "I can have second place with either man." After a lifetime of political deal making, he saw his way forward through more of the same.[8]

In early July 1939 Farley had one of his frequent lunches with Garner, who insisted again that he didn't want to be president but was compelled to "fight any third term for the good of the party . . . I'm the only one who can head up any opposition. I owe it to my friends and to the party." For the first time Garner asked his friend straight out whether he was against a third term. The answer was, "Yes, but don't tell a living soul." For the first time these two traditionalists candidly shared their deep philosophical opposition to a third term. The vice president said the two of them together could stop it from happening. Farley replied that he wasn't sure they needed to, and that if the president didn't raise the topic he could go to him as chairman of the Democratic National Committee and ask him about his plans. Maintaining that he had "no feeling" about the nomination for president or vice president, he said he was nonetheless concerned about the "precedent" set by a third term. Suggesting that this was as much personal as philosophical, he added, "And no one can question my loyalty or faithful service to the President. I must confess I am a bit piqued over the neglect and the kicking around I have been getting." Farley's conflicting feelings and motives are found in the exchange: ambition, self-pity, and resentment wrapped in a binder of undoubtedly genuine concern about a third term. The fact was that as a member of the cabinet, whose loyalties were to the president, and as party chairman, whose responsibilities were to the process that would select the next nominee, Farley, now clearly harboring national ambitions of his own, had put himself in an impossible situation. It would get worse.[9]

A few days later Farley met in New York with Cardinal George William Mundelein of Chicago, at the cardinal's request. FDR had assiduously courted Mundelein over the years, and the cardinal could be counted among the president's strongest allies—within the appropriate confines of the Church, of course. The cardinal said he had just spent two hours with Roosevelt and regarded him as "truly a great man." "I think it is most fortunate that he is where he is and I hope he remains," the cardinal added. "It is my belief that he will run for a third term." The president had not said he would, the cardinal went on, but if FDR did run, he hoped that Farley would support him, adding that Roosevelt had been "extremely generous" in his remarks about Farley. He then said, in great confidentiality, that he did not believe a Roman Catholic could be elected president of the United States in 1940 and could not be "for many years to come." He therefore hoped that Farley—whom he called "James"—would "do nothing to involve the Catholics of the country in another debacle such as we experienced in 1928," referring to Al Smith's failed candidacy.

Farley replied he couldn't talk yet about his "definite views" on the third term, argued that many friends in Congress and elsewhere believed he *could* get elected, and recounted yet again the many slights and lack of appreciation he had suffered at the hand of the president. "There is no reason why the loyalty should all be on my side," he said, summing up his feelings. "It is time that the President be loyal to me."

At several points the cardinal urged Farley to speak with the president to clarify the matter. "I would and will if he ever raises the question," Farley replied. When Farley asked if he could say that they had spoken, if and when he did meet with Roosevelt, Mundelein replied he hoped he would not.

"You are the first person in the Church who has ever attempted to influence me on a political matter," Farley said.

"It is only because I am interested in you and because you have always been considerate of me," the cardinal responded.[10]

Farley, who knew the president's ways, concluded that FDR had asked Cardinal Mundelein to see him. Roosevelt usually preferred an indirect approach in conveying a message, especially an unwelcome message, and he invariably selected exactly the right messenger. It was a process that not only served him well as a rule but gave him considerable pleasure in its creation. It also gave him a measure of deniability. Farley was without much doubt correct in his suspicions, and now he had still another reason to resent the president.

The meeting with Roosevelt that the cardinal had urged occurred just a few weeks later, but at the president's initiative, not Farley's. Press reports about a growing rift between the two were increasing sufficiently that FDR felt he had to stanch the flow. He invited Farley to have dinner and spend the night of July 23 at Hyde Park. When the two of them retreated to a small study in the north wing of the Big House, they immediately got into an argument over the president's attempted purge of 1938. Roosevelt conveyed a report from Tom Corcoran that Farley "did not go along all the way" in the fight, a point that Farley conceded, reminding him that at the time he had told the president that, as party chairman, he had to stay out of intraparty fights and that the president had approved. It was a testy exchange, according to Farley, who described FDR as "frigid during my remarks."[11]

As he was recounting these events years later in his memoirs, Farley took the occasion to offer an observation that was clearly the result of years of watching FDR at close range and that contained insights into the minds of both men. "At heart the President was a boy, sometimes a spoiled boy. Although he had tremendous charm and vitality, he had a few petty attributes which were continually getting him into trouble." In Farley's view, one of these "petty attributes" was that he was always trying to get even with someone for some slight, "real or fancied." A second was that the president was ruled by his heart rather than his mind, and for his decisions, "large and small," he worked by hunches rather than by reason. "Surrounded by genuinely loyal and able people, he would have encountered far less trouble."[12]

Farley thought Roosevelt was slow in getting to the point and, knowing that it was coming, tried to steel himself against FDR's persuasive charm. He was determined, he said, "to impress upon him that I would follow, whatever course of action I decided was right and honorable." The president launched into a survey of possible presidential candidates, all of whom he found wanting: Garner was "just impossible," Wallace didn't have "*It*," he turned his thumb down on McNutt, and various senators and governors were simply "unacceptable." Never mentioned were Hopkins, Hull, Jackson, and, notably, Farley. Then the president turned to what Farley called in his memoirs "the third term issue." It is worth quoting the exchange in full.

"We must save democracy," FDR said with some feeling, according to Farley. "It's the only way to save the country."

"I think it's necessary to have the Democratic Party successful in order the save the country," Farley responded. "And I am more concerned with the country than with the party, because success will come to the party if the country is secure and prosperous as surely as night follows day and maybe I should have put it the other way around—day follows night."

"Jim," Roosevelt said, in what Farley called "a more deliberate tone," "you and I have got to be together in 1940 to work for the good of the country and the party, just as we have in the past." After pausing for effect, he went on: "Now, they're trying to make me run...."

"Just one interruption, Boss," Farley said. "Before you go any further, I want to say that sooner or later you will have to declare yourself. Just when that day should be, I am not prepared to say at this time...."

"Jim, I am going to tell you something I have never told another living soul," Roosevelt whispered. "*Of course I will not run for a third term.* Now I don't want you to pass this on to anyone, because it would make my role difficult if the decision were known prematurely." Farley assured him he would not, and Roosevelt proceeded to explain how he would make his decision known the following year by declining to allow his name to be entered in primary contests. "The thing for us to do now is to get friendly delegations. You and I must work together for the party, the same as we have in the past."

FDR soon changed the subject to one he knew Farley would like. "Jim, you're the only member of the Cabinet I have no reason to criticize for any public utterance. And you're the only one who, at some time or other, has never asked for anything from some other department. And I want to say, here and now, that I appreciate it more than you know."

Before they adjourned, Farley took the conversation back to politics and asked the president what sort of candidate he wanted to see. "All I have to say is that I hope they won't nominate just a yes man, but pick someone who is sympathetic to my administration and who will continue my policies." Farley got the impression that Roosevelt didn't have anyone particular in mind as his successor.

Before turning in, Farley reviewed the conversation (and no doubt jotted down notes on it, since he clearly would not have done so in the meeting; he made it a practice to dictate memoranda to his files soon after important meetings). He was glad there had been no "unpleasantness" and pleased that he had been able to talk "freely and frankly, and without any bitterness over his neglect of me." At the same time he thought Roosevelt had been ill at ease at trying to clarify a situation while at the same time not admitting that he had been guilty of any offense toward Farley. "I took solace from the fact that I had kept my temper and had conducted myself to the best of my ability in a trying period."

The next morning at a news conference the president was asked, with Farley standing nearby, whether the postmaster general was going to resign. "He is not!" Roosevelt replied incredulously and even indignantly, suggesting there had never been anything approaching a rift between them. He had achieved his primary goal from the meeting in putting to rest public speculation on the issue, and Farley had achieved his by getting the answer to the third-term question he had been looking for. They both had reason to be pleased, even though Roosevelt was perhaps disingenuous in failing to mention the war caveat when saying he wouldn't run again. He had done so in an earlier conversation with Harry Hopkins, as he would subsequently with others, but so far there had been no events that required him to mention it to Farley. One can only conclude that he was so eager to put to rest any talk of a rift that he didn't want Farley to think he was equivocating. As for Farley, he prided himself on speaking "freely and frankly" to the president even though he never told him how he really felt about a third term; he had used that kind of candor in opposing the purge, and it had cost him. But the broader lesson of the meeting was that FDR was seeing the issues under discussion in a much broader context than Farley. By talking of "saving democracy," he was looking at what he saw as a likely war in Europe and its effect on the United States; Farley was largely nursing his wounded feelings and looking at the future through the prism of a traditional party leader. They had very different agendas, and at this point in their relationship they were talking past each other.[13]

"I am quite certain that neither Jim nor the President revealed all their cards to one another," press secretary Steve Early wrote fellow White House staffer Marvin McIntyre two days later; "each has some trumps up his sleeve and that there will be another meeting, or series of meetings, at which these trumps will be played by their respective holders and for a showdown."[14]

After a trip to Europe in September 1939, during which Hitler invaded Poland, Farley returned to a different political environment. Now even he could conceive of how the president would have to run again if the country was endangered. That wasn't yet the case, by any means, and after the situation in Europe settled into the Phony War phase, his political mind-set returned to what it had been in the summer: to win a place on the 1940

Democratic ticket. He continued to conspire on the subject with Garner, who gave him all the encouragement he could hope for, and Hull, who was still a reluctant candidate, which is to say not a candidate at all.

Since the midterm elections of 1938, speculation on a possible third term for Roosevelt had been mostly low-volume background noise to events in Europe and of interest primarily to politicians and journalists. But Alf Landon turned up the volume when, following a meeting with the president on September 20, 1939, regarding the Neutrality Act, the *Washington Post* reported that he had urged Roosevelt to "renounce all ambitions of another term in the interest of national unity during the current crisis."[15] "Friends regarded the Landon message as an attempt to put FDR on the spot politically."[16] He didn't bite and deftly deferred comment. Henry Wallace, his agriculture secretary, didn't appear to get the message, and at a news conference in San Francisco on October 25 he called for Roosevelt to run for a third term. The comment "stirred up a furor," according to Ickes, who didn't much care for Wallace, prompting Steve Early to "spank Henry publicly."[17] "It would have been kind and polite of the speaker to have consulted the victim before he spoke," Early said.[18] Wallace in fact had told FDR what he intended to say, and he kept on saying it, but the rebuke served its purpose of quelling the furor in Congress.

In October Ickes again raised the third-term issue privately with the president, who told the interior secretary that Cornelius Vanderbilt Jr., an old friend whose reportorial skills he respected, had written him from the Midwest "to the effect that people are tired of hearing the name 'Roosevelt.'"[19] The same point was reinforced when FDR told Bronx boss Ed Flynn that "Uncle Ted," considering his own third-term bid nearly a quarter century before, "said to friends that the people of the United States were 'sick and tired' of the Roosevelts. 'They are sick of looking at my grin and they are sick of hearing what Alice had for breakfast. In fact, they want a rest from the Roosevelts.' FDR said he felt the same way about his family of Roosevelts: the country was tired of looking at them."[20]

Back in the spring of 1939 Eleanor, who was not being consulted on the third-term question, had a private session with Hopkins, who later made notes on it. The fact that the conversation occurred was a measure of how far their relationship had come. By this time, with Eleanor serving as the guardian of Hopkins's daughter, Diana, the two had become very close. Just as Louis Howe had been something of a bridge between Franklin and Eleanor before he died, Hopkins now played a somewhat similar role. Sitting in the White House gardens, the two had a three-hour chat on what Hopkins later called "the State of the Nation": "Mrs. Roosevelt was greatly disturbed about 1940. She is personally anxious not to have the President run again, but I gathered the distinct impression that she has no more information on that point than the rest of us." Hopkins reported that the First Lady felt that the president had little "zest" to handle the day-to-day business of the presidency and was "probably quite frankly bored." Moreover, if the New Deal couldn't survive him, then "it hasn't as strong a foundation as she believes it has with the great masses of people." She was convinced that her husband still had public support but that the Democrats should make "every effort" to nominate a liberal candidate and elect him. "She has great confidence in his ability to do this, if, and it seems to be a pretty big 'if' in her mind, he is willing to take his coat off and go to work at it."[21]

As revealing as it was, Eleanor's attitude toward the third-term question was not fully explained by Hopkins's account. Given her unusual relationship with her husband, they in fact led very different, and separate, lives. The two of them had the children in common, of course, but they were now grown and largely on their own. She served as Franklin's eyes and ears on various trips and inspection tours, and he appreciated and valued her insightful observations on the mood of the country and the effectiveness of New Deal programs. But she was not part of the decision-making process except to the extent that she could write memos like most anyone else in the administration seeking presidential action. And, despite the fact that she had been tutored by Howe in the art of politics and had proved adept at it, particularly as an asset to his many campaigns, she chose not to be a political advisor. Although she would be the person most directly affected by a third-term decision besides the president himself, she deferred entirely to him. Just as intimacy did not extend to other aspects of their lives, so it did not extend to political decisions, even momentous political decisions.

"I never questioned Franklin about his political intentions," she wrote years later. "The fact that I myself had never wanted him to be in Washington made me doubly careful not to intimate that I had the slightest preference [on the third-term question]."[22]

There was every evidence that Roosevelt was physically tired after seven years in the White House and fretted about the huge problems a third term would bring. In February 1940 the president would be visited by Nebraska's George Norris, the most faithful to FDR's programs of all the Senate progressives. He was there to urge his friend to seek another term, but he got an unwelcome response. "Did you ever stop to think," FDR asked, "that if I should run and be elected I would have much more trouble with Congress in my third term and much more bitterness to contend with as a result of my running for a third term than I have ever had before." Norris protested that the liberals would have nowhere to go if he didn't run. "George, I am chained to this chair from morning till night. People come in here day after day, most of them trying to get something from me, most of them things I can't give them, and wouldn't if I could. You sit in your chair in your office too, but if something goes wrong or you get irritated or tired, you can get up and walk around, or you can go into another room. But I can't. I am tied down to this chair day after day, week after week, and month after month. And I can't stand it any longer. I can't go on with it."[23] There may have been some exaggeration in this statement, but there was also much truth.

Ever since the spring of 1938, when he first encouraged Hopkins to think of the presidency, FDR had left a small caveat in his insistence that he planned to retire in 1941. "I gather from Hopkins' notes that Roosevelt did not entirely rule out the possibility that he might seek a third term," Robert Sherwood concluded in his biography of Hopkins and Roosevelt, published in 1948, after both were dead. "He seems to have left a very slight margin of doubt about it in the event of war."[24] That "very slight margin of doubt," as we shall see, grew incrementally as events in Europe deteriorated and as war loomed. Now, as the new year opened, there *was* a war, It was not yet a shooting war; whether it would become one was the most important question of the day, not least for Roosevelt.

Many observers of the political scene in early 1940 concluded that FDR had decided by this point that he would indeed seek a third term, but there is nothing in the written record to suggest that he had made a decision either way. Some thought he was playing what one biographer later called "a deep, shrewd and duplicitous game" that made it impossible for anyone else to emerge as a serious candidate and that effectively created a demand for his own reelection.[25] Roosevelt was always shrewd and sometimes duplicitous, to be sure, and there were undoubtedly elements of both qualities at work here, but his presumption was still heavily in favor of retirement. Nonetheless, there was the caveat.

As 1939 came to an end, the press was increasingly determined to draw Roosevelt out on the question. Political cartoonists had taken to depicting him as a sphinx who would not yield his secrets. When reporters continued to ask for the answer, FDR would duck and weave, usually with a laugh. Occasionally, in mock exasperation, he would go so far as to tell them to put on a dunce cap and sit in the corner. But they never gave up and invented more oblique lines of questioning. A reporter opened a press conference in late December with the spirit of the season: "We wish you an eventful 1940!"

"Don't be so equivocal," the president replied, laughing.

"We have learned it here, Mr. President," the reporter replied.

"It is all right," Roosevelt said humorously. "That is very sweet of you."[26]

Feeding this speculation was a Gallup poll in November that had offered Democrats their first opportunity to register a preference for president in 1940 from a list that included Roosevelt. An amazing 83 percent of respondents selected him, with only 8 percent supporting Garner and merely 1 percent for Farley. The overwhelming Democratic support for the president, in spite of the supposed third-term barrier, goes a long way toward explaining why there weren't more prominent Democrats exploring 1940 prospects. FDR had effectively frozen the field, as he knew very well.[27]

It was impossible for even longtime intimates of the president to read his thinking on the subject. David Lilienthal, who headed the Tennessee Valley Authority and who saw a good deal of FDR in that and other capacities, was one of the keenest observers. "If anyone could tell from the expressions on his face or from those words what was in his mind about running again," Lilienthal wrote in his journal toward the end of 1939, "or could make out any answer to the enigma from his remarks about a reactionary successor, he's a better reader of signs than I am. I could tell exactly nothing." Lilienthal wrote that while the president had been open about his thinking on other subjects, he had done "a masterful job of keeping his own counsel on the most important question the country has today."[28]

The sphinx was the perfect caricature for Roosevelt, whose deeply ingrained practice was to avoid making decisions, and especially major decisions, until he had to. His rationale was that additional time would yield additional facts to inform the decision or sometimes even obviate the question altogether, and that was often the case. Waiting also allowed him to maintain total control over the situation longer, always an important consideration for him, before others took over the implementation of a decision. If this decision was to be made known—and there was no way to make it known privately without it becoming common knowledge—it would have huge consequences, as he had told Farley in July. Should he admit that he was running for another term, everything he did would be seen as a candidate's political calculation to win reelection. Should he say he wasn't running, he would be a classic lame duck whom foreign leaders and members of Congress could easily ignore.

It was easier to shroud his intentions, Robert Sherwood suggested, when he himself didn't know what they were. "This was a period of impotence when, with all of civilization in peril, the leader of the most powerful nation on earth had to wait, day after anxious day, for his own course of action to be shaped by events over which he had no control."[29] So it had been before events shaped his course in amending the Neutrality Act, and so it would be again in determining his own future.

One of the annual highlights of Washington's political off-season was the winter dinner of the Gridiron Club, to which for more than a half century the capital's leading journalists invited its political elite—presidents, Supreme Court justices, foreign ambassadors, and politicians of all stripes— for an evening of fun and conviviality. On December 9, 1939, an all-male audience, attired in white tie and tails, gathered at one of the city's leading hotels. The reporters' purpose was to poke fun at the men in the audience, who, as even most of them would admit at times, took themselves too seriously. The club members' vehicle of choice for deflating self-importance was a series of satirical musical skits in which the hosts, usually dressed in outrageous costumes and singing off-key, spoofed the newsmakers.

This evening President Roosevelt was in attendance. As we have seen, reporters and cartoonists had begun to depict him as the sphinx for his secrecy. Everyone in the audience that evening knew what was coming when one of the Gridiron members announced that the club "takes you now to a faraway place in the world where a group of Democrats in near desperation have journeyed in search of the most perplexing question of all time. The scene is the Sahara Desert. The time is now. The sphinx is— you guess who!" Onto the stage rolled an eight-foot papier-mâché sphinx with a broadly grinning FDR face, his signature cigarette holder clenched firmly in his teeth. Impersonators for Jim Farley and John Nance Garner sang directly to the president on the dais:

> Here before the Sphinx we stand
> But he's silent in the sand
> Keeping locked the secret
> In his heart of stone.

Facing the president, they made their plea:

> He who knows all things the best
> Answers not our burning quest,
> So we turn to you, now
> You and you alone!

Then came the question:

> Will you run?
> Or are you done?

The gathering broke into uproarious, knee-slapping guffaws, and no one laughed more heartily than Roosevelt himself. He enjoyed the performance so much that he soon arranged to have the prop sphinx secured as an eventual exhibit for the presidential library in Hyde Park, where it remains—silent—to this day.[30]

6

A Year of Consequence

As the new decade dawned, it had all the outward signs of the decade that had just ended. In fact, it would bring enormous change to the United States, as well as to the world, starting with its first year. Not only would the presidential election in November likely determine the future direction of the country, but whether the war in Europe—declared but as yet unfought—would be resolved. Despite this, most Americans were, as usual, focused on their own concerns and, in their spare moments, on the many diversions that a vibrant and changing society provided.

Roosevelt began 1940 much as he had ended the year before, struggling to find the right role to play in the extremely dangerous and volatile scene unfolding in Europe. It was with this challenge in mind that Felix Frankfurter, whom FDR had appointed to the Supreme Court a year earlier and who was not averse to flattering the president in their voluminous correspondence, wrote him a note on New Year's Day: "I feel I know to a considerable measure what the load of the Presidency must be for one who had difficulties no less grave and heavy than those that weighed on Lincoln's soul, and carried them as gallantly as he did and with the inevitable solitude of Lincoln's compassion and wise private humor."[1]

Uncertain though times were, Roosevelt had his certainties. He was convinced that within months a major war would erupt: Britain and France were steadily massing their forces along the heavily fortified Maginot Line opposite the Germans, who were doing the same thing along their similarly fortified Siegfried Line. Thanks to Senator William Borah, the lengthening stand-off between these two forces became known as the "Phony War," and the term stuck (the French called it *drôle de guerre*, "odd war," and German troops on the line called it *Sitzkrieg*, "sitting war"). But the president was unsure what he or his country could do to preserve the peace. In the fall Joe Kennedy and others had importuned him to mediate the differences and secure a lasting peace, but he knew instinctively that agreeing to do so would be a trap. The only settlement the Germans would accept would be one that ratified all of their ill-gotten territorial gains of recent years, and Roosevelt wouldn't be a party to that. He fundamentally detested the Nazis and didn't want anything to do with granting them legitimacy of any kind.

Of greatest concern to the president as the year commenced was the failure of Britain and France to place large orders for armaments now that the Neutrality Act permitted such sales. Two months after repeal of the embargo, the orders that FDR hoped would give his economic recovery efforts a significant boost were at best anemic. With the Phony War showing no sign of ending, the Allies rationalized that they would have years to build up their own manufacturing capacity. Prevented now from buying on credit in the United States, they were determined to husband their gold and dollar reserves. The frustrated president urged Britain and France to coordinate a purchasing mission in the United States, which he hoped would, among other things, avoid conflicts with American military requirements. The latter was a growing problem when larger orders arrived in early 1940, particularly for aircraft, which were in seriously short supply in the U.S. Army Air Corps.

Complicating matters was that Secretary of War Woodring and his assistant secretary Louis Johnson were then engaged in a bitter feud over turf and management styles. The feud demoralized the department and frustrated the too-tolerant Roosevelt. It was exacerbated by top military brass, who opposed any sale of planes, particularly fighter aircraft and medium bombers, that interfered even minimally with U.S. requirements. Meeting with them on January 17, the president said he wanted a certain percentage of all newly manufactured planes to go to France, but the objections continued in what the treasury secretary, Henry Morgenthau, called the "Battle of Washington." Finally, two months later, when the civilian and military chiefs refused the French access to the classified technology in the aircraft they had ordered, FDR told them to stop taking their case to the press and to isolationists in Congress; officers refusing to get with the program would find themselves reassigned to remote islands in the Pacific. When Woodring still resisted in April, Roosevelt, who had put up with the isolationist and ineffective secretary much too long, ordered him to obey or to leave. He obeyed, and one of the results was a quadrupling of aircraft production.

As exasperated as he was by the failure of his low-visibility efforts to get aid to the Allies, Roosevelt began the year still cautious in public pronouncements. The State of the Union message on January 3, 1940, reflected this. His message, boiled down, was that while he understood Americans' fear of being pulled into another war, they couldn't at the same time be oblivious to what was happening: "It is not good for the ultimate health of ostriches to bury their heads in the sand."[2] This was as far as he was willing to go in warning his fellow citizens of the dangers in the world in which they were living. There was little if any sense of urgency to it, and more than a little temporizing. Once again he was more inclined to follow public opinion than to lead it, no doubt still remembering the hostile reception his "quarantine" speech had received, despite the fact that he was personally convinced that the threat to world peace was much more dire and imminent than it had been in 1937. His great quandary was how to alert the American people to see the real dangers they faced without also convincing them that the country would inevitably be brought into the war. Only weeks before he had sought guidance on the matter in a letter to William Allen White that revealed the depth of his quandary. He wrote that if it was likely, as he believed, that a German-Russian alliance would divide up control of Europe between them, and by extension control of the Middle East, Africa, and scattered European colonies as well, "the situation of your civilization and mine is indeed in peril." He added, "Our world trade would be at the mercy of the combine and our increasingly better relations with our twenty [Latin American] neighbors to the south would end—unless we were willing to go to war in their behalf against a German-Russian dominated Europe." What Roosevelt said most worried him was that public opinion "is patting itself on the back every morning and thanking God for the Atlantic Ocean (and the Pacific Ocean)." He for one was not going around thanking God for their physical safety. Events were moving at "such terrific speed" that Americans needed to look further than their backyard. "Therefore, my sage old friend," concluded Roosevelt, "my problem is to get the American people to think of conceivable consequences without scaring the American people into thinking that they are going to get dragged into this war."[3]

The day after the State of the Union address the caution evident in that message was repeated in Roosevelt's budget request, which, against the strong advice of General Marshall and others, recommended only a modest increase in defense spending. With no sense of urgency behind the proposal, the House of Representatives two months later actually cut his request by 10 percent.

Increasingly torn between doing something to promote peace and not challenging isolationist opinion, Roosevelt characteristically settled on an option that split the difference: he would send Sumner Welles to Europe to determine whether there was *any* prospect of serious discussions that could lead to an acceptable and lasting settlement with Germany, using Italy as an intermediary. He also hoped the mission would delay a German offensive so that the western democracies could better supply their needs for the war that he nonetheless was certain was coming. But these were not to be the announced purposes of the trip; Roosevelt insisted it be labeled strictly as a fact-finding mission for the purpose of advising the president, and, to quiet the isolationists, it was emphasized that Welles would have no authority to make proposals or commitments on behalf of the United States. The isolationists were not so easily quieted and complained that this was yet another Roosevelt effort to engage the United States in a foreign war. The internationalists countered with fears that the trip was a mission to promote appeasement, one that would allow Hitler to dictate the terms of any peace.

Cordell Hull, who was still jealous of Welles's close relationship with FDR, was decidedly unenthusiastic about the idea, whose origin he correctly attributed to his deputy. Before Welles left for overseas the president confessed to him that "the chances seemed to him about one in a thousand that anything at all could be done to change the course of events," but Roosevelt felt Welles's mission was worth trying.[4] In the end, nothing substantive came from it. The Italians hinted they might play a mediating role, but Welles quickly discovered that Hitler had foreclosed any possibility of serious negotiations. The diplomat found the French and English, by now wholly distrusting Hitler, equally obdurate on the subject.

Just as the early months of 1940 sharpened Roosevelt's focus on Europe, so did they sharpen his focus on the presidential election that the year would bring. The domestic political scene was largely unchanged. Vice President Garner was now a declared candidate, but the consensus was that the crotchety Texan had limited appeal within the Democratic Party. Jim Farley had convinced himself that his many years as a backroom politician qualified him to be president, or at least vice president, and a number of his fellow professionals encouraged him in that belief. He decided he had to take the matter to the president, and in late January he recalled asking Roosevelt if the president had "any objection" to his entering his name in the New Hampshire and Massachusetts primaries.

"Go ahead, Jim," FDR laughed. "The water's fine. I haven't an objection in the world."

"Now, Mr. President, do not say yes to this arrangement unless you are thoroughly in accord. . . ."

"I think it's a grand idea," Roosevelt replied.

"I don't want you to say so unless you are thoroughly in accord," Farley persisted. "I don't want somebody coming to me . . . saying that you said you could not say no at the time."

"I am in accord, Jim. Go to it."[5]

No new plausible candidates had emerged, FDR's indecision still serving to freeze the field, although some speculation centered on the populist-isolationist senator from Montana, Burton Wheeler. Wheeler had been the first prominent Democrat outside New York State to endorse Roosevelt for president in 1931, but the two had had a serious falling-out over policy differences and real and perceived slights. There was speculation as well about Fiorello La Guardia, the flamboyant and pro–New Deal mayor of New York, who had been encouraged by his old friend Adolf Berle, now the number three official in the State Department. However, La Guardia's recent defeat of the candidate for mayor supported by Tammany Hall, the local Democratic organization, made it unlikely that La Guardia could secure Tammany's support for a presidential nomination. Senator James F. Byrnes of South Carolina, a sometime New Dealer and FDR favorite, was mentioned but seen by many as fatally handicapped by his Catholic birth and then his having formally left the Church. And Secretary of Agriculture Henry Wallace, recently a Republican but now a fervent New Dealer, showed some interest but quickly pulled back.

The Republicans, meanwhile, sensing public exhaustion after eight years of Democratic "one-man" rule and anxiety about the future, saw their opportunity. They had every intention of capitalizing on the lingering economic hardship as well as the prospect of the nation being drawn into another European war. The early field consisted of three serious candidates. The young Thomas E. Dewey, not yet forty, was attracting national headlines as a tough, crime-busting district attorney in New York City. Arthur Vandenberg was a longtime and highly respected senator from Michigan. And Robert A. Taft, son of a former president and barely a year into his first term as a senator from Ohio, had already made a mark for himself as a leader of the hard-core conservatives in Congress. All of them opposed the essential elements of the New Deal, and all, with variations, were isolationists.

In terms of preserving his legacy, Roosevelt could take no comfort from the field in either party. He could take even less comfort in the ability of any plausible candidate, with the exception of Cordell Hull, to shape and implement a foreign policy designed to thwart Hitler's ambitions of conquest while still keeping America out of the war. And among the Democrats, he had no confidence in any potential candidate, again with the possible exception of Hull, of winning in November, which he knew was going to be a very difficult task under any circumstances.

Roosevelt realized, of course, that he had largely created this situation himself by refusing to declare his intentions. He continued to believe that he had no choice. He had to keep open the option of running for a third term, much as he might have preferred to retire to Hyde Park, because all of the other options were so dismal or, in Hull's case, risky. There is no record of his talking with anyone about these issues during this period—the first few months of 1940—but we know they were on his mind and it is reasonable to conclude that with more and more third-term talk being generated in the press and in the country, he was beginning to take the issue more seriously.

A growing number of prominent Democrats started to urge FDR to seek a third term, and as we have seen, they were joined by a prominent Republican, George Norris of Nebraska. A legendary progressive icon, Norris was probably the most ardent New Dealer in the Senate, and as such, he and FDR had a warm friendship. When Norris came to the White House in February, he made an impassioned case that Roosevelt should seek a third term. "I would urge you to run again [even] if I knew it would kill you," Norris said in an odd exchange. "This is war," the president responded, "and in war the life of any one person means nothing."[6]

Henry Horner, the Democratic governor of Illinois, also urged the president to run for a third term, and FDR's response to Horner in late March opens a window onto his thinking. He began by stating that only liberal Democrats stood in the way of Republicans and conservative Democrats "who frankly put property ahead of human beings." The continuance of liberal government shouldn't depend on a single person, he continued, and therefore "we should look at the coming Convention with the following purposes in mind."

First, we should seek a platform of progressive liberalism and candidates who are progressive liberals at heart and not merely in lip service. This first criterion eliminates a good many people whose names you and I could readily agree on. . . .

The second criterion is the practical one of picking a liberal ticket which can win. . . . In this last matter of choice it is too early in my

judgment to attempt to make decisions. Several people who might
be considered available may stub their toes in the next four
months—others may say or do something which will bring them to
favorable public notice.

Especially do I deprecate the attitude of some of our friends that
unless I run, no other Democrat can be elected. That is sheer
defeatism.[7]

On its face this letter suggests a rational course from a liberal perspective, and it "deprecates" the notion that only an FDR candidacy could serve
its ends. Yet it advocates delay in settling on a candidate, and delay was essential to FDR's goal of maintaining options. Admittedly there was no consensus liberal and electable alternative to FDR at this point—Hull came
the closest—but if the uncertainty caused by delay continued right up to
the convention, FDR knew it would create inordinate pressure on him to
run again. Given the way his mind worked, this letter raises the question
of whether it was his purpose here to put himself in that position come
July, when the convention would convene. In late March he clearly had not
made up his mind on running again, but what can be safely concluded is
that the delay he urges on Horner would enable him to have maximum leverage on the convention one way or another; he would remain in control
of the situation.

There were those around Roosevelt, of course, who did not want to see
him run again—Garner and Farley most prominent among them. And
now there was Joe Kennedy, his ambassador to Britain, who just a few
months earlier had surprised many by declaring his support for a third
Roosevelt term and promising to return to London for the duration. This
announcement came shortly after a meeting with FDR in which the ambassador sought to ferret out his intentions, and Roosevelt, after listing
several alternative candidates, added, "There's you." These flattering words
reached very receptive ears, and shortly afterward the *Boston Post* ran a
"carefully planted" story under the headline "Kennedy May Be Candidate." The president told Ickes at the time that Kennedy's actions were to
be expected, for the ambassador was "utterly pessimistic. He believes that

Germany and Russia will win the war and that the end of the world is just down the road."[8]

Now, in March, Kennedy had had a change of heart. Not only had he decided not to run but he had turned on Roosevelt with a vengeance. Certainly the Welles mission had offended him, among other slights real and perceived, and it all became evident when Bill Bullitt, on home leave from Paris, encountered him in the State Department. He listened in disbelief as Kennedy told two journalists that Germany would win the war and that things in France and Britain "would go to hell." He then "denounced" the president, causing Bullitt to leap to Roosevelt's defense. Their argument became so volatile that the embarrassed journalists fled the scene. Bullitt charged Kennedy with being disloyal to the president, whom he served, and told him "to keep his mouth shut." According to Bullitt, Kennedy said that "he would say what he Goddamned pleased before whom he Goddamned pleased." After several similar exchanges, they both stormed out of the room.[9]

For Roosevelt, it was the prospect of war more than politics or anything else that was foremost in his calculations around the third-term question. It may not have been the only consideration, but there can be no question it was the primary one. He returned to the war caveat. "I do not want to run unless between now and the convention things get very, very much worse in Europe," the president had told Henry Morgenthau over lunch on January 24.[10]

FDR and everyone else knew that if the president decided to seek a third term, one of the chief obstacles he would face would be the weight of history, the well-established tradition, not yet a law, that limited presidents to two terms, or eight years, in office. Few chief executives had considered even challenging this tradition, and of those who did none had succeeded. As a student of history and as an incumbent president being urged to challenge the tradition anew, Roosevelt knew how deeply ingrained it had become in the political fabric of the nation. He was especially mindful of the most recent challenge to the tradition, the quixotic and in the end bitter experience of the hero of his youth, his cousin Theodore, in 1912.

The Constitutional Convention of 1787, charging itself with the formidable task of transforming the hopelessly weak Articles of Confederation into a form of government suitable for the new nation, debated at length the powers to be vested in the proposed chief executive. A good part of that debate centered on how long his term of office should be and whether or not he should be "eligible" to serve more than one term. Early in the convention Edmund Randolph had presented the "Virginia plan," which proposed a seven-year term for the president, after which he would be "ineligible" for another term. This formulation came close to being adopted, but further debate prevented an early consensus.

The case for a limit on terms was strongly propelled by fear of anything resembling the kind of monarchy they had just thrown off; the chief executive, it was argued, should be limited in his powers, and that meant limited in his time in office. Gouverneur Morris countered that such limits "tended to destroy the motive to good behavior, the hope of being rewarded by a reappointment."[11] The debate raged on for two months without resolution on either the length of the term or on the question of "reeligibility." Finally, with less than two weeks to go before adjournment, delegate David Bearley of New Jersey proposed a term of four years with no mention of whether a president could succeed himself. Efforts to substitute a six- or seven-year term failed, and on September 6 every state but one agreed to the four-year term. In the absence of language to the contrary, "reeligibility" was assumed.

The first chief executive of the new nation, of course, was George Washington, whose presidency would define the office in ways that the Constitution did not. His heart set on returning to his beloved Mount Vernon after his long absence during the Revolutionary War, Washington agreed to serve not out of ambition but out of a deep sense of duty to his country. As the presiding officer at the Constitutional Convention, he had heard all of the arguments for and against reeligibility, but he had never spoken or written a word on the subject. What was clear was his desire to retire to Mount Vernon after a single term. He was tired, feeling his age, and increasingly disturbed by the growing feud between the two strong-willed principals of his cabinet, Thomas Jefferson and Alexander Hamilton, who disagreed on most everything except the need for Washington to serve another term. After hearing from the president on how displeased he was by their feuding, they agreed to quell the controversy, and Washington again responded to what he saw as his duty: he was unanimously elected to a second term.

He decided early in that term that this one would be his last, although he characteristically kept that information largely to himself. As a result, he came once again under pressure from those who believed the nation would fall into dangerous factionalism if he left. But this time, exhausted by the rigors of the office and especially by the Jefferson-Hamilton feud, Washington resisted; on September 17, 1796, he released his Farewell Address announcing his intention to retire. He never expressed a principled objection to a third term in that document or elsewhere. His decision was based solely on personal considerations.

Jefferson, on the other hand, did have a principled objection to reeligibility. Although not a participant in the Constitutional Convention because he was then serving as minister to France, where he was heavily influenced by what he saw as corruption in the French monarchy, he was adamant in his opposition to perpetual reeligibility. "I was much an enemy to monarchy before I came to Europe," he wrote a friend from Paris. "I am ten thousand times more so since I have seen what they are. There is scarcely an evil known in these countries which may not be traced to their kind as its sources."[12] He was disappointed that the convention had not limited the presidency to a single term, and he expressed hope that a subsequent amendment could remedy the omission. In urging Washington to seek another term in 1792 Jefferson overcame his preference for a single term, but on his own election as president eight years later he immediately announced he would retire after four years. When that time came, however, after heavy Federalist attacks that took their toll, his desire for vindication compelled him to display once more the quality of inconsistency that would be part of his legacy: he allowed himself to be renominated, and an easy reelection followed. He never seriously considered a third term. He continued to express his principled opposition to unlimited terms: "If some period be not fixed, either by the Constitution or by practice, to the services of the First

Magistrate, his office, though nominally elective, will, in fact, be for life; and that will soon degenerate into an inheritance."[13]

Jefferson's example of retiring after two terms, following that of Washington, clearly established the "practice" he sought of limiting presidential tenure. Its effect could be seen in the experiences of his two immediate successors, James Madison and James Monroe, as well as that of Andrew Jackson, all of whom served two terms and none of whom seriously considered seeking a third. The issue became largely moot for a half century until the presidency of Ulysses S. Grant brought it once more to the fore. The great hero of the Civil War very much enjoyed the presidency, and his wife, Julia, enjoyed it even more. His popularity continued well into his second term, giving rise to inevitable talk of a third. Pressed to explain his position, Grant was coy, first saying it was "beneath the dignity of the office . . . to answer such a question" before the nominating convention requested it of him, and then adding, "I do not want [the third term] any more than I did the first. . . . I am not, nor have I ever been, a candidate for renomination. I would not accept a nomination if it were tendered, unless it should come under such circumstances as to make it an imperative duty—circumstances not likely to arise."[14]

This deliberately ambiguous statement was all that Grant's supporters needed to redouble their efforts to create the "circumstances" necessary to justify another term. The more progress they made, however, the more opposition to the idea arose, particularly within the Republican Party. Reformers who were offended by the reports of corruption emanating from the administration as well as those simply opposed to another term in principle built an effective backfire against the third-term movement. It culminated in a resolution offered to the House of Representatives on December 15, 1875: "Resolved that . . . the precedent established by Washington and other Presidents of the United States, in retiring from the presidential office after their second term, has become, by universal concurrence, a part of our republican form of government, and that any departure from this time-honored custom would be unwise, unpatriotic, and fraught with peril to our own free institutions." The resolution carried by the overwhelming vote of 234 to 18, with 88 Republicans joining the unanimous Democrats in sending Grant and his supporters an unmistakable message. At the subsequent convention that ultimately nominated Rutherford B. Hayes, Grant, as much as he wanted to be selected again, was not a factor.

Yet neither Grant nor his hard-core supporters were done with the presidency. They undertook a heavy-handed effort to secure the GOP nomination again in 1880, and Grant was very much in contention, but his candidacy peaked too soon. Most important, the two-term tradition remained a huge stumbling block, and dark horse James Garfield was nominated—on the twenty-fourth ballot.

Theodore Roosevelt, having succeeded to the presidency after McKinley was assassinated in September 1901, was elected in his own right in 1904 by an overwhelming margin. On the very night of his victory he issued a statement that he would come to regret: "On the 4th of March next I shall have served three and a half years and this . . . constitutes my first term. The wise custom which limits the President to two terms regards the substance and not the form; and under no circumstances will I be a candidate for or accept another term."[15]

As 1908 approached, his popularity ensured that there would be serious third-term talk, but TR stuck to his pledge and instead, like Andrew Jackson before him, decided the best way to preserve his legacy was to determine his successor. This he did skillfully in promoting his secretary of war, William Howard Taft. To further that effort and at the same time to kill all talk of a third term for himself, he repeated his pledge of 1904. At the convention a number of delegates, many of whom owed their federal jobs to the president, started to chant, "Four more years of Teddy." In order to quell the demonstration the presiding chairman, Henry Cabot Lodge, was compelled to announce that the president's "refusal of a nomination . . . is final and irrevocable."[16] Taft was both nominated and elected.

TR was respectful of his successor in the early years of his administration and showed every sign of planning to support his renomination in 1912, although Taft and his highly suspicious wife both thought the former president might try for a comeback. A number of progressives in the Republican Party grew restless under Taft's policies after the midterm elections of 1910, and within a year they had decided to challenge him. Their vehicle was to be the voluble populist senator from Wisconsin, Robert A. La Follette, who was eager to lead the charge, but when health issues sidelined him, TR showed immediate interest. By the end of February he had told a reporter in Cleveland, "My hat's in the ring! The fight is on and I'm stripped to the buff!" Just to make it absolutely clear, a few days later he said unequivocally, "I will accept the nomination if it is tendered to me."[17]

Roosevelt was immediately pressed to explain how he reconciled his candidacy with his statement of 1904 that "under no circumstances will I be a candidate for or accept another term." The latter phrase, he argued, meant "of course, a third consecutive term. The precedent which forbids a third term has reference only to a third consecutive term." Also, the situation could be distinguished from other third-term efforts by the fact that if elected it would really represent his second *elective* term. The anti-Roosevelt editorialists and cartoonists had a field day with his awkward attempts to justify his decision.[18]

By the time the delegates arrived at the convention in June, Roosevelt had won most of the contested primaries, then a very recent addition to the nominating process; those victories gave him important bragging rights when it came to popular support. But Taft had a slight majority of the delegates, most of whom were chosen by more traditional means, and his forces used their advantage ruthlessly in seating all two hundred contested Taft delegates. TR, realizing he had no chance of being nominated, was enraged. He and his supporters bolted from the convention, held an impromptu Progressive convention, and nominated Roosevelt as their candidate for president. He gave a brief acceptance speech, declaring, "I am in this fight for certain principles, and the first and most important of these going back to Sinai, and is embodied in the commandment, 'Thou shalt not steal!' Thou shall not steal a nomination."[19]

With Taft as the Republican nominee, Woodrow Wilson running as a progressive on the Democratic ticket, and Theodore Roosevelt heading the Progressive, or Bull Moose, ticket, the die was cast. It was shaping up as a probable Democratic year in any case, and the division among Republicans ensured it. Wilson won 435 electoral votes, Roosevelt 88, and the hapless Taft only 8. The consensus at the time and since is that the third-term issue was not a significant factor in the election; it had "all but dropped out of sight as an important issue," according to one account.[20] The remarkable thing is how close TR came to realizing his 1912 quest for another term in the White House.

Such was the mixed history of the two-term tradition in American presidential politics. It was a Washington-Jefferson legacy designed to clarify a constitutional ambiguity, but it was not inviolable. A few two-term presidents challenged it, and while none succeeded, it wasn't always because of the force of the tradition. The outcomes usually turned on other factors, with the tradition playing a greater or lesser role, and as time passed it was usually lesser. But it still carried some force, and ordinary ambition in ordinary times wasn't sufficient to overcome it. It remained to be seen whether a national "emergency," sometimes cited by opponents of a third-term limitation as a reason not to fix it in law, would make a difference.

James Rowe Jr., an administrative assistant in the White House and one of the ablest of the bright young men around FDR, had a keen interest in politics. Officially tasked to handle political appointments, Rowe said the president had summarized his duties as those of "a bird dog, which was to do, in effect, whatever he told me to do and occasionally I would do things on my own without being told."[21] One of the things he did without being told was to keep track of the letters coming into the White House on the question of the third term. Back in October 1939 he had sent a memo to General Edwin M. "Pa" Watson, the president's principal gatekeeper, indicating that "in the past few months" approximately 1,300 letters on the subject had been received at the White House and "only 35 were unfavorable." His analysis of the letters concluded that the largest number of "organization" letters were the product of labor union efforts, but he added that the "most significant" trend was the large number from career politicians, such as Democratic precinct chairmen, county chairmen, state chairmen, and national committeemen. This group was "most significant," of course, because it contained many individuals likely to be delegates to the nominating convention as well as others who would help determine who the delegates would be.[22]

As FDR had stressed to Jim Farley early in 1939, it was in everyone's interest to see that "friendly" delegations made it to the convention, so there was more than a little interest in Rowe's tabulations when Watson passed them on to the president. The fact that Rowe thereafter sent monthly reports on the letters to Watson could only mean that Roosevelt had asked him to, and the president could not have been disappointed by what he saw. The number of pro-third-term letters grew to 291 in November, 480 in December, 734 in January, and 857 in February; the trend line was obviously moving in the right direction as far as the White House was concerned. Regardless of whatever FDR decided to do when the convention arrived, it was increasingly likely as the spring wore on that he would be assured of "friendly" delegations to help determine who would be the Democratic nominee.

As smoothly as the early stages of the delegate selection process appeared to be going, there were snags, and, where he could, FDR tried to untangle them. In early March he asked Harold Ickes to go to California to heal a breach among the president's supporters in an effort to get them all behind a single delegate ticket in that state's critical primary. It was especially important because Jack Garner had filed a slate in the primary, which he had actually won in 1932. When Ickes reported back to Roosevelt that he had accomplished his mission, the president complimented him profusely, saying he hadn't thought it could be done. Ickes, probably the strongest third-term advocate in the administration, took the occasion to tell FDR that in both California and Illinois "everyone was of the opinion that no one could win on the Democratic ticket except himself."

As Ickes reported in his diary, the president interrupted him impatiently, "Suppose I should become so ill that I could not possibly be a candidate? You oughtn't to talk like that. It only means that a defeatist attitude is being built up."

"My reply to this," noted Ickes, "was that I wanted to tell him of the sentiment that I had discovered, whether it comported with his own opinions or not. I said very frankly that if he refused to take the nomination, the delegates would leave the convention in a spirit of defeat."[23]

Sam Rosenman recalled that the matter "absorbed the interest" of staffers in the White House. Most of the New Dealers were eager to see him run again, yet none of them had any way to read his mind. Because Rosenman had advised FDR longer than nearly anyone around him, he felt completely comfortable advising him on this most sensitive question. Somewhat to his surprise, he found the president as yet unwilling to consider a third term, despite Rosenman's attempts to persuade him. "His mind was then made up; he was going to retire at the end of his second term."[24]

The third-term movement, if it could be called that at this point, three or four months before the Democratic convention, was what Ickes termed a "catch-as-catch-can affair." In fact, it was entirely unorganized, and he decided it needed more focus. If anyone in FDR's inner circle had both the confidence and the ability to take up this challenge, it was Harold L. Ickes. A lawyer and real estate speculator as well as a product of Chicago reform politics—he was close to Jane Addams of Hull House, among others—he had split from the Republicans to help form the Bull Moose Party for Teddy Roosevelt's comeback effort in 1912 but thereafter returned to the GOP fold until FDR's election. Roosevelt barely knew Ickes before plucking him from obscurity for the Interior post. The president soon took to his acerbic humor as well as his willingness to use his verbal skills to defend the administration from its critics. Ickes, who shared FDR's passion for conservation, came to the administration with the conviction of the converted, becoming probably the most fervent New Dealer in the cabinet. However, what the president valued him most for was his role as a political gadfly; they both loved gossip and spent long lunches surveying the political horizon. Happily, most of it would end up in the secretary's detailed and voluminous diary.

So Ickes put together "a little group" to meet regularly on the matter of a third term. He enlisted assistant attorney general Bob Jackson in the effort, as well as troubleshooter Benjamin Cohen, a lawyer Felix Frankfurter had brought in to be part of Roosevelt's "brain trust," and together they persuaded Tom Corcoran to help. The next day Cohen told Ickes that over the weekend he had seen the president, who had suggested that Ickes "ought to take charge of the third-term movement." When Ickes saw Roosevelt Monday morning, however, he noted in his diary that the president "said nothing to me. I do not feel like charging in without some intimation from the President that this is what he wants me to do."[25]

If Cohen's report was accurate, and there was no reason to doubt it, FDR was playing a complicated game. If ultimately he decided to accept nomination for a third term, he didn't want to be seen either then or later as having anything to do with it. He wanted to leave absolutely no fingerprints, and he almost certainly knew that Ickes kept a diary. He definitely knew that Ickes loved to talk politics with a lot of people. So in suggesting to Cohen that Ickes should "take charge" of the movement, it's easy to conclude that he may have been sanctioning the movement while maintaining plausible deniability.

Meanwhile, Jim Farley was smarting from a newspaper article that he was convinced Roosevelt had planted to undermine his presidential ambitions. It quoted "a prominent Democratic politician" to whom the president had declared that he would not run again unless Hitler threatened to overrun Europe and that he preferred Cordell Hull as his successor. The vice presidency, he argued, should go to Bob Jackson, Burton Wheeler, or Paul McNutt, but not to Farley because of his religion. "Roosevelt was reported to have said that he owed more to me politically than to any other person," Farley wrote, "but in the event of my nomination people might say 'we were using Cordell Hull as a stalking horse for the Pope.'" He added that "nothing which ever happened to me politically so wounded me as this article." Although the president denied at his next news conference that he had made the remarks, Farley believed that FDR had deliberately inspired publication of the story "in order to take me out of the picture." If true, he wrote with wounded pride, it would constitute "one of the most unfriendly acts in politics."[26]

Farley commiserated with Hull, who was sympathetic and who later uncharacteristically poured out to Farley his own stories of how insensitive and ungrateful Roosevelt had been to him. "Troubles!" Hull exclaimed. "You don't know what they are!" At the next cabinet meeting Farley, by his own account, "was as cold as ice," reporting he had nothing to say when the president called on him and sulking through the balance of the meeting. Farley soon found himself even more cut off from the White House than he had already been, invited there only when his cabinet position required it and no longer consulted on appointments. Lunching with Arthur Krock of the *New York Times*, Farley said there would have to be a "showdown" with the president in which he would "speak freely."[27]

Ickes had heard FDR say that he believed Farley could not be elected either president or vice president because of his religion, but Ickes never believed Roosevelt was attacking either the Catholic Church or Farley for his Catholicism. "He was merely stating what he believed to be a political fact," one, Ickes noted, with which many Catholic Democrats—including Cardinal Mundelein—agreed. As for being cut off from the White House, Farley, probably the most able and experienced professional politician in the country, should not have been surprised: just days after the hurtful article appeared, Farley issued a statement from Massachusetts indicating that he would enter his name in that state's primary election. Even though he had secured Roosevelt's approval for such a move, the formal announcement of his candidacy could not have been warmly welcomed at a White House teeming with third-term talk. What's more, many of the president's strongest allies were offended that Farley became an announced candidate without resigning either his cabinet or Democratic Party position.

Asked at the news conference whether he thought Farley should resign as national chairman, Ickes replied, "Jim can be relied upon to do the right thing." Nonetheless, Farley didn't do the right thing as far as Ickes was concerned; Ickes later complained that it "is highly improper for a candidate to use the party machinery in his own cause and Jim has been doing that for months."[28] As if to confirm the point, Farley ensured that the Democratic convention would meet in mid-July, which was his own preference, instead of after Labor Day, which FDR had told him he preferred. They at least agreed that it should be held in Chicago, where Mayor Ed Kelly would be controlling the galleries.

As April approached and spring once again made its welcome appearance in Washington, the president of the United States was no doubt reflecting that this could be the last such tranquil time the city, or he, would know for quite a while. Sumner Welles's reports and others from Europe had convinced him that the Phony War would soon be replaced by the real thing. If this happened, it would directly influence his decision on whether to stand for another term; if not, he could retire to Hyde Park as he had planned and as he still hoped to do. Had the decision been his solely, he could retire with full confidence that in two terms he had done for the American people what no other president had been able to do; his legacy was secure. It was his intention at the end of his term, he told a Democratic audience in March, to turn over to his successor his office and "a nation intact, a nation at peace, a nation prosperous." And if it happened that his successor was a Republican who intended to repeal the New Deal, there was nothing to say that FDR couldn't come back in four years and do what his hero and cousin Theodore had attempted to do in 1912, except that he would have a more compelling case to make.[29]

However, with the prospect of imminent war, FDR also believed, self-servingly or otherwise, that the decision was not entirely or even largely in his hands. He couldn't risk leaving the fate of the country to an isolationist Republican who would have neither the courage nor the political skill to send essential aid to Great Britain and France, reinforcing America's first line of defense. And he couldn't see a Democrat, with the possible exception of Hull, who had the understanding of the world situation that he had, *and* who had the ability to steer the country through these dangerous waters on the course he had set, *and* who could get elected. If he was compelled by events to run again, it would be more the result of duty than of desire; as much as he enjoyed being president, and there can be no doubt that he did, more important was his supreme confidence in his own capacity to lead the country facing a dire emergency. Humility was not a factor here; it seldom was with FDR.

Ralph Waldo Emerson had said a century earlier, "Events are in the saddle and ride mankind." For Roosevelt, events were very much in the saddle, and they would ride him as well as mankind.

A Hurricane of Events

As First Lord of the Admiralty, Winston Churchill was drawn to bold ideas for deploying His Majesty's naval forces against Britain's enemies. Holding that position in 1915, during the First World War, he had persuaded the cabinet to authorize a naval attack against the enemy stronghold at the Dardanelles, near Istanbul. Fresh troops from Australia and New Zealand established a beachhead on the Gallipoli Peninsula and were systematically annihilated by the Turks occupying the heights. The result was a humiliating defeat at sea and on land, and Churchill's departure from the war cabinet.

Now, almost exactly a quarter century later, he was once again First Lord of the Admiralty and once again advocating a bold idea. It proposed mining the Norwegian Leads, thereby obstructing German efforts to transport iron ore from Sweden across a narrow stretch of Norway to the northern port of Narvik, then through the Leads to the Baltic and German ports. Hitler correctly suspected that the British were planning such an operation and issued orders for the simultaneous invasions of Norway and Denmark, to commence on April 9, 1940. German troops conquered Denmark within three hours, and they landed successfully in every major port along Norway's 1,000-mile coastline, including Narvik. It was another example of flawless German planning and execution, and it left London deeply chagrined. Few could comprehend how the superior Royal Navy, the pride of Britain, could have allowed the German ships to have slipped so far north undetected. CBS correspondent William L. Shirer captured the sense of the debacle in his diary: "They had a wonderful opportunity to stop Hitler and they've muffed it."[1]

Frustration with the Norwegian fiasco boiled over in Parliament, and it quickly centered on Chamberlain's leadership. During three days of harsh debate he was relentlessly ridiculed for having said only days before Hitler's invasion of Scandinavia, with obviously misplaced confidence, that the Führer had "missed the bus." Finally one of his fellow Tories rose to summarize the feelings of colleagues of all persuasions by quoting to the prime minister the very words that Oliver Cromwell had addressed to the Long Parliament centuries earlier: "You have sat here too long for any good you have been doing. Depart, I say, and have done with you. In the name of God, go!" Within days Chamberlain went, to be replaced by Winston Spencer Churchill, proud descendant of the warrior hero of Waterloo, the duke of Marlborough. Despite his role in the embarrassing Norwegian episode, he had now returned fully from his wilderness years, during which he had been Britain's most forceful, and sometimes only, voice advocating preparedness to meet what he was sure were Hitler's plans for aggression. He was sixty-five years old and, never short on self-confidence, absolutely convinced that he was up to the formidable task that faced him and his country.

Assuming his new office on May 10, he was immediately confronted with the event that everyone feared and most expected—Hitler's all-out assault on western Europe. Finally getting to bed in the early hours of the next morning, he recalled later, he felt "a profound sense of relief . . . I felt as if I were walking with Destiny, and that all my past life had been but a preparation for this hour and this trial."[2]

The evening before Franklin Roosevelt, ensconced as usual in the Oval Study adjacent to his bedroom, had received a call from John Cudahy, the American ambassador in Brussels, reporting that German troops and armor were overrunning Luxembourg and already threatening Holland and Belgium, where, in a bold tactical innovation, paratroopers had dropped behind the lines in a total surprise. The Low Countries, whose neutrality Hitler had promised to honor, would fall within days, and the much-vaunted Maginot Line, which the Germans successfully flanked, proved irrelevant. Although the number of French and British forces nearly equaled those of the invading enemy, they were badly outmatched by the tactical brilliance of the German generals and the flawless execution of their plans by those under their command. German superiority in planes and tanks made the difference up and down the line; the tanks even made it through the Ardennes Forest, which the French had assumed was impenetrable by armor, splitting the French army in half. The Germans had perfected the concept of blitzkrieg— swift and powerful strikes against a complacent adversary at an unexpected time and place—and achieved its apotheosis in May 1940. Scandinavia had been merely a preliminary event, carried out mainly to protect Germany's sea lanes; here was the main event, designed to so demoralize the Allies that Hitler would once again be able to dictate the terms of the peace.

While defeatism began to run rampant through French officialdom, Churchill began his valiant effort to rally Britons with his pledge of "blood, toil, tears, and sweat."[3] The new prime minister also chose this moment to resume his correspondence with Roosevelt, initiated by the president the previous September. It would represent the beginning of his long and relent- less courtship of the president, convinced as he was that only America could provide the weaponry and other material goods that Britain would need to survive the greatest threat it had seen since the Spanish Armada appeared on the horizon 350 years earlier. Instead of identifying himself as "Naval Person," as he had in his earlier cables, he added "Former" to the title and expressed the hope that "although I have changed my office, I am sure you would not wish me to discontinue our intimate, private correspondence."

Churchill described the bleak scene confronting his country, stressing the preponderance of German aircraft, which was then "making a deep impression on the French . . . We expect to be attacked here ourselves, both from the air and by parachute and air-borne troops in the near future, and are getting ready for them. If necessary, we shall continue the war alone, and we are not afraid of that." And then he got to the heart of the matter: "But I trust you realize, Mr. President, that the voice and force of the United States may count for nothing if they are withheld too long. You may have a completely subjugated Nazified Europe established with astonishing swiftness, and the weight may be more than we can bear." What he hoped was that FDR would proclaim nonbelligerency, "which would mean that you would help us with everything short of actually engaging armed forces." He then offered his wish list of arms, beginning with forty or fifty "older" destroyers, several hundred new aircraft, and nearly everything else an effective fighting force required. "We shall go on paying dollars for as long as we can," he wrote, acknowledging the cash-and-carry provision of the Neutrality Act, "but I should like to feel reasonably sure that when we can pay no more, you will give us the stuff all the same."[4]

Roosevelt quickly responded to Churchill's cable, but in a highly unsatisfactory manner as far as the prime minister was concerned. As for the request for destroyers, the president said, that kind of step required the specific authorization of Congress and, as he put it, "I am not certain that it would be wise for that suggestion to be made . . . at this moment." Regarding aircraft, he reported that everything that could be done was being done to make them available, and he was encouraging about prospects for purchasing antiaircraft weapons and ammunition. But he was notably silent on the question of what would happen when Britain's dollar reserves ran out, undoubtedly because he knew that for the moment his hands were tied by the cash-and-carry provision.[5]

As the Allied situation in Belgium and northwestern France continued to deteriorate—the Germans had successfully turned the French right flank and threatened to isolate it from forces in the south—Churchill wrote FDR again immediately and with even greater candor and urgency, stressing that whatever happened, Britain would fight on to the end. Countering this determination, Joe Kennedy counseled both Churchill and the president that the beleaguered nation should negotiate with the Germans for terms while it could.

Both leaders ignored the ambassador's advice, but the clear message from Churchill was that without significant American assistance, particularly in destroyers and planes, there were no assurances the British could survive. "In no conceivable circumstances will we consent to surrender," he assured FDR, but cautioned that it was possible his government could fall and be replaced by another that might be compelled to "parley amid the ruins," most notably with the British fleet. That would be "the sole remaining bargaining counter with Germany . . . and if this country was left by the United States to its fate no one would have the right to blame those responsible if they made the best possible terms they could for the surviving inhabitants. Excuse me, Mr. President, putting this nightmare bluntly."[6]

It was a nightmare indeed, and it could not have been put more bluntly. What Churchill was describing represented Roosevelt's greatest fear. But in his efforts to avoid it he was severely handicapped in part by his own inability to prepare the American people psychologically for the calamity then unfolding in Europe. He had retreated under heavy fire from his first attempt to make the case for collective security in his 1937 "quarantine" speech, and he had never been so bold since. His innate caution had kicked in, and except for repealing the arms embargo he was content to accommodate public opinion on events overseas rather than to shape it. Foreign affairs was not where he had chosen to spend his political capital after his 1936 landslide reelection, when he had a good deal of it; rather, he spent it on a Court-packing plan that proved to be a disaster and then on an equally flawed effort to purge Democratic conservatives in the 1938 election. These missteps were compounded by the "Roosevelt recession," which he had inadvertently triggered by prematurely cutting back on federal spending. The net result of all this was that his standing with the public was at low ebb. He had, at long last, succeeded in amending the Neutrality Act, but it was arguably a case of too little, too late, and Hitler's invasion of Poland had probably done more to make it possible than presidential leadership had. Finally, he had failed to deal with the Woodring-Johnson feud at the top of the War Department, which had seriously hampered his plans to get aircraft to France, and to install new leadership supportive of his own policies.

So the question remains whether FDR could have better prepared the American people for what he clearly saw as the danger to the United States from Hitler's aggression in Europe. Almost certainly he could have, but the question in his mind was a different one—whether he could do so and still maintain the ability to govern effectively given the political environment. Maintaining that ability, he felt, was everything, because without it he could do nothing. While clear majorities of the American people indicated a willingness to help the Allies with "methods short of war," the intensity of the argument in the country, and even more so in Congress, was on the other side. The isolationists were far more vocal than the internationalists, and they played their cards with great skill to receptive audiences: sending aid to the Allies was choosing sides in a European war in which the country had no business, and it could only result in dragging the United States into the conflict. Aside from the economy, isolationism remained the single most important political fact of life in the United States in 1940 and, Hitler's threats notwithstanding, it showed few signs of abating. A poll during this month of turmoil showed that fewer than 8 percent of the American people favored U.S. entry into the war, and only 19 percent believed the country should intervene if the Allied cause appeared doomed; 40 percent opposed intervention under *any* circumstances. "In many parts of America," historian Jon Meacham would write, "isolationism was what we would later call the conventional wisdom."[7]

Now, in mid-May 1940, the question for Roosevelt was, what to do? There is no question what he *wanted* to do: send significant help fast to the Allies and bolster America's "first line of defense." But he had growing doubts about France's ability, or willingness, to stay in the fight, and soon enough these doubts would be confirmed by French accommodation to overwhelming German force. Which left Britain, which now meant Churchill, and Roosevelt hadn't yet taken his measure. They had only met once, in 1918, at a London dinner where FDR believed he was snubbed by the brash young Churchill; the Englishman never remembered the occasion, and the American never forgot it.

More important, Sumner Welles had returned from his recent meeting with Churchill singularly unimpressed by the man, whom he described as a nonstop talker and a nonstop drinker. Bill Bullitt had told Harold Ickes two months before that he had little use for Churchill, and it would be surprising if he hadn't shared the same view with the president. When word reached a cabinet meeting that Chamberlain had resigned, Roosevelt "supposed that Churchill was the best man that England had." It was a less than ringing endorsement. Despite his doubts about the man who now stood almost alone in Hitler's path to conquest of the continent, FDR knew he had to deal with him and hope for the best.

With the outbreak of war it became quickly apparent to most observers that America's defenses were grossly inadequate. For years Germany had been outspending the United States six to one in armaments, and the War Department, both civilian and uniformed, constantly complained that the country could ill afford to send matériel to Europe without also endangering itself. It was an argument that resonated widely, and Roosevelt knew he had to face it. He chose to confront what he called the "hurricane of events" of early May by asking Congress on the sixteenth of the month for an increase of $1.4 billion in defense spending, in addition to an increase he had already requested.[8] The other big news of the address was the president's determination to increase aircraft production from twelve thousand planes a year to fifty thousand. Whether this number was any more carefully calculated than a similar number he had floated to his advisors the previous November is not known, but there can be little doubt that his intention now was the same as the one that General Marshall had suspected then: it was the president's way of getting critical aid to the Allies. "I ask the Congress not to take any action which would in any way hamper or delay the delivery of American-made planes to foreign nations which have ordered them *or seek to purchase new planes*," he pleaded. "That, from the point of view of our own national defense, would be extremely short-sighted."[9] Once again, he didn't make the most forceful case he might have for aiding the Allies, but his intention was unmistakable; he was simply using his favorite device, indirection, to accomplish two purposes at once. He would build enough planes to satisfy critics at home and allies abroad.

William L. Shirer listened to a shortwave broadcast of the president's address in Berlin and was amazed but thrilled that Roosevelt proposed eliminating the gap in aircraft production between the United States and Germany. "This is a truth obvious to all of us here, but when we used to report it we were accused of making Nazi propaganda. . . . It makes you feel good that they're waking up at home at last."[10]

One person "at home" who clearly disagreed with Shirer's assessment and who clearly wasn't "waking up" was Charles Lindbergh, still determined to be the country's voice of isolationism. His fame continued as ever to give him easy access to the news media and especially the radio networks, where he became, in Robert Sherwood's view, Roosevelt's "most formidable competitor."[11] Taking to the airwaves just days after the president's appearance before Congress, Lindbergh condemned his remarks as "hysterical chatter." "We are in danger of war today," he argued, "not because Europeans tried to interfere in our internal affairs, but because Americans attempted to interfere in the internal affairs of Europe." As he had in the past, Lindbergh felt that Americans should not fear invasion, and that peace was at hand by not "asking for war." "Nobody wishes to attack us, and nobody is in a position to do so."[12] Even after the war had begun in earnest, Lindbergh spoke for millions of Americans determined to avoid it at any cost, and he appealed to millions more who were less persuaded but still fearful of the possibility of war.

What had changed was that Lindbergh and the other voices of isolationism no longer had the field to themselves. William Allen White, the small-town Kansas editor seen as middle America's spokesman for down-home common sense, formed a new organization called the Committee to Defend America by Aiding the Allies. The name was a near-perfect description of Roosevelt's own aims, and the committee quickly became the principal private-sector advocate for his policies.

With chapters in virtually every state, White's committee waged the most vigorous fight against isolationism in the country's history, distributing literature and sponsoring radio broadcasts featuring such nonpolitical luminaries as James B. Conant, the president of Harvard; Henry Luce, the publisher of *Time*; and even Lindbergh's mother-in-law, Mrs. Dwight W. Morrow. White was a well-known Republican, and so no one could accuse him of being FDR's handmaiden. Nor could he be accused of being an apologist for Britain, which he blamed for "an avalanche of blunders" early in the year and which he thought could not survive with Chamberlain as its leader. Even before the German blitzkrieg he argued for help for Britain because, with its fleet still intact, "we could have two years in which to prepare for the inevitable attack of totalitarian powers upon our democracy, which must come unless Great Britain wins this war."[13]

White fully expected to be attacked by the isolationists for playing such a prominent role in such a controversial arena, and he was not disappointed. Father Charles Coughlin, the "radio priest" in Detroit, unleashed his vitriol on White in his publication *Social Justice*: "Like thieves who operate under the cover of night, there are in our midst those who operate beneath the cloak of protected auspices to steal our liberties, our peace and our autonomy." Coughlin went on to denounce White's committee as an organization with a "high-sounding name composed of high-handed gentlemen who are leaving no stone unturned to throw everything precious to an American to the dogs of war." William Allen White was nothing but a "sanctimonious stuffed shirt," and he and all the others were "the Judas Iscariots within the apostolic college of our nation."[14] These kinds of ad hominem attacks would only get worse. The stakes for the country could not have been higher, and some obviously felt that they justified any kind of rhetoric or tactic. But White was not one of them. He kept his focus on the issues and trusted the American people to see the merits of his case. He didn't dissuade any committed isolationists, nor did he expect to, but there's no question he blunted the thrust of their argument.

By the last week in May Roosevelt had decided it was time for another fireside chat with the American people. At dinner on Sunday evening, the twenty-sixth, in the residence, with Eleanor, Harry Hopkins, Missy Le-Hand, and a few others, "there was no levity," according to Sam Rosenman. The president mixed cocktails "rather mechanically," an activity he usually embraced with enthusiasm. All the while FDR was receiving and reading depressing cables describing the perilous state of the Allied position in Belgium and France as the entire British Expeditionary Force (BEF) of 350,000 men and an additional 25,000 French troops were retreating toward the port of Dunkirk; it appeared they probably could not make it before being cut off by the rapidly advancing Germans. "All bad, all bad," FDR said as he passed the cables to Eleanor, who then passed them on to

Hopkins. A "grim-looking President" soon sat before the microphone in the reception room downstairs to address the nation. "To those who have closed their eyes . . . to those who would not admit the possibility of the approaching storm—to all of them the past two weeks have meant the shattering of many illusions. They have lost the illusion that we are remote and isolated and, therefore, secure against the dangers from which no other land is free." The president urged listeners not to panic, nor to think the country defenseless, nor to believe that "only by abandoning our freedom, our ideals, our way of life, can we build our defenses adequately, can we match the strength of the aggressors." These, he said, were illusions, and the country should "have done" with them.

The president sought to reassure a nation beset by fears of the unknown, and he did so with his now well-developed style of speaking with confidence in a calm, conversational manner that, just as it had during the early days of the Depression, gave each listener the feeling that the president was speaking to him or her personally: "Let us sit down together, you and I, to consider our own pressing problems." When he came to the subject of the country's military preparedness his reassurances were handicapped by the facts. Given the extraordinary strength exhibited by the German blitzkrieg, there was every reason to question how American forces stacked up. So while he claimed that the United States was strong militarily, he emphasized those resources that were in the appropriations pipeline as well as an innovative plan he had just developed to advance industry federal funds to build plant capacity for arms production as quickly as possible.

He also laid out a preemptive case against any who might be tempted to use the emergency to compromise the New Deal. "We must be sure . . . that there be no breakdown or cancellation of any of the great social gains we have made these past years." Finally, with what could only be seen as a thinly veiled reference to Lindbergh and the others he saw as isolationist extremists, he cautioned against the effects of a "fifth column" in America. "These dividing forces are undiluted poison," he warned in a phrase that Rosenman said FDR found particularly satisfying. "They must not be allowed to spread in the New World as they have in the Old. Our morale and our mental defenses must be raised as never before against those who would cast a smokescreen across our vision."[15]

At a news conference two days later the president was visibly moved by the huge response to his address. He reported that a "flood of mail and telegrams" offering support had poured into the White House, and more than a few included checks for the Red Cross to help displaced civilians in Europe. Following up on his pledge to build the nation's defenses, he announced the resurrection of a mechanism used by Wilson in the First World War: the Council of National Defense, a cabinet-level body still authorized by a 1916 statute. But the more important announcement was his appointment of an advisory commission for the council, consisting of business, labor, and other leaders whose critical task would be to design and implement much of the industrial mobilization plan that Roosevelt had promised. This "advisory commission" would not be advisory at all; it would be fully operational. And it would not be without controversy, particularly among hard-core New Dealers, for placing the lion's share of the rearmament burden on the private sector; it invited worrisome parallels with the earlier experience.[16]

The grim news continued to pour in, and Ambassador Kennedy in London continued to punctuate it. "Only a miracle can save the BEF from being wiped out [at Dunkirk] . . . or surrender," he cabled the day after FDR's fireside chat, and for once it was an assessment with which most observers would agree. He was also on to something when he reported that some British leaders favored seeking an accommodation with Germany "on terms that would be a great deal better than they would be if the war continues," a course he was still urging on the British government. This had to reinforce Roosevelt's doubts about Churchill's backbone, but he was as yet unaware of the momentous struggle then under way in the British war cabinet; if he had known, he would have worried even more about the ultimate fate of the British fleet.[17]

During five days in late May Britain's top ministers wrestled intently with the question of whether Mussolini should be approached to see what terms might be secured from Hitler that could preserve the nation's independence. Lord Halifax, the foreign secretary, who had also served in that capacity under Chamberlain, argued that they owed it to the nation to explore terms because the outlook was bleak and the opportunity would soon disappear. Churchill was adamantly opposed, seeing the move as "being dragged down the slippery slope with France." He believed that peace and security could never be achieved in a German-dominated Europe: "That we could never accept," he told his cabinet. In office just two weeks, Churchill could not afford, and probably couldn't survive, a Halifax resignation, which was at least once obliquely hinted at. So he did a delicate dance with the foreign minister, finally outmaneuvering him to the point where Halifax was dissuaded from pressing the issue. It was a close-run thing, as Churchill would say, and if Roosevelt had seen it, he undoubtedly would have been impressed by Churchill's political skills, which were not unlike his own. The new prime minister had passed his first big test: Britain would fight on alone.[18]

As May wound down and June approached, all eyes focused on the dramatic events unfolding in northwestern France. The BEF and the smaller French force accompanying it made their way slowly but steadily toward Dunkirk on roads teeming with refugees while Stuka dive-bombers pounded both soldiers and civilians from above. The scenes conveyed to the world, as the Germans intended, a sense of terror, doom, and inevitability. With the race on and the odds heavily in Germany's favor, the world was transfixed. Then, mysteriously, the German assault halted for three days; had it not, the Allies almost certainly would have been cut off from the sea and faced either surrender or annihilation. The pressures on Britain to sue for peace would have been overwhelming and perhaps irresistible. But in the event, for whatever reason, the Germans hesitated, and almost the entire Allied force was miraculously rescued and evacuated to Britain on an armada of nearly nine hundred small craft.

On the day of deliverance, June 4, Churchill appeared before the Commons to rally his nation with warrior eloquence not heard in the English language since Shakespeare's Henry V exhorted his "band of brothers" before the Battle of Agincourt. "We shall fight in France, we shall fight on the seas and oceans, we shall fight with growing confidence and growing strength in the air, we shall defend our island, whatever the cost may be. We shall fight on the beaches, we shall fight on the landing grounds, we shall fight in the fields and in the streets, we shall fight in the hills; we shall never surrender, and even if, which I do not for a moment believe, this island or a large part of it were subjugated and starving, then our Empire beyond the seas, armed and guarded by the British fleet, would carry on the struggle, until, in God's good time, the new world, with all its power and might, steps forth to the rescue and the liberation of the old."[19]

The speech deeply moved virtually everyone on both sides of the Atlantic who heard it, including Roosevelt; it reinforced his confidence in Churchill's ability and determination to fight. He could not have missed the reference to the "new world," and he could take satisfaction that even as Churchill spoke, arms were already being loaded onto British ships in American ports.

Though the modest arms shipments may have relieved Britons, the situation in France continued to deteriorate. With half the French army immobile and useless behind the Maginot Line, German armored columns turned south and headed virtually unopposed toward Paris. Premier Paul Reynaud cabled Roosevelt that to survive, the French needed a public declaration of American backing in the form of "aid and material support by all means short of an expeditionary force. I beseech you to do this before it is too late."[20] Mussolini seized precisely this moment to take advantage of France's distress by sending 400,000 Italian troops into the nearly defenseless Riviera and, making good on a promise he had made to Hitler back in March, declared war on Britain as well.

On the day Roosevelt received this news, he was scheduled to deliver the commencement address at the University of Virginia in Charlottesville, where his son Franklin junior would be graduating from law school. "It was a curious trip," Eleanor recalled later. "A trip to one's son's commencement is normal; but that was not a normal and happy occasion. The times were fraught with promise of evil. Franklin's address was not just a commencement address; it was a speech to the nation on an event that had brought us one step nearer to total war."[21]

FDR viewed Mussolini's treachery as a stab in the back to France, and he was so taken with the metaphor that he proposed including it in the speech.

His advisors at the State Department opposed the phrase on the grounds that it was too provocative, and he took it out. On the way to Charlottesville he decided to put it back in. Wearing a crimson academic hood, he addressed the graduates and their families in the university gymnasium as rain fell outside. "On this 10th day of June 1940, the hand that held the dagger has struck it into the back of its neighbor. On this 10th day of June 1940 . . . we send forth our prayers and our hopes to those beyond the seas who are maintaining with magnificent valor their battle for freedom." Roosevelt went on to announce that the country would "pursue two obvious and simultaneous courses." It would offer arms and material to the "opponents of force" and at the same time it would arm itself, such that the country would have the "equipment and training equal to the task of any emergency and every defense." "Signs and signals," he concluded, "call for speed—full speed ahead."[22]

The audience interrupted him with loud cheers and even rebel yells. It was the most direct and most forceful the president had ever been in aligning the United States with the cause of the Allies, and Churchill, who was listening in, could hardly believe his ears. His relentless courtship of Roosevelt had paid off, he believed. He quickly dashed off a cable to the White House: "We all listened to you last night and were fortified by the grand scope of your declaration. . . . I send you my heartfelt thanks and those of my colleagues for all that you are doing and seeking to do for what we may now, indeed, call the Common Cause." He also used the occasion to repeat his urgent request for destroyers: "We can refit them very rapidly. . . . Not a day should be lost."[23]

FDR did not respond to Churchill, but he did respond to a message from Premier Reynaud, who had also taken great encouragement from the Charlottesville speech. The United States, Roosevelt wrote, was "doing everything in its power to make available to the Allied governments the material they so urgently require, and our efforts to do still more are being redoubled."[24] Churchill, on being given a copy of this message by Kennedy, read too much into it, concluding that Roosevelt just might be working with Congress for a declaration of war and American entry into the fighting.

Back in May, during a particularly dark day, Churchill had told his son Randolph, "I think I can see my way through." When Randolph said he didn't see how he could do it, his father replied, "I shall drag the United States in."[25]

Seeing a possible opportunity to "drag the United States in," Churchill pleaded with the president to make the communication between Washington and Reynaud public, believing it would have a huge effect on events and especially on French determination. But he had been wrong in his assumption that it signaled U.S. entry into the conflict. Roosevelt's thinking was not even approaching that kind of decisive action—he apparently had been so buoyed by the reaction to his Charlottesville speech that he got a bit carried away and in his message to Reynaud allowed himself to be uncharacteristically vague on such a critical point—and he gently turned Churchill down on his request. The prime minister, devastated by the response, tried once more, this time citing the threat the French fleet would pose if it fell into German or Italian hands, and repeating the uncertainty of what might happen to the Royal Navy if Britain had to go it alone. Unless Roosevelt assured France the United States would enter the war, he concluded, it would be compelled to seek an armistice.

Before Roosevelt could reply, France itself sought an armistice. On June 22, in the same railway car in the Forest of Compiègne where Germany had signed the armistice of 1918, the tables were now turned. The French were forced to sign away virtually their entire sovereignty: northern France, including Paris plus all of the Atlantic coastline, would now come under direct German control, while unoccupied France was to be governed by a puppet regime in Vichy. It was total humiliation, and a triumphant Hitler thoroughly enjoyed presiding over every minute of it. Only the fate of the French fleet, most of it tied up in French ports in North Africa, remained unaccounted for.

The working strategic assumption in the Roosevelt administration, to the extent that any existed, according to historian David Kennedy, had "implicitly rested on the triad of French land power, British sea power, and American industrial power."[26] Now the first element of that equation had disappeared, and Britain had no choice but to go it alone if it wished to escape the fate of France. Nearly all of Europe had fallen before the Nazi war machine, and the only thing that stood between Hitler and complete domination of the European continent was this stubbornly resistant island nation off its western coast. Churchill had successfully fought back against those ministers who wanted to accommodate Hitler, but after the cabinet learned of the harsh terms the Führer had imposed upon France, there were many fewer such advocates. Churchill was determined to fight, and on June 18 he tried to prepare the nation for the invasion that he was certain would soon come, giving a speech that concluded: "Let us therefore brace ourselves to our duty and so bear ourselves that if the British Commonwealth and Empire lasts for a thousand years, men will still say, 'This was their finest hour.'"[27]

The words again strengthened Roosevelt. He saw clearly the consequences to the United States should Britain go down, and he determined that it wouldn't happen. In the words of Robert Sherwood, the president "had scraped the bottom of the barrel in American arsenals" to ship everything conceivable to Britain. "This was done by means of more legal manipulation in a 'damn the torpedoes' spirit," he said. Sherwood also added that it came at a moment when many of FDR's advisors were "shouting almost hysterically" that helping the Allies would be political suicide and disastrous for the nation, for if Britain was defeated, these arms would be taken by Hitler, who would use them against America.[28]

His advisors may have been in a state of hysteria, but Roosevelt, as usual, was calm, composed, and confident. "FDR's view of himself and of his world freed him from anxieties that other men may have felt, and would have found intolerable," historian William E. Leuchtenburg has concluded. "Not even the weightiest responsibilities seemed to disturb his serenity. One of his associates later said, 'He must have been psychoanalyzed by God.'"[29]

Though Roosevelt was doing what he could, there remained a great disparity between what Washington thought it could do without and what London thought it needed. And it wasn't only Britons who thought the United States should be sending more. William Allen White of the Committee to Defend America by Aiding the Allies was the most vocal American advocate for the cause, and during the second week of June he wired the president: "My correspondence is heaping up unanimously behind the plan to aid the Allies by anything other than war. As an old friend, let me warn you that maybe you will not be able to lead the American people unless you catch up with them. They are going fast. But only you can keep them out of war by giving them some other economic equivalent in aiding the democracies."[30]

At the same time, the president's own military leaders, led by George Marshall, who had been tasked to strengthen America's decrepit forces, complained that "our own stocks were below the safety point" as a result of the transfers.[31] Marshall and his naval counterpart, Admiral Harold Stark, boldly challenged the president's assumption that Britain would survive; sending additional war matériel, they told him, would seriously weaken the country's ability to defend itself and at the same time do the British no good. These conflicting pressures would continue to bear on the president, but he too demonstrated boldness and, as David Kennedy observed, "stuck unflinchingly with his risky bet."[32] All he could do to deal with the pressures without causing irreparable damage on either side of the Atlantic was to keep asking Congress for larger defense appropriations.

As for Churchill's incessant pleas for old American destroyers, Roosevelt didn't think they would be of much use. He was familiar with the vessels and their capabilities from his own service in the Navy Department in the First World War and, as he often did, he was quick to substitute his judgment on naval matters for that of others. In this case he came to a different conclusion than did Churchill, who had even more, and more recent, naval experience than Roosevelt, and who was obviously desperate for the American ships, no matter how obsolete, to replace the growing numbers of British escort vessels sunk almost daily. These heavy losses meant that the merchant ships they were protecting, which provided Britain's lifeline from the rest of the world, were easy prey for German U-boats and surface raiders.

Greater than the military value the ships would convey, Churchill reasoned, was the psychological and political value they would bring to the British cause. Roosevelt no doubt saw this truth as well. Their delivery, David Kennedy noted, "would bolster British spirits, signal Hitler that the patience of the neutral Americans was wearing thin, and, most significant, help drive home to those same Americans their stake in the struggle against

Nazism." In short, the transfer would bring the United States one step closer to belligerency.[33]

At a long lunch with Harold Ickes on June 4, the president conceded he could be wrong in his assessment of the ships' military value, in which case it would have serious results. On the other hand, he added, if he sent the destroyers, they could prove useless and yet would provoke Hitler. There was simply no way of knowing what was the right course. Ickes summarized Roosevelt's conundrum: "If you do send some help with bad consequences to ourselves, the people will blame you just as they will blame you if you don't send help and the Allies are crushed."[34] This was what FDR was facing during the late spring of 1940: any decision carried consequences, and they were greater than ever.

The matter of the destroyers aside—there were particular legal and political issues associated with them that virtually everyone thought were insurmountable—it was in early June that Roosevelt committed himself, and his country, to Britain's survival. The policy had been articulated in his Charlottesville speech and made manifest by overriding his military advisors to dip heavily into American arsenals to send weaponry overseas. While the full meaning of the policy might not have been apparent yet to the world (or even to William Allen White), it was taking firm hold in the president's mind. And the risks inherent in the decision were certainly not generally appreciated. There was no assurance, or even any likelihood, that Britain would survive; the odds favored a successful German invasion, given that nation's recent invincibility on the battlefield and the overwhelming power of its Luftwaffe. In that event, whatever arms America had sent would not only be lost but also, as his military advisors warned him, potentially used against it. A huge public controversy would erupt over Roosevelt's decision to ignore his generals. Given the ferocity of the isolationists—and their representation in Congress—it was not unthinkable that he would be impeached, to say nothing of losing the election.

FDR knew these risks attached to his decision, but he saw it as an overpowering moral issue, involving the preservation of fundamental Western values, and especially the American values of democracy and freedom. Roosevelt's own form of internationalism—first introduced to him by Wilson but tempered over time and adjusted to his own pragmatic sensibilities—was now taking shape. And he took the decision despite his distaste for most things British, particularly the country's commitment to empire, which would be a point of friction between Roosevelt and Churchill in the years to come. This was a decision in which the risks and the dislikes were subordinated to something much larger. It was one of the great gambles of history.

All of this was clearly on Roosevelt's mind the evening of June 5, when he met with a group of fifty young men and women representing left-leaning youth organizations. Having received the suggestion from her young friend Joseph Lash, Eleanor had urged the meeting on her husband. The idea appealed to both Roosevelts in part because a similar meeting on the South Lawn in February had not gone well when FDR grew impatient with his young questioners for their naïveté and failure to understand the complexities of the issues he was facing. They had been particularly vocal about his decision to rearm America at a time when there were so many economic and social issues still demanding attention. He had uncharacteristically allowed himself to get short and even petulant with them, and he had since regretted his handling of the session. He not only wanted make up for it but also wanted to reach out to a generation that could very well soon be asked to put lives on the line for their country. Not least, perhaps, it was a constituency that he might need in the election if he decided to run again.

Seated in the East Room with Eleanor and Harry Hopkins, the latter looking wan and increasingly irritated as the meeting went on, Roosevelt employed his usual charm on his audience. He never showed the slightest annoyance, even when statements and questions crossed the line into rudeness. He was totally disciplined, as he had not been in February.

Foremost in the minds of the young attendees was, again, what they saw as the president's policy of guns over butter, which is to say his abandonment of New Deal goals in favor of ever greater appropriations for armaments. They cited the many issues plaguing the still economically crippled nation—unemployment, hunger, health care, low wages—and they couldn't understand how the objectives he had fought for so valiantly could now be thrust aside before the job had been completed. Social justice, broadly defined, was high on their agenda, and it was no surprise that the group, which was racially mixed, focused as well on rampant discrimination in the country, segregation in the armed services, and the inability of black Americans in the South to vote. Finally, with billions of dollars now going to massive spending on arms of all kinds, why were business leaders being called to Washington to oversee these huge new expenditures? Wasn't this a case of the fox in the henhouse—an invitation to profiteering that would inevitably yield more "war millionaires," something Roosevelt himself had warned against?

FDR should not have been surprised by any of these questions, reflecting as they did the ideals of young liberal activists unencumbered by doubt. He listened to all of it respectfully, and when the time came to address the questions he no longer wore the mantle of commander in chief, which he had been wearing continuously for more than a month. Instead he put on the cloak of educator in chief. Just as he had patiently listened, so now did he try to patiently explain, as candidly as he could, the issues he had to deal with on a daily basis and the choices he had to make. Yes, social welfare issues were very much a part of the nation's defense and they were equally important, but it "is a little difficult in our system to pursue two equally important things with equal emphasis at the same time." He was now confronted with violent Nazi aggression abroad, a threat the United States could not ignore, as well as the still worrisome forces of greed and reaction at home, which he had done his best to combat. He intended to address both concerns, but he also had to make decisions; he didn't have the luxury of occupying the high ground and issuing morally pure pronouncements regardless of what was happening around him. Once again, events were in the saddle, and he had to contend with them.

No president occupies the White House without being constantly reminded that Abraham Lincoln once lived there and grappled with the most fundamental questions a nation could face. Roosevelt was seated just down the hall from George Healy's large portrait of the sixteenth president pondering some great issue. Upstairs in the residence was not only Lincoln's bedroom but also his study, currently occupied by the man seated next to him, Harry Hopkins. And in the East Room itself, the body of the martyred president had lain in state. As a student of history, FDR knew Lincoln well. He was particularly mindful of Lincoln's famous 1864 letter to Albert G. Hodges of Kentucky explaining his position on slavery, and which concluded with a stark admission: "I confess not to have controlled events, but confess plainly that events have controlled me." The president did not cite the quotation to his young audience, though it had been uppermost in his mind for some time. But he did talk about the "great struggle" Lincoln had had with himself between trying to preserve the Union, as he had sworn to do, and confronting the evil of slavery. Lincoln had known the two great issues were related, FDR said, but on assuming the presidency he had to put off dealing with slavery to concentrate first on restoring the Union. He had been compelled to wait on events that would permit him to join the two great causes into one. So, too, must FDR wait on events to deal with other questions later.

An unidentified young man eager to speak for his colleagues—if not for his entire generation—rose and did so at length, covering most of the issues already raised in an articulate and testy oration laced with more than a little arrogance. Again Roosevelt listened patiently. When the young man finally concluded, the president asked him if he had read Carl Sandburg's *Lincoln*, the final volume of which had been recently published; the entire work would be awarded the Pulitzer Prize for history in 1940. When the young man conceded he had not, Roosevelt summarized it for him. "I think the impression was that Lincoln was a pretty sad man because he couldn't do all he wanted to do at one time, and I think you will find examples where Lincoln had to compromise to make a few gains." This made him "one of those unfortunate people called a 'politician.'" Lincoln had been saddened by the fact that "he couldn't get it all at once" but succeeded nonetheless in getting "a great many things for this country" by focusing on those goals that were achievable. Perhaps his young questioner "would make a much better president than I have . . . Maybe you will someday." And if so, "you will learn that you cannot, just by shouting from the housetops, get what you want all the time."[35]

FDR invoking Lincoln as he had was, of course, no coincidence. He revered Lincoln and had studied him closely. Although he hadn't cited the first great quandary Lincoln had faced in his presidency—whether to abandon Fort Sumter, reinforce it, or simply reprovision it—that crisis had in a way paralleled the question Roosevelt now faced in how aggressively to support Britain in its hour of need. Britain's value to the United States, of course, was strategic, whereas Sumter's value to the country had been symbolic. Nonetheless, hanging in the balance over both presidents at the time of decision was war or peace. Stakes for presidents didn't get any higher than that. Roosevelt's quandary was further complicated by the fact that whereas Lincoln had an election just behind him, FDR's second term was now nearly over, and his own political future was yet another quandary.

The Republicans Appear Onstage

No one in or near the administration would have been surprised that Harry Hopkins had shared the stage with FDR and Eleanor in the East Room on June 4. For the past month Hopkins, his health partially restored, had been at the president's side virtually every day. On May 10, the day Hitler invaded the Low Countries, the secretary of commerce had returned to his office for only the second time in nearly a year. That evening he dined with the president at the White House, and when he felt ill his host insisted he stay overnight. Providing what Missy LeHand would claim was the inspiration for Kaufman and Hart's play *The Man Who Came to Dinner*, Hopkins would reside in Lincoln's former study, just down the hall from FDR's bedroom, for the next three and a half years.

Seeing in Hopkins the potential to be an in-house national security advisor, Roosevelt decided to mentor his friend in foreign affairs and geopolitics; they spent hours together poring over cables from Europe. The broad-gauged Hopkins was, as always, a quick study. He was among the first people the president saw in the morning and the last he saw at night, with numerous other sessions in between. Roosevelt didn't have anyone in the White House to work with, or even to talk with, on foreign matters, and he settled on Hopkins, whom he both liked and trusted implicitly, for the role of national security advisor, even though the title was years away from formal use.

Nor did FDR have anyone with whom he could talk serious politics, and Hopkins came to fill that role as well, making him an almost de facto chief of staff. He spent Sundays cruising the Potomac with the president and joined him at Hyde Park for four days in late June, after which he traveled to Chicago to discuss convention arrangements with Mayor Kelly, a task that ordinarily would have fallen to Jim Farley. Robert Sherwood would say later that Hopkins acted "without express instructions" from FDR in political matters, yet "was now moving to take charge of the third term nomination." But this had to be conjecture because, unlike their earlier shared experiences, Hopkins left no memos of or even references to political conversations with his boss. Whether there were "express instructions" remains a question to this day. All we know for certain is that Hopkins was a strong third-term proponent, and since FDR's refusal to declare his decision on the matter was hovering over everything, it's hard to believe that the subject didn't come up more than occasionally.[1]

It is not surprising that Hopkins's newly elevated status in FDR's world caused much comment as well as jealousy and sniping in and around the White House. Pa Watson thought FDR felt "sorry" for Hopkins but also that the latter had his eye on the vice presidency (he had in fact changed his voter registration from New York to Iowa the year before, thereby obviating the constitutional obstacle presented if the presidential and vice presidential candidates came from the same state). Ross McIntire complained that several "deprecatory remarks" about him had been traced to Hopkins. And Harold Ickes, who thrived on this sort of gossip and recorded much of it, lamented the fact that Hopkins "was in the way of becoming a second Louis Howe." If so, he wrote at the time, "it would be altogether too bad. Louis Howe was much abler and he was absolutely disinterested personally." Whereas Howe thought of nothing but FDR's concerns, Harry was "too much interested in Harry and Harry's future."

Ickes also noted that Hopkins was "distinctly susceptible" to rich and famous people.[2]

In fact, Hopkins *was* becoming the new Louis Howe. His primacy in FDR's world was resented not only in the inner circles but also in much of the Democratic Party, where he was seen as not having paid his political dues, as Howe had. Nor did he speak the language of politics or have the deft political skills that Howe had had. Resentment toward Hopkins was soon compounded by his practice of keeping perceived competitors, such as Harold Ickes, Tommy Corcoran, and William O. Douglas, at a safe distance from the president's ear. His ambition, perhaps combined at times with the insecurity that often accompanies such a quick rise to power, would cause him to demonstrate what some saw as ruthlessness.

Since Howe's death in April 1936, before FDR's election to a second term, no one had filled the unique role that he had occupied. The president's oldest son, Jimmy, tried it for a while, but he proved to have neither the talent nor the temperament for the job. Even before Hopkins's illness it was apparent that he had achieved a special status with FDR. In early June he used his new authority to direct press secretary Steve Early to ask members of the administration to "pipe down" on third-term talk because "it serves no useful purpose."[3] Hopkins was absolutely loyal and had proven totally reliable in every job the president had assigned him. So the comparison with Howe was inevitable, and no less keen an observer than Eleanor saw it. "He was a man whom I not only admired but came to have a deep trust and confidence in," she wrote years later. But she had known the two men better than anyone besides Franklin, and she was candid in citing their differences. "In Harry Hopkins my husband found some of the companionship and loyalty Louis had given him, but not the political wisdom and careful analysis of each situation." Harry was more accommodating than Howe, who "would argue until he felt Franklin had seen all sides of a question." Harry was honest about his opinions with the president but also knew that FDR did not like opposition—"as who does?"—and so either agreed with him or was too indirect in changing the president's opinion. Hopkins was the kind of man who waited for what seemed "an auspicious moment" to bring up a subject, and if he felt unsure about his grasp of the subject, he would bring in other people to back him up. "This was not as valuable a service as forcing Franklin," wrote Eleanor, "as Louis did, to hear unpleasant arguments." Eleanor conceded that Howe had advantages in both age and early experience with FDR that enabled him to be "more independent" than Hopkins. "Franklin, in turn, shaped Harry; he widened his horizons and taught him many things about domestic politics and foreign affairs. Consequently Harry's opinion did not carry the weight with Franklin that Louis' had."[4]

For the month or more that the president had been transfixed by events in Europe, he had still managed to keep an eye on political developments at home. It was the peak of the primary season, and he continued to win committed delegates, though he had done nothing to campaign openly for them. He had, of course, done a number of things not so openly to ensure that "friendly" delegations were sent to Chicago, and in that connection he had sent Ickes to California to unify the various Roosevelt factions onto a single slate. The result in early May had stunned Roosevelt: expecting to beat the Garner slate by a two-to-one margin, the president instead bested it by seven to one. The result "had a very buoyant [e]ffect upon [FDR's] spirits," Ickes recorded, adding, "There is no doubt now of the President's absolute control of the convention for himself, whatever he may be able to do with it if he wants to nominate someone else." Roosevelt agreed, observing that control "would result in liberal candidates and a liberal platform."[5]

A few nights later he convened a White House dinner that included Robert Jackson, now the U.S. attorney general, William O. Douglas, whom FDR had appointed to the Supreme Court a year earlier, Tom Corcoran, Ben Cohen, Hopkins, Ickes, and a few others. This was the hard core of the New Deal in the administration, and they began the process of shaping the "liberal platform" that the president had told Ickes he wanted, as well as other convention arrangements.

On June 4, during the same lunch with Ickes at which they had discussed the destroyers issue, the president was still expansive when the subject turned to politics. FDR asked his companion who he thought the Democratic nominee would be, and Ickes recorded the exchange in his diary the next day. "'I know, and if you don't know, someday I will come in and tell you.' He grinned and said, 'Well, there may be a surprise; it may surprise even you.'" Ickes reported his reply to the president: "You have control of the Democratic convention, but I doubt whether you can control it for any-one but yourself." Ickes said he then admitted that Hull might be nomi-nated "but that Hull would make a poor candidate and a poor President." The president professed not to be convinced that this was so.[6]

In fact, the Gallup polls in May and June revealed that Hull was the over-whelming favorite of Democratic voters should FDR not run again. He led Garner by a better than two-to-one margin in both months, with Farley and others far behind.[7] In the April and May polls Hull led potential Republi-can opponents by large margins, larger in fact than Roosevelt's.[8] By any standard—certainly by any standard that FDR would apply—the secretary of state was the sole conceivable alternative to him at this point. Garner and Farley, the only two announced candidates, not only were unelectable in his view but were anathema to the president, politically as well as person-ally. Cordell Hull wasn't ideal by any means, but he was, as they say in the business, viable. Meanwhile, the number of letters coming into the White House, and tabulated by Jim Rowe, urging Roosevelt to seek a third term had soared to six thousand in the month of June.

But the Democratic National Convention wouldn't convene until July 15, six weeks away. Much sooner, on June 24, Republicans would gather in Philadel-phia to select their own presidential nominee. From the perspective of three weeks out, no one could predict the outcome with any confidence. Asked by Ickes at the June 4 lunch who he thought would emerge, FDR predicted it would be Taft but conceded it could be Vandenberg. Should the GOP decide it couldn't win in any case, it might select the young crime-buster Tom Dew-ey "and go through with him." He didn't think the newest entry, utilities exec-utive Wendell Willkie, who was coming up in the polls, had "much chance."[9]

Early on, Republicans had been bullish about the prospect of retaking the White House. Despite all of Roosevelt's initiatives, there were still more than ten million unemployed, and the national debt had soared to an un-precedented $36 billion. While the president hadn't announced his inten-tions, there were no other Democratic prospects who appeared to worry them. And if he did decide to run again, there remained serious opposition in the country as a whole—and especially among Republicans—to the idea of a third term. After Hitler's invasion of Poland, FDR's public approval jumped past 60 percent every month from September 1939 through February of the following year. But during the same months, according to Gallup, approval for FDR seeking a third term never broke 50 percent.[10] Not least, Republicans had been greatly encouraged by the huge gains they had made in the 1938 congressional elections and believed they were a harbinger of even better things to come this year. Unlike in 1936, when FDR's reelection was largely assumed and the GOP nomination fell to the luckless Kansas governor Alf Landon, there would be no lack of serious candidates.

Arthur Vandenberg was the first to announce his "availability"—the euphemism then in use for declaring one's intention to run. The fifty-six-year-old stout, slightly balding Michigander, partial to large black cigars, white suits, and windy speeches, was the very caricature of a U.S. senator, which is precisely what he was.

He represented what he saw as the conservative legacy of his hero, Alexander Hamilton, about whom he had written three books. He nonetheless had supported many New Deal programs but thought they could be tempered and certainly better run. It was in foreign policy, however, where he had his most serious differences with the president and where his Midwestern isolationism took hold. "Repealing the arms embargo probably won't get us into war," he had argued. "But it's like taking the first drink of whiskey. After a while, you're drunk."

Vandenberg's campaign would rely on support from the Midwest—particularly the Wisconsin and Nebraska primaries—and from the Far West, which usually trended Republican. Like other senators seeking the presidency, before and since, he was overly impressed with his own talents and credentials as a legislator and would discover that they did not transfer well to this new pursuit. Because of his national standing, however, he was the instant front-runner the moment he announced.[11]

Hard on his heels was the wunderkind of New York law enforcement, thirty-seven-year-old Thomas E. Dewey. His age may have been a handicap but his growing notoriety as a "racket-busting" district attorney more than made up for it. This was the age of the mobsters, and Dewey had successfully prosecuted scores of them, including some of the most infamous, such as Lucky Luciano, Legs Diamond, and Dutch Schultz. His success in the courtroom inspired movies and even a radio series; the public couldn't seem to get enough of him, and *Life* magazine helped to kick off the presidential boom by calling him the "Number One Glamour Boy of the GOP." His national political standing had been greatly enhanced in the 1938 election when he came within a single percentage point of defeating the popular incumbent governor of New York, Herbert Lehman; he was immediately regarded as a serious presidential prospect. At about the same time that Vandenberg had announced his "availability," Dewey had private polls showing him defeating Roosevelt decisively. While he knew that kind of margin wouldn't last, his whistle-stopping around the country in his own train in early 1940 drew huge crowds everywhere, even in the smallest hamlets of the Great Plains, where his pencil mustache, his diminutive stature, and his eastern dress and mannerisms seemed out of place. Nonetheless, he was a celebrity for his anticrime work, and when he came to town he was a big draw.

His shortcomings were almost entirely personal. In the words of one historian, he was "stiff, humorless and over-bearing." Others found him arrogant, vain, and altogether dislikable. For the most part he managed to conceal these qualities from the public and play the role of the fearless crime fighter. Just as he had been manipulative and calculating in his prosecutions—he paid scant attention to civil liberties and a good deal to illegal wiretapping and unauthorized subpoenas—so he was in his campaign. He may have been the first presidential candidate to hire his own private pollsters, and he got his money's worth from them: he would not take a new position on an issue without poll-testing it, and he was invariably guided by the results. Thus he was reliably isolationist and supported a balanced budget. For the most part he spoke vaguely and in platitudes; his audiences didn't seem to mind, for his popularity grew.[12]

Senator Robert A. Taft of Ohio rounded out the field of the early GOP entrants. As the son of a former president, he had a distinguished Republican pedigree, which gave him instant standing in the party, a standing he enhanced considerably by making a favorable debut in the Senate following his election in 1938. He had brought with him a reputation for honesty and a brilliant mind, which sometimes made him appear professorial—he had been first in his class at both Yale and Harvard Law School. Taft immediately became the most articulate and dogged opponent of the New Deal in that body. A libertarian at heart, he argued that the government had no business interfering in the lives of its citizens or in the workings of the economy. The private economy should lead the way out of the Depression, he maintained, not the deficit spending that FDR had so freely embraced. He saw the New Deal as not only inefficient and laden with waste but essentially socialist in design and operation.

Taft was also a hard-core noninterventionist. He fervently opposed aid to Britain and France on the ground that the ocean protected America from whatever happened in Europe and that no good could come from engagement there. He sometimes joined his libertarian and isolationist strains in his fierce anti-FDR rhetoric: "There is a good deal more danger of the infiltration of totalitarian ideas from the New Deal circles in Washington than there ever will be from activities of the communists or the Nazis."[13] Despite his early success in the Senate, however, his reserved demeanor, coupled with his owl-like appearance and air of supreme confidence, didn't play well on the campaign trail. He centered his strategy for capturing the nomination on skipping the primaries, relying instead on his relationships with the party professionals; it was a strategy that he believed would serve him especially well in a deadlocked convention.

So the race was on. Dewey's celebrity status and extensive campaigning thrust him into an early and impressive lead in the polls. Gallup had reported in January 1940 that he was the favorite of 60 percent of Republican voters, with Vandenberg and Taft trailing with 16 and 11 percent, respectively. At this point the field appeared to be set, but the "internals" of the poll revealed that the numbers were "soft": fully 37 percent of the respondents indicated they were still undecided on whom to support. Gallup's February numbers had shown only a small change, with Dewey dropping to 56 percent and Vandenberg and Taft tied at 17 percent. The same poll revealed a significant finding to which very little attention was paid: 59 percent of

Republicans indicated they preferred to see the party "more liberal" than it had been in 1936, which Gallup interpreted to mean that during those three years "rank and file opinion in both major parties has come to accept a great many of the New Deal's social and economic measures."[14]

April had seen the first key primary, in Wisconsin, where Vandenberg believed his roots in next-door Michigan would stand him in good stead. He also believed that his stature in the Senate would serve him well, and he used his pressing "duties" there as an excuse not to campaign in the state. Dewey saw an opening to stage an upset—the *New York Times* had reported that Vandenberg was a three-to-two favorite—and he seized it with non-stop campaigning. On April 2 Dewey overwhelmed Vandenberg by a better than two-to-one margin, and a week later won again, albeit by a smaller margin, in Nebraska. The easterner had proved that he could solidly beat a midwestern icon in his own backyard, and as a result, there was a new front-runner. That status was confirmed by Gallup in early May when he reported that Dewey's support among Republicans had soared to 67 percent, while Vandenberg and Taft sank into the lower double digits.[15]

Dewey appeared unstoppable at this point, except for one thing: the field that had appeared to be set was in fact anything but. There was a late-comer in the race who seemed to have appeared from nowhere and who was coming on strong. The emergence of this once-obscure lawyer from a small town in the Midwest provided one of the most dramatic, and improbable, stories of American politics in the twentieth century.

Wendell Lewis Willkie was born in Elwood, Indiana, in 1892, the son of two lawyers of German descent whose politics were solidly Democratic and passionately liberal. The Willkies encouraged their children to debate the issues of the day at the family dinner table. Like his father, Wendell tended to favor the underdog in American society and naturally gravitated toward the more liberal political figures of his youth, such as Woodrow Wilson and Robert La Follette. He was a bright student who did well in school and later at Indiana University, where he dabbled in student politics and began to show signs of the magnetic personality that would come to define him. He finished law school in a single year, which then was not uncommon, and distinguished himself in moot court and essay competitions. Returning to

Elwood to open a practice, he faced off against his father in his first court case, a fairly routine one; not surprisingly, he lost. "I believe my son will be a very good lawyer," the elder Willkie said in his closing argument. "He can make so much of so little."[16]

Wendell enlisted in the army after the United States entered the war in 1917 but arrived in France too late to see action. On leave before he shipped out, however, he had married his sweetheart, Edith Wilk, a librarian in Rushville, a small town just down the road from Elwood. They were devoted to each other and the marriage would last, although there would be times when it was not clear that it would. Returning to Elwood after his service, Willkie was tempted to begin a political career by running for Congress, but he was dissuaded by a prominent Indianapolis lawyer who saw unusual potential in the young man and offered to give him an introduction to Harvey Firestone of the Firestone Tire and Rubber Company in Akron, Ohio. The idea of playing on a larger stage appealed to Willkie—as it would throughout his life—and he seized the opportunity when it came. Without the pregnant Edith he moved to Akron, where he immediately melded into the social and political fabric of the community. He joined a host of civic, veterans, and other organizations and made a name for himself as a luncheon speaker. He soon left Firestone to join a prominent law firm, at which he was an instant success both in court and in representing public utilities before regulatory agencies, but he always managed to keep his political oar in the water. He introduced James Cox, the Democratic presidential nominee, when he made a stop in Akron during the 1920 campaign, and four years later he was a delegate to the party's national convention, where he helped lead losing battles to condemn the Ku Klux Klan and to support Wilson's League of Nations. These were, and would remain, fundamental issues for him; he hated discrimination of any kind, and he was convinced that the United States, as a citizen of the world, must work with others to keep the peace.

His success as a lawyer brought him to the attention of Commonwealth and Southern, the owner of Willkie's Ohio utility client. In 1929 he became counsel to the utility's holding company, based in New York. Again, fueled by a healthy ambition and the desire to play on a still larger stage, he accepted. Willkie immediately took to New York, and especially the extra-curricular social opportunities it offered. He and Edith had been gradually growing apart, or, perhaps more accurately, he had been growing in ways that she had not. Whereas Edith had become the traditional stay-at-home mom, Wendell was attracted to the high-octane pace of big business and the extensive travel that went with it. His mussed hair, rumpled clothes, and informal aw-shucks manner appealed to people, and especially to women, at least one of whom observed that he was "very attractive" and exuded "a great deal of masculine charm." The attention flattered the once-awkward Indiana boy, and he took advantage of it.[17]

In January 1933, two months before Roosevelt was sworn in as president, Willkie was named president of Commonwealth and Southern. The ironic confluence of these events meant that Willkie, a strong Democrat who supported the thrust of the New Deal, would now spend most of his professional time fighting regulation of the utility industry, as well as the new Tennessee Valley Authority (TVA) and the unfair advantage he argued it would have over private utilities. Given his charismatic speaking style, he gained increasing notice as an articulate spokesman for business interests and as a reasoned critic of what he saw as excessive regulation. He sometimes criticized his own industry, and particularly some of the unseemly practices of holding companies, which only strengthened his appeal. It became apparent that this was not just another doctrinaire anti–New Deal businessman stridently pleading his case; rather, he came across as a reasonable, thoughtful, and sometimes self-critical midwesterner who spoke the language of common sense.[18]

The utilities industry was alarmed when Roosevelt indicated that he might replicate the TVA in other parts of the country, and as a leader of the industry, Willkie met with the president in December 1934. Nothing of consequence came from the meeting, but afterward Willkie wired Edith (who resented the president's interference in her husband's business): "Charm greatly exaggerated. I did not tell him what you think of him." They met again a month later, after FDR had urged "abolition of the evil holding companies" in his State of the Union message. During a ninety-minute session, Willkie heard FDR explain how the holding companies had disregarded the interests of both consumers and their own operating companies. "During most of this time," David Lilienthal, the director of TVA, recorded, "Willkie said nothing. But I could see he was getting hotter and hotter." When Willkie finally suggested a compromise, the president repeated that he wanted to do away with the holding companies altogether. "Do I understand then," Willkie asked, "that any further efforts to avoid the breaking up of utility holding companies are futile?" The president nodded in agreement. "It is futile," he replied.[19] The gap between the two was too wide to bridge, and subsequent meetings were no more productive; they settled into a frosty and distrustful relationship.

Willkie increasingly took his case to the public, and he found several prominent publications willing to help him, including *Life*, the *Saturday Evening Post*, *Forbes*, and especially *Fortune*. The favorable press he received generated more and more speaking invitations, and one of them arrived in late 1937 from the *New York Herald Tribune* Forum, where he had a fateful encounter with the paper's book editor, Irita Van Doren. An attractive and articulate southerner who exuded charm and intelligence, she caught Willkie's interest immediately, and she was as drawn to him as he was to her. Someone who knew her at the *Herald Tribune* described her as "equally merry and serious with sparkling eyes, a low, gentle Southern voice, a mass of pretty curls, and a slender figure even after bearing three daughters." Another friend said she had a way of combining her charm with an understanding of "the uses of power," a talent that allowed her to move easily in New York's liberal intellectual circles. With the help of the *Herald Tribune*'s owners, Ogden and Helen Reid, it also allowed her to move up on the paper's masthead, first as editor of the book section and soon as a member of the board.[20]

Willkie's marriage to Edith at this point existed in name only, and Irita's marriage to the historian Carl Van Doren had ended two years before. Irita and Willkie collaborated on a book review, and she encouraged him to write for other publications. She also introduced him to such luminaries as Dorothy Thompson, Carl Sandburg, James Thurber, and Sinclair Lewis, and he became as mesmerized by this new world as he was by her. She assigned books for him to read and encouraged him to think seriously about political issues and to develop his own ideas on them. Under her careful tutelage, Willkie acquired growing confidence that he could play on the national political stage. By the summer of 1938 they had fallen in love and were seeing more and more of each other, often spending weekends at her Connecticut farm. While Irita tried to be the picture of discretion, Willkie did little to disguise the relationship.

With his ever-higher profile in the press, it was inevitable that speculation would focus on Willkie as a possible presidential candidate. Indeed, that had been Irita's hope, and he warmed to the idea as well. An impressive performance in his January 1938 radio debate with Robert Jackson on national issues—including, of course, the regulation of utilities—caused a stir, and he again more than held his own debating Felix Frankfurter at the Harvard Club on the merits of the New Deal. Willkie received encouragement from important Republican leaders, including Sam Pryor, a fellow businessman who was the GOP national committeeman from Connecticut, and Charlton MacVeagh, a veteran of both J. P. Morgan and earlier presidential campaigns. With Irita's help, Ogden and Helen Reid became enthusiasts, and Henry Luce, the publisher of *Time*, *Life*, and *Fortune*, also became enamored by this fresh new voice and began to open up his magazines to him.

Probably the most significant convert to the Willkie cause was Russell Davenport, the managing editor of Luce's *Fortune*. After Willkie addressed a forum sponsored by the magazine, Davenport told the would-be candidate that he "took the whole group by storm" and "put into words . . . the things I had been thinking for years."[21] He urged Willkie to run and offered to do anything he could to help. When Willkie said he would like to discuss the matter, Davenport invited him to spend a weekend at his Connecticut house. Thinking the Willkies—Edith came along—would want to be entertained, the Davenports invited a number of friends from the area and planned a variety of activities, but as Marcia Davenport recorded, Willkie had his own idea of relaxation. "He was out on the porch with Russell sprawled in a wicker armchair, one leg thrown over the arm. He had taken off his jacket and necktie and opened the collar of his shirt. He was drinking a whiskey and soda, and chain-smoking cigarettes in such a way that most of the ash fell on his shirt front and most of the butts missed the ashtray at which he threw them. He was talking hard, emphatic, concentrated talk with his blue eyes fixed on Russell's absorbed face."[22]

Willkie's intelligence, enthusiasm, and down-home manner captivated everyone that weekend. With Davenport playing the key role, his team of advisors fell into place, and they used their networks and platforms to spread the Willkie gospel. Davenport's platform was *Fortune* and he used it generously. With his and Van Doren's editorial help, Willkie wrote an article for the April 1940 issue outlining his views on national concerns. Nearly the entire magazine was given over to this new political phenomenon and included a virtual endorsement, but the highlight was Willkie's piece, called "We the People." In it he blamed the federal government for being inept and the New Deal for being too rigid, but, notably, he didn't call for its repeal. Rather, he embraced its premise: "Government, either state or federal, must be responsible not only for the destitute and the unemployed, but for the elementary guarantees of public health." He appealed openly for the support of liberal Republicans, who at this point had no other attractive options. He similarly reached out to those Republicans of an internationalist bent, castigating congressional isolationists for opposing revision of the arms embargo: "We are opposed to war. But we do not intend to relinquish our right to sell whatever we want to those defending themselves from aggression." This was a very different kind of Republican voice, and people took notice, especially after the piece was reprinted in the largest-circulation magazine in the country, *Reader's Digest*.[23] In mid-May, Luce devoted eleven pages in *Life* to the rising star, concluding: "Wendell Willkie is by far the ablest man the Republicans could nominate for President in Philadelphia next month." The editorial bandwagon was rolling, and the *Saturday Evening Post*, *U.S. News*, and other publications soon followed with equally enthusiastic endorsements.[24]

Among those who took notice was a young lawyer at Davis Polk and Wardwell in New York named Oren Root, who decided to make Willkie his cause. The grandnephew of Elihu Root, Teddy Roosevelt's secretary of state and a winner of the Nobel Peace Prize in 1912, he used his contacts to organize an unauthorized petition drive urging Willkie to run and formed local Willkie clubs. The movement caught fire, spreading across the country and feeding the appetite of a party hungry for a new face; it exceeded all of his expectations. "I felt like a surf rider," Root said, "trying to ride this enormous wave I'd started and keep my head above water."[25]

When the very impressive grassroots campaign came to public attention, Willkie and his handlers worried that it would upset their carefully crafted dark horse strategy of being in the right place at the right time in order to break an impasse at the convention. Grassroots politics was something very new and, on this level at least, untested; not yet understanding its potential, they attempted to persuade Root to disband his effort, and when that didn't work Willkie called his friend Thomas Lamont at J. P. Morgan, the principal client of Root's law firm, to intervene. That, too, failed. In a last-ditch effort, Willkie sent Davenport, who by this time had left *Fortune* to manage the campaign, to meet with the eager young man, but instead of Davenport persuading Root to desist, Root persuaded Davenport that the effort was not at odds with the agreed-upon strategy and that it should continue. As a result, Root finally met Willkie, and they agreed that Root would issue a press release saying that Willkie neither approved nor disapproved of the grassroots campaign. He added a statement that he "would not participate in any organized move to that end."[26]

With speaking invitations pouring in after the *Fortune* piece appeared, Willkie fed the press appetite by addressing the nation's political reporters in Washington and then their publishers in New York, charming them all. John and Gardner Cowles, publishers of *Look* magazine, argued that he also had to pay attention to the delegates, and with that in mind they sponsored a trip to Minnesota and Iowa, where they owned the principal newspapers. He spoke to an audience in St. Paul from a prepared script for thirty minutes without visibly stirring them, then abruptly discarded it and said, "Some damn fool told me I had to read this speech. Now let me tell you what I think." Willkie suddenly came to life, and the audience followed; it was a transformative moment, and Willkie would not soon forget the lesson it taught. Four Minnesota delegates immediately endorsed him, and the state's young governor, Harold Stassen, who would keynote the convention, said he was drawn to support him. That night Willkie became a candidate in active pursuit of the nomination, and he soon made more appearances designed to win over delegates, which slowly began to add up. "He could charm a bird from a tree," Marcia Davenport would say.[27]

It took a while for the media spreads and the appearances to be reflected in the polls. By early May Willkie had garnered the support of only 3 percent of Republicans surveyed by Gallup, but by the end of the month he had risen to 10 percent, and Dewey was beginning to drop.[28] The German blitzkrieg on May 10 shocked most Americans into the realization that the president they elected in 1940 likely would have to steer the nation through a major crisis, and the criteria for what kind of person that should be began to change. While Dewey was doing his best to avoid discussing foreign affairs except in vague generalities, it seeped into the thoughts of many that perhaps this otherwise attractive and brash young New Yorker might not be ready for the job. Meanwhile, Willkie unabashedly supported all-out aid to Britain and France. Those two countries, he said in May, "constitute our first line of defense against Hitler . . . It must therefore be in our advantage to help them in every way we can short of declaring war." His policy and even some of his words were identical to those enunciated recently by FDR. Later that month Willkie announced at a dinner party at the home of Ogden and Helen Reid that he would support Roosevelt over a Republican who refused to aid the Allies. Robert A. Taft, a guest who fit that exact description, erupted, and the party descended into a shouting match.[29]

Willkie's rapid ascent in the polls demonstrated how soft the support was for the other candidates. By June 12, with the convention only two weeks away, Dewey had dropped from a high of 67 percent to 52 percent, and Willkie had leaped into second place with 17 percent. Dewey's lead was still significant, but the momentum heading into the convention belonged entirely to the man whom David Halberstam called "the rarest thing in those days, a Republican with sex appeal." Willkie chronicler Charles Peters described him at this point as the nonpolitician "Mr. Smith bound for Washington" who "began to smell like a winner."[30]

Before the Republicans could convene in Philadelphia, however, Roosevelt dropped a bombshell on the GOP. On June 20, with just four days to go before the delegates met, the president announced that he was bringing two of the most prominent and respected Republicans in the country into his cabinet: Henry L. Stimson would be secretary of war and Frank Knox would be secretary of the navy. Stimson had served as secretary of war under William Howard Taft and as secretary of state under Herbert Hoover; a confirmed internationalist with a deserved reputation for rectitude and commitment to public service, he was the embodiment of what would be known as the eastern establishment. Knox, whose robust, high-energy personality and sharp intelligence appealed to FDR (he had been a Rough Rider with Teddy Roosevelt), had been the GOP's vice presidential nominee in 1936. He was currently publisher of the *Chicago Daily News*, whose editorial policy was strongly anti–New Deal but equally strongly in favor of aid to Britain. Both men, it will be recalled, had supported repeal of the arms embargo in the fall of 1939.

Roosevelt knew that he had to make changes in the War Department; not only was Harry Woodring, the current secretary, an isolationist who stubbornly resisted the president's efforts to get warplanes to the Allies, but his poisonous rivalry with his deputy, Louis Johnson, had confused and demoralized others in the department almost to the point of immobility. FDR hated unpleasant personnel decisions, particularly when it involved firing members of his cabinet. He went to great lengths to avoid them, invariably hoping the problem would solve itself. But in this case the problems his indecision had caused were alarming others in the administration.

Harold Ickes was especially concerned and decided to do something about it, but before he sprang his idea on the president, he decided to run it by Missy LeHand. The idea was that at the next cabinet meeting Ickes would announce his resignation on the grounds that circumstances had "so radically changed that I think it is only fair that all of us should resign and leave you [FDR] free to revamp your present Cabinet." LeHand, who after all these years with the president was politically very shrewd, asked if the plan was designed to get rid of Woodring. When Ickes conceded that it was, she said it wouldn't be necessary; the president had already made up his mind to do so. Knowing Roosevelt's reluctance to deal firmly in these matters, Ickes was skeptical, and he raised it at lunch with the president a few days later after Missy had had an opportunity to brief FDR on their conversation. Roosevelt stated unequivocally that he intended to ask for Woodring's resignation, to which Ickes responded, "Mr. President, you'll never do it." Roosevelt got his back up: "You don't know what I can do when I make up my mind," he said. "I will write him a letter." At that point, Ickes recalled, he "went at him in earnest," urging the president to do it "quickly and completely." The interior secretary did manage to learn that FDR was considering Fiorello La Guardia for the job, but he neglected to mention that he, too, was interested.[31]

The idea of bringing more Republicans into his cabinet as the foreign situation deteriorated had long been on Roosevelt's mind (progressives such as Ickes and Henry Wallace had become such fervent New Dealers that they hardly counted as Republicans anymore). Back in the fall of 1939 he had toyed with the idea of making Alf Landon, the GOP's 1936 presidential nominee, the secretary of war, but rejected that notion after Landon called on the president publicly to renounce a third term. For at least six months Ickes lobbied for his friend Knox, whom he had known since their days together in Chicago, to be appointed to a cabinet position, most likely secretary of the navy, where there was only an acting secretary who didn't present a serious personnel problem. FDR liked Frank Knox, and the publisher was interested, but when he was offered the job during the Phony War period, he declined on the grounds that he didn't want to embarrass his party.

The Woodring issue festered until Grenville Clark, FDR's fellow law clerk early in their careers and now a leading lawyer in New York, got involved. He had recently been leading an effort to persuade Congress to enact a conscription bill, which required him to meet with high-ranking officials and officers at the War Department. He was so appalled by the dysfunctional state of the department that he sought guidance from his friend and FDR's close advisor, Justice Felix Frankfurter. At a May 31 lunch at the Supreme Court, the two scoured the landscape for candidates to replace Woodring before settling on Stimson. Although the seventy-two-year-old Stimson was a conservative Republican—they didn't know yet that this would fill FDR's bill perfectly—his experience and reputation for fairness and political impartiality recommended him. He had advocated, albeit unsuccessfully, for collective security measures against Japan in the mid-1930s that could be seen as a precursor to Roosevelt's "quarantine" speech of 1937, and he argued forcefully and consistently for a major buildup of American military strength.

Frankfurter took the Stimson idea to the White House in a personal meeting with the president on June 3, and he soon thereafter told Clark that he thought the idea had "struck fire." But FDR still dithered, fearful of offending Woodring and perhaps triggering a political firestorm through an angry resignation. The issue came to a head two weeks later when the secretary again challenged the president by denying the sale of B-17 bombers to Britain on the grounds that they were needed for U.S. defense and their sale would violate the amended Neutrality Act. This was too much even for FDR, and he immediately asked for Woodring's resignation.[32]

The Stimson candidacy had indeed "struck fire" with the president. They had belonged to many of the same clubs in New York, and he had come to admire the statesman's unabashedly internationalist approach to foreign affairs. In 1930, when FDR was running for reelection as governor of New York, a worried Herbert Hoover had sent several of his cabinet members into the state to verbally rough up the man Hoover saw as his likely opponent in 1932. Stimson, then secretary of state, declined to participate in that kind of blatantly political activity; FDR took note. During the transition following the 1932 election, Stimson came to Albany to brief the president-elect, who was drawn to him even more. And recently Stimson had supported not only revision of the Neutrality Act but also William Allen White's efforts to promote aid to the Allies.

Having settled on Stimson and Knox, Roosevelt, in a curious move, called the latter first on the morning of June 19 to offer him again a seat in the cabinet, this time either the war or navy post. He had to be confident that if Knox accepted either it would be the navy job, but inexplicably he still ran a risk that the Chicagoan would accept the one in the War Department and thereby upset the president's carefully crafted plan. Roosevelt liked Knox a great deal, not least because he had been one of TR's Rough Riders and Bull Moosers and he had many of the same characteristics as FDR's predecessor; it's likely that he was trying to flatter Knox by offering him a choice of two plum positions. In any case, his instinct was correct, and Knox agreed to become secretary of the navy. The president then phoned Stimson, who had been tipped off by Frankfurter and Clark that the call was probably coming, and offered him the war post. The elder statesman accepted, but not before making certain the president knew of his public position favoring compulsory military training. Roosevelt said he was in "sympathy" with his position on the issue, and the arrangement was sealed.

FDR had pulled off an enormous coup. Not only had he greatly strengthened his cabinet in two critical positions, but he had broadened the appeal of his internationalist foreign policy by enlisting two prominent Republicans who were in support of it. This would seriously handicap the ability of the GOP to attack him on the issue in the forthcoming campaign should he run, and in any case it would catch the party by surprise on the eve of its convention and throw its leaders off balance. It was the sort of clever yet principled maneuver that FDR loved to conjure up and that he was skilled at executing: a win-win proposition that furthered an important policy goal while undercutting the political opposition.[33]

News of the appointments hit Philadelphia a mere four days before the GOP convention convened. Most party officials were isolationists and reacted with a fury seldom seen on a public stage. GOP chairman John D. M. Hamilton accused Roosevelt of playing dirty politics, and he damned Stimson and Knox for their treachery and argued that they should be read out of the party. But there were still many internationalists among the Republicans, and again William Allen White spoke for most of them when he applauded the new appointees for doing "the patriotic thing." If some Republicans ignored the growing threat in Europe, he said, they would resemble "bleat[ing] sheep for peace at any price," and he predicted that "my beloved party will not even carry Maine and Vermont," the only two states Republican nominee Alf Landon had carried in 1936.[34]

The big news of early June, however, was the fall of France, reminding Republican delegates pouring into Philadelphia the weekend before the convention was to convene that they had serious business to conduct.

Sobering as the news was, optimism and excitement were in the air as the four major candidates arrived.

Willkie got off his train at Thirtieth Street Station to be met by Russell Davenport, his de facto campaign manager, and Charlie Halleck, a fellow Indianan and rising star in the House of Representatives who had agreed to nominate Willkie. Instead of driving to his hotel, Willkie, wearing a straw hat at a jaunty angle and his trademark rumpled clothes, chose to walk down Broad Street, gathering an assemblage of admirers and reporters as he spread his folksy charm along the way. He stopped in the bar of the Belle-vue Stratford, the convention hotel, and insisted on buying two rounds of drinks for everyone. There is no report that anyone objected to joining Willkie in one of his favorite pastimes. Realizing where his political bread had been buttered to date, the candidate paid special attention to the principal reporters. He went so far as to feign naïveté with Arthur Krock and Turner Catledge of the *New York Times* on the need for a floor manager; he gratefully accepted their advice that he needed to get one.[35]

Feverish campaigning continued right up through Monday, the opening day of the convention, when Willkie managed to meet with more than two hundred delegates. The talk in the hotel lobbies and on the streets was that he was gaining momentum and that Dewey was slipping. This chatter gained impetus from a rumor that a new though as yet unpublished Gallup poll would show Willkie leaping ahead of Dewey as the clear preference of Republicans; the most recent poll, issued just a few days before, had shown Willkie trailing the New Yorker by 47 percent to 29 percent. Again, reports of defections from Dewey added to the sense that Willkie was on the move.

Dewey put on a brave face when he predicted at a news conference that he would receive at least 370 votes, and perhaps as many as 420, on the first ballot, and that he would acquire the 501 votes needed for the nomination by the third ballot. The day before, Willkie, supposedly the novice politician, had shown more savvy in playing the expectations game (always try to *exceed* the expectations) when he said he hoped to receive about 75 votes on the first ballot.

That evening Minnesota governor Harold Stassen delivered the convention's keynote speech, traditionally used by both parties to set the tone for the week to come—primarily by skewering the opposition. Stassen vilified Roosevelt for neglecting the interests of the nation by becoming preoccupied with the politics of a third term. The delegates loved it, and Stassen gave them more. Instead of criticizing the president's appointments of Stimson and Knox to his cabinet, he chastised him for failing to get rid of other "New Deal incompetents." Stassen's role was to stir the blood of the delegates, and he succeeded. He came out squarely against the draft bill, which required young men to register for the first peacetime draft in American history and which was then working its way through Congress with bipartisan support. He compared the measure to "the method of Hitler and Mussolini and Stalin" and hit Roosevelt where he was probably most vulnerable when he declared that "we are too woefully weak to give the Allies the material assistance this nation wants to give them." It was an impressive performance, and Willkie capitalized on it later that evening when, again brought together by the Cowles brothers of *Look* magazine, he persuaded Stassen to endorse him. Following the first faint chants of "We want Willkie!" from the galleries before adjournment, it had been another good day for the dark horse.[36]

However, not everyone was as enthusiastic about Willkie as those in the galleries. He had earlier encountered a group of Indianans in the lobby of the Benjamin Franklin Hotel that included former Senate majority leader James Watson, a conservative of the old school who was supporting Dewey. When Watson told Willkie that he was not "my kind of Republican," the candidate conceded that he had recently been a Democrat. "Well, Wendell," Watson replied, "you know that back home in Indiana it's all right if the town whore joins the church, but they don't let her lead the choir the first night." Everyone laughed at the witticism, but to some of the old-timers, including Watson, it was no joke.[37]

The next day, Tuesday, brought news of Hitler's plans to celebrate his victory over France and his intention to focus all of his military might on conquering Britain. The delegates knew this news was relevant to what they were about in Philadelphia: they could be choosing a man who would have to lead the United States through this dangerous new world. The realization didn't help the young and inexperienced Dewey—it would later be said jokingly that he was the first American casualty of World War II—but in the eyes of some it did bolster the case for the man who, of the four, was most outspoken in calling for American help to the Allies.

The candidates feverishly worked the state delegations, and at the same time they were jockeying with each other for support. Arthur Vandenberg's candidacy was seen as particularly weak—he had barely campaigned—and the others eagerly sought his delegates as well as his endorsement. He turned down Willkie's request for it, arguing that in the end the choice would be between the two of them. Both Taft and Dewey offered Vandenberg the vice presidential nomination in return for his backing. He turned them down as well, offering each the same proposition but in reverse. He went so far as to tell Dewey that if he accepted that arrangement, Vandenberg would agree to serve only one term, which would leave Dewey the clear front-runner for 1944. The senator instructed Dewey's agent, "Tell him if this is too much to swallow at once, I'll make him a sporting proposition. I'll meet him at 11:00 to flip a coin to see which end of the ticket we take." Dewey never got back to him. As events were about to show, the alliance that stood the greatest chance of halting Willkie's momentum was between Dewey and Taft. They held the largest blocs of committed delegates at this point, and, if they could ever agree on terms, they were in the strongest position to stop this usurper from capturing their party. Like Vandenberg, however, each remained confident of his own prospects, and each was determined to see them play out.[38]

First came the party's platform. The foreign policy plank was especially controversial, with confirmed isolationists fiercely resisting the arguments of equally confirmed internationalists. In the end, as often happens with platforms, they split the difference in an effort to give both sides some satisfaction. "We favor the extension of aid to all people fighting for liberty or whose liberty is threatened," the final compromise read, "as long as such aid is not in violation of international law or inconsistent with the requirements of our national defense." The acerbic Baltimore journalist H. L. Mencken observed that it was "so written that it will fit both the triumph of democracy and the collapse of democracy, and approve both the sending of arms to England and sending only flowers." It would be revealed years later that the language had been lifted almost verbatim from an ad that had appeared in the *New York Times* and other papers over the names of isolationist congressmen, written and paid for by Nazi agents. British intelligence was equally diligent in working the other side of the street with the internationalist press.[39]

As the delegates assembled in the hall for the main event, they soon felt as though they were in what Marcia Davenport described as "a hell of sealed-in heat." With no air-conditioning in the hall, the temperature pushed past 100 degrees, and the huge space was filled by "a haze of smoke and noise, with a smell compounded of sweat, anger, and tension from thousands of closely packed bodies." All the while a torrent of some forty thousand pro-Willkie telegrams descended on them, much to the annoyance of most. Hot, crowded, and resentful, only the Willkie delegates, it seemed, had reason to be happy with their circumstances.[40]

Dewey and Taft were the first to have their names placed in nomination, and in each case their supporters dutifully filled the aisles with posters and chants in an effort to create an impressive demonstration. Charlie Halleck's speech nominating Willkie was in an altogether different category, immediately prompting shouts of "We want Willkie!" from the galleries, cries that were answered by loud and persistent boos from Dewey's and Taft's ranks on the floor. When Halleck finished his speech, Willkie's supporters filled the aisles with a demonstration that dwarfed the others in enthusiasm if not in duration. As one journalist reported, "There was more passion packed into one minute of the Willkie demonstration than in the entire 25 of the carefully manufactured Dewey parade." The activity on the floor was accompanied by ever-louder shouts of "We want Willkie!" from above, made possible by Sam Pryor's skillful packing of the galleries with Willkie partisans, one of whom was a young volunteer from Michigan named Gerald R. Ford.[41]

The next morning the *New York Herald Tribune* published a front-page editorial—its first ever—endorsing Willkie, and inside, the influential columnist Walter Lippmann called Willkie "the man obviously best fitted to the circumstances of the hour."[42] When balloting began, the first tally showed Dewey in the lead, as expected, but with a total of 360 votes, 10 shy of the minimum his managers had predicted. Taft was second with 189, followed by Willkie, who exceeded expectations with a total of 105. The momentum was still with the Indianan. The second ballot followed immediately, showing Dewey slipping to 338 votes while Taft's total grew to 203 and Willkie's to 171.

At this point several things were clear to the delegates. First, Dewey, whose people had predicted he would gain at least 50 votes on this ballot, had seriously mishandled the expectations game, and he had compounded the error by failing to hold any delegates in reserve. Second, Willkie's momentum was real and couldn't be denied. Third, it was now a tight three-man race, and if Dewey and Taft could get together, they had enough combined strength to make one of them the nominee and stop Willkie's thrust.

During a brief dinner break Taft's and Willkie's managers tried to persuade the slipping Dewey to step aside; the New Yorker wouldn't budge. On the third ballot Dewey's total declined another 23 votes while Taft gained 9. The big news was that Willkie had picked up 88, propelling him past Taft into second place with 259. Eager to change the dynamic of the convention, Dewey's forces tried to get the proceeding adjourned until the next day. Willkie and Taft each believed momentum was on his side and they thwarted the effort. The fourth ballot was nail-biting time for everyone as delegates waited for the large delegations—California, Pennsylvania, Illinois, Michigan—to reveal significant new trends, but they mostly held back. At its conclusion Willkie had gained 47 new votes for a total of 306 and Taft 44 for a total of 259. They were both still well short of the 501 needed for the nomination. Now it was clearly a two-man race, and speculation was rampant that Dewey, who had fallen to third place, would withdraw.

A nervous Willkie, chain-smoking in his suite at the Benjamin Franklin, became convinced that the momentum had swung to Taft and that the Ohioan would be nominated on the next ballot. He was wrong. The fifth tally showed a gain of 123 votes for each of the new front-runners, with Willkie at 429 and Taft at 377. Willkie had not only maintained his lead but, more important, was now only 72 votes away from the magic number, 501. Suddenly it was Taft's people who wanted to adjourn until the next day, but Willkie's managers persuaded presiding officer Joe Martin, the leader of the House Republicans and someone who was sympathetic to Willkie, to keep going. It was midnight and the delegates were exhausted, but balloting resumed. The momentum swung back and forth as one of them picked up a half dozen new votes and then the other unexpectedly matched or exceeded it. So it went until the roll call reached Michigan, which everyone knew would be crucial. The delegation had been committed to Vandenberg, and when he left for a Senate vote in Washington he instructed the GOP national committeeman, Frank McKay, who had effective control of the delegation, to direct the state's votes to Taft. But McKay was indebted to Willkie supporter John D. M. Hamilton, who now called in the chit. McKay (whom Gerald Ford would later in a different context call a "crook") was prepared to make good on his debt, but he insisted on a clarification: some of his "boys," he said, were concerned about whose voice would be most important in the selection of federal judges if Willkie was elected, "the organization's or the amateurs' running the Willkie clubs?"

Hamilton took the question to Sam Pryor, one national committeeman to another, who in turn took it to the candidate himself. Willkie had told John Cowles earlier that day that he had not had to make bargains to win votes, and he was obviously proud of that fact. But now he was at the moment of truth: Michigan with its 37 votes could make the difference. "To hell with the judges," he told Sam Pryor. "Get the delegates." Michigan announced 35 for Willkie and 2 for Taft. The momentum continued until Virginia, with its 16 votes, dramatically ensured Willkie's nomination. The convention had worked its will.

Willkie celebrated well into the night with friends, finally retiring at 4:30 a.m. Before long he was awakened to deal with the matter of the vice presidential nomination. After extracting himself from a commitment he had made to the governor of Connecticut, he agreed to Charles McNary of Oregon, the GOP leader in the Senate, who was widely admired and who would bring regional balance to the ticket. Since the Republicans still clung to the anachronistic tradition that a nominee had to be "informed" of his selection in his hometown by a delegation before he could formally "accept" the nomination, Willkie gave only brief remarks to the convention.

"I stand before you," he said, "without a single pledge, promise or under-standing of any kind, except in advancement of your cause, the preservation of American democracy." He concluded with words that would bitterly re-mind some of his hard-core opponents in the hall of his very recent conver-sion—and cause a few to wonder if it was complete. "So, *you* Republicans, I call you to join, help me. The cause is great, we must win." Overlooking the stumble, the majority of the delegates, convinced they had nominated their strongest candidate and confident now about their prospects, gave him a standing ovation.[43]

As pleased as most delegates were with their choice, few could have foreseen the long-term consequences of what they had done. If anyone un-derstood the significance of the event, it was the hard-core conservatives who left Philadelphia deeply resentful that the GOP had been captured by what would become known as the liberal "eastern establishment" wing of the party. Years later, Marcia Davenport could still feel "the bitterness of the Old Guard, the adamant resistance to the interloper, the hatred against him and against all of us who had worked for this aim which was, after all, visionary and fantastic." Whatever else it did, Philadelphia gave birth to the bitter proprietary division within the Republican Party, one accentuated by ideology and geography, that would define the party for decades to come.[44]

FDR Decides

Roosevelt was as surprised as everyone else by Wendell Willkie's nomination. He found it hard to believe that the Republicans had not selected a traditional conservative, one of their own, and instead picked a confirmed internationalist who had been a registered Democrat as recently as a year earlier. He had expected Dewey or Vandenberg but now was facing a whole new phenomenon, one that whoever led the Democratic ticket could not dismiss so easily. In an intemperate moment he told Eleanor that Willkie was a "crook" who reminded him of "the sleight-of hand-fellow at the Dutchess County Fair."[1] When he adjusted to this new reality, however, he realized that a Willkie-McNary ticket was the most formidable he could have faced. The charismatic Willkie was a fresh face in national politics; he had no record that he was compelled to defend. The potential strength of his candidacy was confirmed when Gallup reported in his first postconvention match-up that Roosevelt had 53 percent to Willkie's 47 percent among a cross section of voters across the country; the survey had the Indianan "running virtually even with him in the sections of the country with the greatest number of electoral votes."[2] If FDR was going to be the Democratic nominee, 1940 was shaping up to be his toughest election since his first run for governor of New York in 1928.

Roosevelt's first instinct was to figure out how he might run successfully against this political phenomenon. Hoover in 1932 and Landon in 1936 had campaigned as conventional conservatives. Willkie was different. He couldn't be as readily categorized. At the first cabinet meeting following the GOP convention the president surfaced his proposed line of attack: Willkie, he said, "represents a new concept in American politics—the concept of the 'corporate state.'" He pointed out that this phrase had been used by Mussolini in building his fascist state in Italy and had some resonance in the United States. Roosevelt knew that it was a huge stretch to try to connect Willkie with fascism. What he no doubt had in mind was that the otherwise appealing Willkie would become a front for big business interests, such as the utilities company that he had headed. He agreed with Harold Ickes that it would be a mistake to allow Willkie's favorable image to go unchallenged, and he urged those around the table to start softening him up. Ickes cheerfully agreed to do his part.[3]

So the outcome of the 1940 presidential election was very much in doubt. Still, there was one big consolation for FDR, whether or not he ran. According to Robert Sherwood, the president saw Willkie's nomination as a "Godsend to the country" because the Republican candidate's support for all-out aid to Britain meant the isolationist-versus-interventionist issue was not in play and therefore "prevented the splitting of the people into two embittered factions." It also had the advantage of proving to other nations, "and particularly to warring nations," that American foreign policy would not be affected by the election. As events would soon demonstrate, this was no small thing, nor was it entirely accurate.[4]

Over the previous several months, Roosevelt had been moving slowly but steadily toward a decision to run for a third term. Until the Nazi blitzkrieg against the Western democracies on May 10, he was still a good ways from making that decision definitively. But the defeat of France and the isolation of Great Britain, which now feared an imminent invasion, had changed the odds appreciably. Britain was the last force in Europe capable of opposing Hitler, and if it, too, fell to the Third Reich, Hitler would be free to direct his attention, and his strategy of intimidation, toward the Western Hemisphere. Roosevelt had absolutely no doubt that the Führer would do so in that event, the vast Atlantic Ocean notwithstanding. FDR's third-term decision no longer hung primarily on his desire to protect and preserve his domestic legacy. It was now superseded by the Nazi threat to the Americas and all that that involved. He could identify no prominent Democrat, with the possible exception of Cordell Hull, who could step in at this late moment, secure the nomination, win the election, and assume office in January prepared to handle perhaps the greatest crisis facing the country since the Civil War.

This was the sobering reality FDR faced, and there was no doubt that it had moved him toward running again. As he well knew, it was a situation that he himself had helped to create by having frozen the field of potential candidates by playing sphinx and refusing to declare openly his intentions. What he may not have fully realized, at least early on, was that he was presenting the Democratic Party with a sort of Hobson's choice: it could select anyone it wanted as its nominee—so long as it was Franklin Delano Roosevelt, because he was now the only real option it had. Ironically, the choice he had effectively offered the party applied with equal force to Roosevelt himself. He had done a great deal to box himself into this situation, almost surely aware of the consequences of what he was doing. Most observers—Democratic politicians at all levels, labor leaders, factory owners, newspaper writers, teachers, ordinary citizens who were following events at all closely—now saw what Roosevelt saw and understood its meaning. It was no surprise at the White House, then, that the number of telegrams and letters pouring in urging the president to run for a third term had exploded; as we have seen, in June 6,000 messages arrived, more than all that had been received since the previous fall, while the first twelve days of July would see 5,550 more.[5]

Admire though he did the Republicans' shrewdness in nominating Willkie, a nomination he welcomed in that it ensured foreign policy coherence and continuity, it only strengthened the president's inclination to run. The Republican ticket had undeniable appeal, and it would be extremely difficult for the Democrats to assemble one that was competitive without FDR leading it himself. Even with Roosevelt there was no certainty. But without him there was little chance. So politics as well as the threat from Hitler had moved the president toward deciding to run again. Even by mid-June 1940, however, it was not a done deal. There were still the same considerations that had caused him to want to retire in the first place.

As we have seen, the president had taken a series of concrete steps to plan for what he anticipated would be a fulfilling and financially secure retirement. He had designed and built Top Cottage at Hyde Park. He had also designed and broken ground for his presidential library, which would be ready for use in the next year. White House cook and housekeeper Henrietta Nesbitt said that during early 1940, "we were clearing out storerooms . . . in fact, the Roosevelts were closing up." His cousin Daisy Suckley, in charge of the transfer of papers and memorabilia to the new library, reported that FDR brought "gobs of stuff" with him every time he returned to Hyde Park during this period. Moreover, he had signed a handsome contract to write regular articles for *Collier's* magazine, and he had persuaded his longtime chief speechwriter, Sam Rosenman, to help him. Hopkins, too, would be joining him at Hyde Park.[6]

Reinforcing a desire for a more placid life was FDR's concern about his health. Back in February, dining with just Missy LeHand and Ambassador Bill Bullitt in the White House, he suddenly turned white and slumped into temporary unconsciousness. Missy immediately sent for Admiral Ross McIntire, his physician, who, after an examination, tried to reassure her and Bullitt that Roosevelt had suffered "a very slight heart attack."[7] Missy was not reassured, and the incident almost certainly strengthened her belief that this man whom she loved should retire to Hyde Park, where she could give him more of the personal attention she thought he needed, and more than was possible in the public spotlight. Neither the public nor anyone else learned of the episode; a president's health was still considered to be a largely private matter. It's doubtful that even Eleanor knew about it, since she failed to include it when writing about his other health issues. And it is noteworthy though not surprising that there is nothing about the incident in Roosevelt's official or personal files.

The president's most obvious health issue, of course, was his near-death experience with infantile paralysis, or polio, in the early 1920s. The effect of that illness on his legs was apparent to everyone; he needed to be seated except during special occasions. His extraordinary upper-body strength combined with his constantly cheerful nature in public to give a picture of otherwise robust good health. He purposely used the force of personality to distract others from his condition; he wanted pity from no one. Perhaps nothing in the record revealed his ability to accomplish this feat more than a routine episode recorded by David Lilienthal of the TVA after he had dinner with FDR one evening. "When the President sits at a table or even stands speaking, you are entirely unconscious of his disability because of his magnificent head and his tremendously powerful shoulders and arms." Lilienthal therefore found himself shocked when he saw "two great big men"—part of the Secret Service detail—help the president into his overcoat. The men leaned over, and while the president was "still talking vivaciously scooped him up much as you would a child and carried him out the door and out into the night, with him turning his head around and calling good night to us." Lilienthal recalled that he never witnessed "such complete unselfconsciousness or anything quite so touching as the contrast between this indomitable and really gay spirit and this ghastly invalidism."[8]

The "ghastly invalidism" had consequences that were never apparent to the observant Lilienthal or others. In an exchange over the importance of the vice presidency that he would have shortly with Jim Farley at Hyde Park, Roosevelt told him that anyone running with him must have good health, as he couldn't predict how long he would "hold out." "You know, Jim, a man with paralysis can have a breakup at any time. While my heart and lungs are good and the other organs functioning along okay . . . nothing in life is certain." At this point the president lifted and unbuttoned his shirt and showed Farley "a lump of flesh and muscle under his left shoulder," which he explained was "misplaced" because of the necessity of sitting most of the time. "It's essential," FDR continued as he tucked his shirt back in and reached for another cigarette, "that the man who runs with me should be able to carry on."[9]

His outward appearance of vitality notwithstanding, FDR was tired. He was physically tired, and he was tired, as he had told his friend George Norris in February, of being asked by people to do things that he couldn't do or, even if he could, wouldn't do. All of these factors—health, weariness, the need to rebuild his finances, the desire to relax and enjoy the time he had left—had driven his determination to retire from politics. Hitler or no, these factors still pulled hard at him.

There is no other way to explain the president's persistent efforts, almost to the end, to persuade Cordell Hull to step into the void that his retirement would leave. Since late 1938 Roosevelt had urged his secretary of state to be prepared to run for the 1940 nomination, leaving Hull, understandably, with the impression that he had the president's full backing. Hull resisted the idea, believing it would be inappropriate for someone in his office to engage in partisan politics. Moreover, he didn't want to go through the arduous process involved in getting himself nominated and elected. Still, he received encouragement from friends in Tennessee and elsewhere, encouragement loud enough that he was compelled to make a public statement early in the year that he "had no ambitions whatever for the Presidency." He followed that shortly with a letter to friends stating, "There are no such definite indications of personal political recognition as to furnish any serious reason for my consideration of possible eventualities." He went on to say in this letter, which seemed oddly worded and equivocal, that events were moving with such "rapidity as to make the future utterly unpredictable" and that any decision made now "might be subject to reversal or modification a few months hence." In the spring Hull, among others, had noted a public opinion poll showing him doing better than Roosevelt against the likely GOP candidates—which at the time meant Dewey, Taft, and Vandenberg—and beating the last of these handily. There can be no doubt that FDR noticed it, too.

At a White House meeting in the third week of June Roosevelt once again told Hull that he wanted the secretary of state to succeed him. Hull recalled later that the president "gave me no indication that he intended to run again—in fact, just the opposite." He added that "scattered critics" had said that FDR, "in telling a few close friends that I was his choice in 1940, was simply using me as a buffer until he himself got in, and that he was not maintaining good faith with me." Hull didn't then or thereafter buy this line of reasoning. He remained convinced that the president "unquestionably desired my nomination as late as the spring of 1940," by which he meant May or even June.[10]

Though Eleanor and Franklin, so far as we know, never openly discussed the third-term question—he knew she wanted to go home, and the First Lady didn't believe that her personal wishes should be a factor when the country was potentially in peril—there was, as usual, no more perceptive observer of his thinking. "Although I never asked my husband what he himself really wanted to do," she recalled later of this 1940 spring, "it became clearly evident to me, from little things he said at different times, that he would really like to be in Hyde Park, and that the role of elder statesman appealed to him." She knew there were so many things he would like to do—"write on naval subjects, go through his papers, letters, and so on . . . I had, therefore, every evidence to believe that he did not want to run again."[11]

There was no doubt some wishful thinking in Eleanor's conclusion, which was shared by virtually all of her children. "None of us wanted it," his oldest son, James, said later. "The demands of the office are awful, and he seemed tired to us." They argued hard that he should not run, "but he just laughed at us." "In the end," Jimmy recalled, "father, as usual, piloted his own ship. 'I think I'm needed,' he said to me one day. 'And maybe I need it.'"[12]

Sam Rosenman also had an opportunity to observe the president from up close. By the late spring and early summer of 1940, he "took it for granted that the President had decided it was his duty to accept the nomination." Like Eleanor, Rosenman recognized all of the personal reasons that would justify FDR's decision to retire, including the president's confidence "that his own position in history was already secure." Nonetheless, Rosenman cited "compelling reasons" why Roosevelt should continue to serve. The greatest of these, in his view, was the fact that there was no liberal Democrat available who would continue his domestic and foreign policies and who could also be nominated and elected. He feared, as did the president, that if the Democratic nominee was a conservative, he would never receive labor's support, without which "a Democratic victory would be highly improbable."[13]

The most compelling issue moving Roosevelt toward running, however, was the war. Rosenman was convinced that had France not fallen and the war had "developed into a drawn-out stalemate," the president would not have agreed to run.[14] France did fall, and Britain was likely facing the same fate. There was also Hitler's now-evident evil, imprisoning and slaughtering Jews wherever his troops went, snuffing out freedoms, and always moving on to the next victim nation. Roosevelt believed that war was coming to the United States, and the question was, who could lead the country through it and keep it united and focused, as Lincoln had during the Civil War? It was the president's inability to answer this question to his satisfaction that caused him to believe there was no one except himself who had a chance of accomplishing that. Unquestionably, egotism blended with ambition in this conclusion; he very much liked being president, and he identified himself with the office. "He loved the majesty of the position," historian William E. Leuchtenburg has said, "relished its powers, and rejoiced in the opportunity it offered for achievement."[15]

However, to whatever degree egotism was a factor—and FDR was seldom a modest judge of his own abilities—it was outweighed by a realistic assessment of the knowledge and skill he had acquired over the years in foreign affairs and in communicating with the American people. A politician's personal motives when making major decisions are almost always difficult to sort out, not least because they are usually multiple in number and seldom clear-cut. In FDR's case, it can be safely said that he believed he was better prepared to *govern* in a time of national crisis than anyone else, since he had already done so.

In early July 1940, with the Democratic National Convention scheduled to convene in less than two weeks, the president was moving toward a decision. He likely saw it as perhaps the most important decision of his presidency to date, perhaps even of his lifetime. We will never know precisely how he saw it because he faced it alone. His practice of solitary

decision making had begun early for him, an only child raised on an isolated estate that provided few encounters with others and even fewer opportunities for making friends. The practice continued through his youth
and early adulthood until it became deeply ingrained. For all his bonhomie and almost constant need to be around people, Roosevelt had few if
any friends who really understood him, which is to say friends to whom
he really opened up. Robert Sherwood saw in the president a "thickly for-
ested interior" that kept others from penetrating his mind. For whatever
reason, he always withheld something of himself, even from Eleanor. "He
had no real confidantes," she had once observed. "I don't think I was ever
his confidante either."[16] Rexford G. Tugwell, an early advisor who had an
on-and-off relationship with Roosevelt, tried to explain the practice. FDR,
he said, "deliberately concealed the processes of his mind. He would rather
have posterity believe that for him everything was always plain and easy,"
Tugwell wrote, than "admit to any agony of indecision" or "any misgiving
about mistakes."[17]

Roosevelt and Hull met again for a White House lunch on July 3, twelve
days before the official start of the convention, by which time, the secretary
of state recalled, "France had fallen, Britain was making frantic preparations
against invasion, Mussolini had plunged into the war, Japan was preparing
to move, and our own position was grave." The conversation "left such an
impression on me," Hull remembered, that he made notes on it in longhand
as soon as he returned to his office.[18]

After some initial banter, Roosevelt told Hull that he wanted to "talk
some politics" and reported, "in a sort of impatient, incredulous tone," that
"there are many people saying to me, 'you can't afford to let us down.'" He
added that he had been reading Washington's letter to Madison complain-
ing about those who were voicing opposition to a second term for the first
president, and offered that he was thinking about sending a similar letter
to someone such as Senator George Norris, which would conclude by
saying he wanted to go back to Hyde Park. "Of course such a letter would
not delay your nomination by a split second," Hull quickly replied. The
president then speculated how he thought he could defeat Willkie in November, "unless the war should stop." He now spoke, remembered Hull,

"slightly haltingly and disconnectedly," and his tone "was that of deprecating the idea of running." Hull observed that Roosevelt was now "extremely guarded" compared with their previous conversations on the subject, "when he had forthrightly said he considered me his successor."

As the president launched into an assessment of Hull's strengths and weaknesses as a candidate, his luncheon partner interrupted him to say that he did not wish to be considered. By now Hull was convinced that FDR had made up his mind to run, but instead of telling him so, Hull simply said that his health wouldn't allow him to run, and in any case he and his wife were determined that he should get out of politics. The president, undeterred, proceeded to list Hull's weaknesses—his trade policies had made him unpopular in the farm belt, but he could run with the secretary of agriculture, Henry Wallace, to remedy that—before the secretary again said he had no intention of seeking the nomination. He recalled that at the end of the lunch the president's "whole tone and language . . . was a complete reversal of what it had been ten days before, when he was still advocating my candidacy." Leaning on his long political experience, Hull concluded that Roosevelt "must have made up his mind to accept a third term."[19]

Harold Ickes, eager as always to be in on the political action, met with the president two days later to find out what his plans were for Chicago. Who would be his floor leader? Who would make the nominating speeches? Who would be in charge? Roosevelt grinned and said that he was "trusting in God." Ickes responded that he might well trust in God "but still have a vague idea as to what ought to be done." Obviously enjoying the interior secretary's discomfort, FDR launched into a funny story about the psychiatrist who had died and gone to heaven, and "after he had made his obeisance before the great white throne he hurried back to the gates to beg St. Peter to let him go back to the world." The reason he had made this unusual request was that "he had found a being on the throne who thought he was Franklin D. Roosevelt." Ickes stubbornly pursued the matter that evening at a White House meeting of hard-core administration New Dealers to go over the platform and other convention issues with the president. When Ickes asked Roosevelt straight out whether those of his supporters going to Chicago "were to have neither a leader nor a plan," FDR replied that he had nothing to suggest. Robert Jackson picked up the theme and asked the president "whom Paul McNutt would suggest that we consult if he were the candidate." Roosevelt responded, "Jimmy Byrnes." Another participant began to ask a question, but FDR waved him aside: "I haven't anything to say." Roosevelt had settled on his game plan, and he was sticking with it. Not even his closest associates and most ardent supporters would be made privy to it; even to them he would remain a sphinx. In mentioning Jimmy Byrnes, however, he revealed more than they may have understood; as an elected politician, which none of them had ever been, he was saying that if he had to place his political fate in anyone's hands, it would be in those of the man he trusted politically more than any other.[20]

Not for the first time was Ickes frustrated and perplexed by this man whom he admired so much and to whom he was so devoted. Why wouldn't he confide in his friends, those who were about to do battle for him in Chicago? "You are one of the most difficult men to work with that I have ever known," he once boldly told the president.

"Because I get too hard at times?" Roosevelt asked, probably thinking Ickes meant he was too tough on colleagues.

"No," Ickes answered. It was because "you won't talk frankly even with people who are loyal to you. . . . You keep your cards close up against your belly. You never put them on the table." As the Chicago convention quickly approached, FDR's cards were still very close up against his belly.[21]

Almost exactly a year earlier Roosevelt had met with Jim Farley and been less than candid with this seasoned politician, who had successfully managed his two previous campaigns. Even then, several months before Hitler's invasion of Poland, rumors had been circulating that the president was considering running for a third term, and the Democratic chairman had wanted to hear directly from the man at whose side he had served for nearly a decade what his intentions were. Roosevelt had told him then that he would not run again, and was unequivocal about it, promising to make his decision known in early 1940, before the primary season began. He had since said he had no objection to Farley himself seeking the nomination. Much had changed in the last year, and the president now decided that he had to have one last conversation with his old colleague. On the president's mind was whether Farley would allow his name to be placed in nomination for president, thus preventing the possibility of a unanimous Roosevelt nomination, or whether he would withdraw, as FDR evidently now hoped, almost certainly causing Garner to follow suit. As he had the year before, he invited Farley to Hyde Park; it was Sunday, July 7, one week before the convention opened in Chicago.

Arriving at the Big House that morning, Farley was greeted by the president's mother, Sara, who expressed concern at news reports suggesting that he wouldn't be playing a role in the fall campaign. "I want you to be sure to help my boy," she said, prompting Farley to respond, "Mrs. Roosevelt, you just have to let these things run their course." They were joined shortly by Eleanor, who was fond of the chairman and who had also seen the news reports. She volunteered that she was "pleased and shocked with the news," which she explained to mean that she was happy for him if the move from Washington to a business opportunity in New York benefited him, but shocked to think that he wouldn't be around to run the general election campaign. Farley was still in good standing with the Roosevelt women, it was clear, if not with the president.

FDR soon joined them for lunch, together with Hopkins, Missy Le-Hand, Steve Early, and a few other guests. There was "a lot of good natured kidding," according to Farley, before the president turned to the very recent fall of France, which clearly troubled him. Yet he was obviously buoyed by news that the British fleet had effectively disabled French naval forces that had sought refuge in French North African ports. The British had tried to persuade the French admiral at Oran to either disable his three battleships or sail them to the Western Hemisphere for demilitarization. When he refused, the British Royal Navy attacked the French ships, destroying two and disabling the other, killing more than twelve hundred French sailors in the process. At the same time, the British had persuaded the French officer in charge of several ships in Alexandria, under some compulsion, to effectively incapacitate them. The results of these bold events came as a huge relief to Roosevelt, as they obviously were to Churchill; both leaders were determined that that the French fleet should not fall into the hands of the German or Italian navies and thus critically affect Britain's position as the world's dominant sea power. As Hopkins would later tell Churchill, the action convinced the president that Britain was determined to continue the fight.

After lunch Farley joined FDR in the small, spare room that the latter had used as a study as a boy and that he still used regularly on his frequent visits to Hyde Park as president. It was the same room off the back hall on the first floor of Springwood in which they had met a year before. After photographers had been shown in to record the session and then escorted out, the two men removed their suit coats to better endure the hot, humid day. The president rambled for fifteen or twenty minutes, according to Farley, who concluded "he was having difficulty in getting started in the conversation." Finally Roosevelt got to the subject at hand and acknowledged that he had said in the earlier meeting that he definitely would not run for a third term and intended to so declare early in the year. The war had changed everything, he went on, and when the time arrived to make it known to the public and the world that he wouldn't run again, "it would have destroyed his effectiveness as the leader of this Nation."

FDR said that he did not want to run for another term and that "he was going to frankly tell the convention so." Farley replied that if he made it specific, they would not nominate him. The president, reported Farley, said there were "three or four ways" to do it. "One would be to write a letter to someone like Senator George Norris and decline; another would be to broadcast it; another would be to issue a statement; and a fourth way would be to send a letter to me [Farley] to be read at the Convention." Roosevelt explained to Farley that he had to make a statement to prove that he was "definitely opposed" to running for a third term "and in justice to his conscience, he wanted that thoroughly understood."

Farley concurred, and added that the statement "should be so worded that the delegates would be free to nominate someone else." The president, he noted, seemed to agree with this. Farley then launched into a lengthy discussion of why he opposed a third term, making the case that if the Democratic Party couldn't win on its record with another candidate, it deserved to lose; it would be the first time he had made these views known to

Roosevelt. Total candor, never a hallmark of either of these two men, had been further sacrificed in recent months by the growing mutual distrust between them.

The president then asked his guest what he would do in his position. Farley thanked him for the "compliment" and told him he would never be in his position. Nonetheless, he answered: "I would not have waited so long to make my position known; he had made it impossible for anyone else to be nominated." Farley's view was that by not declaring himself, Roosevelt had not "played fair" with the delegates, and that as a result, states had declared their support of the president from a lack of choice. Party leaders were worried that they might be punished "if they did not go along with him." He then offered that were he in the president's position, he would issue a "Sherman-like statement," that is, he would not run if nominated and would not serve if elected.[22] At this point, Farley attributed to Roosevelt a statement (it appears in his memoir *Jim Farley's Story*, but not in the original memorandum dictated soon after the conversation) as follows: "Jim, if nominated and elected I could not in these times refuse to take the inaugural oath, even if I knew I would be dead within thirty days."[23]

Farley then delivered the news Roosevelt most needed to know but didn't want to hear: "I told him frankly that my name and Garner's would go before the Convention." Finally getting the information that he had wanted from the meeting, and concluding that there was nothing further he could do about it, FDR shifted the conversation to a safer subject—Wendell Willkie. He said he was not sure he could defeat the Republican, and Farley concurred, observing that the candidate "looks good in the movies, talks all right and seems to have caught on with the public." The president "admitted it," and offered the prediction that if the war somehow ended before the election, Willkie would be elected. When Roosevelt asked the chairman whether he thought Hull could be elected, Farley answered that he could, "without any difficulty," citing the Gallup poll showing Hull running ahead of the president against possible GOP opponents. Perhaps wanting to rub it in a bit, he added that he believed Hull could win by the same margin Roosevelt had achieved in 1936, which is to say by a landslide; no one was predicting that kind of margin for Roosevelt.

FDR shifted the conversation to possible vice presidential candidates. Farley said he went on the record in urging the president to take on the ticket "a real Democrat," someone who could "carry on" should anything happen to the president. As FDR well knew by now, Farley's definition of a "real Democrat"— an old-time regular, more conservative than liberal—was not the same as Roosevelt's, for Roosevelt believed that the term applied to liberals committed strongly to the principles of the New Deal. Farley cited William O. Douglas, whom Roosevelt had appointed to the Supreme Court the year before and who fit FDR's definition of a "real Democrat," as "too silly for words." As fond as he was of Douglas, the president agreed. The latter then asked—almost incredibly, given how well known it was how much the president and vice president despised each other—whether he thought Garner would agree to run again. Farley responded that the vice president was also opposed to a third term and had been "hurt by the way the President had acted"; he believed that there was no way Garner would agree to run. It was clear here and at other points in the conversation that Roosevelt was simply doing Farley the courtesy of seeking his advice; in some cases, such as this one regarding Garner, he was far from serious about the substance of the questions and had other motives in mind. He was certain that this conversation would be conveyed to Garner within days and that he might be flattered to hear about it. Flattery remained one of FDR's favorite political tools, and he seldom missed an opportunity to use it, even with those he disliked.

Farley suggested a number of other possible candidates, most of whom Roosevelt dismissed with a laugh and a wave of his hand, before the latter asked what he thought about Henry Wallace. Farley responded that he liked the agriculture secretary and had "personal admiration" for him (the word *tremendous* was crossed out in the transcript of the conversation and *personal* substituted for it). Nonetheless, he added that he didn't believe Wallace was "heavy enough" for the job or that he would bring anything to the ticket. "I thought it would be a serious mistake to nominate him for vice president."

When the list of possible vice presidential candidates appeared to be exhausted, Farley suggested that his strong preference would be Cordell Hull, though he was not at all sure that Hull would agree to do it. He urged the president to talk with the secretary of state, and Roosevelt said that he was already doing so. Farley argued that Hull was "an organization Democrat" and "a real Democrat"—that term again—and that he would make a "great" president if anything should happen to Roosevelt. For his part, Roosevelt asked Farley to urge Hull to accept the vice presidential nomination. At this, the chairman demurred, "because," as he put it, "I knew exactly how Hull felt about the third term and the Vice Presidency and I had full realization of his disappointment at the President's attitude toward him," almost certainly a reference to FDR's practice of frequently ignoring or going around Hull at the State Department.

As the afternoon wore on the heat and humidity in the small, cramped room did not let up even with the windows open (Roosevelt had an adamant aversion to air-conditioning, much to the discomfort of his visitors and staff). They moved into a discussion of convention procedure and the platform. Farley offered that the only real point of controversy would be on the foreign policy plank, with the internationalists and the isolationists in strong disagreement. FDR suggested that the entire matter could be covered in just a few sentences, indicating that the United States did not want to become involved in any foreign war "except for the protection of the Western Hemisphere." When Farley asked him about the chances of Britain holding out, the president responded, "One in three."

In looking back on the conversation the next day, Farley noted that it had all been "very friendly," but he also concluded that Roosevelt had not been entirely open with him, or less so than he had been heretofore, and had seemed uncomfortable—*disturbed* was the word he used—during their chat. "It is rather peculiar to realize that the man I have done so much for was the one person who has prevented my nomination for the Presidency or the Vice Presidency." Farley was convinced that had the president not taken the course he did, freezing out other Democratic candidates, he and Hull might have been nominated to run.

There can be little doubt but that Farley was deluding himself on this point; FDR never would have allowed him to be nominated, at least for president. He didn't think Farley was qualified or that he could be elected.

It was apparent that Farley, a seasoned and pragmatic politician who had been in the administration for nearly eight years, had failed to see how dramatically everything had changed since they had met in this same room a year earlier. He had also allowed his sense of self-importance and personal pique to color his definition of loyalty and to whom it was owed, forgetting that one of the immutable rules of politics, especially where the presidency was concerned, dictated that all loyalty must necessarily flow to the man in the Oval Office; in the nature of things, very little is allowed to flow in the other direction.[24]

Nonetheless, each man had gotten the information he had been seeking from the meeting. Farley confirmed that the president would seek another term, and Roosevelt learned, as he must have also expected, that his nomination would not be unanimous. They had nonetheless achieved their shared secondary goal: the mutual desire to avoid a rupture in the relationship, which FDR had feared could cause a breach in the party and affect the election, and which Farley had feared could jeopardize his cherished reputation as a party loyalist as well as his prospects for future employment.

Given that he was going to run again, Roosevelt had to decide which of the four options he had mentioned to Farley for communicating his intentions to the convention he would use. He had tentatively settled on a plan. To help him develop it, he asked Missy LeHand to request that Sam Rosenman come down to Washington for the duration of the convention, now just five days away. This was a signal to anyone reading the tea leaves that Rosenman, well known to be a close advisor as well as FDR's chief speechwriter, had been summoned, as he had been in 1932 and 1936, to assist in writing FDR's acceptance speech to the convention. Canceling his vacation plans but sending his family ahead to Montana, Rosenman arrived at the White House on July 10 and settled into his room in the residence, just steps away from the president's, where he was accustomed to reside during such periods and where he would remain for nine days.

That evening, with Hopkins, Missy, and Grace Tully, he joined the president for dinner in the Oval Study, in the upstairs residence, where FDR could read or relax with his beloved stamp collection without being interrupted. He also frequently used it for informal and intimate meals such as this one in addition to a daily ritual called the "children's hour," in which he and his closest aides would repair to that room at five o'clock for cocktails— always mixed by the president—and light banter on the day's events, plus of course the latest gossip. It was his favorite room in the White House, decorated in a distinctly nautical theme with paintings, prints, models of sailing ships and other memorabilia from his lifelong romance with the sea. It held an eclectic collection of comfortable furniture, including a high-backed red leather chair like the one Thomas Jefferson had designed. Next to the west wall stood a beautifully hand-carved desk, crafted from the remains of the English ship *Resolute*, with a large wastebasket in the front opening to conceal a view of the president's legs. In front of that a lay tiger-skin rug spread-eagled on the floor. This was unquestionably a man's study and, as with any room occupied by FDR, it had an unquestionably lived-in look and feel about it, with books and papers stacked randomly on the floor.

Everyone at dinner that evening had spent countless hours in this room, and all but Hopkins, who would depart the next day for Chicago, would spend many more here during the week ahead. This was where the president would set up his headquarters to follow the events of the convention and to do his best to control them. But "strangely enough," Rosenman noted, there was "no serious discussion" of the approaching convention that evening.[25]

Hopkins, by now a permanent fixture in the second-floor residence, clarified the picture the next morning when he came across the hall to Rosenman's room for a long talk. Both men knew FDR politically as well as anyone else—except Missy LeHand—and could read his intention to seek another term without being told. Moreover, with a major crisis in Europe and no other viable candidate on the scene, they assumed that FDR would be nominated despite his refusal to seek support openly. Since the longtime Roosevelt speechwriter and intimate would be the aide closest to the president left in the White House during the week of the convention, Hopkins, who, like Roosevelt, fully trusted Rosenman, felt the need to fill him in on "various conferences" that had taken place in the White House in recent days. One of those conferences had been a meeting in the president's study with a group of political heavyweights who would be in Chicago: Mayor Ed Kelly of that city; Ed Flynn of New York; Frank Walker from Minnesota, who would replace Farley as postmaster general; and Senator Jimmy Byrnes. Roosevelt told his guests that he had drafted a letter that he wanted Speaker William Bankhead, who would preside over the opening of the convention, to read to the delegates. Hopkins showed the letter to Rosenman, who copied it:

> Dear Will:
>
> When you speak to the Convention on Monday evening will you say something for me which I believe ought to be made utterly clear?
>
> You and my other close friends have known and understood that I have not today and have never had any wish or purpose to remain in the office of President, or indeed anywhere in public office after next January.
>
> You know and all my friends know that this is a simple and sincere fact. I want you to repeat this simple and sincere fact to the Convention.

Those gathered in the study on the evening of July 10, Hopkins reported, to a man had urged the president not to send the letter. "They all wanted him to run," Rosenman reported Hopkins as saying, "and they felt sure that if he kept quiet he would be nominated almost by acclamation." Unstated but clearly implicit in their reaction was the fear that the delegates would take him at his word and that the convention could spin out of control, a scenario that could lead to chaos and a nominee whom no one could now foresee. To them, whose political stock in trade was control, it was a nightmare scenario. But the president was adamant and would stick to his plan; he had instructed Hopkins to take the letter to Chicago and deliver it personally to Bankhead. His was a high-risk strategy, and while he may have sympathized with the politicians, he had his own reasons for proceeding this way.[26]

When Ickes saw FDR again toward the end of the week, a few days before the convention began, the president volunteered his plan for running for reelection if he should be, as he put it, "forced to run for a third term."

With the "international emergency" as his rationale, he wouldn't undertake a conventional barnstorming campaign but rather tend to national security matters by visiting military installations and always remaining within a few hours of Washington. "This would make it possible for him to emphasize what was being done in the way of preparation for war," Ickes noted. Even Ickes, however, came away from the session with a less than firm grasp of the president's intentions: "I gathered nothing from the President to make me feel certain that he had not fully made up his mind to run again."[27]

Meanwhile, Rosenman settled into his accustomed role as speechwriter, advisor, and listener, the last a very important function. The president was used to having a trusted confidant nearby to hear him expound on whatever it was that was on his mind. It was his means of articulating, shaping, and sometimes testing thoughts that were then in formation. First it had been Louis Howe who performed this role for him, with Ickes or another cabinet member on occasion for variety; increasingly now it was Hopkins, but with Hopkins in Chicago the task fell to Rosenman. The day that Hopkins left town Rosenman and the president went for a swim in the White House pool in the west gallery, which connected the West Wing with the White House proper and which had been built with private funds in 1933 to provide relief and therapy for FDR's polio-racked body. Roosevelt talked "quite frankly" about how he sized up the potential vice presidential candidates; not surprisingly, this analysis bore a strong resemblance to the report Rosenman had just heard from Hopkins. "For the first time I heard from his own lips how strongly he favored Wallace for the Vice-Presidency, and how opposed he was to the other candidates."[28]

The next day, Thursday, July 11, Justice Felix Frankfurter swore Frank Knox in as secretary of the navy at a White House ceremony, after which Frankfurter and Rosenman talked "at length" about the acceptance speech; he mentioned some points he thought that the president "ought to make." The justice had been, as Rosenman put it, "a reliable source of ideas and language" for Roosevelt's speechwriters, and Rosenman was not alone in valuing his counsel.[29] FDR valued it as well, and it was likely after this ceremony that he invited Frankfurter to return that evening to discuss an important matter. The justice arrived back at the White House at six-thirty for a lengthy meeting with the president in the Oval Study.[30] Sobered by the enormousness of the decision he was about to make, Roosevelt felt the need for some confirmation that he would be doing the right thing. He also needed to hear how that decision could be put to the American people in such a way that they would understand and support it.

Frankfurter was an interesting and of course symbolic choice of confidant on this crucial matter. He was not a political strategist, as Louis Howe had been; the president wasn't looking for political advice. Nor was he, like Howe or Hopkins, blindly devoted to FDR's interests, although his obsequiousness toward Roosevelt sometimes conveyed that impression. Roosevelt viewed Frankfurter as the heir to what he saw as the tradition of enlightened liberalism shaped on the Supreme Court by Oliver Wendell Holmes Jr. and Louis Brandeis, both of whom FDR revered. Frankfurter at this early point in his tenure on the Court saw himself in the same light. That being the case, the president was likely seeking approval from a higher authority—indeed, from the highest and wisest secular authority available to him, in his view.

Frankfurter had emigrated from Austria at an early age to the United States, where he was raised on Manhattan's Lower East Side. He excelled as a student, and particularly as a law student; his early legal career took him in and out of key posts in Washington, where he earned a reputation as a political progressive, and in some circles as a radical. He demonstrated such legal promise in government as well as in private practice that he was offered a chair at Harvard Law School in 1921, where he found a forum equal to his talents. In 1932 Frankfurter became one of President-elect Roosevelt's key outside advisors, but ironically by this time his political and economic views had tempered to such a degree that he saw his chief role as trying to restrain the more radical views of others in Roosevelt's "brain trust." He further served FDR by being the administration's chief talent scout at Harvard Law, and he sent so many of his bright and otherwise promising students to Washington that they became known as "Felix's Happy Hot Dogs." Prominent among them would be Tom Corcoran and Ben Cohen.

FDR came to like as well as admire Frankfurter even though they didn't always agree, and they carried on a warm correspondence—Frankfurter addressed his letters to FDR "Dear Frank"—during the entire course of Roosevelt's presidency. Much of what Frankfurter did for, and said to, FDR during the first two terms had a subtext, however, and that was to reinforce his own credentials for an eventual appointment to the Supreme Court; chief among these was to persuade the president that he was a loyal friend and would be a dependable supporter on a Court where the president had few. He was often unrestrained in his flattery ("It cannot be mere accident," Frankfurter wrote the president in 1938, "that not since Lincoln has there been a President who possessed in equal measure such a combination of the democratic faith, antiseptic humor, and largeness of view").[31] FDR had the ability to intuit other people's motives, and he certainly understood Frankfurter's, but he didn't consider ambition a disqualifier, and he made the appointment in late 1938.

Now, with the convention just four days away, the two men met in the relaxed setting of the president's study, and they met alone. There is no record, either official or unofficial, of what they discussed. The only known fact about the meeting is that at its conclusion Roosevelt asked Frankfurter to draft a memorandum summarizing the case he had made regarding the third-term decision. Frankfurter said he would do so and asked if he could request one as well from his friend Archibald MacLeish, whom the president had appointed librarian of Congress on Frankfurter's recommendation. MacLeish was a distinguished poet, playwright, essayist, and all-around literary lion who was also wise in the ways of the world, including the political world. The president agreed but urged Frankfurter to keep it all highly confidential and to hurry.

The next evening the justice returned to the White House and delivered a handwritten memo to the president accompanied by a typewritten one from MacLeish. Both justified a decision to run again as a matter of duty to the country in a time of emergency. The president had obviously worried to Frankfurter in their meeting that if he defied the two-term tradition, his critics' charges that he was becoming a "dictator" could jeopardize his reelection. Frankfurter wrote,

Under your leadership we have moved toward a life of economic
as well as political independence for our people who felt the
bludgeoning of misfortune and adversity. . . . In view of this record
you would not be open to the charge of trying to seize power as a
"strong-man." You would in fact be protecting the nation from the
convulsions, dangers and upheavals in a period of acute national
anxiety and world strain that could indeed lead to the establishment
of arbitrary power in Washington by men no longer responsible to
the values of democracy.

When Frankfurter turned to events abroad, it became evident that the
subject had dominated their conversation of the day before. After reciting
the president's efforts to prevent war, condemn aggression, and "awaken the
country to the menace for us . . . in this new attempt to conquer the world,"
the justice appealed to Roosevelt's ego as well as his sense of history:

In all these efforts you have tried to follow the inspiration of the great
men who laid down the principles which must guard the Republic if
it is to remain a sanctuary of freedom. You now look beyond a world
war to the years of peace and you want to play your part in making
sure that these tragedies will never again fall on civilization, that
we will do better than our fathers did when they tried to organize a
system of collective security to restrain or punish aggression, and that
we will succeed in replacing the law of force with the force of law.

He concluded his brief memo in a similar vein:

We have no deeper tradition in our history than resistance to tyranny
and devotion to freedom. In your warnings, you were aware that
the Constitution makes the President the originating impulse and
guardian of our national safety. In all that you have attempted . . .
you can gladly submit your purpose, your achievements, and your
record to the judgment of your countrymen for a third term in the
midst of unprecedented conditions that impose their own duties and

obligations. A President must continue in office when the voice of the people calls him to the continuing task.

MacLeish addressed his memo not to Roosevelt but to Frankfurter, who had requested it, and began by saying that it was "a dangerous thing to ask a man for his two cents worth because he may throw in a couple of bushels of orts." He agreed that FDR should run again as a matter of duty but focused his advice on how the president should characterize his decision, which was clearly why Frankfurter had enlisted him in the cause. MacLeish argued that the president "should not 'accept a call,'" as Frankfurter had probably told him FDR was considering doing. "Undoubtedly the actual truth is that he will be doing precisely that. But to put it that way is to lead with the chin. I can see the cartoons from here." He quickly got to the point that Frankfurter had asked him to articulate.

> What I should like him to say would be something like this: that like most men of his age—most men who have occupied positions of great responsibility—he had made plans for himself; plans for a private life to begin in January 1941. That these plans, like the plans of so many others . . . had been made in a world that now seems as distant as a different planet. That today all private plans, all private lives, have been repealed by a public danger. That in the face of the public danger all those who can be of service to the Republic have no choice but to offer themselves for service in those capacities for which they may be fitted. That if a majority of the members of his party believe he can serve his country best in the capacity in which they have nominated him he has no choice but to accept the nomination. That if a majority of the voters believe as a majority of his party has believed he will have no choice but to accept their judgment.

MacLeish added that he would also "like to hear a statement in explanation of the President's failure to declare himself sooner," but he added that he had no specific advice to offer on that score because he didn't know the president's thinking on the matter. That didn't inhibit him, however, from building on his earlier point: "Obviously a man who faces a crisis so severe that it overrides every other consideration and who believes therefore that every citizen must hold himself ready to serve where he best can, will not declare himself in advance to be unwilling to serve in any capacity whatever. Neither, by the same sign, will he offer himself until the necessity appears."

Frankfurter had asked "Archie" to suggest "a few paragraphs" that FDR could use to explain his third-term decision, and the latter responded with "a few sentences." After citing a series of inescapable "facts" regarding aggression, fascism, and the reduction of men to slavery, MacLeish brought them all together in an effort to suggest language that the president might use:

> This is the fact which dominates our world and which dominates
> as well the lives of all those who live in it. In the face of the danger
> which confronts our time no individual retains or can hope to
> retain the rights of personal choice which free men can enjoy in
> times of peace. He has a first obligation to serve in the defense of
> our institutions of freedom—a first obligation to serve his country
> in whatever capacity his country finds him useful—which must
> override all personal preferences—whether the preferences he
> would establish for himself or the preferences custom and tradition
> would establish for him.

"But you can see, Felix, how impossible it is to go on with this," MacLeish concluded. "For if there ever was a personal document it is this document of which we are thinking. It can be, if it is deeply derived from the emotion and convictions of the man who speaks it, one of the most moving and convincing utterances of which history has record. Or it can be something very different."[32]

These memoranda, which offer probably the best window into FDR's mind on the question of running for a third term, gave Roosevelt the confirmation and guidance he needed. He was indeed justified in running for an unprecedented third term by the unprecedented danger confronting the nation and the world. Events had thrust this role upon him. The traditional rules governing American presidential politics no longer applied, and he *did* have a profound responsibility to respond to this crisis by putting aside his plans for retirement and agreeing to serve further if that was the wish of his party and his fellow citizens. And, it is important to note, Roosevelt had told Frankfurter—for perhaps the first time he had told anyone—that he was looking *beyond* the war to help shape a world at peace, so that, too, was part of his rationale. He eventually returned the memos to Frankfurter, but almost certainly not before making careful notes; however, those notes are not to be found among his papers or anywhere else.

Now that he had decided to run, Roosevelt had to determine how to run—how to make it clear to the convention that his willingness to accept its nomination, if that was what the decision of the delegates should be, was not a matter of personal ambition but rather one of national necessity and personal responsibility. The decision had to be put in the context that Archibald MacLeish had suggested in his memo: he couldn't seek the nomination in a traditional sense, but instead he would "offer" himself to the delegates for their judgment. MacLeish had also warned that the president should avoid ridicule and not "accept a call," even though that is what he would be effectively doing. Roosevelt was moving toward a conclusion that he would have to be drafted by the convention and then approved by the electorate if he was to achieve a third term. He must have wondered, reading MacLeish's advice, about the difference between a "call" and a "draft." He could be forgiven if he concluded that it was a distinction without a difference. "Although he felt that there was no such thing as a bona fide draft by a convention," Sam Rosenman later observed, "he felt confident that the American people wanted him to be President, and believed they should be given a chance to vote for him."[33] In his three decades in politics FDR had never seen such a draft, and his real-life political experience taught him that the system simply didn't permit them.

FDR knew perfectly well that he was often seen, especially by journalists and fellow politicians, as manipulative; when he was honest with himself, which was not always, he had to acknowledge that he even enjoyed being manipulative in seeking larger, and usually honorable, goals. So finding a way to communicate his willingness to serve without conveying personal ambition or, God forbid, manipulation dominated his thinking in these last few days before the convention. In considering his options during the previous few months—in fact, since war had broken out in Europe the year before—he had been determined not to be perceived as doing anything overt to further his chances for the nomination. He never gave even quiet encouragement to his closest aides such as Hopkins, Ickes, and others eager to form a third-term movement. The furthest he went—and this was in full concert with Jim Farley—was to help script the selection of state delegations that would be "friendly" to the Roosevelt cause at the convention, whatever that might end up being. It was all a part of keeping his options open and of maintaining maximum influence with the convention whichever way he decided. Amazingly, however, he never said anything publicly or even privately that asked or encouraged *anyone* to take an action to support his candidacy. It was an enormously disciplined exercise, notable for its restraint.

All Roosevelt was certain of now was that he had to be drafted by the convention, whether that term fit the situation or not, and preferably by acclamation, although his recent meeting with Farley told him that was not possible. There was no question he had a sufficient number of "friendly" FDR delegates to be nominated, but that was not the point. If it was to resemble an authentic draft, it should be so overwhelming as to convince the American people that breaching the powerful and compelling third-term proscription was justified to keep a proven leader in place at a time of great danger to the country.

At Roosevelt's regular Friday morning press conference, reporters bombarded the president with questions related to his role in the convention. As he had for months, he parried the questions effectively, leading one correspondent to conclude, "It is extremely probable now that Mr. Roosevelt will maintain his silence throughout the convention, where his renomination seems assured." The only solid news emanating from the session was FDR's confirmation that he would not be attending the convention. Asked if he was considering sending a message to Chicago regarding his intentions, "he replied that he had not given the matter any thought one way or another." When one reporter was finally satisfied that this press conference would be no more revealing than any others on this question, he announced that he was a representative of the "dunce cap club," which had been formed months earlier when Roosevelt had told a member of the press who had asked an unwelcome question about a possible third term to don a dunce cap and stand in the corner. The reporter announced that the club would meet in Chicago the following week to dissolve its membership, and he asked whether they might expect a message from the president. "Mr. Roosevelt remarked that recent progress had been good and that a large percentage of those once in the corner had been released."[34]

On Saturday the president—as always, drawn to the water—embarked on a weekend cruise on the presidential yacht *Potomac* down the river bearing the same name. The guests included Ross McIntire, Missy, and two of her friends; Rosenman, knowing this drill well from previous years, brought along all of his speech material. Roosevelt read the newspapers, worked on his stamp collection, and "did a little fishing," managing to reel in one rock bass and one eel, a better-than-average catch for him, according to Rosenman. After the others went above to an upper deck, the president and his speechwriter sat at a table in the dining cabin and discussed the convention, now just two days off. "He said that he did not want to give the appearance of making any effort for the nomination." Noting that Jim Farley was determined to wage a floor fight for the nomination, FDR stressed that "he did not want to exercise his prestige or influence . . . to induce the delegates to vote one way or the other." To make this clear to the delegates, he said, he wanted to send them a message "somewhat fuller and more definite" than the one he had entrusted to Hopkins. Rosenman had already concluded as much. He produced from his briefcase a substitute statement, which he handed to the president, who proceeded to rewrite it in longhand. It was, Rosenman recorded, "a combination of the short cryptic one he had given Hopkins and the longer one I had drafted. He then inserted a sentence specifically releasing the delegates." Not only was FDR ignoring the counsel of his political advisors, but he was moving decidedly in the opposite direction.[35]

10

Preparing for the Big Show

Everyone in Washington, it seemed—cabinet members, journalists, members of Congress, political junkies of all kinds—was heading for Chicago and the Democratic National Convention. Everyone, that is, except the incumbent president of the United States, who, most observers assumed, would be its nominee. He had an interest in the outcome of the convention, to be sure, but he was still determined to do nothing overtly to influence that outcome, and that most definitely included not making an appearance there. Nonetheless, he had determined early on that the convention should be held in Chicago, which had hosted the Republican convention in 1860 that nominated Abraham Lincoln and the Democratic convention in 1932 that nominated Franklin D. Roosevelt. So the city had some nostalgic appeal for FDR. More important, it had a mayor, Ed Kelly, who was one of his strongest supporters and who would ensure that the galleries were filled with the right people and that other important arrangements were attended to properly.

The matter of the vice presidency absorbed much of Roosevelt's attention in the final days leading up to the convention. The way in which that selection was made, however, apparently absorbed little if any of his attention. Ever since the political parties began using nominating conventions early in the nineteenth century, delegates to those conventions saw it as *their* prerogative to select not only the presidential candidates but the vice presidential candidates as well. More often than not the latter choice was based on balancing interests such as geography, ideology, and whatever other factors were deemed relevant at the time, all with a view toward creating maximum party unity and public appeal.

In what can only be seen as his own expanded view of the presidency, and certainly of his presidency, Roosevelt now saw the decision as *his* to make. He had been the ultimate decision maker for nearly eight years, and in fact he had structured his government in such a way that virtually every decision of consequence came to him. Why should this decision be any different? This deeply ingrained practice was strongly reinforced by his determination that if he was to run again, he would do so on his own terms, and one of those terms would be to have a vice president of his own choosing. He certainly didn't want the convention to foist another John Nance Garner on him (although he had been a party to that decision in 1932 in a deal that brought him enough votes to be nominated). Thus he would discard more than a century of political precedent, as he had discarded others, and he would do so apparently without discussing the matter with anyone. He simply concluded it was his prerogative to choose his running mate, and so, too, did almost everyone around him. Virtually every future presidential nominee of both parties would see it the same way and follow the precedent created in 1940.

There is no evidence that Roosevelt had anything other than a traditional view of the role of the vice presidency. Like his predecessors, he saw the number two position in the government as simply "stand-by equipment," as Nelson Rockefeller, a future unhappy occupant of the office, would famously call it. If FDR had thought seriously about the position at all, it would have been when he actively sought the Democratic nomination for the office in 1920. That had been an opportunity, in his view, to gain a national identity and the friendship of Democratic politicians throughout the country, and thus to further his long-term presidential ambitions. He waged a low-key campaign among party officials that, combined with his reputation as a Wilson progressive and the advantages of a famous name, won him the slot on the ticket that few others wanted. Nineteen twenty was shaping up to be a Republican year, but for Roosevelt it was a win-win proposition, and he made the most of it.

There was no lack of possible candidates for the job in 1940 and a number of them were actively jockeying for it, but to most observers there was no clear front-runner. Hopkins had reported to Rosenman that the president had discussed "all of the possibilities" with him. The most likely among them were Cordell Hull, James F. Byrnes, William B. Bankhead, Jesse Jones, and Henry A. Wallace. Hull, of course, was Roosevelt's first choice at this point, though it was unlikely that he could be persuaded to run. Byrnes, the senator from South Carolina whom FDR liked, was seen as politically handicapped by having been born into the Catholic Church and then leaving the Church as an adult. William Bankhead was the conservative Speaker of the House from Alabama; FDR had concerns about his health and his age (and, in fact, he would be dead a month after the convention). Jesse Jones was a Texan who had ably headed the Reconstruction Finance Corporation for Roosevelt, who thought he was much too conservative. And then there was Henry A. Wallace, the Republican from Iowa who was now secretary of agriculture and one of the most outspoken New Dealers. His strong commitment to the president's programs certainly didn't escape FDR's attention, though the working assumption among most close observers was that Roosevelt would want a strong liberal on the ticket with him. Wallace's name moved up on many of their lists. Hopkins told Rosenman that he believed the president had "boiled" the list down to three: Hull, Byrnes, and Wallace.[1]

Hull had by now become the president's clear first choice as his running mate. Not only was the secretary of state wholly supportive of all-out aid to Britain, but he had helped to shape that policy. He was not an ardent New Dealer, it was true, but he passed for a liberal in the South, which was something, and FDR believed he would be sufficiently supportive of his domestic legacy that it wouldn't be endangered. Most important, he was held in high regard throughout the country for his integrity. FDR concluded he would be a good president if called upon. He also concluded he would be a huge asset in a close election. So, following the July 3 meeting when Roosevelt in effect conceded to Hull that he was open to a third term, the president "almost immediately" called the secretary back to the White House for a two-and-a-half-hour meeting during which, Hull would later report, FDR "pleaded with me" to run with him. The job of presiding over the Senate "with no authority to participate in the proceedings" held no appeal for Hull. He wrote in his memoirs years later that, recalling Jefferson's unhappy occupancy of the office as "honorable and easy," he told himself he was not interested "in an easy, soft place." He explained to Roosevelt that he could be of much greater value to him "in the troublous days ahead" by remaining at the State Department. "I declined and stood firm in my declination," he wrote in 1948.

A day or two later Hull was summoned back yet again to the White House, where the president once more pressed him on the issue of the vice presidency. As before, the two discussed, as Hull later put it, "every imaginable phase of the present and prospective political situation," but Hull, always respectful, remained adamant in his refusal. An evening or two after this meeting Roosevelt telephoned the secretary at home and renewed his plea "with much emphasis"; Hull still refused to budge.

The president then said, "Let me talk to Frances. I'll convince her, and she can convince you."

Mrs. Hull, who had been standing next to her husband during the conversation, "kept shaking her head. She did not want to be drawn into the discussion."

"Mrs. Hull has gone to bed," Hull told the president in what must have been the only untruth of his time in office. "I can't call her to the phone."

The president was not used to not having his way, particularly when it came to the people around him, and he made his final argument. "If you don't take it," he said, "I'll have to get Henry Wallace to run."

Hull was undeterred: "That's all right with me."

The result of these conversations was that Hull, knowing that Roosevelt could be devious about things he really wanted, instructed the assistant secretary of state, Breckinridge Long, who would be going to Chicago, to ensure that his name was not put into nomination for the vice presidency.[2]

With Hull's refusal to run and Byrnes's potentially disqualifying religious issues, Roosevelt's attention did indeed shift to Wallace. He wanted a committed New Dealer on the ticket with him, as well as one who would sustain his policy of all-out aid to Britain. There were few others who met these criteria. Harold Ickes sometimes entertained notions of national office, though there is no evidence that anyone else, including the president, saw him in that light. And amazingly, after nearly eight years of liberal economic policy defining the nation's recovery, there was no one in Congress, or the statehouses for that matter, who fit the bill. Which left Wallace.

Frances Perkins, the secretary of labor, who had known Roosevelt for thirty years, longer than anyone else in his official family, was herself an ardent New Dealer as well as an astute political observer. Never hesitant to approach the president on a matter she felt strongly about, she confronted him on the vice presidency by making the case for Wallace. He was "very able, clear-thinking, high-minded," she argued, "a man of patriotism and nobility of character." In addition, she said, he would help with the farm vote as "one of the few people with an agricultural background who had begun to make himself comprehensible to the industrial working people of the country." Not least, Perkins added, he had a strong liberal following and that "might strengthen the ticket."

The president agreed that he might well strengthen the ticket: "One has to think of it, he would be a good man if something happened to the President. He is no isolationist. He knows what we are up against in this war that is so engulfing the world." But, according to Perkins, Roosevelt remained indefinite and "did not commit himself."[3]

One New Dealer who was not high on many lists (and who, revealingly, didn't make the one Hopkins shared with Rosenman) was William O. Douglas, a brilliant if somewhat quirky liberal who was now a justice of the Supreme Court. Douglas enjoyed the spotlight that the Court appointment had brought him and had decided he might like an even more prominent role on the national stage. With that in mind, and with Tommy Corcoran's help, he launched a low-key campaign for the vice presidential nomination by stressing his undeniably strong New Deal credentials as well as those of a westerner (he had grown up in Yakima, Washington) who would bring regional balance to an FDR-led ticket. On July 2 he sent a long, ingratiating memorandum to the president arguing that Roosevelt was "the only one who can beat Willkie," that the third-term issue "was pretty well dissolved already," and that his running mate "should be one who can take on Willkie—one who can do a lot of slugging for you." He proceeded to name several candidates who might do just that and then cited reasons they might not be so ideal after all. The implicit suggestion lingered that Douglas himself might be the ideal candidate.[4]

The justice correctly concluded that Wallace was his principal competition for the position, and he also correctly concluded that there was only one person whom it was essential to influence in this covert campaign. The logical extension of these conclusions, in his mind, was that Wallace had to somehow be politically discredited in Roosevelt's eyes. More than a decade earlier, Wallace had been attracted to a Russian-born theosophist named Nicholas Roerich who rejected Christian theology and held to a set of occult beliefs premised on a special mystical insight. Roerich's odd looks and behavior evoked comparisons with Rasputin among many who encountered him; he was clearly out of the American mainstream. Still, Wallace liked him well enough that in 1929 he initiated a correspondence of "Dear Guru" letters with him. As secretary of agriculture, he even found federal funding for an expensive Roerich mission to Mongolia and Manchuria to find drought-resistant plants that could be used in America's dust bowl, but Roerich's behavior on the trip was so bizarre that Wallace decided he had to end the relationship. The letters had not yet surfaced, though Douglas had picked up sufficient innuendo about them to know that they would likely be a serious problem for Roosevelt in the general election.

By at least one account Douglas plotted to use Harold Ickes to bring this potentially explosive issue to the president's attention. Like everyone in the administration, Douglas knew that Wallace and Ickes had tenaciously fought turf wars over the management of public lands for years. He believed that there would be little enough love lost in the relationship, and thus that Ickes wouldn't hesitate to use his political entrée with FDR to convey this potentially scandalous news. Douglas, on the other hand, was a friend of Ickes, so it was natural, according to this version of the story, that the two should meet in the latter's office with Wallace, Robert Jackson (by now the attorney general), Tom Corcoran, Ben Cohen, and a few others. Douglas and Corcoran made the case that disclosure of the relationship and especially the letters would be embarrassing in the extreme to the Roosevelt cause, and that in a potentially close election a Wallace candidacy shouldn't be risked. But Wallace supposedly rose to the occasion and defended himself sufficiently to defuse the issue. The problem with this version is that Ickes, who was meticulous in recording virtually every significant event in his day, never mentioned such a meeting in his diary. It is likely that at some point Douglas did speak with Ickes about the matter, but that Ickes had already decided to go along with the selection of Wallace if FDR wanted him, even though Wallace would not be his first choice for vice president. As a result, he never mentioned the meeting, or the issue, to the president.[5]

Jim Farley had arrived in Chicago early in the week to set up his headquarters in the Stevens Hotel, located conveniently for the delegates and party leaders who traditionally came by at these gatherings to pay their respects and to receive instructions from the party chieftain. This year, however, they did not come in the same numbers as before, and those who did were seldom looking for instructions. It was an awkward situation for most party loyalists, liking and respecting Farley as they did but knowing that he would be opposing the president, to whom they still owed their highest loyalty. Most who came by did so out of personal affection for this man, who was one of them and who had looked out for their interests for so many years, especially against the ardent New Dealers in the administration, whom they dismissed as political amateurs.

A few stopped by with other things in mind, among them Jimmy Byrnes, Frank Walker, and Ed Flynn, all now in the inner circle of FDR advisors. They came separately over the next few days bringing the same message: for party unity Farley should agree to again manage the general election campaign for the president, with a strong implication that the cause of unity would be enhanced if he didn't allow his name to go before the convention.

Farley saw these pleas for what they were and said he was committed to going ahead with his plans, adding that he wasn't doing anything to win more delegates and resented those who would chip away at the delegates already committed to him, which he estimated to be as many as 150.[6]

One of the prerogatives that Farley cherished most about his job as party chairman was the obeisance that others were obliged to pay him in these traditional visits. He was enough of a realist to know why the number of such visitors was much reduced at this convention, although it was too much for him that Harry Hopkins, who had set up shop in the Blackstone Hotel across the street and who had become the "man to see," had failed to pay even a pro forma courtesy call on him. Apparently Hopkins thought Farley should be paying such a visit to him; if so, he was quickly disabused of the notion. When reporters had asked Farley whether he would be calling on Hopkins, he replied that he "would be happy to see everyone who called on me . . . but I would not run around to the hotels calling on anyone else."

Hopkins got the message and phoned Farley Saturday morning, saying he would like to come by. According to Farley, Hopkins began the conversation by asking him what he thought was going on. Farley testily responded that there was no need to tell him because evidently he knew "all about what was happening." When Hopkins stressed that despite what Farley might have heard, Roosevelt really wanted him to manage the fall campaign, Farley replied that he didn't want to talk about it because he had already discussed it with the president. When asked his views on the vice presidential nomination, the party chairman said he hadn't thought much about it except that it should be a "real Democrat." He then offered the comment that "there was no use in kidding each other about what the President intended to do." Hopkins responded with an assurance that he was "not acting as an intermediary" between the president and Farley, to which the latter answered abruptly, "If I had anything to say, I would say it directly to the President, and no one else."[7]

The conversation then turned to the number of delegates Farley expected to receive on the first ballot, and he estimated that "it would be between 125–150, unless pressure was brought to bear." He stressed that he "would not make an effort to get any delegates, and that no effort should be made to take away any pledged to me." Hopkins promised nothing would be done in that regard, though privately Farley was less than certain about that: "I am sure a great deal was done to bring down the size of my vote," he later noted.[8]

By the time Harold Ickes arrived in Chicago on Saturday, he found Hopkins settled in the Blackstone Hotel and "fully established in supreme command of the Roosevelt strategy." Eager as always to be in on the action, Ickes called both Hopkins and Bob Jackson, but there seemed to be no need to get together, as Ickes had hoped. "As a matter of fact," he noted, "there was never any occasion for a conference because Harry was running things to suit himself and he doesn't like to share credit with anyone else."[9]

FDR's most ardent supporters were dismayed when they arrived in Chicago to find such disarray in the Roosevelt camp and such unhappiness among the delegates. Most of the blame for this fell on Hopkins, the novice politician who, they believed, was in over his head in this very challenging environment. Many thought he had no instinct for politics; he seemed to look on the Farley and Garner forces as "enemies" who must be decisively defeated, without regard for the need to heal party wounds for the general election. It was also unclear just what Hopkins's mandate from the president was. Robert Sherwood, who had access to all of Hopkins's papers in preparing his 1948 Pulitzer Prize–winning biography of Roosevelt and Hopkins, found that the handwritten message to Speaker Bankhead to be read to the convention was the only written instruction given to Hopkins before he left for Chicago. Ickes had concluded that either the president had "delegated Harry to represent him, or Harry had assumed authority without being repudiated by the President." The passage of time has not shed new light on this question, and it remains a mystery. The most likely conclusion is that Roosevelt never gave either written or oral instructions to Hopkins, consistent with his determination to leave no trace of anything that could be seen, then or later, as "interference" in the nominating process. At the same time, it is clear that the president and his confidant had more than a few conversations about the political future, and that Hopkins was increasingly able to read FDR's mind and increasingly confident of his ability to act without specific instructions. In short, he was now doing on a much larger stage what Missy LeHand had been doing for years—anticipating the president's wishes without being told.[10]

At the same time, however, Roosevelt apparently had asked Jimmy Byrnes, who had not only faced the electorate successfully as a senator but also attended seven Democratic conventions, to co-manage operations in Chicago with Hopkins. Though the South Carolinian was something less than a full-fledged New Dealer, FDR probably trusted him more than any other Democrat in Congress. They liked each other personally and were kindred political spirits as well; not least, Byrnes was intensely and consistently loyal to the president. Hopkins would be the more visible Roosevelt representative at the convention, yet the savvy and experienced Byrnes would be there when it mattered most.[11]

The president's refusal to state his intentions publicly had created an atmosphere of uncertainty that would have been difficult for even the most skilled politician to manage; for the inexperienced Hopkins, it was nearly impossible. He would later be roundly accused of arrogance, heartlessness, and of course inattention to the views of the party leaders, most of whom had plenty of views to offer. Even Eleanor, who was fond of Hopkins and who would spend convention week at Val-Kill, her personal retreat at Hyde Park, listening to the proceedings on the radio, told friends that Hopkins "was making all his usual mistakes." She concluded that "he doesn't seem to know how to make people happy," which, it could be argued, "was the essence of politics." In her first conversation with her husband after the convention, she later wrote, he had insisted that Hopkins "had had no headquarters and no official authority. Harry had simply gone ahead and acted on his own. I believe it was one of those occasions when Franklin kept hands off because to act was so disagreeable to him; only when he was forced to act by the way things were going did he do so."[12]

Throughout the weekend, reporters in Chicago, with little solid news to report, devoted countless column-inches of print to speculation about what would occur during the following week. They generally assumed that Roosevelt had at least nine hundred committed delegates, more than enough to secure his nomination, and they further assumed that he would accept the nomination. Farley conceded that he knew of the president's plans, but, according to one reporter, he "has been as closed mouth as an oyster." The *Chicago Tribune* had learned that the president had offered the number two spot to the secretary of state and predicted it would be a Roosevelt-Hull ticket. If Hull was reluctant to run, the paper stated, "the president, according to the word reaching the convention leaders, will not hesitate to cause the convention to draft the secretary." More solidly, most reporters were able to identify correctly the principal Roosevelt advisors, the people who would be the ones to watch during the next week: Harry Hopkins, Jimmy Byrnes, and Frank Walker, the last of whom, it was speculated, would replace Farley as Democratic chairman. The more enterprising of the reporters kept an eye on the traffic to and from Hopkins's hotel suite, where the strategy meetings took place and, most important, where a direct line to the White House had been installed.[13]

Shortly after he went to bed Sunday night Rosenman was awakened by a call from Jackson and Walker, who reported that it was the "consensus" of the leaders in Chicago that the president should not send a message to the delegates releasing them. It was the same "strong sentiment" they had expressed to the president a few days earlier in person, one that Rosenman had difficulty appreciating because he had been assured that a majority of the delegates were committed to Roosevelt. Nonetheless, the "strong sentiment" was reinforced by a similar call at 7:00 a.m. from Hopkins, who reported that the president would soon be receiving a call from the leaders themselves. Rosenman quickly dressed and rushed down the hall to the president's bedroom, where he found FDR having breakfast in bed, looking "very fit and . . . in a fighting mood." The call soon came through, and Roosevelt asked Rosenman to stay and listen in on an extension phone. One after another Hopkins, Byrnes, Walker, and Mayor Ed Kelly pleaded with him not to send the message, but he was resolute. "He put it on two grounds," Rosenman recorded: "first, a personal feeling that if he was to be nominated he wanted it to be a free and open nomination by delegates released from any pledge or commitment; second, for purposes of history, he wanted it made clear that he was not actively seeking a third term. He wanted this stated as part of the permanent record of the convention." Roosevelt would not be moved.

The leaders shifted to their fallback position: if the message was to be delivered, it should be read not by Bankhead on Monday night but rather by Senator Alben Barkley in his keynote address on Tuesday evening. The president opposed this argument as well, reasoning that the delegates should have "as much time as possible to make up their own minds what to do." Rosenman wrote that he had never seen the president more stubborn—"although stubbornness was one of his well-known characteristics." Nonetheless, FDR finally relented when he understood that Bankhead wouldn't speak until 10:00 p.m. and therefore wouldn't read the message until close to midnight eastern time, when few people would be listening. Barkley's speech on Tuesday, on the other hand, would be early in the evening and have a much larger audience. "On the basis of that, and that alone," Rosenman wrote, "the President gave in."[14]

At the very time on Sunday that Roosevelt's men in Washington and Chicago were attempting to script the convention, another Roosevelt man—although he certainly would have objected to the term—was boarding a Pan Am Clipper in New York bound for London. William J. Donovan was a much-decorated hero of the Great War, in which he had earned the nickname "Wild Bill." He was also a prominent Republican who had run for governor of New York in 1932 after Herbert Hoover passed him over for an expected cabinet appointment. Now he was a fifty-three-year-old corporate lawyer in New York City with a serious interest in world affairs, and today he was embarked on a secret mission for the administration to assess Britain's ability to withstand an onslaught from Hitler's Germany.

Roosevelt and Donovan had been classmates at Columbia Law, but they were never close and had little in common: FDR was an indifferent student who came from a great family, while Donovan was a conscientious student who came from a modest background. They had clashed when the Republican took on Herbert Lehman for the governorship the same year that Roosevelt was challenging Hoover and couldn't afford to lose New York State. Despite their political differences—Donovan was consistently hostile to the New Deal—they had come in recent years to share a growing conviction that America had to build up its defenses and do all it could to aid

Britain. Donovan began sending the president his observations from trips abroad, generating a two-way correspondence that, over time, persuaded both men of their common views as well as each other's skills, particularly their political skills. When Roosevelt first considered adding one or more Republicans to his cabinet in late 1939 to bolster his national security team, Donovan was on the list of potential appointees, thanks to the advocacy of his friend Frank Knox, whom FDR was then also considering. Six months later the president brought Knox into the cabinet as secretary of the navy and installed Henry Stimson at the War Department instead of Donovan. Once again a cabinet position had eluded Donovan. Nonetheless, he got over it as he prepared Knox for a contentious Senate confirmation hearing and then responded positively to the new secretary's invitation to play a different role in the administration's larger cause.

Roosevelt continued to have serious doubts about Britain's ability to survive a Nazi offensive, and particularly, as we have seen, its will to do so. He was still trying to take Churchill's measure. He had been impressed by the prime minister's decision to destroy the French fleet at Oran and his ability to rally the British people. Still, there were lingering concerns: whether the struggling Royal Air Force could turn back the mighty Luftwaffe, and whether the sea lanes, which were Britain's lifelines, would remain open under relentless assault from German U-boats. It was the question that dominated FDR's thought in July, just as it had for months: did the British military have the leadership and the means to withstand an invasion virtually everyone believed was coming? If an intimidated British government, either Churchill's or that of a successor, ever allowed the British fleet to fall into German hands, it would prove a disaster. Roosevelt didn't know Churchill well, having had only that brief and unhappy encounter with him more than twenty years before, and he needed to know more not just about the prime minister but also about those advising him and how committed they were to seeing this crisis through. Roosevelt needed the answers to these questions because, having decided to seek a third term to steer the country through this war, he was casting his lot with these people. He had committed his administration to giving Britain the means to resist Hitler, and he had to know whether that was indeed a viable strategy or whether the American aid would be wasted and perhaps even end up as German booty.

Churchill's assurances on these questions were welcome yet not dispositive. Roosevelt needed independent confirmation, and he couldn't rely on the usual sources for it. Joe Kennedy had been a strong proponent of Chamberlain's policy of appeasement; now that war had broken out and Chamberlain was gone, the ambassador was convinced that Britain couldn't survive unless it accommodated Hitler. The president used whatever random sources of information he could find—there was nothing resembling a national intelligence apparatus yet—and it was a haphazard exercise that had limited value. Frank Knox, brand-new to the cabinet and sympathetic to the president's needs, had an idea: send Bill Donovan, a savvy and hardheaded internationalist who was in sync with the president's policies, to London to try to get the answers. That a prominent Republican should undertake such a sensitive and secret mission in the midst of a highly charged election was a gutsy suggestion coming from a newcomer to the cabinet, and particularly one who happened to have been the GOP vice presidential nominee just four years before. It says much about Knox that he offered the idea and just as much about Roosevelt that he agreed to it. It also says a good deal about the politics of the time. In any case, Donovan took off that Sunday to try to find the answers the president needed.[15]

11

Chicago
Following the Script

Delegates from across the country poured into Chicago over the weekend and prepared to participate in what should have been an exciting, fulfilling, and uplifting week at the convention. Instead they found confusion, uncertainty, and generally a depressed mood. Indeed, it soon became clear that this was going to be a convention unlike any they had attended before. There were only two announced candidates for the presidential nomination—the incumbent vice president and the incumbent chairman of the Democratic National Committee—and no one believed that either man had a serious chance of being nominated. Instead, looming over the entire proceeding was the incumbent president of the United States, the man who had served two terms and who refused to say whether he would seek a precedent-shattering third. Between the rhetoric of open debate and the overwhelming reality of the done deal was a void that no one seemed able to fill. There was no one on the scene to give the gathering the direction and purpose that the party regulars had come to expect. In short, there was no one in charge.

The conflicts and contradictions of this picture were captured vividly by the national columnists Joseph Alsop and Robert Kintner. Alsop's family relationship to the president—his mother was a niece of Teddy Roosevelt's—gave him enviable access to the White House even though his politics were considerably to the right of the president's; with FDR, blood ties invariably trumped politics. Blood ties or no, the two columnists lowered the boom on the Roosevelt effort in Chicago—though *not* on Roosevelt himself—before the convention even began, writing, "The Democratic Convention resembles nothing so much as a badly managed puppet show in which for want of firm management by the puppet master, the strings moving the figures become entangled, and the figures themselves go in all directions but the right one." They reported that Hopkins maintained that he had no "positive authority" to speak for the president but that nonetheless he and others had been laboring "manfully" to gain several objectives, the first of which was to have the president's appearance on the first ballot appear to be "as large and as spontaneous as possible." The second was to get Farley to stay on as national chairman and manage the Democratic presidential campaign. "Evidently it never occurred to the masterminds in the Blackstone hideaway that these two objectives could possibly conflict," Alsop and Kintner wrote, noting gleefully that on one hand there was an effort to convince Farley not to resign after the convention, and on the other that Farley was feeling huge pressure to release his delegates to Roosevelt.[1]

It was true, of course, that the president had "made no definite arrangements" for his operatives in Chicago to achieve his goals, but that omission was intentional, the ostensible purpose being to have plausible deniability that he was playing the role of "puppet master." What remains unclear, even after nearly seventy-five years, is whether Roosevelt fully understood the price he would pay for this decision. Not only would he be seen as the one pulling the strings, but he would be seen as doing it ineptly, reinforcing his reputation among the party delegates for manipulation. If he did realize there would be such a trade-off, and it seems likely he did, he saw it as an acceptable price to pay. Throughout this week his primary focus would be not on the delegates, who he believed were certain to nominate him, but rather on the people of the country listening in, whose support he would need in November, and, beyond that, on countries either engaged in aggression or its victim, and how their leaders would perceive the American political process. Chicago wasn't just playing to the country; it was playing to the world. Roosevelt was, typically, taking the long view when others were more focused on the immediate.

As Jim Farley was leaving for the hall Monday to open the convention, he received a call from the White House; the president wanted to know "if everything was all right." The chairman replied that it was, and he took the occasion to ask about the message to the delegates that he had understood the president as having promised to show him. Roosevelt dissembled, saying he had just returned from his trip and planned to work on it that day. In fact, he had worked on it with Rosenman on the *Potomac* the day before, and the new draft had already reached Hopkins in Chicago. By this point Farley had concluded as much, since the papers had reported that Rosenman had been on the weekend cruise with the president. "He intimated that he would have it in my possession by tonight," Farley noted. Roosevelt said that the newspapers were filled with stories about the actual need for a ballot, and he agreed that of course there had to be a ballot. In fact, the *Chicago Tribune* had reported that morning that Hopkins had hatched a "daring, spectacular project to 'draft' Roosevelt" by means of an extraordinary procedure; Farley had certainly seen the article. The chairman responded there indeed had to be a ballot and that "any effort to prevent it or a roll call would be just the one thing needed to wreck the Democratic Party in the November election." He promised to do everything he could to manage things along the line of their conference in Hyde Park, noting that "some people were trying to bully the situation and roll over everyone; and if that happened, it would be just too bad." The president, who was in what Farley described as a "friendly frame of mind," agreed.[2]

As Farley entered the convention hall he found what a local journalist called "a festive picture on a massive canvas." The delegates' seats on the floor were painted a brilliant red. A huge portrait of the president dominated the hall. A striking gilded eagle with wings outstretched had been temporarily removed from the Cook County Democratic headquarters and mounted just below the podium, extending out into the enormous space.

And about forty feet above the podium hung "a curious-looking apparatus resembling a beehive" that Thomas Garry, the Chicago superintendent of sewers who had been placed in charge of arrangements in the hall by Mayor Ed Kelly, explained was a loudspeaker system with sixteen horns, representing the very latest in sound technology.[3]

The evening session of the convention convened to hear speeches by Jim Farley, as party chairman, and Speaker William Bankhead, as keynoter. It was widely noted that neither mentioned the president by name; Bankhead once referred to him as "our distinguished president." To Harold Ickes, who chose to listen to the proceedings on the radio in his hotel room, the session was "dead and cold. Everything was dull and bogged down."[4]

Rosenman joined the president and Missy to listen in from the Oval Study, and he, too, noticed the absence of the president's name in either address. "The tone of [Bankhead's] speech showed that he was certainly no friend of the President in that convention," confirming in Rosenman's mind the wisdom of the leaders' advice that Barkley would be a more reliable deliverer of the president's message releasing the delegates. Adding to the intrigue of the evening, Rosenman had a long phone conversation with Hopkins, whom he described as outraged by what Farley and his friends were doing, which was, he said, "spreading all kinds of stories about promises made to Farley by the President." Hopkins was still learning that conventions, particularly when mired in controversy and uncertainty, fed on rumors; they were the staple of the unique species of political animal that thrived on these gatherings.[5]

Ickes, still eager to be a player in the unfolding drama, persuaded himself that control of the convention had to be wrested from Farley and placed in more reliable hands. He enlisted Jackson in the cause, and the attorney general insisted that Hopkins be included; Ickes reluctantly agreed. The three met in the secretary's suite following the evening session, soon to be joined by Byrnes. All were in favor of "doing something," and Ickes was surprised that Hopkins in particular "so readily fell in with our plans." Byrnes argued that the rules committee should be used to shorten the duration of the convention so that consideration of the platform could be deferred until the nomination was settled, and they all agreed to go to work on the plan. But when the same group reconvened on Tuesday morning, Hopkins reported that he had talked in the interim with the president, who had announced that he was pleased with developments so far in Chicago. He was not bothered that Bankhead had failed to mention his name, and he did not want to do "anything to disturb the regular procedure." Ickes said later that he had expected this. His suspicions of Hopkins's ready agreement with "doing something" the night before "were justified." Ickes was "nettled," as he put it, and didn't conceal it. "I remarked that if the Republicans had been running the convention in the interests of Willkie, they could not have done a better job than we were doing." Predictably, the remark irked Hopkins, and "some feelings developed between us." Ickes then resorted to sarcasm, wondering aloud whether "anyone was going to place the president's name in nomination." This comment "really made Harry sore" before it was explained that Senator Lister Hill of Alabama would do the honors. To no one's surprise, this would be the last time Hopkins and Ickes would be in the same room in Chicago.[6]

Meanwhile, back in Washington, Rosenman labored on the party platform that the convention would be asked to adopt. Platforms took on greater meaning in those days, and generally speaking, the public and the press paid close attention to a party's statement of principles and policies; perhaps at no time was this more the case than in the election of 1940. Roosevelt was particularly concerned that it reflect his interests because he likely would be running on this platform, and therefore he saw to it that a reliable ally, Senator Robert Wagner of New York, would be chairman of the platform committee and oversee its provisions. The brief document had been "prepared and revised in the White House," according to Rosenman, who also noted that a "bitter contest arose in the committee over the foreign affairs plank." Everyone could see this fight coming, with the party's isolationists, particularly those in Congress, arguing for restrictions on American involvement in foreign wars and the internationalists arguing for more flexibility.

The issue came to a head when Wagner phoned Rosenman with a draft passage that the isolationists insisted on including in the platform. It read, "We will not participate in foreign wars. We will not send our armed forces to fight in lands across the sea." Roosevelt became disconcerted when he saw this language, according to Rosenman, because "no human being, no political party, could guarantee that we would not get involved in the war." At the same time the president realized that his opponents would make political capital out of his insisting that the plank be entirely removed, carrying with it the implication that he favored intervention. The two discussed it at great length, and the president reached out to Hopkins, Byrnes, and other supporters in Chicago as well as to isolationist leaders such as Senators Burton Wheeler of Montana and David Walsh of Massachusetts. Rosenman finally suggested adding a proviso: "except where necessary to defend and protect our own American interests." Roosevelt was still not satisfied and had further conversations with Byrnes and Hull, after which he wrote out in his own hand: "except in case of attack." Most everyone on both sides took a deep breath and signed off on the compromise, but it took Jimmy Byrnes to seal it. During a break in the platform committee meeting, he escorted three isolationist senators into a vacant ladies' room at the convention hall, locked the door, and announced that no one could leave until they agreed to the "except in case of attack" language. They agreed. The final platform would contain FDR's language, and it would become his standard response to questions about American involvement in the war.[7]

Back in Chicago, Harold Ickes spent the rest of the morning sulking about his inability to affect basic strategy and especially about his bitter exchange with Hopkins. He resolved to withdraw from the field: "I decided that the thing for me to do was to take no active part in the convention at all." His resolve wouldn't last for long. Others who shared his view that the president was being badly served by the chaos in Chicago as well as by the lack of leadership there importuned him to call the president, apprise him of the true feeling of his supporters in Chicago, and urge him to go to the convention and make his case. Ickes told them that he would send a telegram to Roosevelt instead because, he said, it was too easy "to interrupt or divert a telephone conversation and the President is adept at that." "Moreover," he added, "I want a written record."

The wire, sent that afternoon, informed Roosevelt that the latter's friends "have been coming to me in increasing numbers because they are convinced, as I am, that this convention is bleeding to death and that your reputation and prestige may bleed to death with it." Employing the spirit of the MacLeish memo, he argued that, given the world situation, "no man can fail to respond to the call to serve his country with everything that he has." But, he went on, not only must he be willing to accept the nomination, but he must do it in a way that would guarantee a successful campaign. "Here in Chicago are more than nine hundred leaderless delegates milling about like worried sheep waiting for the inspiration of leadership that only you can give them." Ickes went on to say that the "Farley coalition" was out to destroy the president, and that its followers were starting to think that another candidate might be put forward. The upshot of all this, he concluded, was that only the president's presence could clear up "the sordid atmosphere" at the convention. FDR's personal appearance would "raise this political campaign to such a high plane as would be an inspiration to the country." Failure to address this problem would only enhance Willkie's prospects of victory, and "Willkie means fascism and appeasement."[8]

There was validity to much of what Ickes was reporting to the president, and there is no question that many delegates shared his views. But there was also more than a little political paranoia and the kind of exaggeration that inevitably emanates from the heat of politics contested for high stakes. There is no record of Roosevelt ever acknowledging Ickes's telegram.

Labor secretary Frances Perkins had reached the same conclusion as Ickes, who, ironically, disliked her intensely and hoped the president would dismiss her because she was politically naive and too talkative at cabinet meetings. Politics was still very much a man's world in 1940, and women were rarely invited to the table. Nonetheless, Perkins had known FDR longer than anyone else in Chicago, and for equally as long she had been an astute observer of Democratic politics. Roosevelt liked and respected Perkins and, more to the point, he listened to her.

She had concluded, as had others, that Hopkins's management of the Roosevelt effort was causing more problems than it solved. In addition, she personally liked Farley and thought he was being badly treated. As was her custom, she chose a more direct approach to get her message through to Roosevelt than Ickes had: she called him. She got right through and later recorded their conversation. The president wanted to know immediately how she thought things were going. She assured him he would be nominated but stressed "the bitterness and crossness of the delegates . . . the difficulties, confusion, and near fights" that had characterized the convention so far. It would be a "wonderful help," she said, if he could go to Chicago.

Roosevelt replied that he had given the idea full consideration. "I thought it all through both ways. I know that I am right, Frances. It will be worse if I go. People will get promises out of me that I ought not to make. If I don't make promises, I will make new enemies. If I do make promises, they'll be mistakes. I'll be pinned down on things I just don't want to be pinned down to now. I am sure that it is better not to go. I am sure it will come out better the other way."

"Can't you suggest something?" I said. "What can we do?"

"How would it be if Eleanor came?" he asked.

"I think it would make an excellent impression."

"You know Eleanor always makes people feel right," he said. "She has a fine way with her. Would you like her to come?"

"Yes."

"Telephone her. I'll speak to her too, but you tell her so that she will know I am not sending her on my own hunch, but that some of the rest of you want her. Talk to one or two others before you speak to her."

FDR next turned to the vice presidency and asked Perkins what she was hearing. She replied that there were a great number of candidates and that things were getting "tense," and then she asked if he had made up his mind yet. He said he hadn't "really," but asked what she thought about Henry Wallace. She responded that she had always thought well of him, leading him to ask how he would go over with the convention. She said there was as yet no indication of a Wallace campaign, so she couldn't say, adding that he "has a following and is making friends all the time."

"I think Wallace is good," replied Roosevelt. "I like him. He is the kind of man I like to have around. He is good to work with and he knows a lot, you can trust his information. He digs to the bottom of things and gets the facts. He is honest as the day is long. He thinks right. He has the general ideas we have. He is the kind of man who can do something in politics. He can help the people with their political thinking. Yes, I think it had better be Wallace."

"Are you making up your mind?"

"Yes," he said, "it's Wallace, I guess. Yes, it will be Wallace. I think I'll stick to that."

"That's fine," I said. "What shall I do?"

"Would you mind going over to tell Harry? . . . You'd better not telephone. Probably someone is listening in on Harry's wires. You'd better go over yourself and tell him. Will you? That I have decided on Wallace."

"All right, Mr. President."

It was a revealing conversation in several respects. For starters, it was initiated by someone for whom few aside from FDR had much political respect, and who happened to be a woman. It set in motion the enormously consequential trip that Eleanor would make to Chicago. And it again demonstrated Roosevelt's decision-making process, in this case on the vice presidency. He had been leaning toward Wallace but hadn't finally settled on him until he made a case for him to Perkins that he himself found persuasive. His thinking out loud had clinched the matter. Finally, the fact that he hadn't told Hopkins and asked Perkins to do so not only confirms that he hadn't previously settled on Wallace but also suggests his ad hoc management style. Arguably a decision of this importance warranted a personal conversation with his man on the spot—if indeed that is what Hopkins was.[9]

Perkins dutifully conveyed the decision to Hopkins, who was "somewhat surprised, though by no means in disagreement." He said he had had no indication before this, and in fact had called Roosevelt the night before in an effort to get an answer, to no avail. Hopkins called him again for verification of Perkins's message; getting it, he began to spread word that Wallace was "likely" to get the vice presidential nod. Perkins wasn't sure that anyone had thought to inform Wallace, but years later she said that she had finally called him herself.[10]

Eleanor had not been an active participant in the third-term discussions swirling around her husband, though she had of course a huge stake in the outcome. She recognized that it was highly likely that he would be nominated and, if so, "he could not refuse," as she later wrote. Her husband would have been happy—"completely satisfied" was how she put it—to retire, even though he had grown used to being at the very center of world affairs and, like others who have been, could not imagine when that would no longer be so. The president's hesitations all along had been genuine, as he teeter-tottered between "great weariness" and the desire to be his "own master." She saw in him "the overwhelming interest which was the culmination of a lifetime of preparation and work, and the desire to see and to have a hand in the affairs of the world in that critical period."[11]

Her analysis of her husband's thinking was both sympathetic and perceptive; the only major factor she omitted, or at least only hinted at, was the sense of responsibility that he felt in the face of national peril. The week before the convention she had sought to clarify at least one point with him. She noted that he had apparently decided not to go to Chicago, even to deliver an acceptance speech, as he had done twice before, and she hoped therefore that she wouldn't have to go, either. "He said very firmly that it was his definite intention that neither he nor I should go." In that case, she replied, she would spend the convention week at her cottage at Hyde Park with friends, listening in on the radio. Everything was "going very placidly" there, she said, until she got a call from Frances Perkins, who poured out her tale of how miserably things were going in Chicago. The president had to go to Chicago, she argued, if he wanted Wallace nominated, and if he wouldn't go, then Eleanor must. Eleanor replied that it was "utter nonsense" for her to go, and she urged Perkins to talk to her husband, who, if anyone, should be the one to go. The secretary of labor said she would do so, neglecting to reveal that she had already had a conversation with him on the subject.[12]

Perkins called the president again and confirmed that he wouldn't be going to Chicago; he still thought Eleanor should go. Perkins volunteered that everyone except Jim Farley seemed to know what was in the message he had given to Barkley to read to the delegates that evening, and she urged him to call the chairman. Farley was about to leave his hotel for the convention hall when a call came through from the White House. Roosevelt said he had been trying to reach him all afternoon, though Farley had barely budged from his suite that day. "Jim," he quickly went on, "I wanted to tell you that Alben [Barkley] has that statement we talked about. I decided it would be best to release it after the permanent organization was set up." He said he preferred to do it that way rather than release a statement or have Farley read one, as they had discussed at Hyde Park. "I think you'll agree when you think it over. It's short and to the point." FDR didn't offer to read the statement, and Farley wouldn't actually see its contents until he got to the hall. Once he did, he quickly concluded that indeed it was not what they had agreed to at their meeting at Hyde Park. "Apparently the President did not want me to know what was in it, because in our conversations at Hyde Park the last word I had with him was when he said he would surely get the letter to me personally." FDR's call had obviously done nothing to assuage Farley's bitterness.[13]

As the delegates assembled in the hall for the Tuesday evening session they anticipated hearing a rip-roaring, tub-thumping speech by Alben Barkley, the Kentuckian who led the Democrats in the U.S. Senate, a close friend and ally of the president's and his choice to be the permanent chairman of the convention, which position he was now assuming. Farley spoke for many others when he observed that Barkley was "a born orator of the Southern tradition" and, more than that, "one of the best orators of our time." Barkley did not disappoint, although, as usual, he took his time getting wound up to full throttle. About fourteen minutes into his oration, he mentioned Roosevelt's name in passing, sparking a spontaneous demonstration. The floor filled with pro-FDR marchers, which threatened to throw off the "real" demonstration that was planned to "draft" Roosevelt following Barkley's reading of his statement. But not everyone had gotten the message, and Roosevelt's supporters wrestled for state standards to join the parade as cheers rang out from the galleries. The official organist was one of those who didn't get the message as he "whooped it up" by blaring out the popular tune "Franklin D. Roosevelt Jones" (a popular tune of

1938 from *Babes on Broadway* that was enlisted as a campaign anthem). As delegates marched in a "joyous snake dance" past the platform where Farley was seated, the chairman said his "eyes popped in surprise," for there, hopping along with them, was Undersecretary of State Sumner Welles, normally very "impeccable." "I could have been no more surprised if General MacArthur had trotted by in full dress uniform," he noted, and added that Welles didn't look all that happy. "He was going through the motions, but his wan smile was ample evidence that he wasn't really enjoying himself."[14]

Barkley, realizing his mention of the president's name had miscued nearly everyone, tried valiantly to bring the convention back to order. So eager were the Roosevelt supporters to demonstrate, order was restored only when Barkley called for a doctor to treat a woman who had been injured in the demonstration. He then resumed his speech, which quickly became a stem-winder of the old school, praising the New Deal and other accomplishments of the administration. As he spoke, Farley noticed that people with banners, which they kept rolled up, were beginning to fill the aisles, "shifting from foot to foot as the Barkley cadences rolled on."[15] As he had intended, his peroration reached its climax when he finally announced, with great dramatic effect, the revised message he had been given by Hopkins. "I and other close friends of the President have long known that he has no wish to be a candidate again. We know, too, that in no way whatsoever has he exerted any influence in the selection of delegates or upon the opinion of delegates." At the "specific request and authorization of the President," he now hoped to make "this simple fact clear to the Convention": "The President has never had, and has not today, any desire or purpose to continue in the office of President, to be a candidate for that office, or to be nominated by the Convention for that office. He wishes in all earnestness and sincerity to make it clear that all the delegates to this Convention are free to vote for any candidate. That is the message I bear to you from the President of the United States."[16]

For what seemed to many who were there like a very long time, the delegates sat in stunned silence as they tried to absorb the meaning of the message they had so eagerly awaited. Most of them had expected clarity; instead they had gotten more confusion and uncertainty. What were they supposed to think? What were they supposed to *do*? The pregnant quiet was finally broken by a "thundering" voice booming through the public address system, "We want Roosevelt!" As the chant from the mysterious voice continued, the demonstrators waiting in the aisles came to life, unfurled their banners, and began doing what they were there to do—demonstrate. Farley noticed that while most faces registered surprise, that of Chicago mayor Ed Kelly "beamed" as the galleries he had packed with friends emptied out to flood the aisles. One of the marchers yelled up as he passed the mayor's box, "Hey, Ed, we planned it that way!" For forty-five minutes the voice from the loudspeakers, loud enough to carry over the noise of the demonstration, exhorted the hall with "Chicago wants Roosevelt!" "The party wants Roosevelt!" "New York wants Roosevelt!" "The world wants Roosevelt!" "Illinois wants Roosevelt!" "America needs Roosevelt!" "Everybody wants Roosevelt!" All of it was accompanied by the band playing "Happy Days Are Here Again," the Roosevelt theme song from the 1932 convention, blended together into a cacophony of sounds that to those in the hall was overwhelming. And to most of them it was also exhilarating, as they at last realized why they were there and what they were supposed to do.[17]

An enterprising reporter, Warren Moscow of the *New York Times*, determined to identify the voice that had started the whole thing, found that it belonged to Thomas D. Garry, Chicago's superintendent of sewers, whom the mayor had placed in charge of the arena. His assignment had been to sit in the basement of the convention hall before a microphone connected to the loudspeakers upstairs, the one that looked like a beehive and which he had installed. When he got his cue, he was to start the chant that now echoed through the hall. Farley claimed later that during the demonstration, "a half dozen times [Garry] darted out of his basement cell to bask in Kelly's approval and to see the scene; then he would go back to his chant." He also claimed that the mayor himself had selected Garry for the task, which was undoubtedly true. "It was a job right up my alley," he told reporters with great pride the next day. "I figured out a lot of my own angles." So it was no surprise when Roosevelt's opponents labeled the incident "the voice from the sewers."[18]

The next morning's *Chicago Tribune* revealed that Frances Perkins had characteristically said publicly what no one else in Roosevelt's "official family" had dared to say: the president had "examined his conscience" and would certainly accept the convention's nomination.[19] The day's papers also revealed that columnists Alsop and Kintner were still on Hopkins's case. Observing that the first days of the convention had gone "horribly sour," they said that "the president's favorite crony" was receiving the blame for it from both pro- and anti-third-term advocates. The columnists had obviously used Farley as their source for the column, dutifully laying out in detail all of the chairman's laments on how unfairly he had been treated and faulting Hopkins's "amateurish efforts" for virtually all of it.[20]

Perkins again called Eleanor and pleaded with her to go to Chicago, saying her husband supported the idea. Eleanor responded, "Franklin may be willing, but how do I know how Jim Farley feels about it? I certainly am not going out there unless he invites me." She was aware that there was ill feeling between Hopkins and the Democratic chairman, and this was in part due to Hopkins not having been "very tactful." She was not going to do anything to make it worse. Perkins asked whether she would go if Farley wanted her to, and Eleanor replied that she would have to talk with her husband first. She did just that after she rang off from Perkins; she reported on the conversation and asked what he wanted her to do. Later she quoted her husband as saying, "It might be very nice for you to go, but I do not think it is in the least necessary." She replied, "If Jim Farley asks me to go, do you think it would be wise?" The president, she said, had replied, "Yes, I think it would be."[21]

When Farley reached the convention hall that afternoon he was told Mrs. Roosevelt was trying to call him. Reaching her at Hyde Park, he heard her say that Frances Perkins "insists that it is absolutely necessary that I come to Chicago," relating the bleak story the labor secretary had shared with her. "Frances doesn't like the look of things out there and feels that my appearance would do a lot to straighten things out. Now, I don't want to appear before the convention unless you think it is all right." As Farley recalled the conversation, he had given his blessing.

"Why, it's perfectly alright with me," Farley responded.

"Please, don't say so unless you really mean it."

"I do mean it and I'm not trying to be polite. I feel and mean what I am saying. Frankly, the situation is not good. Equally frankly, your coming will not affect my situation one way or the other. From the President's point of view I think it desirable, if not essential, that you come."

"Thanks, Jim. I appreciate this. I'll come."[22]

When the convention convened on Wednesday it first took up the platform and the foreign affairs plank that Roosevelt had spent so much time cobbling together in an effort to satisfy everyone and to protect his political flank. It was adopted without controversy before the session moved on to the main event of the evening: the nomination and seconding speeches of candidates for president and the roll call to follow. When the roll of the states was called for nominations, Alabama, as always, was first and announced that Senator Lister Hill would place Roosevelt's name before the convention. Robert Jackson had told Harold Ickes, who had finally decided to attend a session, that Hill was a "fine speaker," but Ickes was unimpressed. "He made a rotten speech," he recorded in his diary. Reflecting his own unhappiness with the convention, he added, "There wasn't a decent speech made that night and some were almost terrible." The obligatory demonstration for Roosevelt that followed Hill's desultory address seemed to reflect it; although it lasted for a half hour and was "a fair one of its kind," Ickes concluded that the crowd "had pretty well shouted itself out" the night before.[23]

When Arkansas was called on next for nominations, it deferred to Virginia, which announced that its senator, Carter Glass, would nominate James A. Farley. Glass was one of the most senior Democrats in the Senate and also one of the most conservative. He and Farley had developed a natural affinity, based in large part on their resentment of Roosevelt's imperious nature as well as their opposition to a third term and their shared conservatism. Although he was frail and apparently ill, Glass got out of his sickbed to come to Chicago to stand up for his friend and the issues he represented. Farley was deeply moved not only by Glass's appearance but even more by the fact that, at last, his name was being placed in nomination for the presidency of the United States. He had had a number of thrills in politics, he later concluded. "But that night in the dingy old stadium office"—which was where he listened to the proceedings—"all previous thrills paled into insignificance . . . Tears came to my eyes and spilled over."[24] Harold Ickes had a very different reaction to the same moment, calling both the Glass speech and the Farley demonstration that followed "pitiful."[25]

After similarly unmemorable speeches and demonstrations for Garner and Senator Millard Tydings of Maryland (whom FDR had tried, unsuccessfully, to purge in 1938), it was time for the delegates to cast their ballots. The outcome was never in doubt, and the final tally revealed the expected and overwhelming preference for Roosevelt, whose total came to 946, with Farley trailing far behind with 72 and Garner with 61. Farley, who would be forever loyal to the party if not to the president, moved that the nomination be made unanimous.

The president had successfully overcome the first major barrier to a third term, though it was not by the unanimous vote that he had hoped for, nor with the unbridled enthusiasm that had greeted his candidacies in 1932 and 1936. The surliness and frustration of the delegates had been largely contained but had not disappeared, at least to the eye of William Allen White, the staunch Republican from Kansas who was FDR's great ally in arguing for all-out aid to Britain but who was in Chicago as a syndicated columnist. The president's message to the delegates, he wrote, "did not in the least clarify the situation, did not at all remove the depressed confusion which one felt here among all the delegates. Mr. Roosevelt's ardent supporters were on the defensive even though they were in the majority."[26] The "depressed confusion" would not only hang like a dark cloud over Chicago. The next day it would find its voice and nearly upend the convention—and the Democratic Party.

12

Chicago
Unscripted

The events of Thursday, July 18, the final day of the convention, flowed directly from a conversation the president had late the night before with Chicago mayor Ed Kelly, who had called to report on the evening in the convention hall, in which he had proudly played no small part. Everyone had left the Oval Study except Sam Rosenman, whom Roosevelt asked to stay behind. When the conversation turned to the vice presidency, Rosenman heard FDR say for the first time that he favored Henry Wallace and gathered from his boss's expression that the name "was not too enthusiastically received by the Mayor."[1]

In Chicago, Wallace's longtime aide Paul Appleby found his boss "bleary-eyed" at seven-thirty that morning in his hotel suite working on an acceptance speech. "Shake hands with the vice president," Wallace said. Knowing there were a number of other serious aspirants for the honor at the convention and that Wallace's name was certain to stir opposition, they decided that their best strategy was to persuade the president to call a half dozen of those who were bound to be disappointed and to "soothe any bruised feelings." Among the prospective candidates were men of considerable standing in the party, including Senators Jimmy Byrnes and Burton Wheeler, Paul McNutt, Jesse Jones, Sam Rayburn, Louis Johnson, and William Bankhead, among others. The president flatly rejected the suggestion that he call them and indicated that Wallace and Hopkins would have to make the calls.[2]

Meanwhile, as Mayor Kelly passed on his conversation with the president, news of the Wallace choice spread quickly through the hotels and bars of Chicago, wherever delegates and reporters were gathered, and almost nowhere was it received as good news. Frustration with Roosevelt's aloofness from the convention in many cases turned to anger when delegates realized they were being asked to nominate someone who had only recently been a Republican, yet whom conservatives in the party saw as another liberal New Dealer; many of those conservatives thought the ticket should be balanced with one of their own. Most delegates, and certainly the local party leaders, still saw the vice presidential nomination as the prerogative of the convention itself. FDR was now changing that tradition, as he had changed others.

The delegates had dutifully followed his wishes in "drafting" him the night before, but now the president was trying to strip them of their traditional right. They had been prepared to be a rubber stamp where his own renomination was concerned, in part because they had no other real choice. Now they had a choice and many, especially the conservatives, were determined to exercise it. Roosevelt may have been their leader, but more than a few now saw him anew as arrogant and imperious.

Hopkins called Rosenman early that morning to ask whether reports of the Wallace selection were accurate. When the speechwriter confirmed that they were, Hopkins, who knew he was about to have a very bad day, replied, "There's going to be a hell of a lot of opposition. So far there must be at least ten candidates who have more votes than Wallace. It'll be a cat-and-dog fight, but I think the Boss has enough friends here to put it over." The president was unsurprised when Rosenman interrupted his breakfast to relay his conversation with Hopkins. "Well," he said, "I suppose the conservatives in America are going to bring pressure on the convention to beat Henry.

The fellow they want is either Jesse [Jones] or [William] Bankhead. I'm going to tell them I won't run with either of those men or with any other reactionary—I've told them that before and I'll tell them again." Then, as Rosenman recalled, the president's face and voice took on a grim quality, and he articulated a thought that was apparently just forming in his mind: "I won't deliver that acceptance speech until we see whom they nominate."[3]

Roosevelt and Farley spoke early in the morning—Rosenman claimed Farley placed the call, Farley maintained that FDR did. In any case, the president said that he had settled on Wallace as "the best man to nominate in this emergency." Farley replied that he intended to support Jesse Jones, and Roosevelt responded that he didn't believe Jones was in good health and that he needed someone to "carry on" if something should happen to him. Farley disagreed and continued to press the case for Jones while the president did the same for Wallace. Farley went to some lengths to express his "extremely high regard" for Wallace but said that "people look on him as a mystic, and I think you'll regret it," signaling his conviction that Wallace's beliefs—and history with the "guru" Nicholas Roerich—would become a serious campaign issue. Rosenman heard the president respond, "Jim, Henry's not a mystic, he's a philosopher, a liberal philosopher, and I'm sure he'll be all right." The chairman answered, "This is your party, Mr. President, and it is up to you to select the man you want to ride along with you." Rosenman concluded that Farley was "quite aroused" because the call ended abruptly.[4]

Calls continued to pour into the Oval Study from Chicago, most of them expressing concern, including one more from Frances Perkins, who reported on the preparations for Eleanor's visit and then said there was "a fight coming" over the vice presidential nomination. A little later the president was reading a newspaper and came across a picture of Perkins and Farley "in a closely whispered conversation." He laughed, called for Grace Tully, and dictated a note to the labor secretary: "After all these years I believed that I could let you go to Chicago without a chaperone. You really must not let the camera men catch you when you are so truly coy!"

It was proving to be as bad a day for Roosevelt in Washington as it was for Hopkins in Chicago. The president still found amusing a telegram he received that morning from Ickes, recommending that he select Robert

Hutchins, the chancellor of the University of Chicago, as his vice president. After making the case for him, Ickes added, "I say also that if Hutchins does not appeal to you, I would feel honored to be considered as your running mate."[5] "Dear old Harold," the president chuckled as he read it. "He'd get fewer votes even than Wallace in that convention."[6]

More calls from Chicago arrived in the Oval Study during the afternoon. Speaker Bankhead, angry that he had been passed over for the vice presidency, spoke "very sharply" with the president, failing to understand how the liberal Wallace—"never an organization Democrat"—could have been selected over him. Jimmy Byrnes, another disappointed aspirant, also called and argued with the president over the choice of Wallace. FDR genuinely liked the South Carolinian and expressed "great personal regret" to Byrnes that he couldn't go along with him, "for reasons with which he said he knew Byrnes was familiar," according to Rosenman. The president stressed that he had given the matter much thought, he was sure that Wallace was the best candidate, and he hoped that he would be nominated. Seeing that he wasn't going to change Roosevelt's mind, Byrnes said he would "go down the line for his candidate and would try to put him over," but he wasn't positive it could be done. Listening to FDR's end of the conversation, Rosenman concluded that the president was beginning to worry about what would happen at the convention that night.[7]

Jim Farley went to the airfield late that afternoon to meet the plane carrying Eleanor and Franklin junior. After a brief interview with reporters, they drove into town with Farley pouring out his woes: the president had not talked with him since the convention began and had never told him who his choice for vice president would be (in fact, they had spoken three times, including once that morning). Eleanor, who was, as we've seen, genuinely fond of Farley, was appalled that things had come to this point between him and the president. Turning to the vice presidency, the chairman made his now familiar case against Wallace and for the selection of a "real Democrat." Eleanor insisted that it was essential for him to speak with her husband, and they stopped at Farley's hotel, where she placed the call. She relayed the car conversation to FDR and suggested "he talk with him and tell him how he felt." Farley would later say that Eleanor "agreed" with him on the matter of the vice presidency and in particular that Jesse Jones would be a better choice. She strongly disputed that assertion in her own account of the day. "I expressed no preference for any candidate," she maintained. The account Farley had given in his book, an account that paralleled his contemporaneous memorandum of the conversation, was merely his "impression of what I said rather than what I actually said." "I never expressed a preference or an opinion on matters of this kind," reiterated Eleanor, "and I am sure I did not change my habits on this occasion."

At the hotel, after speaking with her husband, Eleanor then handed the phone to Farley, who argued—"rather halfheartedly," remembered the First Lady—when the president told him, again, why he wanted Wallace. After a few minutes of back-and-forth, Farley said (according to his own account of the conversation) that he would vote for Jones if he ran, otherwise for Bankhead, because the Democrats wanted a "real Democrat." Realizing that Roosevelt was adamant on the subject, he began to give way: "I proceed upon the theory the Presidential nominee of a party has some right to select his own Vice Presidential nominee." Again, Eleanor later gave a different account, reporting that after arguing the point with the president, Farley said, "You're the boss. If you say so I will do all I can to nominate Wallace, but I will have to work fast." Eleanor and Farley may very well have been fond of each other, but on this day at least they were using different scripts.[8]

They reached the convention hall, and soon it was time for Eleanor to address the delegates, which was why she had come; however, she hadn't any prepared remarks except for a few notes. "I made up my mind that what I said would be brief," she recounted later. "I decided to base my short speech on the conversation I had heard in the hotel. If Franklin felt that the strain of a third term might be too much for any man and that Mr. Wallace was the man who could carry on best in times such as we are facing, he was entitled to have his help; no one should think of himself but only of the job that might have to be done."[9]

When the woman universally admired by Democrats of all stripes stepped to the podium to deliver her brief message, the convention hall went totally quiet. The delegates on the floor and the visitors in the galleries listened with rapt attention to the case that she was making openly and honestly for Wallace, without mentioning his name. She was known to them as a truth-teller, and whatever their views on the matter at hand, they listened respectfully. Whoever became president, she said, would face "a heavier responsibility, perhaps, than any man has ever faced before in this country . . . You cannot treat it as you would an ordinary nomination in an ordinary time." Her message was that by nominating her husband each delegate had assumed a "grave responsibility," and that now the delegates had to rise above partisanship. "No man who is a candidate or who is President can carry this situation alone. This is only carried by a united people who love their country."[10]

It was immediately clear as soon as she finished that her presence and her words had had an effect. "She has done more to soothe the convention bruises than all the efforts of the astute Senators," the New York *Daily News* would intone the next day.[11] Candidates for the vice presidency who hadn't already withdrawn during the morning did so now, led by Paul McNutt, the former Indiana governor who had considerable support in the hall and who the Roosevelt forces believed had the best chance of "stampeding the convention against Wallace," according to Rosenman.[12]

All withdrew, that is, except Bankhead, who remained bitter. Meanwhile, Hopkins and Byrnes frantically worked the floor, pleading with delegations to go along with the president. To strengthen his case with wavering delegates, Byrnes called the White House and got FDR's permission to repeat his threat to reject his own nomination if Wallace wasn't selected as his running mate. "For God's sake," Byrnes shouted to delegates, "do you want a President or a Vice President?"[13] Hopkins would later tell Roosevelt and Rosenman that Byrnes "had performed as he had promised." "It was," added Hopkins, "a fine display of political loyalty."[14]

Back at the White House, Roosevelt had gathered once again in the Oval Study this evening with an "unusually large crowd" that included Rosenman, Pa Watson, Ross McIntire, Steve Early, Missy LeHand, and Grace Tully in addition to several others. The president liked to have people around even—and perhaps especially—when the situation was tense. The scene there was getting very tense indeed, and it did not help that the midsummer Washington heat and humidity in the un-air-conditioned room made the atmosphere stifling. The president was seated at a card table, simultaneously listening to the convention proceedings on the radio and playing a game of solitaire. The tension rose when everyone heard the convention resume its boisterous and contentious tenor following Eleanor's address. Every time Wallace's name was mentioned, a chorus of boos would ring out from the floor and the galleries, countered by cheers whenever Bankhead's name came up. It was a two-man contest now, and the lines were clearly drawn. FDR's preference was known, but the residual resentment toward him and the New Dealers was the driving force behind Bankhead's candidacy. Everyone, including the president, knew that and took it very seriously.[15]

Since Hopkins was not a delegate, he had gained admittance to the convention floor to work the delegates only after being designated a deputy sergeant at arms by Mayor Kelly. Rushing from one place to another, he was, remembered Rosenman, "feverishly telephoning the White House from minute to minute while the radio in the president's study blared forth the raucous expressions of discord." At one point an impassioned delegate shouted into the microphone, "Just because the Republicans have nominated an apostate Democrat, let us not for God's sake nominate an apostate Republican."[16]

Wallace's biographers John Culver and John Hyde characterized the scene in the convention hall as "something close to a mob mentality." The boos and hisses for Wallace contrasted sharply with the thunderous approval for his opponent. Wallace seemed stunned by it all. Frances Perkins saw "agony" in his face as well as "utter, blank suffering." She had never witnessed anything quite like it.[17] Eleanor was seated next to Wallace's wife, Ilo, during all this, and reached over and took her hand. "Why do you suppose they are so opposed to Henry?" Mrs. Wallace asked.[18] Eleanor didn't answer the question. Later Harold Ickes did. He did not believe that the anti-Wallace catcalls were about Wallace personally; rather, he thought, they were about the manner in which the whole thing had been handled. "The President, in my judgment, mishandled this whole convention and he was particularly inept with respect to the Vice Presidential nomination."[19]

Rosenman heard the nominating and seconding speeches for Bankhead as "quite bitter" and the tenor of the proceedings as increasingly "acrimonious." Radio commentary "made it clear that a strong revolt was developing against the nomination of Wallace."[20]

Finally the roll call of the states began. Bankhead jumped to an early lead, largely because southern and other conservative states were among the first delegations asked to report. The president, clearly agitated, put aside his game of solitaire and asked Missy for a pencil and notepad. No one in the room had any idea what he was doing. They had to resist the temptation to sneak a look over his shoulder as he wrote out five pages in total silence. When he finished, he turned to Rosenman and said, "Sam, take this inside and go to work on it; smooth it out and get it ready for delivery. I may have to deliver it very quickly, so please hurry it up." He calmly resumed his game of solitaire.[21]

Rosenman took the papers and left the room, followed by Missy and Watson. He sat down at a desk outside the study and began to read, with his two colleagues leaning over his shoulder. It was a message addressed to the convention, which Roosevelt obviously intended to deliver if Wallace lost. It laid out the Democratic Party's historic role as "the champion of progressive and liberal policies and principles" but then cited its failure whenever it had been "controlled by interests which think in terms of dollars instead of in terms of human values." That was the fundamental issue dividing the party, and FDR could not in honor go along with it. It "would be best for America to have the fight out," and therefore he was declining the nomination.

Missy, who despite her loyalty to the president had consistently opposed a third term, said, "Fine, I'm glad," and returned to the Oval Study. Pa Watson had the opposite reaction. "Sam," he said, "give that damned paper to me—let's tear it up." At first Rosenman thought he was joking, but soon saw that he was completely serious. Watson, with what Rosenman saw as "a religious fervor," argued that the president would regret it in the morning. No one could care less who was going to be vice president. "The only thing that's important to this country is that fellow in there. There isn't anyone in the United States who can lead this nation for the next four years as well as he can." Rosenman replied that he hoped the president would never have to read the statement. He told Watson that he was also convinced that if Bankhead got the nomination, Roosevelt would read it, "and nobody on earth is going to stop him." Rosenman knew as well that this was not a sudden impulse on Roosevelt's part. He had seen the idea take form over breakfast that morning when he had told the president of the serious trouble developing in Chicago over the Wallace choice; he had since authorized Byrnes to use the threat in persuading delegates to go along with that choice.[22]

Roosevelt, having decided to run, had determined to do so on his terms. That meant, among other things, having a vice president of his own choosing. But his draft statement was also a reversion to the mind-set of 1938's attempted purge of conservative congressional Democrats, when he had sought to purify the party ideologically. It was a strong but infrequently articulated tenet of his political philosophy that the Democratic Party should be the party of liberalism, and he had recently come to believe it should be the party of internationalism as well. FDR was now in a position to leverage his dominance of the Democratic Party to cement those goals. The party needed him desperately at this moment—there was no one else—and he knew it; he was willing to gamble *everything* to have his way. As often was the case with Roosevelt, stubbornness bordered on arrogance, and the arrogance sometimes on hubris. He was used to having his way, and he would have it here or he would go home, as he had originally planned to do. Given all this, what was, and remains, hard to grasp is his willingness to risk not only his New Deal legacy but also his deeply principled policy of all-out aid to now imperiled Britain if he didn't get his way on an office that most Americans saw as insignificant—the "bucket of warm piss," as Garner had described it. Pa Watson had been right about that perception. The moment revealed the paradox that was Roosevelt at times, when stubbornly adhering to a smaller matter of principle could stand in the way of achieving a much greater one. Probably no episode of his presidency captured it better than this one. His overreach in both the Court-packing plan of 1937 and the attempted purge of 1938 bore many of the same characteristics, but neither of those potentially threatened his entire presidency as this one did.

Rosenman took the paper into his air-conditioned room across the hall and did what he did best: he took the president's sentiments and faithfully embodied them in words, using as much of the original as possible because Roosevelt, too, had a feel for language, and changing too much would risk losing the intention that lay behind his choice of words and phrases. When he thought the message was ready for public consumption, he returned to the study—it had only been ten or fifteen minutes—where the president was still playing solitaire. The others were standing around in small groups and discussing the situation. "Missy was all smiles, saying that the President was doing the only thing he could do," Rosenman recalled. "Pa Watson was almost in tears, and looked up at me angrily for bringing the sheets back." Everyone apart from Missy LeHand was opposed to this course and trying to convince the president to change it. "But if I ever saw him with his mind made up it was that night."[23]

The president copied most of Rosenman's suggestions onto the typewritten copy of his original draft and added a new paragraph of his own. The speechwriter took the document back to his room and reworked it again before returning it to the president. After reading it over, Roosevelt said, "This will do; don't bother to retype it. I'll read it like this." Then he returned once more to his game of solitaire. The final draft, which probably represented the most accurate explication of his mind at this point, read as follows:

MEMBERS OF THE CONVENTION:

In the century in which we live, the Democratic Party has received the support of the electorate only when the party, with absolute clarity, has been the champion of progressive and liberal policies and principles of government.

The party has failed consistently when through political trading and chicanery it has fallen into the control of those interests, personal and financial, which think in terms of dollars instead of in terms of human values.

The Republican Party has made its nomination this year at the dictation of those who, we all know, place money ahead of human progress.

The Democratic Convention, as appears clear from the events of today, is divided on this fundamental issue. Until the Democratic Party through this Convention makes overwhelmingly clear its stand in favor of social progress and liberalism, and shakes off *all* the shackles of control fastened upon it by the force of conservatism, reaction and appeasement, it will not continue its march to victory.

It is without question that certain political influences pledged to reaction in domestic affairs and to appeasement in foreign affairs have been busily engaged behind the scenes in the promotion of discord since the Convention convened.

Under those circumstances, I cannot, in all honor, and will not, merely for political expediency, go along with the cheap bargaining and political maneuvering which have brought about party dissension in this Convention.

It is best not to straddle ideals.

In these days of danger when democracy must be more than vigilant, there can be no connivance with the kind of politics which has internally weakened nations abroad before the enemy has struck from without.

It is best for America to have the fight out here and now.

I wish to give the Democratic Party the opportunity to make its historic decision clearly and without equivocation. The party must go wholly one way or wholly the other. It cannot face in both directions at the same time.

By declining the honor of the nomination for the Presidency, I can restore that opportunity to the Convention. I so do.[24]

By any measure this has to be considered one of the most remarkable documents in American political history, and it had the ring of history built into it. When he said the Democratic Party "must go wholly one way or wholly the other," at least one biographer has noted that he was echoing Lincoln's "House Divided" speech on slavery.[25] Written and approved at a moment when it appeared likely that Bankhead would be nominated, it was using that eventuality as a watershed. While we will never know what FDR would have done had that happened, his state of mind and his behavior up to this point give every indication that he would have delivered the remarks to the convention precisely as written. So did his lifelong practice of decision making: he almost never changed his mind once it was made up. He had already made two highly controversial decisions leading up to this convention—to release his delegates and to select Wallace as his running mate—and he never seriously reconsidered either one once it was made. The decision to decline the nomination if Wallace was rejected was of a piece with these other two, reinforced as they all were by Roosevelt's determination to seek reelection on his own terms.

In a larger sense the decision was also of a piece with his failed efforts to pack the Supreme Court and to purge recalcitrant Democratic senators and congressmen who had opposed his policies. There had been, to his mind, a fundamental principle at issue in both of these efforts: the purpose of Democratic government was the enactment of progressive policies, and that could happen only if the Democratic Party was a party of unalloyed liberalism. Ideological consistency if not purity in the Democratic Party had been a long-held tenet of Roosevelt's and, as this incident demonstrates, it went deep into his political soul. Making the outcome of the Wallace decision so consequential can also be seen as a way, perhaps even a proxy, for the manner in which FDR had achieved his party's nomination for a third term. He had been, as we have seen, highly manipulative and at times duplicitous in preempting the field so that he would have the option, which he finally took, of running again. By risking everything on a matter of fundamental principle, he was in a way absolving himself of the "political chicanery" that he now saw in his adversaries; he was running for office for the loftiest of reasons and not for personal gain. In the process, of course, Roosevelt was trying to have it both ways—he was willing to select what a later generation might call the "nuclear option" to get his way on Wallace by couching it in principled terms that had the added benefit of obscuring his own behavior. Again, FDR was trying to achieve his goals by indirection. As Frances Perkins and many others have observed, he was a very complicated man.

Rosenman had watched FDR make decisions since their early days together in Albany. "I was amazed that he never seemed to worry," the speechwriter recalled. "Having come to a decision, he would dismiss it from his mind as finished business. He never went back to it to worry about whether his decision was right." At one point the president explained the process to him: "Once you've made a decision, there's no use worrying about whether you were right or wrong. Events will soon prove whether you were right or wrong, and if there is still time you can change your decision. You and I know people who wear out carpets walking up and down worrying whether they have decided something correctly. Do the very best you can in making up your mind, but once your mind is made up go ahead."[26]

Back in Chicago Wallace surprised nearly everyone when he eventually pulled ahead of Bankhead and barely secured the nomination with 627 votes out of the 1,100 cast. Farley attributed the outcome to Eleanor: "There is no doubt in my mind that Mrs. Roosevelt's appearance before the convention saved the nomination for Secretary Wallace."[27] No one offered the traditional motion to make the nomination unanimous; virtually everyone knew that it was not and never would be a unanimous choice, and everyone was spared an embarrassment by the omission. Similarly, Wallace, who had worked hard on his acceptance speech, was almost certainly spared more boos and hisses when Byrnes persuaded him not to attempt to deliver it.[28]

As soon as Wallace's nomination had been secured, Eleanor left the convention hall and headed for the airport. As her plane was taxiing on the runway, it was waved back to the gate for the First Lady to receive a call from the president. "He told me that he had listened to my speech and that I had done a very good job." Hopkins was waiting on another line "and he said practically the same thing." When Hopkins conceded that he had made mistakes during the convention, she replied, "You young things don't know politics." She then dashed back to the airplane for her nighttime flight back to New York.[29]

Though both Roosevelt and Hopkins thought she had done "a very good job" in Chicago, neither they nor anyone else ever fully acknowledged the critical, indeed decisive role that Eleanor and Frances Perkins played to keep the convention from unraveling completely. It was a time when women weren't expected, or even permitted, to play an important role in politics, and if they should unexpectedly do so, it wasn't a time when men were inclined to credit them for it. Each of these women was in the process of making history in her individual role, Eleanor breaking the traditional mold of First Ladies by using her talents to further her husband's goals, Frances Perkins the first woman in any president's cabinet and one, not incidentally, who was advocating tirelessly for the interests of working men and women. It would be years yet before other women would be serious players in American politics (Republican Clare Boothe Luce would be one of the next to do so) and decades before they would do so regularly and in large numbers. Their political involvement would inevitably grow as American society evolved, but what these two women did in Chicago in 1940 gave it all an important impetus.

Before the acceptance speech could be delivered, the deliverer would have to refresh himself. FDR looked "weary and bedraggled," according to Rosenman, while his shirt "was wilted from the intense heat of the Oval Room and he generally needed a freshening up." Wheeled to his bedroom, he washed, changed his shirt, combed his hair, and returned, remembered Rosenman, "looking his usual, jaunty, imperturbable self." Roosevelt and his entourage went downstairs to the diplomatic reception room on the ground floor, where he quickly shed his suit coat; the speech would be broadcast by a shirtsleeved president simultaneously to the convention and to radio stations around the country and the world. Rosenman looked around the room of Roosevelt's friends and noted that all were "happy and smiling except one." Missy LeHand, he noted, was "in tears."[30] For a brief moment it had appeared that Missy's dream of retiring to Hyde Park, where she could care for this man she loved, would come true, but the moment was soon gone.

The president, Rosenman recalled later, had been working on a public pronouncement about his feelings about a third term, and in general the conflict between "deep personal desire for retirement on the one hand, and that quiet, invisible thing called 'conscience' on the other.'" Rosenman added that FDR was aware that his motives in accepting the nomination would be "misconstrued" by some, and that in the end, whatever the combination of elements that had gone into his decision to run again, he would have to trust to "the good faith and common sense of the American people to accept my own good faith—and do their own interpreting." However, before leaving matters to that trust, he needed to situate the context for his own intentions, and they directly related to the war in Europe. In doing so, he would follow MacLeish's advice to explain his "failure to declare himself sooner."

When the conflict first broke out last September, it was still my intention to announce clearly and simply, at an early date, that under no conditions would I accept reelection. . . .

It soon became evident, however, that such a public statement on my part would be unwise from the point of view of sheer public duty. . . .

Every day that passed called for the postponement of personal plans and partisan debate until the latest possible moment. The normal conditions under which I would have made public declaration of my personal desires were wholly gone.

And so, thinking solely of the national good and of the international scene, I came to the reluctant conclusion that such a declaration should not be made before the national Convention. It was accordingly made to you within an hour after the permanent organization of this Convention. . . .

Lying awake, as I have, on many nights, I have asked myself whether I have the right, as Commander-in-Chief of the Army and Navy, to call on men and women to serve their country, or to train themselves to serve and, at the same time, decline to serve my country in my own personal capacity, if I am called upon to do so by the people of my country. . . .

The right to make that call rests with the people through the American method of a free election. Only the people themselves can draft a President. If such a draft should be made upon me, I say to you, in the utmost simplicity, I will, with God's help, continue to serve with the best of my ability and with the fullness of my strength.

One observer in the convention hall noted that the delegates, whom he characterized as "jaded and scarcely happy" after hours of political contention, sat "intently quiet" while Roosevelt explained why he was shattering a time-honored American tradition in the name of a greater tradition.[31] The president then left what Rosenman called the "personal side," where he had closely followed MacLeish's rationale and even used some of his language, to make it "unmistakably clear that he would continue full blast" his policy of helping Britain to resist Hitler and all that Hitler stood for:

> I would not undo, if I could, the efforts to prevent war. . . . I do not now soften the condemnation expressed by Secretary Hull and myself from time to time for the acts of aggression that have wiped out ancient liberty-loving, peace-pursuing countries. . . . I do not recant the sentiments of sympathy with all free peoples resisting such aggression, or begrudge the material aid that we have given to them. I do not regret my consistent endeavor to awaken this country to the menace for us and for all we hold dear. . . . As long as I am President, I will do all I can to ensure that that foreign policy remains our foreign policy.

Roosevelt concluded that because of the emergency he would not have either "the time or the desire" to actively campaign for reelection, although he shrewdly—and unsurprisingly—left himself some room to maneuver. "I shall never be loath to call the attention of the nation to deliberate or unwitting falsifications of fact, which are sometimes made by political candidates."[32]

Most of the delegates in Chicago were relieved to see this convention come to an end. They were eager to get home. The journalists, at least, couldn't leave before rendering judgment on the drama they had witnessed. A good many were predictably unkind to the president and especially to his motives. Conservative columnist David Lawrence argued that it was not believable that the so-called draft could have occurred without Roosevelt's knowledge, since members of his cabinet had been working overtime to bring it about. The isolationist and equally conservative *Chicago Tribune* editorialized that throughout his second term Roosevelt "was determined to have the third if he could get it. He knew that the judgment of the country would be against him unless the nation could be thrown into a state of great alarm and worked into a sense of great national emergency."[33]

Alsop and Kintner called the convention "grimly depressing" and continued to heap scorn on Harry Hopkins. But this time they put the president himself directly in their sights, attributing the anti-Wallace revolt to resentment against FDR's undoubted influence—or lack thereof—on the proceedings in Chicago. "The behavior of the delegates had something in it of tenantry who know their farms have been thatched and painted and their children schooled and fed at the expense of the squire, but who will burn down the squire's hall if they have a chance."[34]

By trying to have it both ways—secretly plotting a "draft" but failing to give the effort direction—Roosevelt achieved his primary goal of renomination, but he paid a large price in the confusion of the convention and the resentment it caused among the party faithful. The unhappiness of the delegates had never been a big concern for Roosevelt, of course; his attention was focused on the general election and the need for a story line that included a genuine "draft" that could help him transcend the third-term issue with the electorate. The deception served to deepen the cynicism of his critics, which was to be expected. However, it also angered more sympathetic observers, many of whom were in Chicago. Was the deception necessary in order for him to achieve his objectives? Probably not. His renomination was ensured under virtually any scenario, and he almost certainly allowed his stubbornness—read arrogance—to cloud his usually acute political instincts. There were ways to deal with the complex issues of a third term by being more open and transparent, perhaps even flying to Chicago to rally his troops, as he had in 1932. He firmly rejected them all as he charted his course according to his own designs.

There was no one like Louis Howe to call him a "damned fool" when he was too full of himself and on the verge of making a big mistake—and to whom he would listen. This failure to invite and accept candor and to weigh it honestly, reinforced by the intimidating nature of the presidency to anyone but the president himself, was, and remains, the curse of the office. In this instance at least FDR did nothing to remedy it. As usual, Eleanor understood the phenomenon better than anyone. She recalled how often she had seen people heading into the Oval Office to tell her husband how strongly they disagreed with him "in no uncertain terms." When they emerged, she noted, "they usually looked at me blandly and behaved as though they never had disagreed at all." The question is whether this results from the office or depends upon its tenant. To Eleanor, it was both; she attributed the change partly to "the effect of Franklin's personality" and partly to "the person's awe of the office itself." She reflected that he invariably listened patiently to advice that was offered but that in the end, she concluded, "I have never known anyone less really influenced by others."[35]

Ernest K. Lindley of the *Washington Post* was astounded by the risks Roosevelt assumed in seeking a third term—the risk of losing, the risk of winning narrowly without a mandate, the risk to his prestige, the risk to his health. "Only a man of supreme daring and disregard for himself could have assented to a third nomination," he noted. The more one focused on the risks involved, he wrote, the clearer it became, at least to Lindley, that Roosevelt had not initially set out to win the nomination for himself. What he intended was "to control the convention" for the purpose of nominating a worthy successor, one who would be "loyal to his policies. To do that he had to let his name be used to corral delegates." Lindley came closer to the historical truth about FDR's intentions in this regard than most of his journalistic colleagues.[36] He suggested the complex ways in which the president had determined that he had both nothing to lose and everything to lose.

As for Roosevelt's observations on the convention, as usual he didn't spend much time looking back, though he did offer some views to his good friend George Norris, the progressive Republican senator from Nebraska who had urged him early on to seek another term. Responding to Norris's message of congratulations, Roosevelt told him that a week before the convention he "wrote out in longhand a letter to you which . . . carried essentially the same thoughts" as his acceptance speech. But, he went on, the letter was never sent; "all of the more liberal leaders" had pleaded with him not to send it, since the "old line conservative element" had acquired a larger-than-expected hold on the convention. "I was, frankly, amazed by the terrific drive which was put on by the old-line conservatives to make so many things adverse to liberalism occur that I would have to decline and disassociate myself from anything further to do with the restoration of control to the conservative element." Joining them, he added, was what he and Norris had called "The Hater's Club"—those who had opposed him in 1932, who were heartened by the midterm election of 1938, and who thought this convention would give them a fighting chance to put control of the Democratic Party back where it had been in 1920, 1924, and 1928. "On the nomination of Wallace they made their final stand. They were sure to be beaten by a fairly small margin, but their stupidity in making a violent issue out of Wallace will cost the ticket a great many votes this Autumn."[37]

From Roosevelt's perspective, this was what it had been all about when a few days earlier he had left his game of solitaire and drafted a statement declining the party's nomination, to be released if Wallace was denied the vice presidential nomination. Rightly or wrongly, for him the soul of the Democratic Party was at stake. He was so determined to prevent its return to its more conservative roots, which Bankhead represented, that he was prepared to decline its nomination and bring chaos down on the party. He was less prepared to concede that his method of bringing on that show-down, a combination of stubbornness and brinksmanship, had contributed significantly to the turmoil of the convention and to nearly derailing what he most hoped to accomplish at it.[38]

At the same time, Roosevelt was looking at the world—the world be-yond Chicago, of course, but especially the world beyond the United States—in ways that almost no one else was. He knew that America's des-tiny was about to become linked with events abroad, and that realization provided yet another, and indeed larger, lens through which he saw and affected the proceedings in Chicago. It was, after all, the reason he was seek-ing a third term.

13

Drafts and Destroyers

While the president and his people had been struggling to follow the renomination script in Chicago, Bill Donovan had spent the week in London scoping out Britain's preparedness and determination to fight Hitler. Initially Churchill's government was skeptical as to why they should pay attention to an Irish American Republican lawyer. But Lord Lothian, Britain's ambassador in Washington, was prompted by Frank Knox to persuade colleagues in London that Donovan was close to the navy secretary and could be influential on the matter of aid. As a result, official doors all over London swung open, including the big one at Buckingham Palace, which was the envoy's first stop. The king warmly received the American before showing him a three-day-old battle order from Hitler to his commanders, obviously intercepted, concerning the Führer's plans to destroy Britain. Donovan was meant to be impressed, and he was. Whatever his earlier assessments of Britain's intelligence capabilities, he raised them. Soon he was taken to the labyrinth of tunnels beneath Westminster that served to protect the prime minister and his war cabinet from the bombs falling daily on London. In what came to be called the War Rooms, Churchill, dressed in his signature siren suit, effectively filled the role he had been assigned to play, persuading Donovan that Britain would never surrender on his watch.

The American received detailed briefings from top generals and admirals as well as senior economists who gave estimates on industrial and agricultural production. He peppered them all with so many questions he had brought over from U.S. policy makers that seven men were assigned to write up the answers. He traveled outside of London to inspect airfields and naval facilities, and he was even given highly classified intelligence briefings, a rarity for foreigners. Churchill's own intelligence briefer, Stewart Menzies, sensing that Donovan was a kindred spirit, expressed the hope that the United States would establish an intelligence apparatus on the British model so that the two nations could collaborate. As events would reveal, he was speaking to receptive ears. (Donovan would soon become the godfather of the Office of Strategic Services, the predecessor of the CIA.)

The three-week courtship of "Wild Bill" Donovan had the desired effect. He had arrived in London already sympathetic to Britain's plight and predisposed to sending what the country needed to survive; everything he now saw and heard only strengthened that inclination. He told his hosts he would strongly recommend that the United States send the aid they were seeking, particularly military equipment to replace that lost at Dunkirk and—the prime minister's top priority—the destroyers Churchill had been asking for since May. Donovan believed that Britain could thwart a German attack, and he even volunteered a few bits of strategic advice on how they might do it. Needless to say, British officialdom was thrilled with this unlikely but very charismatic envoy and his support. Whitehall went so far as to suggest to the State Department that Donovan would be an ideal candidate to replace as ambassador the defeatist Joe Kennedy, whom this government loathed. But in the immediate term they wanted him back in Washington as soon as possible to deliver his message to the policy makers who mattered; they quickly put him on another flying boat, thoughtfully furnished with a bottle of champagne and a volume of Edmund Burke's speeches and writings.

In Washington Knox arranged for Donovan to brief members of the president's national security team, who were delighted to hear his optimistic appraisal of Britain's prospects and to see the fulsome responses to their questions. The navy secretary next arranged for the envoy to brief the president, and on August 9 the two of them joined Roosevelt on his train from Hyde Park to Portsmouth, New Hampshire, where he would inspect the navy yard before boarding the *Potomac* for a cruise to Boston. For a day and a half on land and at sea, Donovan attempted valiantly to get his message of optimism and aid to the ears of the president, which was not all that easy: when FDR wasn't engaging in long monologues, he was usually either fishing, reading the latest cables, or otherwise being interrupted by aides. The ever-confident Donovan persisted, unafraid to interrupt the president to make his points, principally that Britain had a very good prospect of surviving *if* it had the destroyers and other weaponry it was asking for.

FDR appeared to be convinced, but in his typical way he wanted the advocate to take his message to others who could help change public opinion. So Donovan soon trooped up to Capitol Hill to talk with key members of Congress and anyone else who would listen. Not long after that he addressed a national radio audience on the need to build up America's defenses to avoid the fate of those nations in Europe that had fallen under Germany's boot.

Bill Donovan came across as someone who appeared to know what he was talking about. This Republican was a genuine war hero whom no one could accuse of being a toady to Roosevelt, which made his message all the more salient. Frank Knox had done both the president and Britain a great service by enlisting him in the cause.[1]

※

Wendell Willkie had observed the proceedings in Chicago from the luxurious Broadmoor Hotel in Colorado Springs, where he spent six weeks, from July 9 to mid-August, recovering from the rigorous campaign trail he had been on as well as planning for the one he would resume in the fall. But rest would be hard to come by until he could get out from under a huge volume of phone calls and people wanting to see him. It was already the consensus of his advisors that the Willkie campaign had wasted time and lost momentum during its long stay in Colorado. "We let what was the hottest thing in the world get cold," one of them would conclude. Sam Pryor, Willkie's early supporter from Connecticut, put it more bluntly. "All the screwballs in the United States visited him while he was out there," he later told a friend. "He was mentally fagged out before the campaign started and didn't recover from it until the day he died."[2]

Willkie's opponent in the election was not only a more seasoned candidate but, more important, the incumbent president of the United States, and he therefore entered the contest with distinct advantages. His immediate post-convention strategy could not have been more different, stressing as it did his role of commander in chief rather than that of candidate. It was no coincidence that on the day that Willkie formally accepted the GOP nomination, the president reviewed nearly a hundred thousand officers and men in the First Army in upstate New York. And he made news that day when he met with Canadian prime minister Mackenzie King and announced plans for defense of the Western Hemisphere.

Wearing the cloak of commander in chief may have been the political strategy Roosevelt had settled on earlier, but now it was also demanded by events. The war in Europe, and particularly the threat to Great Britain, had escalated to such a dangerous level that it required his full attention. In particular, the staggering amounts of money authorized and appropriated by Congress, at the president's urging, had reached unprecedented levels. Following Hitler's May blitzkrieg in the west, FDR had dramatically increased his requests to Congress, and virtually all of them had been granted; by October the total amount in the defense pipeline came to more than $17 billion. The only way this money could be effectively and quickly spent to provide the weaponry necessary to arm an expanded American fighting force and to help Britain was by converting private industrial capacity to that purpose. He therefore enlisted such captains of industry as William Knudsen, the president of General Motors, and Edward Stettinius Jr., the board chairman of U.S. Steel, to the cause, persuading them to serve on the newly formed Council of National Defense. Each of the council members reported directly to the president. In keeping with his management style of long standing, he refused to delegate decision-making authority; as always, he kept that squarely in his own hands.

All of this money and effort was intended, of course, to arm and equip a military force that would be capable of dealing with the potential threats posed by an aggressive Hitler in Europe and an equally aggressive Japan in the Far East. Both the president and Congress envisioned that force to include an army of at least a million men, a credible two-ocean navy, and a modernized and greatly expanded air force. What was not envisioned anywhere, it seemed, was where the manpower would come from to operate such a force. The current rate of enlistments wouldn't come close to doing so, and few thought that was likely to change soon.

The only real option was a system of compulsory military training for young men of a certain age—in short, a draft. Given the decidedly mixed receptions to the draft systems imposed during the Civil War and the First World War, there was little appetite in the country currently for anything similar. The United States had never instituted a peacetime draft, and of course this was an election year and few, including the president, were prepared to get too far ahead of public opinion on the matter. Roosevelt had made mention of a "draft" in his recent acceptance speech to the Democratic National Convention, although it was in reference to his own decision to run for a third term. It is likely, however, given the way his mind worked, that his use of the term in that context was his way of introducing the more traditional concept of a draft into the public conversation. Having thought about the issue extensively and having proposed a huge expansion of the American military, he knew that a draft was the only way to deal with the manpower issue, and he privately supported its enactment. He also believed that his public endorsement of the idea would hurt the cause more than help it, a belief no doubt reinforced by his political caution in the midst of an election that he was convinced would be close. So, as was his practice, he kept quiet on the matter in hopes that events would compel public opinion to catch up with what he believed needed to be done.

Grenville Clark, who had been a Harvard classmate and fellow law clerk with FDR during his brief legal career and was now a senior partner in one of New York's most prestigious law firms, was among those who knew that a draft was the only way to prepare America for the emergency it faced. He had been among those to whom Roosevelt in 1907 had casually outlined

his political career, paralleling that of his uncle Ted, and at the time neither Clark nor his peers thought it implausible for him to think in terms
of the White House. Clark, who had only infrequently kept in touch with
Roosevelt, had in mind in early June using the relationship to further his
efforts to enact a draft. He and others of a similar mind, mostly from the
business and legal elite of New York, who frequented such places as the
Harvard Club and the Century Association, sought to rise above the politics of the moment to promote a policy they saw as essential to America's
security. They patterned their efforts after those of a similar group seeking
a draft before the First World War. They were essentially what later came to
be known as the eastern establishment—well-born, conservative, accomplished in their fields, and pro-British—and they expanded their ranks to
include such kindred spirits as Henry L. Stimson, Frank Knox, and William
J. Donovan. By anyone's standard they constituted a heavyweight group,
and it was Clark who, as chairman of the planning committee, provided the
impetus for the effort and who emerged as its leader.

In preparation for the first large meeting of the group, Clark wired the
president that its members were considering placing their energies behind
supporting "compulsory military training" and asked whether he thought
this was the right moment. Roosevelt responded two days later that he saw
no reason that Clark and his group should not advocate military training,
adding, however, that "if it is to be 'compulsory' I am inclined to think that
there is a very strong public opinion for universal service of some kind so
that every able-bodied man and woman would fit into his or her place."
Eleanor had been urging such a universal service program for some time,
and supporting it in this context served several of FDR's objectives, the
chief one being getting the idea of compulsory service of some kind into
the public debate.

Clark was sufficiently encouraged by the response to put before the
president three resolutions his group would be voting upon: support of
mandatory conscription, all aid "short of war" to the Allies, and the training
of civilians as army pilots. Roosevelt again replied equivocally and without
much explanation except for the observation that he could do only what
Congress permitted him to do. He elaborated a bit in response to a letter

from Helen Reid, whose husband was publisher of the New York *Herald Tribune*, who urged him to speak out publicly for conscription. "You say you have been a pacifist all your life," he told her in a response that one biographer called "distinctively Lincolnian prose," "but now you are for universal service. From what extremes do pendulums swing as individuals. Governments, such as ours, cannot swing so far or so quickly. They can only move in keeping with the thought and will of the great majority of our people." He then added what he saw as the paradox of American government and its relationship to the governed: "Were it otherwise the very fabric of our democracy—which after all is public opinion—would be in danger of disintegration."[3]

In both responses Roosevelt was making it clear that there was not yet sufficient backing in Congress to enact a conscription bill, and that only greater public support for the idea could change that. He hoped that groups such as Clark's and newspapers such as Reid's could play a significant role toward that end, and he pointedly did nothing to discourage them.

Clark's group embraced the three resolutions wholeheartedly, and momentum for conscription began to build. The movement now became based largely on the Century Association, where FDR had been a member since 1922, picking up new recruits from William Allen White's Committee to Defend America by Aiding the Allies. It was a time when bipartisan establishment opinion could still affect policy makers in Washington, and the emerging consensus of the Century Group that America's defense required manpower that could only be provided by a draft was being heard where it mattered. On June 20 Senator Edward Burke, a conservative Democrat from Nebraska who had been targeted in FDR's 1938 purge, introduced a "selective service" bill to train a sixteen-million-man reserve, and the next day James W. Wadsworth, a Republican moderate from New York, introduced a similar bill in the House.[4]

Activity on the measures was suspended as Congress recessed for the two conventions, but public support for conscription continued to grow, as Roosevelt had hoped. In August Gallup reported that 65 percent of Americans now supported a draft, up from about 50 percent in June. The difference, besides the advocacy of the Century Group, was the effect of the fall of France and the more imminent danger the American people could see to their own country from across the ocean. But as strong as these numbers were, the intensity of the argument was still on the side of the opposition. Senator Burton Wheeler of Montana, speaking for many isolationists, said, "If you pass this bill, you slit the throat of the last democracy still living." Labor leader John L. Lewis predicted the measure would lead to "dictatorship and fascism" in the United States. Despite such rhetoric from many of his own supporters, Willkie, still ensconced in Colorado, was of a mind to take a stand on the issue. Joe Martin, the House minority leader, whom Willkie had made chairman of the Republican National Committee, told him he needn't get involved. "People don't want their sons in uniform," he said. But while Willkie was now the nominee of a party that was largely isolationist, he was still himself a committed internationalist who saw the danger of ignoring the clear warning signs in Europe.

Traveling home to Elwood, Indiana, in mid-August to deliver his formal acceptance speech before 250,000 supporters, he stated forthrightly that he would prefer to lose the election than make conscription a political issue in the campaign. Relieved that the issue was safely removed from partisanship, the president soon offered his own public support. Willkie demonstrated his conviction on the matter when the Burke-Wadsworth bill came up for a vote: he privately persuaded the two Republican leaders, Charles McNary in the Senate, who was his running mate, and Joe Martin in the House, who was his party chairman, both of whom were inclined to oppose the measure, to vote for it. Republican senator Hiram Johnson of California observed that Willkie "broke the back" of those opposing the first peacetime draft in American history. By courageously going against the grain of opinion in his own party for a strongly held belief in the midst of a presidential campaign, it was one of Willkie's finest moments. Even FDR, who called the bill "America's answer to Hitlerism," would concede that the bill could not have been enacted without his opponent's support.[5]

Meanwhile, in Europe developments were taking an even more dangerous turn. On July 16 Hitler had ordered his commanders to prepare for an invasion of the British Isles. While Churchill and his colleagues were unaware of the decision, they had long believed that an invasion of their homeland was the Führer's logical next step, and the evidence to support that assumption—including the intercepted German message that the king had shown Donovan—was not long in coming. In order for any invasion to be successful, Germany would need total control of the airspace over the English Channel as well as over England itself, and it was with that end in mind that the Luftwaffe launched an all-out assault on southern ports and Channel shipping. The sea-lanes now under heavy attack were Britain's life-sustaining arteries from the outside world, bringing much-needed food-stuffs and war matériel to the isolated country. To keep them open, British fighter squadrons scrambled many times a day to engage the bombers in what came to be known as the Battle of Britain. They took a heavy toll on German aircraft but couldn't halt the ongoing damage to the British destroyers that were escorting the merchant ships and that were indispensable to thwarting an invasion armada. Only destroyers and smaller torpedo boats were capable of maneuvering in the narrow Channel, and thus they were absolutely essential to the nation's survival.[6]

By the end of July the steady loss of destroyers had reached a critical point, and Churchill renewed his correspondence with Roosevelt, pleading with him to "leave nothing undone to ensure that fifty or sixty of your oldest destroyers are sent to me at once." He had first made the request for these rusting and antiquated First World War ships to be transferred to Britain in May, but Roosevelt had been unresponsive, convinced that Congress would never approve such a move. ("The Americans treated us in that rather distant and sympathetic manner one adopts towards a friend one knows is suffering from cancer," Churchill would later recall of the long dry spell in his correspondence with Roosevelt.)[7] "The Germans have the whole French coastline from which to launch U-boats and dive-bomber attacks upon our trade and food, and in addition we must be constantly prepared to repel by sea-action threatened invasion in the Narrow Waters," Churchill now wrote the president.

All this in the advent of any attempt which may be made at invasion! . . . We could not sustain the present rate of casualties for long, and if we cannot get a substantial reinforcement the whole fate of the war may be decided by this minor and easily remediable factor. . . . Mr. President, with great respect I must tell you that in the long history of the world this is a thing to do *now*.[8]

This was Churchill at his best—urgent and persuasive, and appealing to Roosevelt's sense of destiny and drama. At the same time the prime minister told Joe Kennedy that if he couldn't get the American destroyers "we will all go down the drain together."[9] All this couldn't help but further move the president, who was increasingly impressed by Churchill's—and Britain's—fighting spirit, particularly that exhibited by the daring Royal Air Force pilots during the Battle of Britain. By this point Roosevelt was convinced beyond doubt that helping Britain was essential to American defense, and in implementing that policy he began more muscularly to overrule his military commanders, who even after the fall of France argued that the meagerly equipped American forces could not spare much-needed matériel for a beleaguered Britain, which, many believed, would soon go the way of France. Joe Kennedy, for his part, kept reinforcing this point with his unfailing pessimism of Britain's ability to survive, which is of course why the British were keen for him to go. Roosevelt knew that his commanders' argument was a plausible one and that there was a substantial risk of losing all the equipment shipped to Britain if that country should collapse. It was not a risk he was eager to assume, especially in the heat of a political campaign. He decided to assume it in a typically Rooseveltian way: he asked Congress to appropriate funds to satisfy both American and British needs, emphasizing the former and somewhat obscuring the latter.

As the president must have known, the American destroyers Churchill sought would not fall into a category of aid that could be so easily obscured. David Walsh, an isolationist Democrat from Massachusetts who chaired the Senate Naval Affairs Committee, successfully attached an amendment to an appropriations bill that prohibited the transfer of ships unless the navy declared they were not needed for defense of the United States. In fact, the navy had recently declared that the aging destroyers were needed for U.S. defense and should be refitted for that purpose. Such a declaration could only be overcome, Roosevelt reasoned, by seeking a special act of Congress, which he saw as having two large downsides: first, it would take a very long time to accomplish, if it could be accomplished at all; and second, it would represent a swift kick to the hornet's nest that was isolationism and thereby, even if it had the support of the pro-British Willkie, escalate campaign charges that he was leading the country into war. There had to be another way.

Close observers of the war who were sympathetic to Britain had already learned of that nation's urgent need for the destroyers, and British authorities were only too happy to furnish them the details. The Century Group, William Allen White's Committee to Defend America by Aiding the Allies, and influential columnists—including Joseph Alsop, despite his lambasting of the president at the Democratic convention—increasingly sounded the alarm and urged Congress to act. Their efforts to move public opinion were only modestly successful until they persuaded America's greatest living war hero, General John "Black Jack" Pershing, to make a radio address urging transfer of the destroyers. The idea had been suggested by FDR, who, typically, was reluctant to get too far ahead of public opinion on the grounds that his speaking out now would only politicize the issue. He preferred that events, in this case the speech by Pershing, should change public opinion. The general's address on the evening of July 31 had the desired effect, resulting in a torrent of hugely favorable press coverage and editorial comment. Not incidentally, it totally overshadowed a radio speech by Charles Lindbergh the same evening, urging "cooperation" with Germany if Britain fell. Gallup polls showed that over the course of the summer Americans had significantly improved their assessment of Britain's chances of surviving the war, and even larger numbers favored sending food and war matériel even if it appeared the country was unlikely to survive.[10]

Nonetheless, despite growing support for sending the destroyers to Britain—a Gallup poll taken after Pershing's speech showed that 62 percent of Americans favored selling the ships—the legal and political obstacles to doing so still appeared insurmountable.[11] Walsh's amendment was the law of the land, and any effort to get around it with special legislation was sure to stir the isolationists, as well as the Republican establishment, perhaps even including Willkie, sufficiently to make it a campaign issue that could threaten Roosevelt's election. No one could see a way to overcome these obstacles until, on August 1, the Century Group suggested that Roosevelt send the destroyers in return for assurances that if Britain fell to an invasion, her fleet would sail to North America or, alternatively, for "immediate naval and air concessions in British possessions in the Western Hemisphere." The group argued that under an arrangement that would bring such obvious benefits to America's defense, it would be unnecessary to seek congressional authorization.[12]

That evening Lord Lothian, Britain's ambassador in Washington, who was under orders from Churchill to do everything he could to pry the destroyers loose, asked Secretary of the Navy Knox to meet with him immediately on a matter of great urgency. Lothian needed an advocate for the cause who had Roosevelt's ear, and he saw Frank Knox, whom he had come to know and respect, as the best candidate. Knox heard the ambassador argue that the fate of Great Britain hung in the balance and that having the destroyers could mean the difference between survival and defeat. It was such an emotional appeal that Knox would tell Harold Ickes the next morning that Lothian "had been almost tearful in his pleas for help and help quickly." Knox was fully sympathetic, but he was compelled to cite the serious barriers on the American side to a transfer of the ships. He asked whether the British government would be open to conferring use of the naval bases in the West Indies in order to make the transfer more palatable to Congress, pointing out that in any case defense of those bases would fall to the United States. Knox left the embassy convinced that the basic elements to solve the dilemma were now on the table, and decided that he would raise the matter at the cabinet meeting scheduled for the next day.[13]

When Roosevelt extensively redesigned the Oval Office shortly after becoming president, he did the same with the Cabinet Room nearby. He gave these two rooms in the West Wing the essential appearance they still retain, with only minor variations. The most visible addition he gave the Cabinet Room was a large oval mahogany table that stretched most of the nearly forty-foot length of the room, with each member of the cabinet assigned a seat determined by protocol according to the date his department had been created. At 2:00 p.m. on August 2 the president wheeled into the room and took his customary place at the middle of the table with his back to the French doors looking out on the Rose Garden to the east. He faced the vice president's chair directly across from him, empty this day, and behind that he looked on portraits of two Democratic icons, Jefferson and Jackson. Woodrow Wilson, under whom he had served in the Navy Department during World War I, adorned the north wall above the fireplace.

For most of Roosevelt's presidency, weekly cabinet meetings had been largely informational, with members reporting on important developments in their areas of concern and with the president voicing whatever views he wished to share along with whatever information he had independently gathered. These were not decision-making sessions—everyone understood clearly that only the president made the major decisions—and only rarely since the early days of the administration were there substantive debates; even cabinet members were often reluctant to challenge a president's views. But today's cabinet meeting would be very different.

After several routine matters were discussed, Knox sought recognition and reported on his conversation with Lothian the night before. Echoing the ambassador's sense of urgency, he culminated the report with a plea that the aging destroyers be sent immediately in return for America's right to use British naval and air bases along the Atlantic coast. Secretary of War Stimson, whose support Knox had already enlisted, strongly seconded Knox's recommendation.

The question now was where Cordell Hull would come down. The secretary of state voiced concerns that Latin American governments, to which he had recently been paying much attention on a related matter, would react badly to the idea. Roosevelt, revealing his penchant for both secrecy and pragmatism, wondered whether there might be some way to conceal a lease of the bases. As the debate continued, it became evident, at least to Ickes, "that the President and Cabinet generally were much more sympathetic" to Knox's idea of a destroyers-for-bases swap. Even Hull, Ickes noted, "was in favor of doing something," though he was the one to surface "the one preoccupying thought on the Hill"—what would happen to the Royal Navy if

Britain collapsed or if, as happened in France, a government sympathetic to Germany was installed in London?[14]

Everyone in the room, including the president, assumed that any exchange like the one they were discussing would require congressional approval, and this was no small point. Congress would want assurances that the fleet would sail to the Western Hemisphere or, at the very least, would not be allowed to fall into Nazi hands. No one around the table could find a way that Churchill's government could guarantee that that wouldn't happen. The consensus was that nonetheless the United States should seek whatever assurances it could.

With cabinet sentiment now clearly favoring a deal, the conversation moved to how it could be implemented. Roosevelt worried that congressional Republicans, if they could not defeat the measure, could certainly delay it and turn it into a major campaign issue. His way to forestall this potential threat was to persuade Willkie to publicly endorse the deal and to enlist his efforts to convince the GOP leaders to support it as well (as he would do shortly with the draft bill). The president decided that he would enlist his friend and confidant William Allen White as his emissary to Willkie. Everyone strongly concurred in the decision.[15]

That evening the president, who almost never recorded his own account of important meetings, dictated one of this meeting, revealing that, three months after Churchill had first raised the issue, he was finally persuaded. "It was the general opinion without any dissenting voice that the survival of the British Isles under German attack might very possibly depend on their getting these destroyers," he wrote. It was further agreed, he said, that failure to secure Republican support beforehand "would meet with defeat or interminable delay." It would also be necessary to get British assurances that their fleet would not fall into German hands "under any conceivable circumstances."[16]

The president finally reached White that evening and asked him to seek Willkie's support for the destroyer deal and also that of the Republican congressional leaders, McNary and Martin. Roosevelt told the Kansas editor that he was prepared to send the necessary legislation to Congress if White was successful in this mission. White readily agreed to take on the assignment, relishing the opportunity to help get critical aid to Britain. But before he could reach Willkie, White discovered that Archibald MacLeish had already contacted the nominee's chief advisor, Russ Davenport, and put the matter to him. Willkie said he personally supported the transfer of the destroyers but was skeptical of getting the support of the congressional leaders. When White traveled to Colorado Springs, the candidate told him as well that he personally supported sending the destroyers, prompting the intermediary to assure FDR that Willkie would not publicly criticize the swap.

In fact, Willkie was becoming hugely discomfited by the corner he saw Roosevelt trying to squeeze him into. On one hand, his support of all-out aid to Britain was a core belief of his principled internationalist approach to the dire events unfolding in Europe, and he had been unequivocal in expressing it publicly. On the other hand, his experience with Roosevelt, going back to their meetings on holding-company legislation, caused him to distrust the president deeply, and he had no desire to be FDR's cat's paw in this business. Moreover, he doubted he could persuade Republican congressional leaders to support transfer of the ships, and even attempting to do so would further exacerbate his already fragile relations with his newly adopted party. Influential leaders of that party, as well as journalist Arthur Krock of the *New York Times*, told him that if he acquiesced to Roosevelt on the destroyers, he was effectively forfeiting the larger issue of the war itself and the argument that Roosevelt was leading the country into it. The isolationist *Chicago Tribune* editorialized that the transfer of destroyers to a belligerent nation "would be an action of war." The war, and who was best suited to lead the United States in a time of great peril, was already emerging as the central question in the campaign, and polls indicated that Roosevelt was winning it by a wide margin. So the age-old quandary of principle versus opportunity landed with a thud on Willkie's political doorstep, and how he addressed it would define not only him but also the campaign.[17]

Clearly conflicted, on August 9 Willkie released a statement that attempted to obfuscate the issue: "My general views on foreign policy and the vital interests of the United States in the present international situation are well known. As to specific executive and legislative proposals, I do not think it appropriate for me to enter into advance commitments and under-standings." This was not what either White or the president had hoped for or expected, and White immediately tried to resurrect an "understanding" between the two by wiring a more optimistic message to Roosevelt: "It's not as bad as it seems. I have talked with both of you on the subject in the last ten days, and I know there is not two bits difference between you on the issue pending."[18] Roosevelt was not assuaged by these words from White; he worried, perhaps too much, that with isolationist sentiment running so strong, he might even be impeached if he proceeded with the transfer.

As far as the prospects for congressional approval of a destroyer deal were concerned, things *were* as bad as they looked, if not worse. Senator David Walsh, whose chairmanship of the Naval Affairs Committee gave him something approaching a stranglehold on the issue, remained adamantly opposed after a three-day charm offensive on the *Potomac* by the president had failed to move him. Senator Claude Pepper of Florida, who supported the deal, told Stimson the votes simply weren't there for it. Fortuitously, however, events were already moving swiftly toward another way of execut-ing the transfer.

Joe Alsop, like Arthur Krock on the other side of the issue and others in the same line of work, was not content to confine his advocacy to his column. At the urging of the Century Group he approached Ben Cohen, the brilliant young staffer who had crafted much of FDR's New Deal legis-lation, to find a legal means of circumventing Congress on the issue and al-lowing the president to act on his own. Cohen threw himself into the issue and soon became convinced that there was probably sufficient authority in the Constitution as well as under existing law to provide the rationale he was seeking. After the president reacted coolly to his preliminary findings, Cohen looked for reassurance on the matter. Like Roosevelt himself back in July, he consulted a higher authority and, again like Roosevelt, that au-thority was Felix Frankfurter, his former mentor and sponsor. Cohen had been one of the first of "Felix's happy hot dogs," recruited to the New Deal cause right out of Harvard Law.[19]

Frankfurter, as we have seen, was no more constrained by his official job description than the journalists were by theirs, and he quickly agreed to help. He saw that the law was if anything ambiguous. He saw also that the politics were as important as the law. Which meant that public opinion—the very fabric of and yet danger to American democracy—had to be taken into account, which in turn meant that Cohen's legal case needed the most credible possible advocate. He soon settled on Dean Acheson, a distinguished forty-seven-year-old Washington lawyer, for the assignment. Acheson was highly respected for his legal acumen as well as for his integrity; he had served briefly as undersecretary of the treasury before resigning—quietly, in a way that Roosevelt appreciated—over a matter of monetary policy. Frankfurter was understandably drawn to him because Acheson had effectively blunted critics of Frankfurter's own nomination to the Court in his Senate confirmation hearings. Not least, Acheson too was a member of the Century Association and fully supportive of aiding Britain.

Settling into Cohen's New York apartment, the two lawyers set out to draft a public memo, what today would be called an op-ed piece, though it was shrewdly disguised as a legal brief. And though it would be intended ostensibly for the general public, it was really intended for only two men: the president of the United States and his attorney general, Robert Jackson, who would have to give his boss the legal sanction to act unilaterally.[20]

Acheson and Cohen blended legal research with the public case for the transfer of the destroyers, drawing heavily on the rationale that General Pershing's words offered—that the law "is not only compatible with, but is vitally important to, the safeguarding [of] our national defense." The draft went on to state that they wouldn't have proposed such a course if they hadn't believed there was adequate congressional support for the move, but time was of the essence. Given that they believed that opinion in Congress and the country was in favor of a deal, "we are loath to see time lost to secure authority which already exists when time may be vital to the preservation of our own liberties." In fact, this claim was dubious; no one had accurately measured opinion in and out of Congress. It nonetheless sought to protect the president from the inevitable criticism that he was circumventing Congress. But their key point was that the president possessed sufficient constitutional and legal authority to act without seeking sanction from Congress. They both knew the president well enough to know that he would be strongly inclined to take this course if he could be persuaded he could do so within the bounds of existing law and that Congress would not erupt. FDR had already been assured by Charles McNary, the Senate minority leader, who was his favorite Republican in the body and who was now Willkie's running mate, that while he would vote against a destroyer deal if it came to the Hill, he would not object if the president could find a way to do it on his own.[21]

With the message finalized, Acheson next focused on the messengers to deliver it, again with the intended audience in mind. He settled on three other distinguished lawyers well known to the president: Charles Burling-ham, Thomas D. Thacher, and George Rublee, the latter two recognizable Republicans.[22]

The only thing left was to determine the best vehicle for the message. Acheson decided to approach an old friend, Charles Merz, the editor of the *New York Times*, to ask if the paper might be interested in running it. The paper was indeed interested, and on Sunday, August 11, the Acheson-Cohen document ran as a letter to the editor over the names of the four attorneys. The piece occupied half the space on the page under the headline "No Legal Bar Seen to Transfer of Destroyers: Ample Authority for Sale of Over-Age Naval Vessels Exists in Present Laws, According to Opinion by Leading Lawyers." Its prominent display couldn't help but attract readers, most of whom couldn't be faulted if they concluded it carried the endorse-ment of the *New York Times* itself.

Acheson and Cohen were not content to leave it at that and acted to bring the message directly to the attention of both Roosevelt and Jackson. Cohen sent a copy of the piece to Missy LeHand asking that she share it with the president, while Acheson tracked down an irritated attorney general, camp-ing with his daughter in the Poconos of Pennsylvania, to warn him that this hugely consequential issue was coming to his desk for a legal opinion.[23]

Two days after the letter appeared, Roosevelt called Stimson, Knox, Sumner Welles (representing the absent Cordell Hull), and Henry Mor-genthau to his office for a discussion centered not on whether to negotiate a destroyers-for-bases swap with the British but *how* to do such a deal. Only a short time earlier, the cabinet discussion had persuaded him that Churchill needed the ships to defend against an invasion and he was prepared to seek congressional approval of the transfer. Now, barely a week later and almost certainly influenced by the heroic fight British pilots were waging over the Channel, he was prepared to act on his own. He never made mention of the Acheson letter, but it was apparent to the others that it had affected him.

The question he put before the group assembled in his office on August 13 was whether he should notify Congress before or after he negotiated terms with Churchill. Only Morgenthau argued that he should tell Congress first; the decision went the other way. The president asked his attorney general whether he had the authority to act independently, and Jackson gave him the answer he was looking for. He drew heavily on the reasoning of the Acheson letter, allowing him to consider the net benefit of the trade to the United States. It was a liberal interpretation of the law, to be sure, but it was not an unreasonable one. "The Chief of Naval Operations may, and should, certify . . . ," Jackson wrote in his opinion, "that such destroyers are not essential to the defense of the United States if in his judgment the exchange of such destroyers for strategic naval and air bases will strengthen rather than impair the total defense of the United States."[24] Now, at last, everything was in place.

The negotiations with Churchill began immediately, and it was soon apparent that the issues wouldn't be as quickly or as easily resolved as they had hoped. Roosevelt was eager to present a deal that would benefit the country's defense. He also wanted one that showed the American people, and especially Congress, that the United States had gotten the better of the bargain: giving up a bunch of obsolete vessels in return for strategically valuable bases along its Atlantic coast was unarguably a very good deal for the United States. Churchill, seeing FDR's game and determined to prevent such an interpretation from reaching his own shores, tried to separate the issues and proposed instead that America simply *give* the destroyers and he would simply *give* the bases, all of it being done in friendship. Lord Lothian had to remind the prime minister that the Walsh Amendment wouldn't permit such an arrangement. Only *trading* the vessels for the more valuable bases would bring a net benefit to the United States and thereby satisfy U.S. law; simply *giving* them, even in friendship, wouldn't do it.

When a series of cables in both directions couldn't resolve the contentious issue—each side was driven now by its own political imperatives—Roosevelt decided to use a transatlantic call with Jackson on the line to explain the law to the prime minister. The attorney general did his best to make the case that only a trade, or, as he said, a "bargain," could satisfy the legal constraints the administration was under to get the ships to Great Britain, but Churchill was not persuaded.

"Empires just don't bargain," he said when Jackson had finished.

"Well, republics do," Jackson replied.

Roosevelt, in an effort to put the matter in a context Churchill could understand, told him: "The trouble is I have an Attorney General and he says I have to bargain."

The prime minister, still unmoved, rejoined: "Maybe you ought to trade these destroyers for a new Attorney General."[25]

The impasse continued until Hull convened a meeting in his office of his top advisors on August 24. His chief legal advisor, Green H. Hackworth, had been mulling the issue for two weeks and announced that he may have found a solution. Why not, he asked, split the bargain/gift problem right down the middle by allowing Britain to give the northernmost bases, Newfoundland and Bermuda, to America unencumbered by a quid pro quo, but explicitly trade the more valuable (because of their proximity to the Panama Canal) Caribbean bases for the destroyers? It was a classic compromise that gave each side something of what it wanted, including something that was important for Churchill: a means of saving face. The prime minister, weary of the back-and-forth, agreed to the proposal; it was done.[26]

All that remained for Roosevelt was to get Wendell Willkie on board before announcing the deal. On his visit to Colorado Springs, William Allen White had already laid the groundwork for the candidate's support, reinforcing his pledge of "wholehearted support to the president in whatever activities he might take" in order to give "the opponents of force the material resources of the nation." White and others in the Century Group continued to press Willkie to come out publicly in favor of the swap (this at a time when it was still thought congressional approval would be required) but, unknown to them, the freewheeling Arthur Krock of the *New York*

Times and Herbert Hoover, among others, urged Willkie not to do so. The nominee was beginning to feel the heat from his new party, and he was uncomfortable about it. Nonetheless, he sent word to Archibald MacLeish and others in the Century Group gathered in the Hay-Adams Hotel across Lafayette Park from the White House on August 30 that while he wouldn't publicly endorse the deal, neither would he publicly oppose it. That was good enough for Roosevelt.[27]

At the end of a thinly disguised campaign trip through the upper South, during which the president dedicated a dam and a national park and inspected defense facilities, his train was headed back to Washington from Charleston, West Virginia, when he summoned the traveling press corps back to his private car. He told the reporters that while he didn't have any news for them, he nonetheless wanted them to know of the announcement then being made in the capital of his message to Congress on the destroyer deal. Repeating disingenuously that it was a Washington story and that he didn't have any news for them, he gave them a quote he knew would be irresistible: "It is probably the most important thing that has come for American defense since the Louisiana Purchase." Pressed from all sides with questions about the details of the deal and Jackson's opinion, he gave them all the same response without stepping on his favorite line: "It is a fait accompli." He did elaborate on the Louisiana Purchase analogy, however, when he noted that Thomas Jefferson, finding Napoleon receptive, had concluded that going to Congress "would have involved a delay," and this, too, was a fait accompli in that it never required a treaty. It would do him no harm to be seen in the company of the iconic Jefferson in the wake of what surely would be seen by some as an excessive act of executive authority. He made certain to mention Churchill's pledge to send his fleet to the Western Hemisphere if necessary, but added that it was not part of the destroyer deal; its timing now, he said, was "fortuitous."[28]

The next day the *New York Times* ran a banner headline across the front page: "Roosevelt Trades Destroyers for Sea Bases; Tells Congress He Acted on His Own Authority; Britain Pledges Never to Yield or Sink Fleet." Most other publications gave the announcement similar play, and the editorial comment was largely favorable, even from unexpected sources, thanks in part to the efforts of Joe Alsop and Henry Luce to organize it ahead of time. The staunchly isolationist *Chicago Tribune* opined, "Any arrangement which gives the United States naval and air bases in regions which must be brought within the American defense zone is to be accepted as a triumph." Even Herbert Hoover called the bases "important contributions to our defense," and many Republicans in Congress agreed. But the verdict was by no mean unanimous. A number of Republicans chose to attack the "dictatorial" means the president had used rather than the result he had achieved; the *St. Louis Post-Dispatch* compared it to "the edicts forced down the throats of Germans, Italians and Russians by Hitler, Mussolini and Stalin."[29]

Willkie found himself politically boxed in by the announcement. He had recently pledged his wholehearted support to the president to get material aid to those opposing aggression, and the destroyer deal fit squarely into the literal meaning of that statement. Furthermore, he had sent word to the Century Group, which he knew would be forwarded to the White House, that he would refrain from criticizing the deal. On the other hand, if he had any hope of closing the gap in the polls with FDR, he couldn't remain mute on what potentially could be the biggest issue in the campaign. His way out of this conundrum was to echo those editorial writers who accepted the result but attacked the means of achieving it. "The country will undoubtedly approve of the program to add to our naval and air bases and assistance given to Britain," he said in a statement released September 4. "It is regrettable, however, that the President did not deem it necessary . . . to secure the approval of Congress." Americans needed to be mindful, he added, of not threatening the very nature of the democratic process at a moment when democracy around the world was under siege.

It was the mildest of criticisms, and in the view of hard-core isolationists in his new party it was pap. Senator Arthur Vandenberg and others pounced on the nominee, telling him he had to draw a much sharper line in the political sand if he was to have any chance in November. The result was another Willkie statement a few days later terming the deal "the most dictatorial and arbitrary act of any President in the history of the United States."[30] While the new statement was no doubt well received by the isolationists, it had to have caused consternation among Willkie's friends in the Century Group, who had received assurances that he would not criticize the deal. That wouldn't have been the case with FDR, who, while certainly disappointed, understood the exigencies of politics in the midst of a heated campaign in which the war issue was the only arrow in Willkie's quiver.

On September 5, the first of the fifty destroyers, fresh from a $50 million refitting in American yards, set sail from Boston and Philadelphia for Halifax, where British crews would board them for the voyage across the ocean. There Churchill waited to welcome them as important additions to his fleet and, even more important, as a huge step in his consuming effort to bring the United States closer to a full war footing. He ironically saw the deal much as the American isolationists did: a serious compromise of neutrality that left the two countries "somewhat mixed together in some of their affairs for mutual and general advantage." In fact, as James MacGregor Burns and others have pointed out, the deal effectively signaled the end of American neutrality. To the prime minister, it was only the beginning of a beautiful relationship: "I could not stop it if I wished; no one can stop it. Like the Mississippi, it just keeps rolling along."[31]

If Willkie's support of the draft bill at a critical juncture represented his moment of courage in the campaign, the same could be said of Roosevelt's embrace of the destroyer deal. During the last weekend in August, when he was at Hyde Park dictating a memorandum on the understanding, he turned to Grace Tully and said, "Grace, Congress is going to raise hell about this but even another day's delay may mean the end of civilization. Cries of 'war monger' and 'dictator' will fill the air but if Britain is to survive we must act."[32] There was more than a little Rooseveltian exaggeration in that statement, but there was also some truth. To act unilaterally on such a significant matter, which everyone, including the president, had believed until recently must be submitted to Congress, was uncharted territory. As yet another extension of presidential authority, it was certain to be attacked. Still, the unprecedented nature of such an action made it uncertain what the net political effect would be. In ordinary times this was the kind of risk FDR didn't need and wouldn't be inclined to take but, as Eleanor had said recently in Chicago, these were not ordinary times. Rather, this was at the core of why he was running for a third term—to steer the country through a dangerous period by helping Britain to survive.

If that was the case, however, it raises the question of why it took Roosevelt three months to act after Churchill first asked for the destroyers. There was the Walsh Amendment, of course, which appeared to be an insuperable obstacle and which the navy used to oppose the transfer. There was the isolationist sentiment in the country that was certain to gel in Congress, which meant at the least a protracted debate and at worst a defeat. There were FDR's serious doubts about Churchill's commitment to defeating Hitler, and even about Churchill's, and Britain's, ability to survive. Related to this, there was his lack of confidence in the value of the destroyers to Britain's defense. And finally, there was the preoccupation with the conventions; it wasn't until late July and really August that he began to focus seriously on Churchill's increasingly desperate plea for the ships.

For whatever reasons, Roosevelt was slow in coming to the decision that he needed to find a way to get the destroyers to Britain. In the Battle of Britain, then being waged in the skies, the nation was fighting literally for its life, to forestall an invasion it was certain was coming; British destroyers and other escort vessels were being lost at an alarming rate, and the only short-term hope lay in the aged American ships across the Atlantic. Had the president been convinced of their potential value to the Brits, he could have tasked his deputies to come up with a way to get them transferred quickly. He prided himself on coming up with creative solutions to seemingly intractable problems, even when dealing with foreign policy issues, but here he didn't. It would have been a perfect assignment for Harry Hopkins, whom he was then training to be his de facto national security advisor.

But this is a view formed in retrospect. The fact at the time was that he did act, and acted decisively, once he was persuaded Britain needed the ships and he saw the path to getting them in British hands. The episode demonstrates vividly how comfortable he was in the exercise of presidential authority, and also in pressing the limits of that authority (there was, and remains, a question as to the constitutionality of his action). It was a courageous thing to do at any time, and it was a particularly courageous thing to do in the midst of a hotly contested presidential election. In the short term it would change the nature of Britain's defense posture (or at least so it was thought at the time) as well as America's relationship with that nation. In the long term it would change the nature of the presidency, with some critics arguing that it began the "imperial" nature of the office. Dean Acheson, for one, was having none of it. As for complaints that the president should have sought congressional approval, he told John J. McCloy in a letter on September 12 that he had no patience with those who saw the action as a threat to American institutions and democracy. "The danger to them seems not in resolving legal doubts in accordance with the national interest but in refusing to act when action is imperative."[33]

14

The Politics of War

However much Roosevelt may have feared the political repercussions of the destroyer deal, his fears turned out to be largely
unfounded. In a poll taken before the September 3 announcement but
released a few days after, 60 percent of Americans approved of sending
the ships to Britain. The president's standing was clearly enhanced by the
strong and decisive action he had just taken to help that besieged nation,
enabling him to open a lead over Willkie in what had appeared to be a
tight race up to that point. Sentiment for aiding Britain with war matériel
had steadily grown, as had the belief that Germany would set its sights
on America should Britain fall. In addition, these developments reflected
both FDR's ability to use the advantages of incumbency and Willkie's
inexperience as a candidate; in purely political terms, it was the master
versus the novice.[1]

As we have seen, Willkie was painfully slow in getting his campaign off to
an effective start. Resting in Colorado for those six weeks, he didn't travel
to Elwood, Indiana, to formally accept the Republican nomination until

mid-August, and then he lingered for a month in neighboring Rushville, where he owned several farms, to burnish his credentials as a product of rural America. He finally left Indiana on September 12 for Coffeyville, Kansas, where he had once taught in the high school and where he would formally begin his campaign. It had been two and a half months since his nomination in Philadelphia.

The degree of disorganization in the campaign was embarrassingly evident to outsiders as well as to those struggling inside. At least four people—Joe Martin, Russ Davenport, Sam Pryor, and John D. M. Hamilton—had been given major responsibilities, and each reported directly to the candidate, but none was first among equals. Keeping authority in his own hands was the corporate model that Willkie knew and that had served him well, and he wasn't about to abandon it. However, what may have worked in a holding company's boardroom didn't translate to the campaign trail, where the candidate's chief responsibility was to focus on his message while leaving most other matters to his staff. The resulting chaos appalled virtually every close observer, including his former rivals for the nomination. "I feel that the campaign has demonstrated one thing so far," Senator Robert Taft wrote Tom Dewey in mid-September, "that is that no convention should nominate a candidate who has never been engaged in a political campaign before." The journalist Ray Clapper came to essentially the same conclusion. "Seldom has there been more chaos in a presidential campaign," he wrote; if this dire situation foretold what would happen in a Willkie administration, "the government would be almost paralyzed."[2] No one explained the disorganization more vividly, perhaps, than Pierce Butler, a senior aide, who was compelled to tell a disgruntled local official, "Have you ever been in a whorehouse on a Saturday night when the Madam was away and the girls were running it to suit themselves? That's how this campaign train is run."[3]

The campaign nonetheless managed to put together a twelve-car train, dubbed the *Willkie Special,* that over the next seven weeks would carry the candidate and his entourage and traveling press corps nearly nineteen thousand miles through thirty-one states. Settled comfortably in his mahogany-paneled private car at the rear of the train both day and night—he would spend only five nights in hotels—he was forever hopping back to the rear platform for brief appearances before assembled crowds in hundreds of small towns and then returning to speechwriting and strategy sessions with his team. It was exhausting work, and it took a toll on the candidate. His voice became an early casualty, causing him to speak more briefly and more softly, contrary to his normal practice. Doctors with remedies were summoned, but the nominee resisted their ministrations, and his voice continued to fail him. At one point he was forced to allow a surrogate to read his speech while he waved smilingly to the crowd. "The spirit is willing," he murmured into the microphone at another stop, "but the flesh is weak."[4] The loss of his voice seemed to symbolize his faltering campaign.

Willkie's principal difficulty was his failure to find a message that resonated with voters. During a random September encounter in the Waldorf-Astoria barber shop, Jim Farley—of all people—urged him to stress the third-term issue, which of course was the issue Farley had used to rationalize his own failed candidacy. Willkie took a few tentative stabs at it, but his heart wasn't in it, and he soon dropped it.[5]

The Republican candidate's inability to settle on a message that dramatized his differences with Roosevelt was handicapped by the fact that there were few real differences between them. Only recently he had been an unabashed New Deal Democrat on most domestic matters, and in foreign affairs he was a committed internationalist who favored all-out aid to Britain as strongly as FDR did. The issue he felt most strongly about, and on which he sharply disagreed with the president, was the latter's advocacy of government entities such as TVA competing with private utilities. This simply wasn't an issue that resonated with many voters, however, including many Republicans; Willkie's own running mate, Senator Charles McNary, was a strong partner of Roosevelt's on the issue, having been instrumental in creating such public power facilities on the Columbia River as Bonneville and Grand Coulee. In a similar vein Willkie advocated removing federal regulations to provide private industry an incentive to create new jobs, but this embrace of corporate capitalism also served to reinforce the public's perception of the GOP as the party of big business and of Willkie as a big-time industry executive. Historian David Kennedy has summarized Willkie's economic case as denouncing the Democrats "as having acquired a vested interest in the Depression and therefore as having throttled the wealth-making and job-creating potential of private enterprise."[6] In any case, it wasn't selling.

Harold Ickes had early on referred to the Indianan as "the barefoot boy from Wall Street," and the appellation stuck. What also stuck was Willkie's vow to continue most New Deal programs and even to expand some, such as Social Security, farm credit, and rural electrification. With millions of Americans still out of work, he vowed to provide jobs for everyone able and willing to work. On these issues there was no way to set him apart from the man who had first championed them and who had turned them into actual programs. Willkie, observed Norman Thomas, the minister and sometime Socialist Party candidate, "agreed with Mr. Roosevelt's entire program of social reform and said it was leading to disaster."[7]

At the same time his efforts to make the economy a salient issue were undercut by FDR's ramping up of defense production, which required more and more manpower. During August and September this need alone removed nearly a million workers from the unemployment rolls; by Election Day 3.5 million unemployed Americans would have found work since the depth of the "Roosevelt recession" of 1937–38. From a purely political point of view, more important than the fact that 14.6 million people would still be unemployed at the end of the year was the direction the economy was taking, giving hope to those who were still hurting. Just as the sudden rise in unemployment back in 1937 had hurt Roosevelt's standing after he had let up on federal spending, so now its decline gave him a boost.

The Republican nominee's efforts to explain himself on foreign policy, and especially on aid to Britain, were similarly unavailing. "We must rid ourselves of the fallacy that democracy can be defended with words, with poses, with political paraphernalia designed to impress the American people and no one else," he said in a thinly veiled reference to FDR. "We must send, and we must keep sending, aid to Britain, our first line of defense and our only remaining friend." As passionately as he stated this theme, it went largely unheard after Roosevelt unveiled the destroyer deal, the most dramatic assertion of presidential authority in such a matter that the country had ever witnessed. What's more, Willkie's views on foreign aid were almost directly opposite those of the isolationist core of his new party, a contradiction that was widely noticed. "Mr. Willkie cannot make speeches advocating conscription and the policy of extending to Great Britain 'the material resources of the nation,' and expect the people to follow him if his own party does not follow him," columnist Walter Lippmann wrote in mid-August.[8]

It was evident to the Roosevelt camp that Willkie's speeches were not making the case that a challenger needed to make in order to defeat an incumbent president. "Some of these speeches were good," said Ed Flynn, the Bronx Democratic leader whom FDR had installed as Jim Farley's replacement at the Democratic National Committee, "but their chief import was that while he agreed with the President in both foreign and domestic policies, he asked people to believe that he could carry out those policies better than President Roosevelt, who had created them." Willkie's failure to draw a contrast with Roosevelt on fundamental policies was a function of principle—he really *agreed* with most of the president's policies—but if it continued, it would prove politically fatal.[9]

Willkie was on solider ground when he criticized the president's failure to prepare the country militarily to face potential threats abroad, but here, too, he was sailing into strong headwinds. Nearly every public appearance FDR made in these early months of the campaign was as the leader of the nation's military forces and never as a candidate for reelection. The commander in chief, it seemed, was ubiquitous. When he was not announcing new initiatives to increase defense spending or to convert industrial facilities to arms production, he was inspecting shipyards, army bases, or munitions factories. "Franklin Roosevelt is not running against Wendell Willkie," a Republican congressman shrewdly observed. "He's running against Adolf Hitler." Added another Republican wag, "With Willkie a poor third." Roosevelt was pursuing the strategy that he had settled on months earlier of ignoring his opponent and concentrating exclusively on military preparedness. This wasn't solely or even primarily a political decision. He was convinced that the country was at risk and that his most solemn responsibility as president was to prepare it for whatever might come. There is no question, however, that he used the opportunity shrewdly with his announcements and his appearances. If making the American people aware of his efforts to protect them was also a sound political strategy, so much the better. In any case, it left Willkie shadowboxing with his elusive opponent, unable to land a solid blow.[10]

Whereas Willkie and Roosevelt had emerged from the conventions on a roughly equal political footing with voters—people had been attracted to the down-home charisma and nonpolitical freshness and honesty of the Republican, while the machinations in Chicago had reminded them of the president's propensity for manipulation—public perceptions had changed in two months. With the skies over Britain filled with German bombers that were now mercilessly pounding population centers at night, and with a cross-Channel invasion still expected, the war in Europe eclipsed all other issues for the American electorate. There was a growing sense that this could become America's war, too, and whom could they trust to lead them through it? It wasn't so much Roosevelt's buildup of the nation's defense forces that began to break the race open for him as it was the perception of him as a strong and tested leader on the international stage. These were very dangerous times, and fewer and fewer Americans were willing to trust their fortunes to someone who would have to learn on the job. Though many were tiring of Roosevelt after nearly eight years, it was ironically the experience he had acquired during those years that had become his hole card. "We're living in a crisis right now," an Ohio farmer's wife told one of Gallup's pollsters. "I'd hate to change Presidents when we need somebody in there who knows about things." A waitress in Chillicothe went a step further: "If there wasn't a war, I'd say try someone else besides Roosevelt. But he's been in there, and he's better acquainted with conditions." Gallup wrote that she summed up the attitude of many voters who "admitted that their support of Roosevelt was definitely related to the conflict abroad."[11]

The result was that the president began to open a nearly double-digit lead over his Republican opponent. Unless something dramatically changed, it would be game over for Wendell Willkie. But where was the game changer that could reverse this outcome? Back in August officials at the Republican National Committee thought they might have the answer. In an exercise that a later generation of political operatives would call opposition research, they learned about, and managed to acquire, several of Henry Wallace's "Dear Guru" letters. Through a reporter friend Hopkins had acquired photostatic copies of several of the letters, many of them handwritten by Wallace. In one letter Wallace said he "must read Agny Yoga [a seventeen-volume spiritual "teaching" by Roerich and his wife, Helena] and sit by myself once in a while. We are dealing with the crude beginnings of a new age." One of the most potentially explosive letters was written in code: "The rumor is the Monkeys [the British] are seeking friendship with the Rulers [the Japanese] so as to divide the land of the Masters [Manchuria] between them. The Wandering One [Roosevelt] thinks this and is very suspicious of Monkeys. . . . He does not like the Rulers and wants adequate preparation for two of three years hence." Here was a high official in the Roosevelt administration writing in a weird cipher to a Russian "mystic" whose loyalties were unclear about a sensitive national security concern. The president, Wallace had written, suspected the British planned to divide Manchuria with the Japanese.[12]

After conferring with Sam Rosenman, Hopkins and the speechwriter took the letters to FDR over breakfast one morning with a report that the Republicans were shopping the story, with the letters as evidence, to sympathetic newspapers. The president never considered replacing Wallace on the ticket, as Hopkins had just days before. He suggested instead that Paul Appleby, Wallace's top aide who had verified the authenticity of the letters to Hopkins, be sent at once to Chicago to serve as a minder for Wallace to prevent him from confirming the story to reporters.[13]

At the very least, release of the story would change the dynamic of the campaign by placing Roosevelt on the defensive; at its worst, it could be made to badly damage his judgment on a critical decision. Selecting a vice president was unarguably one of the most important decisions a president could make, and FDR had decided that he would be the first presidential nominee to make it himself rather than leave it to the convention. Should his judgment be brought into question on Wallace, could it also be brought into question on his conduct of foreign affairs and his stewardship of the nation through a time of great peril, currently his strong suit in the election? FDR didn't need all this spelled out for him. He saw the danger clearly and was prepared to deal with it decisively. If that was the game the Republicans were going to play, he could counter it with a story even more damaging to Willkie: his affair with Irita Van Doren. In a recorded conversation in late August with his aide Lowell Mellett, Roosevelt mused aloud about how that relationship might factor into the election if the Republicans were determined to inject the Wallace-Roerich relationship.[14]

The story of how this conversation came to be recorded is almost as interesting as its content. Roosevelt had been furious on the morning in late January 1939 when he read on the front page of the *New York Times* that he had told the Senate Military Affairs Committee the day before that America's frontier was on the Rhine River. He was certain that he had said no such thing, certain that he had never mentioned the word "Rhine," and a close examination of the official stenographer's transcript bore him out. That hadn't prevented one of the senators from leaving the meeting and giving a reporter his own embellished interpretation of what he thought FDR had said. The president wanted to be protected from such inaccurate reports, especially from his often casual utterances at news conferences, and Henry Kannee, the White House stenographer, set out to find a way to solve the problem. At this time there were no tape-recording machines, or indeed recording machines any other kind yet in existence, so Kannee's assignment was not an easy one.

After many months he settled on the methodology employed by filmmakers in their soundtracks, and RCA agreed to construct and install an experimental "Continuous-film Recording Machine" in the Oval Office. It was personally presented to the president in June 1940 by RCA chief executive David Sarnoff. A microphone was placed somewhere on the president's desk, probably in his reading lamp, and a connecting wire went through the floor to the recording device on the lower level of the White House.[15]

It was a crude device, and one that made it difficult and sometimes impossible to discern what was being said and who was saying it. But the value of the tapes to historians proved immeasurable, as FDR scholar and biographer Arthur Schlesinger Jr. noted. They offered, he said "the excitement of immediacy: FDR in casual, unbuttoned exchange with members of his personal staff." Schlesinger noted how little the president's "private voice" and his "public voice" differed. He was also impressed by Roosevelt's tone, his "rich and resonant tenor." As other have noted, the president was a remarkable performer, particularly evident when he acted out "imagined dialogues," such as between Willkie and J. P. Morgan.

Although the president had an activating switch in his desk drawer, there is no indication that he ever used it. The machine's chief and probably only purpose was to give an accurate account of his twice-weekly news conferences. Since a news conference was by definition a public event, he had no reservations about recording them, even secretly; these sessions were already being openly recorded by a stenographer, and moving the process to this device was simply a more foolproof means of doing what was already being done, or so it was thought. It recorded fourteen of the twenty-one news conferences the president held during the time the system was in operation, from August 23 to November 8, 1940, shortly after the election, when Roosevelt apparently ordered it stopped. However, no one, including Henry Kannee, who controlled the system, could account for the seemingly random conversations it picked up during those eleven weeks.

So it was that the device picked up a conversation in late August between Roosevelt and Mellett in which the president was rambling about a fanciful theory that he had acquired in 1920 when he was running for vice president. A Warren Harding operative named Henry Daugherty, according to Roosevelt's account, had deliberately spread rumors of Harding's supposed African American ancestry to gain sympathy for his candidate. It was the spreading-of-rumors element of the story that was foremost in the president's mind when he launched into a monologue, most of which found its way into the machine.

FDR: Now, I agree with you that there is, so far as the other man goes [read Willkie], we can't use it (tape garbled) spread it [the Irita Van Doren relationship] as a word of mouth thing, or by some people way down the line. We can't have any of our principal speakers refer to it but people down the line can get it out. I mean the Congress speakers and the state speakers, and so forth. They can use raw material as a matter of fact. Now, now, if they want to play dirty politics in the end, we've got our own people . . . Now, you'd be amazed at how this story about this gal is spreading across the country.

Mellett: It's out.

FDR: [. . .] Awful nice gal, writes for the magazine and so forth and so on, a book reviewer. Nevertheless, there is the fact. And one very good way of bringing it out is by calling attention to the parallel in conversation. Jimmy Walker [the flamboyant and corrupt mayor of New York City whom Roosevelt, as his party's nominee for president but still governor of New York, had to decide whether to remove from office] once upon a time, was living openly with this gal all over New York, including the house across the street from me . . . and she was an extremely attractive little tart . . . very happy. Jimmy and his wife had separated . . . And it came to my trial [wherein FDR had to determine Walker's political fate] . . . and Jimmy goes and hires his former wife, for ten thousand dollars, to come up to Albany on a Saturday . . . lives with him ostensibly in the same suite in the hotel, and on Sunday the two of them go to Mass at the Albany Cathedral together. Price? Ten thousand dollars (laughter).

Now, now, Mrs. Willkie may not have been hired, but in effect she's been hired to return to Wendell and smile and make this campaign with him. Now, whether there was a money price behind it, I don't know, but it's the same idea.

Mellett: Doesn't have to be a money price. It's a nice place to live.[16]

It's impossible to imagine that FDR would have wanted this conversation recorded. It reveals among other things his fascination with historical parallels, in this case with past scandals either real or imagined, and his apparent willingness to use those parallels to justify his own use of scandal to counter those propounded by his opponents. Yet this is not a conversation that sets Roosevelt on a specific course of action. Rather, it reveals his way of thinking through a situation that must somehow be handled—by looking at similar situations that he is familiar with, and floating ideas of how to proceed before a sympathetic audience. Close aides such as Mellett were expected to be generally approving of the exercise, but at the same time they knew better than to take it as an actionable decision. Rather, it was FDR's way of formulating his thoughts, which, once articulated, would gestate and evolve over time until he became comfortable enough to act on them. Some people put thoughts down on paper to achieve this goal. Roosevelt preferred to enact them through conversations with himself, whether or not he was alone.

In any case, Paul Appleby flew to Chicago and made certain that Wallace avoided reporters who might have been on to the story. It turned out there were none, at least not yet.

During most of the summer and fall Charles Lindbergh was unusually silent, focusing much of his time organizing the new America First Committee, which became the isolationists' chief vehicle for arguing that America should stay out of the war. The closest he came to venturing into the political thicket came on October 14 in a national radio address in which he bemoaned the absence of men such as the Founding Fathers: "What we lack today is the type of leadership that made us a great nation; the type that turned adversity and hardship into virility and success." Regarding the forthcoming election, without mentioning names he said the United States depended on men "regardless of their party, who will lead us to strength and peace, rather than to weakness and to war." Two days later Henry Wallace, reflecting Roosevelt's view, called Lindbergh "the outstanding appeaser of the nation."[17]

While the president may have appeared to the outside world during August and September as a single-minded commander in chief, attempting to protect the nation from aggression, those who knew him best knew also that he was heavily invested in the role of strategist in chief of his own reelection campaign. Nowhere was this fact more evident than in an exchange in the Oval Office on October 4 with Speaker of the House Sam Rayburn and majority leader John McCormack. Immediately after the president's regular Friday morning news conference—the 686th of his presidency—the two Democratic leaders were shown into the presence of a still-voluble Roosevelt eager to speak what was on his mind. He launched into an extended monologue on the current political situation as he saw it. The device that had recorded the press conference was still on.

FDR: And of course, on the strategical end of things, I said about the first of August—I said you watch these polls, you watch the Republican timing of this campaign. I think the polls couldn't possibly make it Willkie. Let them show Willkie, ah, in pretty good shape the first part of August. Then they're going to put him through a bad slump, bad slump, so that I'll be well out ahead on the first of October. And my judgment is that they are going to start Willkie pickin' up, pickin' up, pickin' up, from the first of October on. And you know what a horse race is, it's like, what they're going to do is have their horse three lengths behind, coming around the stretch. And then, in the stretch, in the first hundred yards, he gains a length, and the next hundred yards he gains another length, and gives the people the idea that this fella still can win, he's got time to win, he can nose out the other horse. Now, I don't know whether that's their game, but I'm inclined to think it 'tis. I'm wrong on my dates. They didn't start the first of October. Next Sunday, in the Gallup poll, we'll have a great many—too many— [electoral] votes handed to us, five hundred. A great many, too many.[18]

Two days later, the Gallup poll showed that Roosevelt had indeed opened a wide lead and was currently ahead in forty-two states, with Willkie favored in only six; those numbers translated to 499 electoral votes to 32. The president was on the money, most likely because his personal intelligence network had given him advance word on the poll results; Eugene Meyer, publisher of the *Washington Post*, liked to call press secretary Steve Early with them before publication. The more interesting revelation from this discourse was Roosevelt's belief that he was in a horse race that was about to become close and that would go down to the wire.[19]

If that belief wasn't yet shared by Willkie and the Republicans, it certainly represented their aim, and they were determined to do whatever was necessary to start gaining a length or two on the front-runner. It began to happen in late September when Willkie used a campaign speech for the first time to make the war a major campaign issue. "If [Roosevelt's] promise to keep our boys out of foreign wars is no better than his promise to balance the budget," he declared, "they're already almost on the transports."[20] It is unclear whether the statement represented a strategic decision to inject the war into the public debate or whether it represented a frustrated candidate's momentary impulse. Either way, the result was immediate. It struck a barely suppressed fear in the electorate that perhaps, just perhaps, the president's policies of aiding Britain (and offending Germany) were bringing the United States closer to war. Willkie's isolationist advisors, such as former GOP national chairman John D. M. Hamilton and his successor, Joe Martin, had been trying to convince the candidate for weeks that there was only one issue the voters cared about, and it was the war. Willkie's stock speeches filled with generalities and encomiums to the free enterprise system, they argued, weren't cutting it with electorate, and continuing with that strategy meant certain defeat.

Influential publishers, such as Colonel Robert McCormick of the *Chicago Tribune* and Roy Howard of Scripps-Howard, strongly reinforced the point. Their encouragement strengthened Willkie's own relentless drive to win, causing him to escalate the charges against Roosevelt, his favorite being to call him a "warmonger." He could sense on the campaign trail that he was finally getting traction with the crowds; more important, he could see it in the polls, which began to move. "We shall not undertake to fight anybody else's war," he told a large Boston audience of Irish and Italian Americans already upset by the president's policy of aiding Britain and the "stab in the back" charge aimed at Mussolini. "Our boys shall stay out of European wars." Willkie began to taste victory and, his long-held commitments to Britain and internationalism notwithstanding, he was throwing everything into the pot.

One development that gave Willkie greater confidence to take on the war issue was then occurring in the skies over the English Channel. By the time he offered his provocative "transports" comment, it was apparent that the Luftwaffe was losing the Battle of Britain. The Royal Air Force was, as we've seen, destroying three German planes for every one of its own that was lost, and when Goering abruptly changed his strategy from engaging the deadly British Spitfires during daylight to the bombing of London and other population centers at nighttime, it signaled that a cross-Channel invasion was no longer imminent.

The realization that Britain would survive as a fighting force, at least for the time being, meant that the United States too was in less imminent danger; that in turn made it politically safer for Willkie to thrust charges such as "warmonger" at the president. He would not have dared to do so earlier, even if his convictions had permitted. He had consistently been every bit as much a committed internationalist as Roosevelt, and he had even suggested that he would be open to retaining Cordell Hull, the co-architect of the administration's policy, as secretary of state.

In Philadelphia Willkie accused Roosevelt of causing "a drift toward war," and he was prepared to stop that drift. "We must stop that incompetence. Fellow Americans, I want to lead the fight for peace." Willkie set out to secure the support of such isolationist Republicans as Senator Hiram Johnson. He even eulogized the late William Borah, the dean of Senate isolationists. He became fully committed to the new strategy, encouraged by his advisors and confirmed by the polls, but more than anything driven by his own growing determination to make this a horse race. He enthusiastically embraced the strategy for the balance of the campaign.

Willkie's near-total conversion from principled internationalist to opportunistic isolationist was too much for some who had been attracted to his earlier idealism, which they had thought was innate. Among them was Dorothy Thompson, the influential columnist with the *New York Herald Tribune*, who met personally with the candidate to tell him how disappointed she was; she soon endorsed FDR, a decision that would cost her her position with the staunchly Republican paper. Another was Walter Lippmann, also of the *Herald Tribune*, who wrote privately, "I hoped and believed [Willkie] would be the man this country needs, but I think he set his campaign on a fundamentally wrong line." He had been inclined to support the Republican, but he announced now that he would endorse neither candidate.[21] Summing up the views of several other commentators, Richard H. Rovere observed, "Willkie was as much in opposition to the man he had been a few months earlier as he was to his opponent."[22]

If his steadily improving poll numbers told Willkie that he now had a resonant message, they told FDR the same thing, confirming his prediction that their numbers would continue to narrow and that it would be a close race in November. That realization was soon shared by Democratic leaders, who were seeing and hearing firsthand evidence of it in their neighborhoods and communities. The White House began to receive dozens, and soon hundreds, of letters and telegrams from Democrats on the ground who were alarmed by what they were hearing and increasingly worried about what it meant for the party's candidates down the ticket who were relying on presidential coattails. Jim Rowe was closely monitoring the White House mail from party leaders as well as ordinary citizens, and in mid-October he alerted Hopkins to unmistakable concerns that were developing. Both groups, he said, were hearing Willkie's charges, and they wanted to hear from the president whether or not they were true. No one else would do.[23] Party leaders pleaded with Roosevelt to take to the campaign trail and to answer the charges of "warmonger" and "secret agreements."[24] The stream of pleas "rose to a flood," according to one observer, and threw the Roosevelt camp "into a state of near panic."[25] "This fellow Willkie is about to beat the Boss," an alarmed Hopkins told a colleague.[26]

Eleanor, on a cross-country trip to California, as usual had her ear close to the ground and picked up these same alarm bells. Her acute political antennae, ever more refined since Louis Howe began tutoring her in the art of politics during the 1920 vice presidential campaign, were attuned not just to the local politicians she encountered but also to the attitudes of ordinary citizens. She became convinced that unless Franklin shifted to an all-out campaign mode, answering Willkie's charges and making his own case, he would lose. "Dearest Franklin," she wrote him on October 11, "I hope you will make a few more speeches. It seems to me essential that you make them now as political speeches. The people have a right to hear your say in opposition to Willkie between now and the election."[27]

Harold Ickes, by now largely recovered from the slights he had suffered in Chicago, shifted to full campaign mode himself with the single purpose of dislodging Roosevelt from his "inspections" tours, which he and others had concluded were basically deceptions. He, too, wanted FDR to fight back, and he sent him several memos making the case for a shift of strategy. Ickes wired his concern to the president from Buffalo on October 14: "Sentiment here among influential leaders, who are your friends, is that Willkie is now gaining. They have volunteered the hope that you would make some fighting speeches. They expect you to carry the state only after a hard fight."²⁸

When that appeal failed to get any results, Ickes took a more direct approach and enlisted Missy LeHand and others in the White House in the effort. He reminded them that the president had inserted a caveat in his acceptance speech in which he reserved the right to correct any "misrepresentations or misstatements," and that Willkie's recent rhetoric had given him more than ample justification to start answering Willkie's charges. Ensuring that his views would be heard where they mattered, Ickes told them all he "wouldn't bet a nickel that the President would win" unless he put up a fight. Meeting with the president a few days later, Ickes was gratified to hear him say that he agreed that he needed to use the caveat he had left himself to answer the charges, and the secretary urged him to reveal his new plans immediately.²⁹

On October 18 the White House announced that the president would deliver five speeches before November 5, Election Day. He would answer directly the "falsifications" that Willkie and his surrogates had been propagating. "I am fighting mad," he told Ickes when the secretary called to congratulate him.³⁰

At about the same time in mid-October, the "Dear Guru" letters of Henry Wallace reappeared as a potentially embarrassing campaign issue for the Democrats. Since Roosevelt's musings about how to deal with them back in August, they had slipped below everyone's political radar, but now, two months later, they again got the full attention of the White House. Through a circuitous route the letters had come into the possession of Paul Block, publisher of the *Pittsburgh Post-Gazette*, and he was discussing how to use them with GOP officials and other publishers. Hopkins learned that Block had assigned one of his top investigative reporters, Ray Sprigle, to write a series of stories on Wallace's relationship with Nicholas Roerich, the "guru" recipient of the letters, and he had even managed somehow to acquire copies of some of Sprigle's drafts. Guessing correctly that the reporter would attempt to confront the vice presidential nominee with the letters, Hopkins showed the draft stories to Wallace and instructed him to avoid any contact with Sprigle.

The newsman and his quarry played cat-and-mouse as Wallace headed west on his final campaign swing until, on October 19, it was learned in Chicago that Sprigle had finally made it onto the campaign train. Stationing himself outside Wallace's compartment, Sprigle was startled to see the candidate suddenly emerge and ask him how he spelled his name. Wallace quickly jotted it on the top of a two-page statement that he thrust into the reporter's hands before abruptly shutting the door. The material in the stories, the statement said, represented the "desperation" of Willkie's supporters and was certain to be seen as a sign of "political bankruptcy." Even the "most psychopathic Roosevelt hater" would be offended by the publication of the stories, it went on, "since your first proposed article, as drafted, is not only libelous and outrageous in its departure from the truth but clearly is designed to raise in the midst of our citizenry minority religious suspicions and hatreds." For whatever reason Sprigle's stories never appeared, and the Roosevelt-Wallace camp breathed more easily.[31]

Congressman Joe Martin, Willkie's choice to chair the Republican National Committee, claimed later that he had feared the stories would be seen as "a last-minute smear" and that he killed the idea. "I didn't know anything about this fellow Guru," he wrote in a passage that had to astonish anyone even remotely familiar with the episode. "Maybe he had a great many more followers than any of [us] realized. Why kick away their votes? Everything considered, therefore, I decided that the Republicans would not use them." Others said Willkie himself had nixed the idea, with one version claiming that Hopkins had phoned Willkie and personally threatened to unleash the Irita Van Doren rumors if the "Dear Guru" letters were printed. If so, neither Hopkins nor anyone else ever took credit.[32]

15

To the Finish Line

It was a tall order to produce five major speeches in such a short time, but on this task Sam Rosenman would have help. Over the summer he and Hopkins had persuaded a major talent in the form of Pulitzer Prize–winning playwright Robert Sherwood to join the staff as a full-time speechwriter. Sherwood had not only a gift for language but an intuitive sense of politics, and he was wholly in sync with Roosevelt and his policies. Under tremendous pressure during the next few weeks, Rosenman, Sherwood, and Harry Hopkins (when he was available) would mesh their talents with FDR's political instincts in an effort to blunt, and even reverse, the momentum the Republicans had been able to generate. They would have to do so not only in a short time frame but also in a limited geographic sphere, as Roosevelt had announced in late summer that he wouldn't travel more than twelve hours by train from Washington—the Secret Service forbade him to fly—in case of an emergency. So the five speeches would be focused in the Northeast, though of course they would all be carried on national radio networks.

In preparing for the speeches, the president focused hard on the task at hand. He saw his reelection prospects possibly slipping away, and he was determined not to let that happen. He began by assessing the opposition's strengths and weaknesses. The Republicans' greatest strength was the undeniable pull of Willkie's charismatic personality and refreshing style. Their greatest weakness was the history of obstructionism Republicans had shown in Congress to virtually every major initiative he had put forth, both foreign and domestic. And as appealing as Willkie might be personally, FDR was convinced that he and his policies would be subsumed by the reactionaries in his party; the candidate's recent rhetoric showed signs that such a process was already under way. Therefore Roosevelt wouldn't attack Willkie directly, and in fact he would never mention his name. Rather, he would go after those whose records reflected what he regarded as the true core of the Republican Party and which he believed was at odds with what the country wanted its next president to represent. By implication he would wrap Willkie in those records and portray him as the captive of all of the worst instincts of his newly adopted party. Some might see it as guilt by association, but if so, FDR saw it as entirely legitimate because Willkie had eagerly sought the association.

The president opened this new and final stage of the campaign in Philadelphia on October 23. He delighted a large crowd of partisans by declaring at the outset, "I am an old campaigner, and I love a good fight!" So did the crowd, and they showed it with their enthusiasm. He then launched an assault on what he regarded as Republican hypocrisy in its newfound concern for the working men and women of the country, whose votes Willkie had been openly seeking. "The tears, the crocodile tears, for the laboring man and laboring woman now being shed in this campaign come from those same Republican leaders who had their chance to prove their love for labor in 1932—and missed it." Rather than help workers, they had greeted them with "troops and tanks," and rather than embrace the thought of a minimum wage or maximum hours of work, they "raised their hands in horror." The tune they were playing now is "played against a sounding board of Election Day. It is a tune with overtones which whisper: 'votes, votes, votes.'"

Shifting from ridicule to a more serious tone, Roosevelt took on directly Willkie's charge that the administration had entered into "secret agreements" that would bring the United States into the war. "I give to you and to the people of this country this most solemn assurance: There is no secret treaty, no secret obligation, no secret commitment, no secret understanding in any shape or form, direct or indirect, with any other Government, or any other nation in any part of the world, to involve this nation in any war or for any other purpose." Sherwood said later that the Philadelphia speech had not been one of Roosevelt's "better efforts," but it was effective at the time because it signaled that he was back in action. The roars of the partisan crowd, the speechwriter added, "were as important when broadcast as anything specific that he said."[1]

Sherwood later wrote that to some it appeared that Willkie had been "shaken" by the Philadelphia speech. His perspective on the GOP candidate at this point in the campaign reflected almost certainly the views of the man for whom he was writing and with whom he was spending several hours a day. When Willkie started charging that a foreign war would break out within five months in the event of a Roosevelt victory, his "campaign really descended to the lower depths and became, pretty much for two impassioned weeks, pretty much of a national disgrace." Contemptible as they were, the charges succeeded in the short term, and the advice Republican professionals were giving Willkie was "unhappily sound."[2] The appeal of Willkie's new message was enhanced by his campaign persona. His awkward and sometimes stumbling style of speaking, while initially off-putting to some, grew on many listeners as sincere if not polished, and it contrasted sharply with the often too-smooth delivery of the president.

Willkie spent the final weeks of the campaign pounding the theme that had finally gained him traction. He was now in a mad dash across the country in the "*Willkie Special*"—he would make some five hundred speeches in just over fifty days—lambasting the president's policies, which, he argued, would drag the country into the European war. "We do not want to send our boys over there again," he told a St. Louis audience at one point. "If you elect the third-term candidate, I believe they will be sent."[3]

Five days after Philadelphia, Roosevelt spent fourteen hours touring the boroughs of New York—and being cheered by an estimated two million people—before arriving at Madison Square Garden for the main event. He had decided that this was the forum in which he would answer the charge that he had been slow to rebuild the nation's defenses. He told his speechwriting team that he wanted to lay out all that he had done, but he also wanted the voting records of the Republicans. "They opposed nearly everything we tried to do to strengthen our defenses," he told them. The records proved him right—the GOP leaders had argued almost unanimously before 1940 that the country was spending too much on defense—and it was an easy decision to go on the offensive. With that in mind, the speechwriters saw an opportunity for FDR to indulge his favorite rhetorical devices, including sarcasm and ridicule, by rhythmically linking the names of three principal House Republicans who had been in the forefront of the opposition: minority leader Joe Martin of Massachusetts, Bruce Barton from the Upper East Side of Manhattan, and Hamilton Fish from Roosevelt's own Dutchess County. The president immediately saw what the speechwriters were up to: "his eyes twinkled," Rosenman recalled, "and he grinned from ear to ear."[4]

Roosevelt's speech in the Garden ignored Willkie while taking direct aim at congressional Republicans who, he claimed, had opposed virtually every defense initiative he had sent to the Hill. In short, the president said, they were "playing politics" with the issue of national defense. Until now, the Republican leaders had been maintaining that America's defenses were more than enough, but now they were announcing that the armed forces were being "starved." "Yes, it is a remarkable somersault. I wonder," Roosevelt went on, his voice dripping with sarcasm, "if the election could have something to do with it."[5]

He then cited in dramatic detail the votes that backed up his assertion, and he listed the names of Republican leaders who had opposed the proposals: Senators McNary, Vandenberg, Nye, and Johnson, and "Congressm[e]n Martin . . . Barton . . . and Fish." Britain never would have received "one ounce of help from us," he said to underscore his point, "if the decision had been left to Martin . . . Barton . . . and Fish." This time the crowd, which loved what Rosenman had called the "euphonious and rhythmic sequence" of the names, joined in: as soon as they heard the president say "Martin," it was their cue to shout out the other two names. Picked up by Democratic partisans on the radio, it became an audience favorite wherever FDR spoke for the remainder of the campaign. Roosevelt concluded the speech with a list of everything he had done to keep the United States out of the war, which he called an "affirmative, realistic fight for peace"; it included, incredibly, a favorable reference to the Neutrality Act of 1935, which he had regretted signing.[6]

The next day, October 29, only one week before the election, the president presided over a ceremony in Washington at which the first draft numbers were drawn under the recently enacted Selective Service Law. He had the authority to schedule the event after the election, which his political advisors unanimously and strenuously urged him to do, but he refused. He had supported the law, he reasoned, and as president of the United States, he had a moral obligation to be identified with its implementation, especially after suggesting in his acceptance speech that he, too, was submitting to a "draft." But in his remarks at the ceremony he never used that word; the historian in him, reinforced by the politician in him, harked back to the days of the Revolutionary War, preferring to call it a "muster." Before the cameras focused on Secretary of War Henry Stimson, blindfolded, drawing numbered blue capsules from a fishbowl, Roosevelt spoke directly to the young men of the country who would be directly affected by the random selections. He recalled for them the army that was first "mustered" together to "achieve independence and to establish certain fundamental rights for all men."[7] In the next few weeks some sixteen million men between the ages of twenty-one and thirty-five would register for the "muster."

Sherwood wrote later that letters and telegrams in unprecedented numbers now flooded the White House with "evidences of hysteria" about the prospects for war. Sympathetic reporters told of "waves of fear throughout the country which might easily merge into tidal proportions by Election Day and sweep Willkie into office." The growing fear of war, Sherwood wrote, was "unreasoning" and fueled by a sense of panic. Reports coming in from Democratic national headquarters in New York were even more alarming, all of them saying essentially much the same thing: "Please, for God's sake, Mr. President, give solemn promise to the mothers of America that you will not send their sons into any foreign wars." They warned that if he didn't, the president would lose.[8]

That message had been strongly reinforced when a few days earlier one of the most powerful labor leaders in the country, John L. Lewis of the Congress of Industrial Organizations (CIO), broke ranks with the president and endorsed Willkie. In the 1936 campaign, Lewis's United Mine Workers had been Roosevelt's largest contributor, but a series of personal and policy piques since had disabused him. Frances Perkins recounted an incident in which Lewis told FDR that all third-term objections would disappear if he was chosen to be on the ticket with the president. Needless to say, it was not to be, and in January 1940 Lewis had shocked his labor colleagues by charging that the New Deal had "not preserved faith" with American workers and predicted that FDR would go down to "ignominious defeat" if he was renominated.

Now, on October 25, Lewis tore viciously into the president as a would-be dictator who couldn't be trusted. He asked organized labor to join him in repudiating Roosevelt and pledged to resign his position with the CIO if that didn't happen. Then he spoke directly to the young men among the thirty million listeners in his radio audience: "You, who may be about to die in a foreign war . . . should you salute your Caesar?" And to their mothers he added: "May I hope" that on Election Day they might "lead the revolt against the candidate who plays at a game that may make cannon fodder of your sons?" Roosevelt had seen the attack coming and had asked other labor leaders to prepare their rank-and-file for it, which they did with considerable success. The speech's potential impact was fatally undercut as well by its obvious vitriol and personal animus toward FDR, which most independents and even more workers didn't share; members of his own CIO quickly labeled Lewis a "traitor." But Willkie liked it, wiring Lewis that it was "the most eloquent address I ever heard." As Election Day rapidly approached, Lewis was one more prominent speaker giving voice to the rising fear of war.[9]

If Roosevelt had discounted the effect of John L. Lewis's endorsement of Willkie and done nothing to dissuade him, it was a very different story when rumors reached him in late October that Joe Kennedy planned to do the same. The defeatist envoy had told Clare Boothe Luce earlier in the year that he was "absolutely certain Roosevelt is going to push us into the war."[10] Receiving reports of such statements by his top diplomat in London, FDR saw him as an inveterate appeaser and distrusted him to faithfully represent his views. As much as he would like to replace Kennedy, he feared the political consequences of angry Catholic voters, so he simply ignored him.

That was getting harder to do. As the slights accumulated, most recently on the destroyers-for-bases negotiation, so did Kennedy's resentments, which inevitably came to the attention of powerful Roosevelt adversaries in the United States. Henry Luce wired the ambassador in July that he "should return to this country immediately and tell what you think about everything totally, regardless of ordinary antiquated rules."[11] Such rules, of course, precluded an ambassador from publicly criticizing his government, not to mention his president. Kennedy was torn: he was sorely tempted to voice his many frustrations with Roosevelt and his policies, and he had gone so far the previous spring as to tell Clare Boothe Luce, "I'm going to come home, get off the plane, and endorse the Republican candidate for president." Now, in the midst of the campaign, he threatened Cordell Hull with the publication of an article attacking the administration for "having talked a lot and done very little."

FDR's political instincts went into high gear when he received these reports, and he instructed Hull to deny the diplomat home leave. Roosevelt's Mussolini stab-in-the back speech in Charlottesville had already cost him with Italian American voters, and his all-out support for Britain hadn't endeared him to those of Irish decent. Kennedy had the potential to do more political damage to Roosevelt than any other American should the ambassador lend credence to Republican claims that the president had made "secret agreements" with Churchill's government. Should Kennedy, who happened to be one of the leading Catholic laymen in the country, now endorse Willkie and repeat Republican charges that Roosevelt was leading the nation into war, it could cost the president the election.

Not surprisingly, others in the Roosevelt camp were also concerned about the Catholic vote. It may have surprised some to know, however, that one of them was Felix Frankfurter. The Jewish associate justice of the Supreme Court was obviously no authority on the Catholic vote. Nonetheless, he knew where to find someone who was. Newly arrived on the Court as FDR's latest appointee was Frank Murphy, a savvy and seasoned former governor of Michigan who was a committed New Dealer. Murphy told his fellow justice that the best way to get Catholics back on the Roosevelt reservation would be a full-throated defense on his behalf by Joe Kennedy. Adding William O. Douglas to their mission, the three justices trooped to the White House to urge the plan on Roosevelt and Hopkins. The view was unanimous that only Roosevelt personally could make it happen.

Unquestionably one of Roosevelt's greatest talents in the public arena, if not his greatest, was his ability to make those listening to his fireside chats believe that he was almost in their living rooms and that he cared personally about their concerns. It was a talent that translated with even greater force and effect in private quarters; he rarely failed to make a visitor across the table from him believe that he had the president's entire attention, that he cared deeply about whatever the visitor was saying, and that he agreed with whatever complaints or requests were being made. Joe Kennedy was about to get an all-out FDR charm offensive.

Realizing that the justices' advice offered a unique opportunity to turn a potential political disaster into a political gain—FDR relished nothing more than precisely this kind of challenge—he approved Kennedy's home leave after Sumner Welles assured him the State Department would get him straight to the White House before the ambassador saw anyone else. As Kennedy boarded a Pan American Clipper in Lisbon, he received a note from Roosevelt asking that he come straight to Washington without speaking to the press. Another message awaited him in Bermuda asking that he and his wife, Rose, already in New York, come immediately to the capital and spend the night at the White House. Finally, upon his arrival in New York, the White House operators managed to get him on the phone even before he saw his waiting family. FDR was having lunch with House Speaker Sam Rayburn and his new protégé and rising star from Texas, Representative

Lyndon B. Johnson, but he interrupted it to speak directly with Kennedy. "Ah, Joe," he began in his warmest and most mellifluous tones, "it is so good to hear your voice. Please come to the White House tonight for a little family dinner. I'm dying to talk with you." Johnson reported later that when the president hung up the phone, Roosevelt dramatically drew a finger across his throat. Neither Rayburn nor Johnson doubted that it was Kennedy's throat that was at issue.[12]

The ambassador dutifully put off a press scrum—reporters suspected something was afoot—before he and Rose boarded a flight to Washington. He failed to call the Luces, who apparently believed they would be dining with him that evening to discuss his resignation and his endorsement of Willkie. It was with this in mind that Rose Kennedy on the flight to Washington reminded her husband of the likely consequences of such an action. "The President sent you, a Roman Catholic, as Ambassador to London, which probably no other President would have done. . . . You would write yourself down as an ingrate in the view of many people if you resigned now."[13]

Joining them for an intimate dinner that evening in the White House were Senator Jimmy Byrnes and his wife, social friends of the Kennedys. FDR had asked Byrnes to take the lead in urging Kennedy to deliver a radio address urging the president's reelection. The South Carolinian made a soft pitch for the idea before dinner, noting that radio time had in fact been reserved for just that purpose a few days hence, but Kennedy demurred; he had to unburden himself of a few things, he said. During most of a dinner that consisted of scrambled eggs and sausage, a Roosevelt favorite on Sunday evenings, the ambassador reported on the effects of the Blitz on London and on his last conversation with his friend Chamberlain. Byrnes again suggested a radio address for Roosevelt, and the president reinforced the idea, but Kennedy still failed to respond. He was clearly awaiting his opportunity to be alone with the president to pour out his grievances, but, realizing that he wouldn't have that opportunity, he suddenly gave voice to his frustrations: "Since it doesn't seem possible for me to see the President alone, I guess I'll just have to say what I am going to say in front of everybody."[14]

He proceeded to complain bitterly about the way he had been treated, particularly the way he had been ignored by U.S. envoys as they had come traipsing through London on official business. In the face of all this and more he had remained loyal to Roosevelt, he protested, and had even come out for the third term. Yet he had not even been informed of the destroyer negotiations. He was fed up, he said, and he would not be returning to London. Throughout this tirade FDR listened attentively without comment, until he finally offered Kennedy his full sympathy and support. He didn't know any of this, he claimed, and he was outraged that his ambassador had been treated so shabbily. The State Department was guilty of callous behavior that would be remedied with a total overhaul after the election. *How could this have happened?* he seemed to be saying. The president was so strongly backing up Kennedy's complaints, Byrnes said later, that he thought the ambassador was "even beginning to feel a touch of sympathy for the State Department boys."[15]

At this point Roosevelt moved the conversation into the political future, casually suggesting that he would be favorably disposed toward Kennedy for the Democratic presidential nomination four years hence, or at least so the ambassador's son John later claimed. Leaving a visitor with the impression that he agreed with him on such a cherished ambition—Kennedy had clearly harbored visions of the presidency for some time—was of course a frequent FDR tactic. If that was what occurred here, it was successful: when the president again asked the ambassador to deliver a speech on his behalf, he agreed to do so, but he insisted that he would pay for the radio time himself and that he would write his own speech.

Missy LeHand promptly called the Democratic National Committee asking that the radio time it had reserved for the following Tuesday be relinquished to Kennedy. News of the scheduled address immediately buoyed hopes in the Willkie camp that a Kennedy endorsement was forthcoming.

On October 29, exactly one week before Election Day, Kennedy took to the airwaves to report that he was "renewed in my conviction that this country must and will stay out of war." He admitted that he had had serious disagreements with the president, but firmly denied that there were any "secret agreements" with the British that would bring the United States into the war. Now was the time for continuity, he argued: "In light of these considerations, I believe that Franklin D. Roosevelt should be re-elected President of the United States."[16]

FDR could not have hoped for a more effective speech. Not only was potential disaster averted, but Kennedy had reassured many listeners, and especially Catholic listeners, that the president would keep the country out of the war. Favorable telegrams inundated the White House and the Democratic National Committee, with local party leaders urging Kennedy to repeat his message continuously until Election Day. Roosevelt's ploy had worked, perhaps better than he imagined. But what he really thought of Kennedy was revealed four months later in a letter to his son-in-law John Boettiger: "The truth of the matter is that Joe is and always has been a temperamental Irish boy, terrifically spoiled at an early age by huge financial success; thoroughly patriotic, thoroughly selfish, and thoroughly obsessed with the idea that he must leave each of his nine children with a million dollars apiece (he had often told me that)." As a result, he was determined to prevent any kind of change. "To him, the future of a small capitalist class is safer under Hitler than under Churchill. This is sub-conscious on his part and he does not admit it."[17]

Needless to say, Henry and Clare Boothe Luce were stunned at the turn of events, and Willkie himself was hugely disappointed, convinced that the president had misled Kennedy about the likelihood of war. They knew they had been seriously outmaneuvered, but they didn't know exactly how. Sixteen years later Clare Boothe finally asked Kennedy what had happened. "I simply made a deal with Roosevelt," she said he told her. "We agreed that if I endorsed him for president in 1940, then he would support my son Joe for governor of Massachusetts in 1942."[18]

Willkie meanwhile continued his focus on the war issue that was gaining him so much traction, but in a play for the black vote he began to weave his lifelong commitment to civil rights into his speeches. He may have been the first presidential candidate to emphasize the issue seriously, and it won him the endorsement of leading black newspapers and the legendary Joe Lewis. When Father Coughlin's anti-Semitic *Social Justice* endorsed him, Willkie repudiated it: "I don't have to be President of the United States, but I do have to keep my beliefs clear in order to live with myself." Emotions were running high in these final days before the election, and the Republican found himself the target not just of slurs aimed at his German heritage but of numerous fruits and vegetables as well, some of which hit their mark, including a potato in Boston and an egg in Chicago. "He had more assorted sizes and kinds of vegetables thrown at him," *Time* magazine said, "than anyone since the old Mississippi showboat days." Tempers were fraying and things were getting nasty.[19]

On the train to Boston the day after the Selective Service event, FDR worked with his speechwriting team between rear platform appearances on the address he would deliver that evening. The major issue facing them all was how to deal with the growing fear of being dragged into the war. Democratic chairman Ed Flynn was "particularly insistent" that Roosevelt offer assurances to the mothers of America that their sons would not be sent overseas.

Sitting in a low-backed armchair in his private car, the tastefully appointed *Ferdinand Magellan*, surrounded by Hopkins, Rosenman, Sherwood, Missy LeHand, and Grace Tully, he was shown this plea from his handpicked party leader together with others that had arrived by wire at the latest stop. "How often do they expect me to say that?" Roosevelt protested. "It's in the Democratic platform, and I've repeated it a hundred times." He was referring, of course, to the formulation he had persuaded the platform committee in Chicago to adopt, which pledged that American boys would not be sent to foreign wars "except in case of attack." Sherwood, the junior member of this team, quickly replied to FDR's question: "I know it, Mr. President, but they don't seem to have heard you the first time. Evidently you've got to say it again—and again—and again."[20]

Rosenman suggested that he use the same platform version of the pledge that he had been using in his previous speeches, but to his surprise Roosevelt "suddenly got stubborn about it." The president tried to rationalize leaving out the qualifying language: "It's not necessary. It's implied clearly. If we're attacked it's no longer a foreign war . . . Or do they want me to guarantee that our troops will be sent into battle only in the event of another Civil War?" Clearly the urgent pleas were having an effect on the president. That evening the text he delivered was an effort to satisfy them as well as the broader fears they represented: "And while I'm talking to you mothers and fathers, I give you one more assurance. I have said this before, but I shall say it again and again and again: Your boys are not going to be sent into any foreign wars."[21]

Hearing the speech on the radio, Willkie exclaimed, "That hypocritical son of a bitch! This is going to beat me." It was the only time Roosevelt made this statement without the attacked-first proviso, and it would cause him "a lot of headaches later" when it was thrown back at him, according to Rosenman. Like other presidents running for reelection, he couldn't always reconcile his role of chief executive with that of candidate. A day earlier he had shown political courage in presiding over the first draft lottery; he saw it as his solemn responsibility in his role as a commander in chief facing a dangerous world. Today he yielded to political expediency essentially so that he could *continue* in that role, convinced as he was that his reelection was essential to America in facing that world. It may have been a momentary lapse—if indeed he saw it as a lapse, and he never admitted as much—but throughout the year he had recognized political calculation as a legitimate factor in making larger strategic decisions. He had no difficulty justifying the practice, and most of the time he was aware of its limits. However, on this occasion it was too much even for Eleanor, who gently reproved her husband in her "My Day" column: "No one can honestly promise you to-day peace at home and aboard. All any human being can do is to promise that he will do his utmost to prevent the country being involved in war."[22]

James Roosevelt questioned his father about the "dishonesty" of what he had said in Boston. "I knew we were going to war," FDR replied, according to James. "I had to delay until there was no way out of it. I knew we were woefully unprepared. . . . But I couldn't come out and say a war was coming, because the people would have panicked and turned from me. I had to educate the people to the inevitable, gradually, step by step . . . So you play the game the way it has been played over the years, and you play to win."[23]

The next day it was Charles Lindbergh's turn to be in New England. Kingman Brewster, an undergraduate at Yale who was the head of the university's America First Committee (and who would one day become president of Yale as well as ambassador to Great Britain), had recruited the aviator to rebut the growing number of alumni who opposed the isolationist viewpoint on campus. ("We are resentful of the deceit and subterfuge which has characterized the politics of foreign policy," Brewster would later tell the Senate Foreign Relations Committee.) A standing-room-only crowd of three thousand jammed into Woolsey Hall that evening to hear him introduce Lindbergh to heavy applause. "Most of us were for the first time in the flesh-and-blood presence of our boyhood hero," one student recalled, "the most famous American of our childhood, and you could feel the electricity because of that and because of the sheer magnetism of his presence." Lindbergh recounted what he saw as the folly of events since the First World War that had led to yet another conflict for which America was ill prepared; the country should deal with its own internal problems, build up its defenses, and stay out of Europe, he argued. "We must decide whether we are going to place our security in the defense of America, or in an attempt to control the affairs of the rest of the world." That security, he added, should be built upon "the bedrock of our own continent and its adjacent islands" in pursuit of "the independent American destiny that Washington outlined in his Farewell Address." Lindbergh had expected that he would be heckled in this, his longest speech to date, but instead received a "prolonged standing ovation."[24]

By coincidence, Roosevelt came through New Haven that same day on his way back from Boston, and he, too, spoke about the war. Addressing some two thousand rain-soaked fellow citizens for ten minutes from the rear platform of his train, the president bemoaned what Sherwood called the "contemptible" attacks that his opponents had shamelessly introduced into the campaign and that had given rise to war "hysteria." Mindful that he was in a college community of draft-age young men, he skirted over the recently enacted Selective Service Act: "We have started to train more men not because we expect to use them, but for the same reason your umbrellas are up today—to keep from getting wet."[25]

On November 1 Roosevelt was back in New York, this time to address a rally in Brooklyn. The Boston speech and its pledge had left a bad taste in virtually everyone's mouth, and the speechwriting team was eager to put it behind them. Rosenman remembered a sense of cheer and relief, an "undefined feeling that the worst was over." The speech that evening, he said, represented "a vast improvement over its unworthy predecessors in this strange campaign." They built the core theme of the president's remarks around the "evil" combination within the Republican Party of "the extreme reactionary and the extreme radical elements in this country." He reminded his listeners "what the collaborative understanding between Communism and Nazism has done to the processes of democracy abroad," implicitly warning that democracy in America could also be at risk. But the highlight of the speech was an unwitting gift from *New York Times* columnist Arthur Krock, a Willkie supporter who that morning had pointed out several "blunders" the Republicans had been making in attacking Roosevelt. "The President's only supporters are paupers," Krock had quoted a Pennsylvania GOP official as saying, "those who earn less than $1,200 a year and aren't worth *that*, and the Roosevelt family." A staffer read the quote to FDR, who immediately saw the possibilities even without having it pointed out to him that half of American families had incomes below $1,200. "I think we might as well forget the Roosevelt family," said the president in his speech, but who were these "paupers" Krock referred to? "They are only the common men and women who have helped build this country, who have made it great, and who would defend it with their lives if the need arose." He for one did not believe that any American who earned $100 a month did not "lose their devotion to social and economic justice." "'Paupers' are not worth their salt—there speaks the true sentiment of the Republican leadership in this year of grace." The Pennsylvania Republican denied making the remark Krock had attributed to him, and Krock himself came in for no little resentment for having served up such an easy pitch for FDR to knock out of the park.[26]

Then it was on to Cleveland for the final speech of the campaign. Boarding the train at midnight, Roosevelt asked his team if they had anything prepared for that obviously important event, and they had to confess sheepishly that they did not. "Well, don't stay up too late," he said as he went off to bed. Rosenman and Sherwood worked through most of the night—the ill Hopkins had retired much earlier—sifting through material they had sought from Dean Acheson, Archibald MacLeish, and Dorothy Thompson. Rosenman, who had written for Roosevelt for fourteen years and who knew his voice better than any other person, and Sherwood, the gifted newcomer, worked as though they had been collaborating for years. They wrote separately, then they edited each other, then they wrote together, and then they repeated the process all over again until they finally got out the scissors and did a classic cut-and-paste job that was intended to sum up all that Roosevelt stood for in this campaign. It was a herculean effort that was completed only at 6:00 a.m., when they sent the draft back to Roosevelt's car for his breakfast reading.[27]

But the real process of writing this speech was only just beginning. After a few hours of sleep the speechwriters joined the president for lunch in his car, but Sherwood was shocked by what he saw. Roosevelt looked "gray and worn and sagging." It was his introduction to the burdens of the office, and, he wrote, he almost hoped that the president would lose the election, "for it seemed that flesh and blood could not survive another six months—let alone four years—in this terrible job." Then Sherwood witnessed what he called Roosevelt's "powers of recuperation in action." The president began reminiscing about his sailing days off the Atlantic coast years earlier, telling stories about Maine lobstermen that apparently everyone present already knew by heart. Sherwood noticed that the grayness of the president's face had been replaced by "a healthy color, the circles vanished from under his eyes, the sagging jowls seemed to tighten up into muscles about his jaw-bone." By the time lunch was over FDR turned to his team and said, "Now! What have you three cutthroats been doing to my speech?" Hopkins and Rosenman had seen this performance many times before, but to Sherwood it was an amazing and totally unexpected feat of self-revival, a preparation in this case for the campaign's final act. For the next six hours they worked on the speech, interrupted only when they arrived at a stop where the president was compelled to put on his leg braces and walk to the rear platform on the arm of Pa Watson.[28]

Rosenman and Sherwood agreed that the speech that FDR delivered that evening before an enthusiastic Cleveland crowd was the best of the campaign. It appealed to workers, farmers, intellectuals, conservationists, liberals, parents of school-age children, and others who constituted the New Deal coalition to come together once again, as they had in 1932 and 1936. It seamlessly wove together the principal themes of his previous speeches—the vigor of democracy, keeping the United States out of war, the obligations of government to its people—and concluded with what Rosenman called one of the most moving and eloquent passages ever uttered by Roosevelt:

> I see an America where factory workers are not discarded after they
> reach their prime, where there is no endless chain of poverty from
> generation to generation, where impoverished farmers and farm
> hands do not become homeless wanderers, where monopoly does
> not make youth a beggar for a job.
>
> I see an America whose rivers and trees and valleys and lakes—
> hills and streams and plains—the mountains over our land and
> nature's wealth deep under the earth—are protected as the rightful
> heritage of all the people.
>
> I see an America devoted to our freedom—unified by tolerance
> and by religious faith—people consecrated to peace, a people
> confident in strength because their body and their spirit are secure
> and unafraid. . . .
>
> There is a great storm raging now, a storm that makes things
> harder for the world. And that storm is . . . the true reason that I
> would like to stick by these people of ours until we reach the clear,
> sure footing ahead. We will make it—we will make it before the next
> term is over . . . When that term is over there will be another
> President and many more Presidents in the years to come, and I
> think that, in the years to come, that word "President" will be a word
> to cheer the hearts of common men and women everywhere.

When the audience heard the president say "another president," shouts of "No! No!" rang through the hall. Worried that the radio audience might conclude that a fourth-term demonstration was under way, Roosevelt never paused in his delivery but moved closer to the microphone and raised his voice in an effort to drown out the protests in the hall. Later, when everyone was unwinding on the train ride back to Washington, George Allen, a political operative with a well-recognized sense of humor, turned to FDR and referred to the "another president" passage: "Mr. President . . . that's going to cost us a million votes in 1944." Everyone burst out laughing, never imagining it could be anything but a joke.[29]

The electorate meanwhile was transfixed by this election, which they sensed would be hugely consequential to their country and to them personally. Willkie hammered the war issue so hard and so persistently that it obscured every other issue in the campaign. He would only send aid to Britain with the approval of Congress, he said, and not by means of the "slick legal short-cuts" Roosevelt had been using (a reference almost certainly to the destroyer deal that Willkie had earlier approved but then denounced as "dictatorial").[30]

After a brief stop in Washington, Roosevelt headed north to Hyde Park, where he would vote and receive the returns, as he had every election year since 1910, when his name first appeared on a ballot for state senator. This was the place that was more important to him than any other—where he had been born, where he had roamed the fields with woodchucks as a young boy and discovered nature, where he learned to fend for himself, where the unqualified love of his parents gave him the confidence to nurture great dreams and the confidence to pursue them. Hyde Park was home, but it was more than that, too: it was where he came for renewal nearly two hundred times as president. Now, after nearly eight long and trying years in the White House, it was the place to which he came to learn if his countrymen wished him to continue as their president. He was not at all sure they would—the still-struggling economy, the threat of war coming to the United States, the third-term taboo, and an able opponent effectively arguing these and other charges all stood in the way. He was worried about the outcome, and the most recent polls gave him good reason to worry. "Once more I am in the quiet of my home in Hyde Park," he told a national radio audience in his traditional election eve address.

As I sit here tonight with my own family, I think of all the other American families . . . sitting in their own homes. They have eaten their suppers in peace, they will be able to sleep in their homes tonight in peace. Tomorrow they will be free to live out their ordinary lives in peace—free to say and do what they wish, free to worship as they please. Tomorrow, of all days, they will be free to choose their own leaders who . . . become in turn only the instruments to carry out the will of the people . . . And when you and I stand in line tomorrow for our turn at the polls, we are voting equals . . . Last Saturday night I said that freedom of speech is of no use to the man who has nothing to say and that freedom of worship is of no use to the man who has lost his God. And tonight I should like to add that a free election is of no use to the man who is too indifferent to vote.

Several weeks earlier he had said he wanted to close this traditionally nonpartisan election-eve speech with a prayer that he remembered from the Book of Common Prayer at Groton nearly a half century before. It had been a favorite of the Reverend Endicott Peabody, who had urged his young charges, mostly unsuccessfully, to seek public service, but the message had resonated strongly with the young Franklin; he credited Peabody with having influenced him more than anyone else outside his family. The Library of Congress produced dozens of prayer books, but none of them contained the precise quote that Roosevelt sought. When he returned from Cleveland, however, the library had finally found it, and now he voiced it again, almost certainly for the first time in decades: "Endue with the spirit of wisdom those to whom in Thy Name we entrust the authority of government, that there may be peace and justice at home, and that, through obedience to Thy law, we may show forth Thy praise among the nations of the earth. In the time of prosperity, fill our hearts with thankfulness, and in the day of trouble, suffer not our trust in Thee to fail."[31]

The Republicans made no effort to be nonpartisan and inspirational on election eve. "When your boy is dying on some battlefield . . . crying out, 'Mother! Mother!'" a GOP radio advertisement warned, "don't blame

Franklin D. Roosevelt because he sent your boy to war—because YOU sent Franklin D. Roosevelt back to the White House!"[32]

There would be yet one more national radio address that evening, this one delivered by Lincoln scholar and poet Carl Sandberg, who admired Roosevelt and saw to it that the president had received his classic multi-volume biography of the sixteenth president. FDR had studied Lincoln for years, especially since entering the White House, and there was no one who could draw a parallel between the two presidents more persuasively than Sandburg. In a five-minute broadcast—paid for by the Democratic Party—he quoted an Illinois congressman, Owen Lovejoy, on his deathbed in 1864, the year that Lincoln's reelection was very much in doubt. "I am satisfied," Lovejoy said, "as the old theologians used to say in reference to the world, that if [Lincoln] is not the best conceivable President he is the best possible. . . . And although he does not do everything that you and I would like, the question recurs whether we could elect a man who could."[33]

The next morning the president, accompanied by Eleanor and his mother, Sara, drove to the polling place to cast his vote. As usual on such occasions, FDR exuded optimism, cheerfully obliging photographers who urged him to wave at nearby trees. Eleanor, on the other hand, was more reserved; the day before, she had written her aunt Maud, "Frankly, I hate the next four years in Washington and dread what it may do to us all but there seemed nothing else for F. to do."[34]

After lunch at the Big House, the president joined Ross McIntire, Pa Watson, and Harry Hopkins in a poker game designed to take their minds off the election returns, which would be coming soon enough. With the same purpose in mind, Eleanor went for a long walk with her young friend Joe Lash through the woods from her retreat at Val-Kill to her husband's at Top Cottage. Later, everyone except FDR and his mother came to Val-Kill for supper before finding their way back to the Big House, which had been prepared to receive the returns. Radios tuned to news broadcasts had been stationed throughout the house, but the main action was in the family dining room, where the president, his coat off and his tie pulled down, had established himself at a table equipped with tally sheets, sharpened pencils, and telephones with direct lines to the White House as well as to his national chairman, Ed Flynn, at the Biltmore in New York.

In a small cubicle off the dining room three wire service teletype machines, clacking loudly, began spewing out early returns, which were quickly torn off and given to the president as soon as they appeared. Staff and family members constantly entered the room to get the latest information. Roosevelt, as ever, liked to be surrounded by people, and even the unhelpful tension that his very nervous neighbor and treasury secretary, Henry Morgenthau, brought into the room didn't appear to bother him. The president seemed his usual relaxed and confident self, concentrating on the early returns, while Eleanor was more intent on being the perfect hostess and seeing that everyone was both comfortable and informed. Periodically given brief reports from Missy, she passed them along calmly to others, "as if nothing out of the ordinary were taking place," Joe Lash observed; "she made everyone feel at home and included, but she was detached about the returns, an observer rather than a participant in the mounting excitement."[35]

Mike Reilly, the head of Roosevelt's Secret Service detail and an astute observer of his traits, stood guard over the president outside the dining room door. Suddenly FDR turned and abruptly instructed him: "Mike, I don't want to see anybody in here." Taken aback by Roosevelt's unusually sharp tone, he noticed that the president had broken into a heavy sweat. At first he thought he might have taken ill, but he quickly rejected the thought and concluded that something had upset him. He would say later that the president's nerves had failed him, the first time he had ever witnessed such an occurrence.

"Including your family, Mr. President?" he asked.

"I said *anybody*," came the response.

Reilly dutifully closed the door, informed Eleanor what he had been told to do, and began turning away everyone who came looking for the latest returns. Hugely disappointed, they were compelled to rely on radio reports for the better part of an hour.[36]

Reilly had been correct that something had upset the president, and it was clearly something that he had seen in the early returns. Virtually everywhere Willkie was running ahead of Alf Landon's pace of four years before, and he was running well ahead in places, such as New York State, that FDR needed in order to produce an Electoral College majority. He was an experienced student of election returns, well versed in what the early ones foretold. It was an art refined over three decades of reading such numbers and extrapolating them into likely results, and tonight they were almost certainly reinforced by the reports Ed Flynn was getting from party leaders around the country. These early trends more than disturbed him; they shook him to the point that one of the most observant people around him believed that he lost his nerve. During nearly eight years in the presidency no one else had ever witnessed anything close to that in him. To virtually everyone in Roosevelt's world he was the picture of steadfast confidence— always. It was his defining characteristic. Suffering personal defeat in the Court-packing fight and the attempted purge, he had never lost his nerve, nor did he lose it in the face of the nation's worst economic calamity and more recently the prospect of another world war. But he apparently lost it that night.

Some of Roosevelt's biographers have speculated on what must have been going through his mind during the time he was closeted in the dining room staring at the numbers that he believed signaled his defeat. Kenneth Davis, for example, imagined that FDR was certain that his defeat would represent "the triumph of forces of immense evil in American life . . . forces aimed straight at the kind of civil strife out of which, in other lands, the corporate state had risen."[37]

No one will ever know exactly what he was thinking, of course, because he never wrote about the episode and it wasn't in his nature to talk of such personal experiences with anyone, even Eleanor. One thing that can be reasonably concluded, however, is that he didn't know how to *act* in these new and alarming circumstances. How else to explain why this ebullient man who *always*, even in the most tense situations, wanted to be surrounded by people, now insisted on being alone for nearly a hour? Roosevelt was quintessentially an actor, a talent he had developed as a child and perfected as a politician; it defined him to such an extent that it was impossible to separate the actor from the man. He had reportedly once told Orson Welles that they were the two best actors in America. Now, apparently on the verge of political and personal defeat, his ability to act failed him, and he closeted himself in the dining room of the Big House.

It's more difficult to surmise what went through his mind in these moments, but it would have been surprising had he not been consumed with dark thoughts about what a Willkie victory would portend for the country and the world. He had spoken with great feeling in Brooklyn just a week before about the combination of forces arrayed against him, all of them determined to destroy his vision for America. At risk now was all that he had done during the New Deal years to harness the power of government to give hope and opportunity to millions of struggling Americans. He had persuaded himself that if elected, Willkie, no matter what he was saying publicly, would become captive to the most reactionary forces within the Republican Party. Willkie was already becoming captive, in Roosevelt's view, to the most isolationist forces in the country in his desperate decision to use the fear of war as his chief campaign issue.

It would have been surprising as well had the president not revisited his decision, gestating for nearly a year and reached finally in July, to run for a third term. Scholars are divided as to whether or not he wanted to run, and many have concluded that it was his plan as far back as early 1939—or even earlier—to do so. Being in charge was too much a part of his being, they argue, for him to give it up. The one thing we know for certain about FDR on this question, William Leuchtenburg has observed, is that he never left the presidency voluntarily.[38] But the evidence we have shows that his mind was set on retirement so that he could relax, write, tend to his health and financial security, and simply enjoy the years he had left. Roosevelt was not a martyr or deluded by grandeur. He knew his limits, and he yearned for peace. He had put all of that aside when the outbreak of war in Europe threatened to reach the United States, and he became determined to prevent that from happening. He had come to believe that only he could overcome the deep isolationism of the country, only he could persuade his fellow Americans that their interests were tied directly to the survival of Britain. In the end he couldn't persuade himself that there was another Democrat committed to the New Deal and committed to Britain who could be elected. So, strengthened by the justifications offered by Frankfurter and MacLeish, he decided he had to run—to challenge the third-term taboo and therefore do what no president before him had ever done. Whether from a stern sense of duty, overweening ambition, or both, he had concluded that he had no choice. Of course, decisions always stem from choices, and the one he had made in July that now appeared to be crashing down on him was arguably the most important decision of his presidency, if not of his lifetime. For all the hindsight certainty we now ascribe to it, it had been a choice filled with risk. Now, at the end, he was besieged by the doubt that attended it. Had he miscalculated the power of the third-term issue? Had he misjudged public support for his national security agenda by trumpeting the destroyer deal and presiding over the first peacetime draft in American history in the midst of a campaign? In short, was he was trying to reach a political bridge too far?

The early election returns told him he would be returning to Hyde Park after all. He desperately didn't want to return this way, which is to say involuntarily. Since he had been a boy here he had tried to live life on his own terms, and in that he had largely succeeded, even as the victim of the polio that crippled him. Now, it appeared, he would be returning to Hyde Park not on his own terms. It was a dark moment for him, almost certainly one of the darkest he had experienced, and by his own choice it was also a crushingly solitary moment. Once again he was where he had not been before: how would he explain such a devastating defeat to his family, his friends, and his fellow Americans?

At the same time, ironically, Wendell Willkie was convinced that *he* would lose the election. Chain-smoking Camels in an overstuffed chair on the fourteenth floor of New York's Commodore Hotel, he saw early encouraging returns disappear when the industrial states started to report. He clung to the hope that the rural and small-town vote would yet save him, but the reality of the overall electoral picture was settling in.[39]

Back in the dining room at Hyde Park, the gloom finally lifted. Whether through a message from Flynn or someone else, it became evident to the president that the electoral landscape looked very different than it had when Mike Reilly had closed the door less than an hour before. Roosevelt told him to open it, and into the dining room poured family, staff, and friends, jubilant at the latest returns, which showed FDR surging to a significant lead in the most heavily populated states—New York, Pennsylvania, Illinois, Massachusetts. Others soon followed, and though Willkie showed no sign of conceding defeat, everyone in the Big House that night had no doubt of the outcome. That included a newly buoyant president, once again jocular and full of smiles.

It also included the people of Hyde Park, who at midnight appeared at the front door in the form of the traditional torchlight parade accompanied by a band playing, teasingly but affectionately, "The Old Gray Mare." The parades had become a staple of Democratic electoral victories since Roosevelt's childhood, and they took on a more personal significance after he won his state senate seat in 1910; like virtually every ritual associated with Hyde Park, it was one that he loved. His own part in it required him to feign surprise that his neighbors had so honored him, and they, knowing their own role in the charade, let him know how much they admired his acting skills. A boy added to the hilarity when he pushed to the front of the crowd with a sign on which the words "Out at third" had been crossed out, with "Safe at third" replacing them. FDR loved it.

With four generations of his family assembled outside the front door—Sara and Franklin junior were beside him, while young Franklin the third was watching from an upstairs window—Roosevelt reminisced about the first time he had witnessed a torchlight parade: it was 1884, Grover Cleveland had just been elected to his first term as president, and Franklin was one and a half years old. His family's disclaimers to the contrary notwithstanding, he maintained that he remembered the event, perhaps because he often liked to embellish his own narrative and perhaps because it reminded him of the time he actually met Cleveland, a few years later. His father, a staunch Democrat, had taken the five-year-old Franklin with him to the White House to see the only Democratic president elected since the Civil War. "My little man," Cleveland said after putting his hand on FDR's head, "I am making a strange wish for you. It is that you may never be president of the United States."[40]

Now, in the first week of November 1940, not only was he president of the United States, but he had just been elected to a third term to that office. His own wishes, fueled by a healthy ambition and a desire to follow Endicott

Peabody's admonition to serve his country, had long ago obscured that of his predecessor. He had been much more ambivalent in seeking this third term but in the end had thrown himself into the pursuit with total commitment. And his effort yielded the result that he had sought, with numbers not as impressive as his first two elections to the White House but impressive still. His vote totals surpassed those of Willkie's by nearly 5 million—27,243,000 to 22,304,000; his Electoral College margin was even wider—449 votes from thirty-eight states as against Willkie's 82 votes from ten states. Jewish, Polish, Anglophile, and other voters who most strongly supported his war policies bolstered that margin, while those of Irish, Italian, and German descent who seriously questioned them cut into it. The participation of 50 million Americans in the election smashed all previous records, signaling that they, too, knew what was at stake and that they wanted their voices heard.

Polls showed that if 1940 had been an ordinary year, one in which war was not threatening the United States, Roosevelt almost certainly would have lost decisively to Willkie. Too many people were tired of the New Deal and too many were tired of FDR. As Eleanor had famously said, however, this was not an ordinary time, and the voters had looked at the election differently. They saw it through the prism of war and decided they needed a tested and trusted leader, his faults notwithstanding, to lead the country down the perilous road ahead. They didn't know where that road would lead, nor did Roosevelt, although he had a sense—and dread—of what lay ahead.

The journey down that road would start soon enough, but tonight he and his family and neighbors and friends were still here, in Hyde Park. "We are facing difficult days in this country," he told them, "but I think you will find me the same Franklin Roosevelt you have known a great many years. My heart has always been here. It always will be."[41]

Elmer Davis, the dean of radio commentators, had told the nation at 11:00 p.m. that Franklin Roosevelt has been reelected to a third term. A subdued Willkie took the news stoically. He would issue a gracious and conciliatory concession statement, but not until the next morning. "Congratulations on your re-election.," he wired FDR on Wednesday. "I wish you all personal health and happiness." Roosevelt responded with his "sincerest thanks" and "heartily" reciprocated Willkie's "good wishes." It was over. At last.[42]

Epilogue
The Mandate

If anyone was more relieved than Roosevelt by the election returns, it was Winston Churchill. He had followed the election "with profound anxiety," he wrote later. "No newcomer into power could possess or soon acquire the knowledge and experience of Franklin Roosevelt. None could equal his commanding gifts."[1]

The day after the election he sent the president a cable of congratulations: "I did not feel it right for me as a Foreigner to express my opinion upon American politics while the Election was on, but now I feel you will not mind my stating that I prayed for your success and that I am truly thankful for it."[2] It was a flattering, thoughtful, and tactically brilliant letter that Churchill had taken great pains to draft himself, as he did all of his communications to FDR. It was never answered, never even acknowledged, which had to have extended and probably deepened the anxiety Churchill was feeling during the election. What did this silence mean? The prime minister never got over the slight, if that is what it was.

Two days after the election a crowd of several thousand people warmly welcomed Roosevelt at Washington's Union Station while another two hundred thousand cheered his motorcade on the short trip to the White House. He was back at the seat of government with a strong mandate to help Britain withstand, and even reverse, Hitler's merciless onslaught from the air and on the sea. What would he do with that mandate? It was well known that Britain was running out of the money needed to purchase American goods under the cash-and-carry requirement. To underscore the point, Lord Lothian stepped off a plane from London at LaGuardia and announced, "Well, boys, Britain's broke. It's your money we want." Would the president call for amending the Neutrality Act—again—so that the United States could make loans to belligerents, or the Johnson Act, so that it could make loans to those who had defaulted on their debts from the Great War?[3]

On December 3 FDR left for a cruise on the USS *Tuscaloosa* in the Caribbean, ostensibly to inspect naval bases; in fact, it was a vacation, neither the first nor last time he would use a warship to rest up, and to think. Aside from his personal staff, only Harry Hopkins accompanied him, but the two conducted little official business. For the most part they watched the latest movies and fished. From his home in Cuba, Ernest Hemingway, a world-class sport fisherman as well as a renowned writer, thoughtfully radioed locations of the best fishing grounds in the area. The information failed to improve FDR's consistently poor experience with the sport. The daily routine was broken only by the regular arrival of navy seaplanes delivering the mail and official dispatches, and on December 9 Roosevelt received a four-thousand-word letter from Churchill. It was, the prime minister would say, "one of the most important" of his lifetime, and again he had taken great pains, with the assistance of Lothian, to draft it. It was, in the words of Jon Meacham, "classic Churchill—long, well-argued, and passionate yet practical."[4]

The prime minister gave the president a detailed assessment of conditions facing British forces around the world before moving on to the desperate need for more shipping and war materials of all kinds. He concluded the long document with an expression of confidence that America would see them through this great trial, but he offered no suggestions as to how that might be done. Hopkins would later tell Churchill that Roosevelt "read and re-read this letter as he sat alone in his deck chair, and that for two days he did not seem to have reached any clear conclusion." Adding his own touch to the imagined scene on the *Tuscaloosa*, Churchill wrote later, "He was plunged in intense thought, and brooded silently."[5]

Hopkins said of the period following the letter's arrival: "I didn't know for quite awhile what he was thinking about, if anything. But then—I began to get the idea that he was refueling, the way he so often does when he seems to be resting and carefree. So I didn't ask him any questions." Finally, Hopkins recalled, FDR "suddenly came out with it—the whole program." Roosevelt had determined to provide England with the means to survive. "He didn't seem to have any clear idea how it could be done legally. But there wasn't a doubt in his mind that he'd find a way to do it." This "refueling process," as Sherwood called it, was a "vital function" for Roosevelt; no one seemed to know quite how it worked because he didn't talk about the subject under consideration, nor did he seek the advice of others on it. In that sense it was similar to his decision during the late spring and early summer to run for a third term. In this instance, Sherwood concluded, "One can only say that Roosevelt, a creative artist in politics, had put in his time on this cruise evolving the pattern of a masterpiece, and once he could see it clearly in his own mind's eye, he made it quickly and very simply clear to all."[6]

The "whole program" that emerged would soon become known as Lend-Lease, Roosevelt's unique way of getting aid to Britain without giving it outright or loaning funds for its purchase. The United States would produce the ships and other matériel and simply lend them to Britain without the expectation of payment; rather, the United States would expect the return of the goods, or their replacement in kind, at the end of the duration, whenever that might be. The idea of using such a concept for cargo ships had been circulating in Washington for several months, and the president simply extended it, apparently to cover all aid sent to Britain. The overall plan and its timing, Robert Dallek observed, "was strictly the product of Roosevelt's fertile political imagination."[7] If he didn't have all the details worked out, that was what he had cabinet departments for, and he returned to Washington on December 16 to direct them to come up with the answers.

The next day he teased the White House press corps when he said he didn't have "any particular news," but the veteran reporters in the Oval Office that day knew from his demeanor that they could expect something big. He had been reading a good bit of foolishness lately about how to finance wars, he began, but most of it missed the mark. The basic fact, he said, was that "in all history no major war had ever been won or lost through lack of money." And then he explained just how this new idea would work by employing the fire-hose analogy. "Suppose my neighbor's house catches on fire, and I have a length of garden hose four or five hundred feet away. If he can take my garden hose and connect it up with his hydrant, I may help him to put out his fire. Now what do I do? I don't say to him before the operation, 'Neighbor, my garden hose cost me $15; you have to pay me $15 for it.' What is the transaction that goes on? I don't want $15—I want my garden hose back after the fire is over."

Similarly, he went on, the United States would send war matériel to Britain "with the understanding that when the show was over, we would get repaid something in kind."[8]

FDR decided to employ once again his favorite vehicle for public persuasion, the fireside chat. He tasked Hopkins, Rosenman, and Sherwood, barely recovered from campaign duty, to help him prepare for it over the Christmas holidays. On December 29, seated before the microphones in the Diplomatic Reception Room, Roosevelt talked directly to the American people about the crisis their country was facing. He began by comparing it with the crisis they had faced eight years earlier when banks were closing, millions were out of work, and the country was in near-despair. But the United States had faced that economic crisis with "courage and realism," he said, and it needed to do the same in facing this crisis. He reminded his listeners that in September Germany, Italy, and Japan had signed a Tripartite Pact, the purpose of which was world domination. "The experience of the past two years has proven beyond doubt that no nation can appease the Nazis," he said. "No man can tame a tiger into a kitten by stroking it. There can be no appeasement with ruthlessness. There can be no reasoning with an incendiary bomb. We know now that a nation can have peace with the Nazis only at the price of total surrender." Should the Axis powers take control of Europe, Asia, Africa,

Australasia, and the world's seas, they would bring their forces to bear on the United States. "It is no exaggeration to say that all of us, in all the Americas, would be living at the point of a gun—a gun loaded with explosive bullets, economic as well as military." Rather than wait "tamely" for an Axis victory, the United States needed to be "the great arsenal of democracy." [9]

In just five words FDR summed up perfectly what he proposed to do with his new Lend-Lease program. The phrase "the great arsenal of democracy" was apparently first coined by Jean Monet, the French economist and financier, who, when he mentioned it to Felix Frankfurter, was persuaded by the justice to allow it to be appropriated by the president; FDR loved it the first time he heard it and made it his own.

The president had barely finished with his fireside chat before turning to yet another speech, his annual message to Congress, set for January 6, which would be his first of the new year and his last before being inaugurated for a third term two weeks later. The official transmittal of his Lend-Lease legislation to Congress was to be its main focus. Meeting with his speechwriters one night in his study going over the third draft that had just come back from the State Department, Roosevelt announced that the speech needed a peroration and he had an idea for what it should be. He leaned back in his swivel chair and gazed at the ceiling for so long that Rosenman found it "uncomfortable." Finally FDR leaned forward, turned to Dorothy Brady, who was taking dictation, and borrowed a line from George M. Cohan's hit show *I'd Rather Be Right*: "Dorothy, take a law." Suddenly, Rosenman would recall, "the words seemed to roll off his tongue as though he had rehearsed them many times to himself."

> We must look forward to a world based on four essential freedoms.
>
> The first is freedom of speech and expression—everywhere in the world.
>
> The second is freedom of every person to worship God in his own way—everywhere in the world.
>
> The third is freedom from want—which, translated into world terms, means economic understandings which will secure to every nation everywhere a healthy peacetime life for its inhabitants.

The fourth is freedom from fear—which, translated into international terms, means a world-wide reduction of armaments to such a point and in such a thorough fashion that no nation anywhere will be in a position to commit an act of physical aggression against any neighbor.[10]

The previous July the president had mentioned what would become known as the Four Freedoms in a "offhand answer" to a reporter's question about his "long-range peace objectives," and he had obviously been mulling them over in his mind ever since. These freedoms were the values, the goals, that he sought to preserve through Lend-Lease and all that he was doing to thwart aggression. They constituted his vision for the world when that effort was finally successful; they were the context for everything he was trying to do.

When he finished his dictation, he invited reactions from his speechwriters, as usual. Hopkins questioned the phrase "everywhere in the world" as the president had applied it to the first two freedoms. "That covers an awful lot of territory, Mr. President. I don't know how interested Americans are going to be in the people of Java."

"I'm afraid they'll have to be some day, Harry," Roosevelt replied. "The world is getting so small that even the people of Java are getting to be our neighbors now." The phrase not only survived but was extended to all four freedoms.[11] They would soon be seen as an abbreviated form of the country's war aims, and historian David Kennedy noted that at least two of them—those dealing with freedom from want and fear—represented the "unmistakable continuity between Roosevelt's domestic policies during the Great Depression and his foreign policies during the war."[12]

The challenge of enacting Lend-Lease, FDR concluded, required enlisting Wendell Willkie in the cause. As it happened, the former Republican nominee was coming to the same conclusion. Just six days after the election Willkie had addressed a national radio audience with a message of reconciliation. "We have elected Franklin D. Roosevelt President," he said. "He is your President. He is my President. We all owe him the respect due his high office, and we will support him with our best efforts for our country."[13]

As he rested for six weeks in Sam Pryor's winter cottage in Florida, however, his critics wouldn't let him get his mind off the grueling campaign. Herbert Hoover and others charged that he would have won had he run a traditional Republican campaign. Willkie interrupted his vacation to give a speech in New York decrying the "dispassionate discussion" of the campaign and calling for national unity. He concluded the address with a toast "to the health and happiness of the President of the United States." Thirty-six hundred people rose to their feet cheering, some of them chanting, "We still want Willkie!"[14]

Wendell Willkie had consistently supported all-out aid to Britain as the best strategy to thwart Hitler and to keep America out of the war, and if he had hedged on the destroyer deal and accused Roosevelt of being a warmonger during the fall, well, that was politics in the midst of a hotly contested campaign. Now was the time to put politics aside, he decided, and simply do what was best for the country. If he was getting over the heated resentment of the election so quickly, however, most other prominent Republicans were not; the opposition to Lend-Lease among the GOP leadership was intense and nearly unanimous. Herbert Hoover and Alf Landon, two previous Republican standard-bearers, harshly denounced it, as did Senator Robert Taft, who showed a talent for the catchy analogy when he said, "Lending war equipment is a good deal like lending chewing gum. You don't want it back." The *Chicago Tribune* and senators such as Charles McNary said the bill would give the president dictatorial powers, reprising a favorite campaign theme. Senator Burton Wheeler, the isolationist Democrat from Montana, said passage of the bill "will plow under every fourth American boy." Roosevelt called the charge "the rottenest thing that has been said in public life in my generation."[15]

Willkie, whose prestige was still high despite a campaign that had been uneven—desultory at first but ultimately impressive and competitive—came under intense pressure to fall into line, especially if he wanted to seek his party's presidential nomination again in 1944. He was not uninterested in that prospect, but he resisted the pressure because he saw the issue as one of principle. "I remained silent after the campaign for a couple of months," he wrote a friend, "but when Messrs. Hoover, Landon, Dewey,

Taft and Vandenberg all came out in a frontal assault on the Lend-Lease Bill, I thought I owed a duty to speak for it." He announced his support for the measure on January 13, 1941, arguing that granting extraordinary powers to the president was the only way to defend democracy. "The United States is not a belligerent, and we hope shall not be," he said. "Our problem, however, is not alone to keep America out of war, but to keep war out of America." He boldly went on to chastise the bill's opponents, many of whom had only recently been his supporters: "Appeasers, isolationists, lip-service friends of Britain will seek to sabotage the program . . . behind the screen of opposition to this bill." Willkie added that he planned to visit Great Britain to assess the war situation for himself.[16]

Roosevelt, always alert to opportunities to co-opt the opposition, had been thinking of ways to enlist Willkie in his administration. William Stephenson, a ranking official in British intelligence, suggested that he send Willkie to London as his representative to demonstrate American unity and thereby bolster morale. Immediately recognizing the potential of the idea, Roosevelt seized it; no one could better symbolize bipartisan support for Britain than the most recent GOP standard-bearer. What's more, he would certainly return home deeply affected by the war-ravaged nation and the spirit of its valiant people and in a position to be a credible and persuasive advocate for Lend-Lease. Felix Frankfurter, once again privy to just about everything going on in the White House, mentioned the idea at a New Year's Eve party to Irita Van Doren, who by now had been reunited with Willkie. She passed it on to him, and he responded positively.[17]

Few other Republicans liked the idea, and House minority leader Joe Martin—of "Martin, Barton, and Fish" fame—did his best to dissuade Willkie from going to London by arguing that it could only damage him within the party: "All I can say is that Roosevelt is trying to win you over. This won't be well received by the Republicans."[18]

Willkie was not dissuaded. He came to Washington to pick up his passport at the State Department, where Cordell Hull, at the president's instruction, intercepted him and brought him to the White House for dinner on the eve of Roosevelt's third inaugural. It was the first time they met without contentious issues dividing them, and they quickly decided they liked each other. FDR had told Grace Tully that he wanted an outside chef to come in and prepare some terrapin that had been sent to him, and he didn't want to be disturbed by anyone. "It was clear to me the two men enjoyed being together," Tully noted after hearing gusts of laughter drifting out of the Oval Study that evening. The president suggested people Willkie should see in London, including Averill Harriman, who was then coordinating U.S. aid in Britain, and Harry Hopkins, who would be there on a separate mission for Roosevelt.

In the relaxed and candor-friendly atmosphere that evening, no doubt fueled by a few glasses of wine, Willkie asked what otherwise might have been seen as an inappropriate or even impertinent question: "Why do you keep Hopkins so close to you? You surely must realize that people distrust him and resent his influence." Willkie would later quote FDR as expressing a sentiment held by other presidents, even if they never expressed it: "Some day you may well be sitting here where I am now as president of the United States. And when you are, you'll be looking at that door over there and knowing that practically everybody who walks through it wants something out of you. You'll learn what a lonely job this is, and you'll discover the need for somebody like Harry Hopkins who asks for nothing except to serve you."[19]

The dinner didn't adjourn until close to midnight, but not before Roosevelt gave his new envoy a handwritten note addressed to "a former naval person" that he wanted delivered to Churchill. "Wendell Willkie will give you this," he wrote, "he is truly trying to keep politics out over here." He added a verse from Longfellow that he had written down earlier that day from memory and which he told the prime minister "applies to you as it does to us" (and which had brought Lincoln to tears on hearing it read during the Civil War).

Sail on, O Ship of State!
Sail on, O Union strong and great!
Humanity with all its fears,
With all the hopes of future years,
Is hanging breathless on thy fate![20]

Willkie had a whirlwind tour of London, eager to see everything and everyone. Fascinated by the Blitz and its effects, he wandered the streets during the worst of the bombing until the prime minister, hearing of his recklessness, sent him six white helmets and three gas masks. Getting the message, Willkie thereafter headed for the shelters when he heard the sirens and came away enormously impressed by the strength and resilience of the British people. Official doors opened for him as they had earlier for Bill Donovan, because once again everyone knew what was at stake and they pulled out all the stops; he had an audience with the king and a bonding session with Churchill.

Willkie met with Hopkins as well and he promised to do everything he could to help with Lend-Lease. On his return to Washington he found the debate raging furiously on the Hill, but he was determined to go forward. Leading the administration's offensive before the Senate Foreign Relations Committee were Secretaries Hull, Morgenthau, Stimson, and Knox, who testified that Britain could be invaded in the next few months and that the United States could be next if the Royal Navy fell into Nazi hands. Only a grant of the widest possible discretionary powers to the chief executive could cope with this unprecedented threat, they argued. They were vague, at Roosevelt's insistence, on the questions of cost and whether U.S. convoy escorts would be necessary to ensure safe passage of the "leased" goods.

The lead-off witness for the opposition was Joseph Kennedy, still officially the American ambassador to London and still conflicted over his pessimism regarding Britain's chances for survival and his loyalty to Roosevelt. As a result, he awkwardly managed to oppose Lend-Lease while arguing for greater aid to Britain. (FDR observed that "most papers got the feeling that he was blowing hot and blowing cold at the same time—trying to carry water on both shoulders.")[21] Norman Thomas spoke eloquently of the threat to American democracy and civil liberties. The principal witness for the opposition, however, was Charles A. Lindbergh. Now the chief spokesman for the newly formed America First Committee, the aviation hero argued that the United States was invulnerable to air attack, and that in any case the country had no stake in the war currently under way. Lend-Lease, he said, would only protract the war unnecessarily. Under questioning he refused to say if he favored a British victory. In an effort to explain that answer, he said that achieving such a victory would involve years of war, which "would create prostration, famine and disease in Europe—and probably in America—such as the world has never experienced before."[22]

Willkie appeared at the climax of the debate, obviously tired from the transatlantic flight but eager to say his piece, and he made the case for the legislation with a carefully reasoned argument leavened by passion and conviction. He had the overflow audience in the large hearing room with him. "Britain needs more destroyers," he said. "She needs them desperately. The powers [granted in the bill] are extraordinary. But in my judgment, this is an extraordinary situation." Lend-Lease, he argued, represented the "best clear chance" for keeping the United States out of the war. "If Britain can stand through the summer, then at last the effects of our long-term assistance will begin to be felt." Isolationist senators tried hard to poke holes in his testimony, but Willkie effectively stood his ground. The most persistent and certainly the most strident of the questioners was Champ Clark of Missouri, who worried about American-made bombers falling to the Nazis and being used against the United States. "If all the hazards of war go against us," the witness responded, "we will get whipped." When Clark raised the subject of Willkie's campaign speeches and specifically his charges that Roosevelt would lead the country into war, he responded, "I made a great many statements about him. He was my opponent, you know."

"You would not have said anything about your opponent you did not think was true, would you?" the senator asked.

"Oh no," came the answer, "but occasionally in moments of oratory in campaigns we all expand a bit."

Clark pressed the point, prompting Willkie to declare there was nothing to be gained by revisiting old campaign speeches. "I struggled as hard as I could to beat Franklin Roosevelt and I tried to keep from pulling my punches. He was elected President. He is my President now, and I expect to disagree with him whenever I please." The room erupted in applause.[23]

The *Chicago Tribune* nonetheless kept up its relentless attack on what they and other isolationists saw as committing the United States as Britain's co-belligerent "in all but name," and calling Willkie "the Republican Quisling."[24]

After tempers cooled and the rhetoric died down, the Lend-Lease bills passed both chambers comfortably, by 260 to 165 in the House on February 8 and exactly a month later by a two-to-one margin in the Senate.

According to a Gallup poll, Willkie's testimony played a significant role in building public support for the bill; even a plurality of Republican respondents said they backed it. Roosevelt never forgot Willkie's contribution to the victory, and in fact thought it was critical. At one point during the war Robert Sherwood heard Harry Hopkins make a "slurring remark" about Willkie: "Roosevelt slapped him with as sharp a reproof as I ever heard him utter. He said, 'Don't you ever say anything like that around here again. Don't even *think* it. You of all people ought to know that we might not have had Lend-Lease or Selective Service or a lot of other things if it hadn't been for Wendell Willkie. He was a Godsend to this country when we needed him most.'"[25]

Roosevelt signed the measure into law on March 11, asked Congress to appropriate $7 billion for its implementation, and immediately sent lists of available weaponry to London. He had boldly exercised his mandate just four months after he had earned it.

Once the gears of government and the machinery of industry began to turn, huge quantities of goods and weaponry started to be sent to where they were needed. In an unmistakable signal of the priority he gave to the swift and efficient administration of the program, he named Hopkins to head it. Food and materials for industry began to arrive in Britain by mid-year, and tanks and planes were soon being off-loaded in Egypt for the British thrust into Libya. When Germany invaded the Soviet Union in June, the latter country, too, was declared eligible for assistance and began to receive arms at Murmansk. Supplies arriving in China by way of the Burma Road tripled. After Pearl Harbor, when the United States became a belligerent, Lend-Lease was broadened dramatically in both scope and volume. By mid-1944 the "arsenal of democracy" had shipped nearly 30,000 planes, 27,000 tanks, 637,000 other military vehicles, 1,800 merchant ships, and 1,400 naval vessels to thirty-eight different nations. Thirty-eight billion dollars' worth of those and other supplies ended up in Great Britain, which not only survived but became an indispensable force in the ultimate defeat of the Nazis. Winston Churchill, who had once been skeptical of Lend-Lease, now told Parliament that it was "the most unsordid act in the history of any nation."[26]

As successful as Roosevelt had been in enacting Lend-Lease, he was furious that members of Congress as well as the press had attacked the program so viciously in the days before his inauguration. He had held his fire on them all of these months, but now that it was over he decided to unleash his pent-up fury. The forum was to be the White House Correspondents' Dinner, and one evening he started dictating what Sherwood called "one of the most scathing, most vindictive speeches I have ever heard." After an hour of haranguing, the president appeared to tire of the exercise and retired. The horrified Sherwood went across the hall to tell Hopkins how depressed he was by Roosevelt's "petulant tone" and how surprised he was that he hadn't been more magnanimous to his critics. Hopkins said that was exactly what the president would ultimately do; he was "just getting it off his chest." Then Hopkins "spoke in a way that was very unusual for him," as Sherwood put it. "You and I are for Roosevelt because he's a great spiritual figure, because he's an idealist, like Wilson, and he's got the guts to drive through against any opposition to realize those ideals." When he tried to appear "tough and cynical and flippant," he was putting on "an act." The "real Roosevelt" was the one who articulated ideas such as the Four Freedoms. "And don't get the idea that those are any catch phrases," Hopkins warned Sherwood, with emphasis. "*He believes them!* He believes they can be practically attained."[27]

Although execution of the decision to run for a third term was often messy, unattractive, and laced with arrogance, its essence came from Roosevelt's moral core. He was convinced that preserving civilization as he knew it meant the pursuit of the Four Freedoms that he had enunciated. Thus defeating Hitler was a *moral* imperative, and he was prepared to take great risks, for himself as well as for the country, to see it through.

However, Roosevelt was quintessentially a politician who factored political realities into every decision he faced. To him political realities were not only a legitimate part of the governing process but essential ones when deciding great questions. He agreed fully with Lincoln, who had said in his first debate with Steven A. Douglas: "Public sentiment is everything. With public sentiment, nothing can fail; without it, nothing can succeed." Thus FDR was sometimes cautious in pursuing bold initiatives, such as preparing the country for war; he needed public opinion behind him before hugely consequential ideas could be realized. "You have led public opinion by allowing it to get ahead of you," King George VI would tell him in 1941.[28] Just as Lincoln had had to wait for a victory at Antietam before announcing the Emancipation Proclamation, so Roosevelt had had to wait for Hitler's thrust into France and the Low Countries before mobilizing the country to meet the threat. Given the way his mind worked, he knew his voice alone was not enough to shape public opinion; he needed events to help shape it. He needed acts.

No one could have foreseen even six months before that 1940 would be the year that the historic wall of isolationism in America was first breached. It was the horrific news from Europe that constituted the tip of the spear, especially as its meaning was conveyed so dramatically over the radio by Edward R. Murrow from London, William Shirer from Berlin, and Elmer Davis from New York. Increasingly Americans realized that what was happening in Europe could happen to them. A "shaky balance of power" had given isolationism "a sort of intellectual respectability for isolationism in America," Richard Ketchum observed, but it was a respectability that could not last.[29]

Charles Lindbergh and other "America Firsters" would persist through 1941 in their quest for an isolated America until further events, culminating at Pearl Harbor, rendered their efforts moot.

No one could have predicted, either, that granting such broad discretionary powers to the chief executive under the Lend-Lease Act would presage the emergence of a national security state whose president was in practice if not always in law authorized to dispatch troops and to intervene in faraway places on his own initiative. Isolationists charged in 1941 that Lend-Lease would make Roosevelt a dictator, but even they could not foresee the latitude that future presidents believed they had when facing foreign crises. Just as his New Deal had fundamentally expanded the role of government in domestic affairs, so had his destroyer deal of 1940 and his Lend-Lease

Act of 1941 fundamentally expanded the powers of the presidency in foreign affairs. After Roosevelt it would be a very different presidency leading a very different country in a very different world.

One of the consequences of that development would be the way in which the electorate viewed the presidency—and those who sought it. From the advent of World War II through the Cold War, the Vietnam era, and the time of jihad terrorism, it mattered more than ever who was commander in chief. Thus since 1940 presidential candidates have been viewed through a prism of how qualified and competent they are to protect the American people—the most fundamental responsibility of the office. Economic and domestic issues might still dominate a particular election, but never to the exclusion of potential foreign threats. The question is now routinely asked: is a candidate familiar with foreign affairs and national security issues and able to deal with them? It's unlikely that a candidate who fails to answer this threshold question satisfactorily can be elected. The electorate of 1940 was the first in the American experience to ask it seriously, and the polls showed that they answered it decisively in Roosevelt's favor.

That year he was more than anything the great bulwark between civilization and the abyss, and no one knew that better than Churchill, who made enlisting the United States in the cause of freedom his highest priority. The skill that FDR brought to the leadership of the Allied effort then and later during the Second World War made a monumental difference, arguably the critical difference. If the president of the United States after 1940 had been anyone else, it is anyone's guess what the outcomes would have been, but they would not have been the same. All of which makes the election of 1940 one of the most consequential American elections since 1864. In both 1864 and 1940, elections took place during extraordinary times, and in each case the American electorate was being asked to judge the incumbent president—to cast a vote in moments when peace was nowhere to be seen, and in circumstances in which the context was wholly unfamiliar. Roosevelt's running for a third term was an act of self-faith that required from voters a similar act of faith. The voters employed their intuitive wisdom to confirm Roosevelt's decision, and in that sense it was a shared decision that set the nation on an unprecedented and hugely consequential course. That is what democracy is all about at pivotal times in a nation's history. Although Roosevelt used extraordinary skill in making the American system work at a critical time, the electorate deserves much credit as well, certainly more than it has been given.

The dilemma the president and the electorate faced in 1940 never would have to be faced again. Following Franklin Roosevelt's death and final Allied victory over the axis powers in 1945, the newly elected Republican Congress made one of its first acts in 1947 the adoption of an amendment to the Constitution limiting future presidents to two terms. The nation finally resolved the ambiguity over "reeligibility" left by the Founding Fathers when the necessary three-fourths of the states ratified the Twenty-second Amendment to the Constitution in 1951, thereby codifying in law the practice Washington and Jefferson had established more than a century and a half before.

APPENDIX

President Roosevelt met with Justice Felix Frankfurter in the White House on the evening of July 11, 1940, four days before the Democratic National Convention would convene in Chicago. They discussed whether the president was justified in running for a third term and, if so, how to explain the decision to the American people. At the conclusion of the meeting Roosevelt asked the justice to prepare a memorandum summarizing the advice he had just offered. Frankfurter asked if he could solicit one as well from Librarian of Congress Archibald MacLeish, and the president agreed. He returned to the White House the next evening with the two memoranda, which are reprinted here in their entirety.

Felix Frankfurter's Memorandum

The task of safeguarding our institutions is two-fold. One must be accomplished, if necessary by guns and bombs and tanks, by ships and planes, on land and sea and in the air, by the Armed Forces of the nation. The other, by the united but diversified efforts of the many men and women of the country, individually and banded together in trade unions and farm granges, trade associations and cooperatives, and in that common effort of all of the people which is the Government. For we must continue to pursue our two great actions at the same time: we must be ready to defend the right of our democracy to continue to exist; we must have a democratic society worthy of survival.

Whatever its new trappings and new slogans, tyranny is the oldest and most discredited rule known to history. And whenever tyranny has supplanted a more humane form of government it has been due more to internal causes than external. Democracy can thrive only when it enlists the devotion of those whom Lincoln called the common people. And it can hold their devotion only when it adequately respects their dignity by so ordering society as to assure to the mass of men reasonable security and to stir in them confident hope for themselves and for their children.

If democracy becomes merely a set of negations, or degenerates into empty political forms in which insecurity and hopelessness become the lot of many, the road is open for the so-called "strong-man" with all his meretricious promises. We know only too well what happens to these promises once the "strong-man" comes to power. Trade unions are banned; the cooperative movement is taken over; freedom of the press is at an end—and, indeed, so is every freedom that gives dignity to man.

In the last eight years under your leadership much has been done to make effective, in the lives of the mass of our people, the hopes and principles to which this country is dedicated—a life of dignity, of liberty not in the abstract or on paper, but the liberty of a free man who is able to serve his nation and engage in the pursuit of happiness. Under your leadership we have moved toward a life of economic as well as political independence for our people who felt the bludgeoning of misfortune and adversity when you first were summoned to the headship of our nation. In view of this record you would not be open to the charge of trying to seize power as a "strong-man." You would in fact be protecting the nation from the convulsions, dangers and upheavals in a period of acute national anxiety and world strain that could indeed lead to the establishment of arbitrary power in Washington by men no longer responsible to the values of democracy and the wishes of Lincoln's common people.

I now turn to foreign policy and suggest these thoughts for your consideration: You would not undo, if you could, the efforts you made to prevent war from the moment it was threatened, and to restrict the area of carnage down to the last minute before Italy entered the struggle. Nor do you now soften the condemnation expressed from time to time by Secretary Hull and yourself for the acts of aggression that have wiped out ancient, peace-preserving, liberty-loving countries which had scrupulously maintained their neutrality and independence. Nor do you recant the sentiments of sympathy with all free peoples who are resisting such aggression. Nor do you regret your consistent endeavor to awaken this country to the menace for us and for all we hold dear in this new attempt to conquer the world, to establish the despotic rule of an aggressive tyranny, and to extinguish the lights of the human spirit. In all these efforts you have tried to follow the inspiration of the great men who laid down the principles which must guard the Republic if it is to remain a sanctuary of freedom. You now look beyond a world war to the years of peace and you want to play your part in making sure that these tragedies will never again fall on civilization, that we will do better than our fathers did when they tried to organize a system of collective security to restrain or punish aggression, and that we will succeed in replacing the law of force with the force of law. That is the great aim, the great hope and sustaining purpose, by which you now chart your course.

You know, and you must hope none has yet forgotten, that in these last few months and years you pursued your campaign against the aggressors, and pursued your campaign to preserve the world's endangered peace, against the opposition of powerful newspapers and leading public men who charged you with being guilty of hysteria and war-mongering. But you have no apologies to offer, no excuses to make. History will judge your actions, and every day your motives are becoming clearer for all to see and understand.

You felt it your duty to arouse your countrymen with a great sense of urgency to the new and dangerous forces loose in the world and to emphasize the hazards which they presented for us in this beloved land. In this conduct of our foreign relations you were guided by the principles which have brought our country to its present greatness. You knew how vast a prize we were for the pride and greed of the dictators, and you were resolved that they would never lay their evil and brutal hands on America, if all of us, recognizing the danger and standing together, could stop them from carrying out their wicked design of conquest and enslavement.

For we have no deeper tradition in our history than resistance to tyranny and devotion to freedom. In your warnings, you were aware that the Constitution makes the

President that originating impulse and guardian of our national safety. In all that you have attempted, in your efforts to maintain the peace of the world, in all that you have done to maintain the peace of this country and to prepare it morally and well as physically for whatever dangers yet may come, you can gladly submit your purpose, your achievements, and your record to the judgment of your countrymen for a third term in the midst of unprecedented conditions that impose their own duties and obligations. A President must continue in office when the voice of the people calls him to the continuing task.

Archibald MacLeish's Memorandum
Dear Felix:

It's a dangerous thing to ask a man for his two cents worth because he may throw in a couple of bushels of orts. But you have and you'll have to take it.

The more I turn it over on my tongue the more certain I am that the President should not "accept a call." Undoubtedly the actual truth is that he will be doing precisely that. But to put it that way is to lead with the chin. I can see the cartoons from here.

What I should like him to say would be something like this: that like most men of his age—most men who have occupied positions of great responsibility—he had made plans for himself; plans for a private life of his own to begin in January 1941. That these plans, like the plans of so many others, like so many other plans, had been made in a world which now seems as distant as a different planet. That today all private plans, all private lives, have been repealed by a public danger. That in the face of the public danger all those who can be of service to the Republic have no choice but to offer themselves for service in those capacities for which they may be fitted. That if a majority of the members of his party believe he can serve his country best in the capacity in which they have nominated him he has no choice but to accept the nomination. That if a majority of the voters believe as a majority of his party has believed he will have no choice but to accept their judgment.

I should like, also, to hear a statement in explanation of the President's failure to declare himself sooner. I think the people are entitled to such a statement and will surely demand it. Obviously I am not in a position to supply such a statement myself but I should suppose that the development of the line suggested above might supply the words. Obviously a man who believes his country faces a crisis so severe that it overrides every other consideration and who believes therefore that every citizen must hold himself ready to serve where he best can, will not declare himself in advance to be unwilling to serve in any capacity whatever. Neither, by the same sign, will he offer himself until the necessity appears.

However—for the main point. You ask me for a couple of paragraphs. Here are a few sentences for whatever they may be worth. . . .

In times like these—in times of great tension, of great crisis, the compass of the world narrows to a single fact. The fact which dominates our world is the fact of armed aggression, the fact of successful armed aggression, the fact of successful armed aggression aimed at the form of government, the kind of society we in the United States have chosen and established for ourselves. It is a fact which no one any longer doubts—which no one is any longer able to ignore. In the early days of Fascist aggression it was said and it was believed that the struggle was a war of rival imperialism. Later and after the first

Fascist successes by force of arms in Europe, it was still said and it was still sometimes believed that the war was an imperialistic war, the end and aim of which was land and goods. But with the unambiguous successes of Fascism in Europe in the spring of this year, and above all with the conquest of France, it was no longer possible to say this or to believe it. For the purpose of this aggression is now declared in the irrefutable and unarguable terms of the results which it has itself accomplished. Now that successful Fascism has imposed upon defeated France not only its will but its image, it is no longer possible for any man to doubt what the consequences of successful Fascism will be. It is not a war of imperialism which threatens all men everywhere; it is a revolution imposed by force of arms not from within but from without. It is a revolution which proposes not to set men free but to reduce them to slavery—and to reduce them to slavery in the interest and to the advantage of a dictator who has already demonstrated the nature and the extent of the advantage which he hopes to obtain.

This is the fact which dominates our world and which dominates as well the lives of all those who live in it. In the face of the danger which confronts our time no individual retains or can hope to retain the rights of personal choice which free men can enjoy in times of peace. He has a first obligation to serve in the defense of our institutions of freedom—a first obligation to serve his country in whatever capacity his country finds him useful—which must override all personal preferences—whether the preferences he would establish for himself or the preferences custom and tradition would establish for him. . . .

But you can see, Felix, how impossible it is to go on with this. For if ever there was a personal document it is this document of which we are thinking. It can be, if it is deeply derived from the emotion and convictions of the man who speaks it, one of the most moving and convincing utterances of which history has record. Or it can be something very different.

Yours,
Archie

ACKNOWLEDGMENTS

I am extraordinarily fortunate to have had the help of so many historians and students of history in the writing of this book. Historians not only like to share their love of history but are invariably eager to help those who aspire to the craft. They are, I have found, among the most generous of people with their time, their ideas, and their encouragement. Ernest B. (Pat) Furguson first surfaced the idea of FDR and the 1940 election several years ago as one that he was thinking of pursuing himself. Ultimately forgoing it, he bequeathed it to me, a very generous gift for which I will always be grateful. Pat has given me sound advice from the beginning, and he and his wife, Cassie, have been among the strongest supporters of the project.

As has Michael Janeway, who knows the literature of FDR and the era as well as anyone and who spent many hours steering me to relevant but not always obvious sources. His early memos scoping out key issues were invaluable, as was his ongoing willingness to explore new avenues with an amateur historian and to offer insights and suggestions throughout. Both Mike and Pat took the time to read early drafts and to provide valuable comments. I am hugely indebted to them, as I am to my good friends Peter Decker and Mike Andrews, who plowed through the same material and emerged with very helpful suggestions.

There is no one to whom I am more indebted for my interest in American history than David McCullough, my friend and teacher, who in conversations and visits to historic places over many years showed me some of the remarkable people who shaped the American story. His skill in bringing that story to life for countless readers has been, and remains, a huge inspiration to me. In this project David graciously opened doors on his own initiative and constantly urged me on. Even earlier James MacGregor Burns lit in a young student the fire that became my deep interest in government and politics. He later introduced me to Franklin Roosevelt, and while that fire took longer to light, it eventually did, and I thank him for that as well.

Over the eight years I worked for him and beyond, Walter Mondale imparted to me the relevance of a sense of history to the contemporary practice of politics. He and Jimmy Carter gave me a unique opportunity to observe the presidency at close hand for four years, an experience that aided greatly in the writing of this book. My late friend Harry McPherson embodied that same sense of history and combined it with an uncommon ability to write and talk about it with insight and enthusiasm, especially over lunch.

Other historians who graciously shared their thoughts on FDR and the period include Robert Dallek, William Leuchtenburg, Charles Peters, Jeff Shesol, and Lynne Olson, and I very much appreciate their help. Similarly, David Douglas shared his relationship with and knowledge of his grandfather Henry Wallace. My friend Don Lamm generously brought to bear the wisdom of a lifetime in publishing, helping to explain the vagaries of that changing industry and offering suggestions along the way. Veteran author and friend Hedrick Smith also taught me much about the book business, for which I am equally grateful.

I was very fortunate to be able to enlist probably the premier researcher of American history to assist me in this project. Mike Hill is a longtime friend and former White House colleague who has earned a deserved reputation as the best in the business. In this case, however, he was an important advisor as well. His comments on early chapters were invaluable, and his suggestions throughout were invariably on the mark. Mike's competence is fully matched by his thoughtfulness and his essential kindness, and it has been an uninterrupted pleasure to work with him throughout the project.

Bob Clark, the estimable chief archivist at the FDR Library, has been an important source of information and encouragement to both Mike and me during our visits to Hyde Park. We thank him and his splendid staff, particularly Matthew Hanson, for their many courtesies. Similarly, we both thank Jeff Flannery, the head of the Manuscripts Reading Room at the Library of Congress, and his staff for their wonderful assistance. Tim Corcoran allowed me access to the papers of his father, Thomas J. Corcoran, at the Library of Congress, and Jon Cuneo shared with me the unpublished manuscript of his father, Ernest Cuneo. I am grateful for these kindnesses.

In a typically thoughtful gesture, Bob Dallek introduced me to his agent of twenty years, John Wright, who agreed to take me on. Very happily for me, he found the manuscript a home at Oxford University Press and its Pivotal Moments in American History series. I'm enormously grateful to John for his belief in the project and his skill in bringing it to the right place.

I was further blessed to find myself at Oxford in the hands of Tim Bent, who heads the trade history section there and who is as impressively versed in American history as he is in the precision of language. He helped me to sharpen the book's focus, particularly its "pivotal moment" elements, and worked with me to clarify the chronology and to keep the narrative moving. Always encouraging but always probing, Tim is everything a good editor should be, and I couldn't have been more fortunate to have had him at my side throughout. Special thanks go to Tim's talented assistant editor, Keely Latcham, who was unfailingly helpful in a myriad of ways. I am also hugely indebted to three distinguished historians who serve as the editors of Oxford's Pivotal Moments series— James McPherson, David Hackett Fischer, and David Greenberg—for welcoming the book into the series and for their insightful comments and suggestions. Joellyn Ausanka masterfully oversaw all aspects of the book's production, and Sue Warga copyedited the manuscript splendidly. Others at Oxford who contributed in important ways include Christian Purdy, Coleen Hatrick, Brady McNamara, Andy Varhol, and Tara Kennedy.

Eric, Andrew, and Alex have constantly inspired me over the years with their unique abilities to create. That inspiration and their encouragement have meant the world to me in writing this book. No one has inspired me longer or to greater effect, however, than

Julia, who over nearly fifty years of marriage has enabled me to do things I never could have done otherwise. In this case she has been an invaluable critic and advisor, unafraid to question assumptions or conclusions. More important, she has once again been my indispensable partner by selflessly giving her preoccupied husband the understanding, patience, encouragement, and work environment he needed. It's no easy thing being the spouse of a cloistered writer whose attention is frequently elsewhere. I've been hugely lucky in that respect, and I thank Julia from the bottom of my heart for believing in me and in this book. I dedicate it to her with all my love.

NOTES

Introduction

1. Alsop and Kintner, *American White Paper*, 58–60.
2. Davis, *FDR: Into the Storm*, 487.
3. Roosevelt, *Autobiography of Eleanor Roosevelt*, 211
4. Goodwin, *No Ordinary Time*, 15.
5. Leuchtenburg, ed., *Franklin D. Roosevelt*, 20.
6. Davis, *FDR: Into the Storm*, 487–88.
7. Smith, *FDR*, 435.
8. Dallek, *Franklin D. Roosevelt and American Foreign Policy*, 199.
9. Tully, *F.D.R., My Boss*, 235.
10. Halberstam, *The Powers That Be*, 15.
11. Rosenman, *Working with Roosevelt*, 188–89.
12. Beschloss, *Kennedy and Roosevelt*, 200.
13. Brands, *Traitor to His Class*, 393.
14. Ibid., 396.
15. Ketchum, *The Borrowed Years*, 215.
16. Brands, *Traitor to His Class*, 420.
17. Lindbergh, *Wartime Journals*, 255–56.
18. Berg, *Lindbergh*, 419–20.
19. Ibid., 420.
20. Sherwood, *Roosevelt and Hopkins*, 377.
21. Ibid., 124.

Chapter 1

1. Quoted in Dallek, *Franklin D. Roosevelt and American Foreign Policy*, 101.
2. Nixon, ed., *Franklin D. Roosevelt and Foreign Affairs*, 2:630–33.
3. Rosenman, *Working with Roosevelt*, 165.
4. Ibid.
5. Dallek, *Franklin D. Roosevelt and American Foreign Policy*, 148–49.
6. Rosenman, *Working with Roosevelt*, 166–67.
7. Dallek, *Franklin D. Roosevelt and American Foreign Policy*, 148.
8. Rosenman, *Working with Roosevelt*, 167.
9. Davis, *FDR: Into the Storm*, 135–36.
10. Smith, *FDR*, 424.

11. Freidel, *Franklin D. Roosevelt: A Rendezvous with Destiny*, 289.
12. Burns, *Roosevelt: The Lion and the Fox*, 385.
13. Dallek, *Franklin D. Roosevelt and American Foreign Policy*, 166.
14. Quoted in ibid.
15. Churchill, *Blood, Sweat and Tears*, 55–66.
16. Davis, *FDR: Into the Storm*, 346.
17. Berg, *Lindbergh*, 369.
18. Ibid., 380.
19. Davis, *FDR: Into the Storm*, 348.
20. Berg, *Lindbergh*, 383.
21. Ibid., 382.
22. Lindbergh, *Wartime Journals*, 70.
23. Berg, *Lindbergh*, 396.
24. Press conference, November 15, 1938, PPA, 7:596–98, FDRL.
25. Blum, *From the Morgenthau Diaries*, 2:48–49.
26. Pogue, *George C. Marshall*, 323.

Chapter 2
1. Ketchum, *The Borrowed Years*, 396.
2. Sherwood, *Roosevelt and Hopkins*, 22.
3. Davis, *FDR: Into the Storm*, 217.
4. Ibid., 44.
5. Sherwood, *Roosevelt and Hopkins*, 94–95.
6. Ibid., 99 (Sherwood's emphasis).
7. Jackson, *That Man*, 31–32.
8. Cuneo, *Autobiography*, 18.
9. Ibid., 20.
10. Ibid., 42–46.
11. Ibid.
12. Hull, *Memoirs*, 856.
13. Berle and Jacobs, eds., *Navigating the Rapids*, 270.
14. Hull, *Memoirs*, 856.

Chapter 3
1. Rosenman, *Working with Roosevelt*, 182.
2. Leuchtenburg, *The FDR Years*, 9.
3. Rosenman, *Working with Roosevelt*, 182–83.
4. *New York Times*, January 5, 1939.
5. Devine, *The Illusion of Neutrality*, 234–35.
6. Quoted in Davis, *FDR: Into the Storm*, 401.
7. Ibid., 402–6. The entire transcript of the conference appears in Schewe, ed., *Franklin D. Roosevelt and Foreign Affairs*, item 1565.
8. *New York Times*, February 2, 1939.
9. Davis, *FDR: Into the Storm*, 410.
10. Quoted in Dallek, *Franklin D. Roosevelt and American Foreign Policy*, 181–82.

11. *New York Times*, February 22, 1939.
12. Richardson, *A Compilation of the Messages and Papers of the Presidents*, 1:221–23.
13. Ibid., 1:323.
14. Wilson, *Papers of Woodrow Wilson*, 6:18–19.
15. Jonas, *Isolationism in America*, 143–48.
16. Gallup and Robinson, "American Institute of Public Opinion—Surveys, 1935–38," 388.
17. Schlesinger, *Coming of the New Deal*, 528.
18. Churchill, *The Gathering Storm*, 345–46.
19. Ibid., 346.
20. Alsop and Kintner, *American White Paper*, 44–46.
21. Lindbergh, *Wartime Journals*, 186.
22. Rosenman, *Working with Roosevelt*, 24.
23. Lindbergh, *Wartime Journals*, 186–87.
24. Ibid., 187.

Chapter 4

1. Burns, *Roosevelt: The Lion and the Fox*, 398.
2. Usher Burdick to Franklin Roosevelt, September, 1939, OF 1561, FDRL.
3. Alsop and Kintner, *American White Paper*, 75.
4. Transcript, conference of the President with Democratic and Republican congressional Leaders preceding the opening of a special session of the Congress, September 20, 1939, 52, OF 1561, FDRL.
5. Ibid., 64.
6. Rosenman, *Working with Roosevelt*, 189–90.
7. Davis, *FDR: Into the Storm*, 497–98.
8. Dallek, *Franklin D. Roosevelt and American Foreign Policy*, 201–2.
9. Lindbergh, *Wartime Journals*, 275.
10. Davis, *FDR: Into the Storm*, 503.
11. Ibid.
12. Ibid.
13. Ibid., 504.
14. Dallek, *Franklin D. Roosevelt and American Foreign Policy*, 207.
15. Davis, *FDR: Into the Storm*, 152–53, 152n.
16. Sherwood, *Roosevelt and Hopkins*, 170.
17. Ibid., 117.

Chapter 5

1. Timmons, *Garner of Texas*, 235.
2. Farley, *Jim Farley's Story*, 158.
3. Ickes, *Secret Diary*, 95.
4. Farley, *Jim Farley's Story*, 217–18.
5. Ibid., 68–70.
6. Ibid., 111.
7. Ibid., 109–11, 142–43.

8. Ibid., 153
9. Ibid., 170–72.
10. Ibid., 174–78.
11. Ibid., 181–83.
12. Ibid., 183–84.
13. Ibid., 183–91.
14. S. Early to M. McIntyre, July 26, 1939, Stephen Early Papers, Box 23, FDRL.
15. *Washington Post*, September 24, 1939.
16. Ibid.
17. Ickes, *Secret Diary*, 49.
18. Culver and Hyde, *American Dreamer*, 201.
19. Ickes, *Secret Diary*, 36.
20. Flynn, *You're the Boss*, 154.
21. Sherwood, *Roosevelt and Hopkins*, 117–18.
22. Roosevelt, *Autobiography of Eleanor Roosevelt*, 214.
23. Quoted in Morgan, *FDR—A Biography*, 519–20.
24. Sherwood, *Roosevelt and Hopkins*, 94.
25. Davis, *FDR: Into the Storm*, 532.
26. Quoted in Burns, *Roosevelt: The Lion and the Fox*, 409.
27. Scroop, *Mr. Democrat*, 177–78.
28. Lilienthal, *Journals*, 140.
29. Sherwood, *Roosevelt and Hopkins*, 137.
30. Brayman, *From Grover Cleveland to Gerald Ford*, 354–55.

Chapter 6

1. Frankfurter to FDR, January 1, 1940, in Freedman, ed., *Roosevelt and Frankfurter*, 457.
2. PPA 1940, 1–10, FDRL.
3. FDR to White, PPF 1939, 1196, FDRL.
4. Welles, *Time for Decision*, 73–74.
5. Farley, *Jim Farley's Story*, 223–24.
6. Lilienthal, *Journals*, 157.
7. FDR to Henry Horner, March 27, 1940, in *F.D.R.—His Personal Letters*, 1011–12.
8. Ickes, *Secret Diary*, 85; Ketchum, *The Borrowed Years*, 520.
9. Ketchum, *The Borrowed Years*, 520.
10. Morgenthau diaries, April 29, 1940, FDRL.
11. Farrand, ed., *Records of the Federal Convention of 1787*, 2:33.
12. Jefferson to A. Donald, February 7, 1788, quoted in Stein, *The Third-Term Tradition*, 33.
13. Jefferson to Thomas Weaver Jr., quoted in Stein, *The Third-Term Tradition*, 37.
14. Stein, *The Third-Term Tradition*, 78.
15. Ibid., 145.
16. Ibid., 161, 163–64.
17. Ibid., 185.
18. Ibid., 186.

19. Ibid., 199.
20. Ibid., 204.
21. Rowe, oral history interview, September 30, 1969, Harry S. Truman Library.
22. Rowe memorandum to Watson, October 23, 1939, James Rowe Papers, Box 24, FDRL.
23. Ickes, *Secret Diary*, 153–54.
24. Rosenman, *Working with Roosevelt*, 192–93.
25. Ickes, *Secret Diary*, 158.
26. Farley, *Jim Farley's Story*, 225–26.
27. Krock, *Memoirs*, 199.
28. Ickes, *Secret Diary*, 154–55.
29. Ketchum, *The Borrowed Years*, 407.

Chapter 7
1. Shirer, *Berlin Diary*, 323–24.
2. Churchill, *The Gathering Storm*, 667.
3. Ibid., 15–26; Freidel, *Franklin D. Roosevelt*, 331.
4. Meacham, *Franklin and Winston*, 48–49.
5. Davis, *FDR: Into the Storm*, 546–47.
6. Ibid., 547–48.
7. Meacham, *Franklin and Winston*, 54–55.
8. Burns, *The Lion and the Fox*, 419.
9. PPA, 1940, 202, FDRL (emphasis added).
10. Shirer, *Berlin Diary*, 343–44.
11. Sherwood, *Roosevelt and Hopkins*, 153.
12. Ibid.
13. Ibid., 165–66.
14. Ibid., 166.
15. Rosenman, *Working with Roosevelt*, 195–98.
16. Davis, *FDR: Into the Storm*, 552–53.
17. Meacham, *Franklin and Winston*, 56.
18. Lukacs, *Five Days in London*, 109, 149.
19. Quoted in Meacham, *Franklin and Winston*, 58.
20. PPA, 1940, 265, FDRL.
21. Roosevelt, *This I Remember*, 211.
22. *New York Times*, June 11, 1940.
23. CWP, 2:287–88.
24. PPA, 1940, FDRL, 166–67.
25. Meacham, *Franklin and Winston*, 51.
26. Kennedy, *Freedom from Fear*, 440.
27. CWP, 2:368.
28. Sherwood, *Roosevelt and Hopkins*, 149.
29. Leuchtenburg, *The FDR Years*, 8.
30. W. A. White to FDR, June 10, 1940, PPF 1196, FDRL.
31. Langer and Gleason, *The Challenge to Isolation*, 569.

32. Kennedy, *Freedom from Fear*, 448.
33. Ibid., 453–54.
34. Ickes, *Secret Diary*, 199–200.
35. Davis, *FDR: Into the Storm*, 563–65; a full description of the meeting is in Press Conference File, 1940, FDRL.

Chapter 8
1. Sherwood, *Roosevelt and Hopkins*, 172–73.
2. Ickes, *Secret Diary*, 206–7.
3. Hopkins to Early, June 7, 1940, Stephen Early Papers, Box 24, FDRL.
4. Roosevelt, *This I Remember*, 167–68, 172.
5. Ickes, *Secret Diary*, 172.
6. Ibid., 201.
7. *New York Times*, June 30, 1940.
8. Ibid., April 14, 1940; May 5, 1940.
9. Ickes, *Secret Diary*, 201.
10. *New York Times*, March 1, 1940.
11. Neal, *Dark Horse*, 57–59.
12. Ibid., 59–61.
13. Peters, *Five Days in Philadelphia*, 21.
14. *New York Times*, January 7, 1940; February 11, 1940.
15. *New York Times*, May 8, 1940.
16. Peters, *Five Days in Philadelphia*, 25–28.
17. Ibid., 30–31.
18. Ibid., 32.
19. Lilienthal, *Journals*, 1:46–47; Neal, *Dark Horse*, 30–31.
20. Peters, *Five Days in Philadelphia*, 33–34.
21. Neal, *Dark Horse*, 48.
22. Davenport, *Too Strong for Fantasy*, 262.
23. Willkie, "We the People."
24. Peters, *Five Days in Philadelphia*, 39.
25. Ketchum, *The Borrowed Years*, 418.
26. Neal, *Dark Horse*, 70.
27. Ketchum, *The Borrowed Years*, 416.
28. *New York Times*, May 8, 1940; May 31, 1940.
29. Peters, *Five Days in Philadelphia*, 21.
30. *New York Times*, June 12, 1940; Peters, *Five Days in Philadelphia*, 49–50.
31. Ickes, *Secret Diary*, 179–80.
32. Davis, *FDR: Into the Storm*, 572–73.
33. Ibid., 574–75.
34. *New York Times*, June 22, 1940.
35. Krock, *Memoirs*, 193–94.
36. Peters, *Five Days in Philadelphia*, 57–76.
37. Neal, *Dark Horse*, 89.
38. Peters, *Five Days in Philadelphia*, 84.
39. Ibid., 91–92.

40. Ketchum, *The Borrowed Years*, 432–33.
41. Ibid., 93–96.
42. *New York Herald Tribune,* June 27, 1940.
43. Peters, *Five Days in Philadelphia*, 98–113.
44. Ketchum, *The Borrowed Years*, 440.

Chapter 9
1. Beschloss, *Presidential Courage*, 172.
2. *New York Times,* July 12, 1940.
3. Ickes, *Secret Diary*, 223–24.
4. Sherwood, *Roosevelt and Hopkins*, 174.
5. Rowe memoranda to Missy LeHand, July 3, 1940, and July 12, 1940, James Rowe Papers, Box 24, FDRL.
6. Sherwood, *Roosevelt and Hopkins*, 377; Goodwin, *No Ordinary Time*, 108.
7. Bullitt, ed., *For the President*, 289–99.
8. Lilienthal, *Journals*, 46.
9. Farley, *Jim Farley's Story*, 254–55.
10. Hull, *Memoirs*, 1:856–57.
11. Roosevelt, *This I Remember*, 212.
12. Roosevelt, *My Parents*, 162–63.
13. Rosenman, *Working with Roosevelt*, 200–203.
14. Ibid., 203.
15. Leuchtenburg, *The FDR Years*, 8.
16. Ketchum, *The Borrowed Years*, 399–400.
17. Dallek, *Franklin D. Roosevelt and American Foreign Policy*, vii.
18. Hull, *Memoirs*, 858.
19. Ibid., 858–59.
20. Ickes, *Secret Diary*, 235–36.
21. Dallek, *Franklin D. Roosevelt and American Foreign Policy*, vii.
22. Farley memorandum, July 1940 Hyde Park Conference, Ernest Cuneo Papers, Series: Roosevelt and Farley, FDRL.
23. Farley, *Jim Farley's Story*, 251.
24. Farley memorandum, July 1940 Hyde Park Conference.
25. Rosenman, *Working with Roosevelt*, 204–5.
26. Ibid., 206.
27. Ickes, *Secret Diary*, 238.
28. Rosenman, *Working with Roosevelt*, 207.
29. Ibid., 207–8.
30. White House Usher's Log, July 11, 1940, FDRL.
31. Frankfurter to FDR, May 18, 1938, in Freedman, ed., *Roosevelt and Frankfurter*, 457.
32. Freedman, ed., *Roosevelt and Frankfurter*, 531–35. The Frankfurter and MacLeish memoranda are reprinted in their entirety in the appendix.
33. Rosenman, *Working with Roosevelt*, 203.
34. *Washington Star,* July 12, 1940.
35. Rosenman, *Working with Roosevelt*, 208–9.

Chapter 10

1. Rosenman, *Working with Roosevelt*, 205–6.
2. Hull, *Memoirs*, 860–61.
3. Perkins, *The Roosevelt I Knew*, 129–30.
4. Douglas to FDR, July 2, 1940, Hopkins Confidential Political File, FDRL.
5. Feldman, *Scorpions*, 188–93.
6. James Farley, memorandum, Chicago, July 11, 1940, Ernest Cuneo Papers, Series: Roosevelt and Farley, FDRL.
7. James Farley, memorandum, Chicago, July 13, Ernest Cuneo Papers, Series: Roosevelt and Farley, FDRL.
8. Ibid.
9. Ickes, *Secret Diary*, 240–43.
10. Sherwood, *Roosevelt and Hopkins*, 177; Ickes, *Secret Diary*, 243.
11. Robertson, *Sly and Able*, 291–94.
12. Lash, *Eleanor and Franklin*, 619; Roosevelt, *This I Remember*, 218.
13. *Chicago Tribune*, July 13, 1940; *Washington Star*, July 14, 1940.
14. Rosenman, *Working with Roosevelt*, 211–10.
15. Waller, *Wild Bill Donovan*, 14, 44, 55–56.

Chapter 11

1. *Washington Star*, July 14, 1940.
2. Farley memorandum, Chicago, July 15, 1940, Ernest Cuneo Papers, Series: Roosevelt and Farley, FDRL; *Chicago Tribune*, July 15, 1940.
3. *Chicago Tribune*, July 15, 1940.
4. Ickes, *Secret Diary*, 243.
5. Rosenman, *Working with Roosevelt*, 211.
6. Ickes, *Secret Diary*, 243–46.
7. Rosenman, *Working with Roosevelt*, 211–12; Robertson, *Sly and Able*, 292.
8. Ickes, *Secret Diary*, 247–50; Ickes to FDR, July 16, 1940, PSF, Document 24, FDRL.
9. Perkins, Frances, *The Roosevelt I Knew*, 130–33.
10. Ibid., 133.
11. Roosevelt, *This I Remember*, 213–14.
12. Ibid., 214.
13. Farley, *Jim Farley's Story*, 278–79; Farley memorandum, Chicago, July 16, 1940, Ernest Cuneo Papers, Series: Roosevelt and Farley, FDRL.
14. Farley, *Jim Farley's Story*, 279–80.
15. Ibid., 280.
16. Rosenman, *Working with Roosevelt*, 212.
17. Farley, *Jim Farley's Story*, 280–81; Davis, *FDR: Into the Storm*, 596–97.
18. Farley, *Jim Farley's Story*; Ketchum, *The Borrowed Years*, 464.
19. *Chicago Tribune*, July 17, 1940.
20. *Washington Star*, July 17, 1940.
21. Roosevelt, *This I Remember*, 214–15.
22. Farley, *Jim Farley's Story*, 283.

23. Ickes, *Secret Diary*, 254–55.
24. Farley, *Jim Farley's Story*, 284–87.
25. Ickes, *Secret Diary*, 255.
26. *Washington Star*, July 18, 1940.

Chapter 12

1. Rosenman, *Working with Roosevelt*, 212–13.
2. Culver and Hyde, *American Dreamer*, 218.
3. Rosenman, *Working with Roosevelt*, 213.
4. Farley, memorandum, Chicago, July 18, 1940, Ernest Cuneo Papers, Series: Roosevelt and Farley, FDRL; Rosenman, *Working with Roosevelt*, 213.
5. Ickes, *Secret Diary*, 257.
6. Rosenman, *Working with Roosevelt*, 213–14.
7. Ibid., 214–15.
8. Roosevelt, *This I Remember*, 215–17; Farley memorandum, Chicago, July 18, 1940; Farley, *Jim Farley's Story*, 299–300.
9. Roosevelt, *This I Remember*, 217.
10. Lash, *Eleanor and Franklin*, 623.
11. New York *Daily News*, July 19, 1940.
12. Rosenman, *Working with Roosevelt*, 215.
13. Robertson, *Sly and Able*, 293–94.
14. Rosenman, *Working with Roosevelt*, 215.
15. Ibid.
16. Sherwood, *Roosevelt and Hopkins*, 179.
17. Culver and Hyde, *American Dreamer*, 221.
18. Roosevelt, *This I Remember*, 217–18.
19. Ickes, *Secret Diary*, 262.
20. Rosenman, *Working with Roosevelt*, 215.
21. Ibid.
22. Ibid., 216–17.
23. Ibid., 217.
24. Ibid., 218.
25. Davis, *FDR: Into the Storm*, 601.
26. Rosenman, *Working with Roosevelt*, 36.
27. Farley, memorandum, Chicago, July 18, 1940.
28. *Chicago Tribune*, July 19, 1940.
29. Roosevelt, *Autobiography*, 218; Goodwin, *No Ordinary Time*, 135.
30. Rosenman, *Working with Roosevelt*, 218–19.
31. *Washington Star*, July 19, 1940.
32. Rosenman, *Working with Roosevelt*, 219–21.
33. *Chicago Tribune*, July 20, 1940.
34. *Washington Star*, July 19, 1940.
35. Roosevelt, *This I Remember*, 3–5.
36. *Washington Post*, July 19, 1940.

37. FDR to George W. Norris, July 21, 1940, in *F.D.R.: His Personal Letters 1928–1945*, 2:1046–7.
38. FDR's biographers are divided as to how serious Roosevelt was in his threat to decline the nomination. Frank Freidel (*Franklin D. Roosevelt*, 346) writes that he was simply "venting his feelings," while Jean Edward Smith (*FDR*, 462) argues that it is "clear" he would not have run for a third term if Wallace had lost.

Chapter 13

1. Waller, *Wild Bill Donovan*, 59–62; Shogan, *Hard Bargain*, 132–35.
2. Neal, *Dark Horse*, 130–32.
3. Davis, *FDR: Into the Storm*, 569.
4. Ibid., 568–71.
5. Neal, *Dark Horse*, 138–39.
6. Friedlander, *Prelude to Downfall*, 113; Davis, *FDR: Into the Storm*, 605–7.
7. Churchill, *Their Finest Hour*, 401–2; Freidel, *Franklin D. Roosevelt*, 351.
8. Churchill, *Their Finest Hour*, 402.
9. Beschloss, *Presidential Courage*, 176.
10. Shogan, *Hard Bargain*, 149–56, 160; Ketchum, *The Borrowed Years*, 477.
11. *New York Times*, August 19, 1940.
12. Dallek, *Franklin D. Roosevelt*, 244.
13. Ickes, *Secret Diary*, 283; Shogan, *Hard Bargain*, 162.
14. Ickes, *Secret Diary*, 292.
15. Shogan, *Hard Bargain*, 165–67.
16. FDR memorandum, 4:1050, FDRL.
17. Neal, *Dark Horse*, 139–40; Davis, *FDR: Into the Storm*, 608–9; Shogan, *Hard Bargain*, 167–69, 174; *Chicago Tribune*, August 6, 1940.
18. Davis, *FDR: Into the Storm*, 608–9.
19. Peters, *Five Days in Philadelphia*, 168; Shogan, *Hard Bargain*, 178.
20. Shogan, *Hard Bargain*, 187–89.
21. *New York Times*, August 11, 1940; Shogan, *Hard Bargain*, 178.
22. Chace, *Acheson*, 79.
23. *New York Times*, August 11, 1940; Shogan, *Hard Bargain*, 190–91.
24. Shogan, *Hard Bargain*, 218–19.
25. Ibid., 222.
26. Davis, *FDR: Into the Storm*, 610–11; Shogan, *Hard Bargain*, 224–25.
27. Peters, *Five Days in Philadelphia*, 167–70.
28. Shogan, *Hard Bargain*, 237–39.
29. *New York Times*, September 4, 1940; Shogan, *Hard Bargain*, 242–44.
30. Quoted in Davis, *FDR: Into the Storm*, 611.
31. Quoted in Dallek, *Franklin D. Roosevelt*, 247.
32. Tully, *F.D.R.: My Boss*, 244.
33. Chace, *Acheson*, 80.

Chapter 14

1. *New York Times*, August 4 and 25, September 6, 15, and 22, 1940.
2. Neal, *Dark Horse*, 149.

3. Ibid.
4. Ibid., 143, 147.
5. Ibid., 153.
6. Kennedy, *Freedom from Fear*, 455.
7. Ketchum, *The Borrowed Years*, 467.
8. Neal, *Dark Horse*, 155; Davis, *FDR: Into the Storm*, 612.
9. Flynn, *You're the Boss*, 168.
10. Neal, *Dark Horse*, 150.
11. *New York Times*, October 1, 1940.
12. Morgan, *FDR: A Biography*, 531–33.
13. Culver and Hyde, *American Dreamer*, 232–33.
14. Butow, "The FDR Tapes."
15. Butow, "The Story Behind the Tapes"; Davis, *FDR: Into the Storm*, 670n.
16. Small Collections: Roosevelt, Franklin D.: Transcript of White House Office Conversations, 1940, FDRL. Transcript also appears in Butow, "The FDR Tapes."
17. Duffy, *Lindbergh and Roosevelt*,154–55.
18. Small Collections: Roosevelt, Franklin D.: Transcript of White House Office Conversations, 1940. FDRL. Transcript also appears in Butow, "The FDR Tapes."
19. *New York Times*, October 6, 1940.
20. Quoted in Davis, *FDR: Into the Storm*, 614.
21. Neal, *Dark Horse*, 159–60.
22. Quoted in Freidel, *Franklin D. Roosevelt*, 354.
23. James Rowe Jr. to Hopkins, October 17, 1940, Hopkins Papers, FDRL.
24. Davis, *FDR: Into the Storm*, 615.
25. Burns, *Roosevelt: The Lion and the Fox*, 446.
26. Kennedy, *Freedom from Fear*, 462.
27. Eleanor to FDR, October 11, 1940, Box 16, Roosevelt Family Papers, FDRL.
28. Ickes to FDR, October 14, 1940, PSF, FDRL.
29. Ickes, *Secret Diary*, 351–52.
30. Ibid., 352.
31. Culver and Hyde, *American Dreamer*, 240–41.
32. Ibid., 241–42.

Chapter 15

1. Sherwood, *Roosevelt and Hopkins*, 186; Burns, *Roosevelt: The Lion and the Fox*, 447; Rosenman, *Working with Roosevelt*, 238.
2. Sherwood, *Roosevelt and Hopkins*, 186–87.
3. Kennedy, *Freedom from Fear*, 462.
4. Rosenman, *Working with Roosevelt*, 239–40.
5. Ibid.
6. Davis, *FDR: Into the Storm*, 619–20; Rosenman, *Working with Roosevelt*, 239–41.
7. Rosenman, *Working with Roosevelt*, 241–42.
8. Sherwood, *Roosevelt and Hopkins*, 187–88.
9. Perkins, *The Roosevelt I Knew*, 126–27; Dubofsky and Van Tine, *John L. Lewis*, 358–59; Davis, *FDR: Into the Storm*, 534, 618.

10. Beschloss, *Kennedy and Roosevelt*, 213.
11. Ibid.
12. Beschloss, *Kennedy and Roosevelt*, 214–15; Davis, *FDR: Into the Storm*, 618.
13. Beschloss, *Kennedy and Roosevelt*, 215–16.
14. Ibid., 217.
15. Ibid., 217–18.
16. Ibid., 219–20.
17. FDR to John Boettiger, March 3, 1941, John Boettiger Papers, Box 5, FDRL.
18. Beschloss, *Kennedy and Roosevelt*, 221. However, Joe Kennedy Jr. died in an airborne explosion over Europe in 1944.
19. Neal, *Dark Horse*, 164–65.
20. Sherwood, *Roosevelt and Hopkins*, 191.
21. Ibid.
22. Rosenman, *Working with Roosevelt*, 242; Freidel, *Franklin D. Roosevelt*, 355; Hastings, *Inferno*, 185.
23. Roosevelt, *My Parents*, 160–61.
24. Ketchum, *The Borrowed Years*, 512–14.
25. Ibid., 514–15; Sherwood, *Roosevelt and Hopkins*, 187.
26. Rosenman, *Working with Roosevelt*, 245–47.
27. Ibid., 247–48.
28. Sherwood, *Roosevelt and Hopkins*, 196; Burns, *Roosevelt: The Lion and the Fox*, 450.
29. Rosenman, *Working with Roosevelt*, 251–53.
30. Morgan, *FDR: A Biography*, 539; Freidel, *Franklin D. Roosevelt*, 355.
31. PPA 1940, 554–57, FDRL; Sherwood, *Roosevelt and Hopkins*, 197.
32. Freidel, *Franklin D. Roosevelt*, 355–56.
33. Carl Sandburg to FDR, November 9, 1940 (with the attached speech), PPF 4509, FDRL.
34. Lash, *Eleanor and Franklin*, 631.
35. Ibid., 631–32.
36. Slocum, *Reilly of the White House*, 66.
37. Davis, *FDR: Into the Storm*, 623.
38. Interview with the author, June 19, 2012.
39. Neal, *Dark Horse*, 174.
40. Smith, *FDR*, 23.
41. Davis, *FDR: Into the Storm*, 625; Burns, *Roosevelt: The Soldier of Freedom*, 4.
42. Neal, *Dark Horse*, 174–75; Moscow, *Roosevelt and Wilkie*, 203.

Epilogue

1. Churchill, *Their Finest Hour*, 553.
2. Ibid.
3. Sherwood, *Roosevelt and Hopkins*, 221; Kennedy, *Freedom from Fear*, 465.
4. Meacham, *Franklin and Winston*, 77.
5. Churchill, *Their Finest Hour*, 567.
6. Sherwood, *Roosevelt and Hopkins*, 224–25.
7. Dallek, *Franklin D. Roosevelt*, 255.

8. PPA, 1940, 604–8, FDRL.
9. Rosenman, *Working with Roosevelt*, 260; Burns, *Roosevelt*, 29 (emphasis added).
10. Rosenman, *Working with Roosevelt*, 262–63.
11. Ibid., 263–64.
12. Kennedy, *Freedom from Fear*, 470.
13. Moscow, *Roosevelt and Willkie*, 204.
14. Neal, *Dark Horse*, 178–80.
15. Ibid., 187; Kennedy, *Freedom from Fear*, 472–73.
16. Neal, *Dark Horse*, 187–88.
17. Ibid.
18. Martin, *My First Fifty Years in Politics*, 128–29.
19. Tully, *F.D.R., My Boss*, 58; Sherwood, *Roosevelt and Hopkins*, 2–3.
20. Neal, *Dark Horse*, 192; Beschloss, *Presidential Courage*, 194.
21. FDR to John Boettiger, March 3, 1941, John Boettiger Papers, Box 5, FDRL.
22. Burns, *Roosevelt*, 45–46; Berg, *Lindbergh*, 439–40.
23. Neal, *Dark Horse*, 204–5.
24. Kennedy, *Freedom from Fear*, 472.
25. Neal, *Dark Horse*, 314.
26. Churchill, *Their Finest Hour*, 569.
27. Sherwood, *Roosevelt and Hopkins*, 266.
28. Quoted in Beschloss, *Presidential Courage*, 190.
29. Ketchum, *The Borrowed Years*, 468.

SOURCES AND SELECTED BIBLIOGRAPHY

FDRL   Franklin D. Roosevelt Library, Hyde Park, New York
PPA   Public Papers and Addresses of Franklin D. Roosevelt
PPF   President's Personal File
PSF   President's Secretary's File
PL   Personal Letters (of Franklin Roosevelt)
LOC   Library of Congress

Alsop, Joseph, and Robert Kintner. *American White Paper: The Story of American Diplomacy and the Second World War*. New York: Simon and Schuster, 1940.

Baker, Ray Stannard, and W. E. Dodd, eds. *Papers of Woodrow Wilson*. New York: Harper and Brothers, 1925–27.

Berg, Scott A. *Lindbergh*. New York: Putnam, 1998.

Berle, Beatrice Bishop, and Travis Beale Jacobs, eds. *Navigating the Rapids, 1918–1971: From the Papers of Adolf A. Berle*. New York: Harcourt Brace Jovanovich, 1973.

Beschloss, Michael. *Kennedy and Roosevelt: The Uneasy Alliance*. New York: Norton, 1980.

————. *Presidential Courage: Brave Leaders and How They Changed America, 1789–1989*. New York: Simon and Schuster 2007.

Blum, John Morton. *From the Morgenthau Diaries*, vol. 2, *Years of Urgency: 1938–1941*. Boston: Houghton Mifflin, 1965.

Brands, H. W. *Traitor to His Class: The Privileged Life and Radical Presidency of Franklin Delano Roosevelt*. New York: Doubleday, 2008.

Brayman, Harold. *From Grover Cleveland to Gerald Ford . . . The President Speaks Off the Record—Historic Evenings with America's Leaders, the Press, and Other Men of Power, at Washington's Exclusive Gridiron Club*. Princeton, NJ: Dow Jones Books, 1976.

Brinkley, Alan. *Franklin Delano Roosevelt*. New York: Oxford University Press, 2010.

Bullitt, Orville H., ed. *For the President: Personal and Secret Correspondence Between Franklin D. Roosevelt and William C. Bullitt*. Boston: Houghton Mifflin, 1972.

Burns, James MacGregor. *Roosevelt: The Lion and the Fox*. New York: Harcourt Brace and World, 1956.

————. *Roosevelt: The Soldier of Freedom*. New York: Harcourt Brace Jovanovich, 1970.

Butow, R. J. C. "The FDR Tapes—Secret Recordings Made in the Oval Office of the President in the Autumn of 1940." *American Heritage*, February/March 1982.

Chace, James. *Acheson: The Secretary of State Who Created the American World*. New York: Simon and Schuster, 1998.

Churchill, Winston S. *Blood, Sweat and Tears*. New York: Putnam's, 1941.

————. *The Gathering Storm*. Boston: Houghton Mifflin, 1948.

————. *Their Finest Hour*. Boston: Houghton Mifflin, 1949.

Culver, John C., and John Hyde. *American Dreamer: A Life of Henry Wallace*. New York: W. W. Norton, 2000.

Cuneo, Ernest. *Autobiography*. Unpublished; property of Jonathan Cuneo.

Dallek, Robert. *Franklin D. Roosevelt and American Foreign Policy, 1932–1945*. New York: Oxford University Press, 1981.

Davenport, Marcia. *Too Strong for Fantasy*. New York: Scribner's, 1967.

Davis, Kenneth S. *FDR: Into the Storm, 1937–1940*. New York: Random House, 1993.

Donahoe, Bernard F. *Private Plans and Public Dangers: The Story of FDR's Third Nomination*. Notre Dame, IN: University of Notre Dame Press, 1965.

Dubofsky, Melvyn, and Warren Van Tine. *John L. Lewis: A Biography*. New York: Quadrangle/New York Times, 1977.

Duffy, James P. *Lindbergh and Roosevelt: The Rivalry That Divided America*. Washington, DC: Regnery, 2010.

Edgerton, David. *Britain's War Machine: Weapons, Resources and Experts in the Second World War*. New York: Oxford University Press, 2011.

Isaacson, Walter, ed. *Profiles in Leadership: Historians on the Elusive Quality of Greatness*. New York: W. W. Norton, 2010.

Farley, James A. *Jim Farley's Story: The Roosevelt Years*. New York: McGraw-Hill, 1948.

Farrand, Max, ed. *Records of the Federal Convention of 1787*. New Haven, CT: Yale University Press, 1937.

Feldman, Noah. *Scorpions: The Battles and Triumphs of FDR's Great Supreme Court Justices*. New York: Twelve, 2010.

Flynn, Edward J. *You're the Boss*. New York: Viking, 1947.

Frankfurter, Felix. *From the Diaries of Felix Frankfurter*. Ed. Joseph P. Lash. New York: W. W. Norton, 1975.

Freedman, Max, ed. *Roosevelt and Frankfurter: Their Correspondence, 1928–1945*. Boston: Little, Brown, 1967.

Freidel, Frank. *Franklin D. Roosevelt: A Rendezvous with Destiny*. New York: Back Bay Books, 1990.

Friederlander, Saul. *Prelude to Downfall: Hitler and the United States, 1939–1941*. New York: Knopf, 1967.

Gallup, George, and Claude Robinson. "American Institute of Public Opinion—Surveys, 1935–38." *Public Opinion Quarterly*, 2, 1938.

Goodwin, Doris Kearns. *No Ordinary Time*. New York: Simon and Schuster, 1994.

Gugin, Linda C., and James St. Clair, eds. *The Governors of Indiana*. Indianapolis, IN: Indiana Historical Society, 2006.

Halberstam, David. *The Powers That Be*. New York: Knopf, 1979.

Hasting, Max. *Inferno: The World at War, 1939–45*. New York: Knopf, 2011.

Hodgson, Godfrey. *The Colonel: The Life and Wars of Henry Stimson, 1867–1950*. New York: Alfred A, Knopf, 1990.

Hull, Cordell. *The Memoirs of Cordell Hull*. New York: Macmillan, 1948.

Ickes, Harold L. *The Secret Diary of Harold Ickes*, vol. 3, *The Lowering Clouds, 1939–1941*. New York: Simon and Schuster, 1955.

Jackson, Robert H. *That Man: An Insider's Portrait of Franklin D. Roosevelt*. New York: Oxford University Press, 2003.

Janeway, Eliot. *The Struggle for Survival*. New York: Weybright and Talley, 1951.

Janeway, Michael. *The Fall of the House of Roosevelt: Brokers of Ideas and Power from FDR to LBJ*. New York: Columbia University Press, 2004.

Jenkins, Roy. *Franklin Delano Roosevelt*. New York: Times Books, 2003.

Jonas, Manfred. *Isolationism in America, 1935–1941*. Chicago: Imprint Publications, 1990.

Kennedy, David M. *Freedom from Fear: The American People in Depression and War, 1929–1945*. New York: Oxford University Press, 1999.

Ketchum, Richard M. *The Borrowed Years, 1938–1941: America on the Way to War*. New York: Random House, 1989.

Krock, Arthur. *Memoirs: Sixty Years on the Firing Line*. New York: Funk and Wagnalls, 1968.

Langer, William L., and S. Everett Gleason. *The Challenge to Isolation: The World Crisis of 1937–1940 and American Foreign Policy*. Gloucester, MA: Peter Smith, 1952.

———. *The Undeclared War, 1940–1941*. New York: Harper, 1953.

Lash, Joseph P. *Eleanor and Franklin: The Story of Their Relationship Based on Eleanor Roosevelt's Private Papers*. New York: Norton, 1971.

Leuchtenburg, William E. *The FDR Years: On Roosevelt and His Legacy*. New York: Columbia University Press 1995.

———, ed. *Franklin D. Roosevelt: A Profile*. New York: Hill and Wang, 1967.

———. *In the Shadow of FDR: From Harry Truman to Ronald Reagan*. Ithaca, NY: Cornell University Press, 1983.

Levy, Herbert. *Henry Morgenthau, Jr.: The Remarkable Life of FDR's Secretary of the Treasury*. New York: Skyhorse, 2010.

Lilienthal, David. *The Journals of David E. Lilienthal: The TVA Years, 1939–1945*. New York: Harper and Row, 1964.

Lindbergh, Charles A. *The Wartime Journals of Charles A. Lindbergh*. New York: Harcourt Brace Jovanovich, 1970.

Lukacs, John. *Five Days in London: May 1940*. New Haven, CT: Yale University Press, 1999.

Martin, Joseph. *My First Fifty Years in Politics*. New York: McGraw-Hill, 1960.

Meacham, Jon. *Franklin and Winston: An Intimate Portrait of an Epic Friendship*. New York: Random House, 2003.

Morgan, Ted. *FDR: A Biography*. New York: Simon and Schuster, 1985.

Moscow, Warren. *Roosevelt and Willkie*. Englewood, NJ: Prentice Hall, 1968.

Neal, Steve. *Dark Horse: A Biography of Wendell Willkie*. New York: Doubleday, 1984.

Nixon, Edgar B., ed. *Franklin D. Roosevelt and Foreign Affairs: January 1933–January 1937*. Cambridge, MA: Belknap Press, 1969.

Olson, Lynne. *Citizens of London: The Americans Who Stood with Britain in Its Darkest, Finest Hour*. New York: Random House, 2010.

——. *Those Angry Days: Roosevelt, Lindbergh and America's Fight over World War II, 1939–1941*. New York: Random House, 2013.

Perkins, Frances. *The Roosevelt I Knew*. New York: Viking, 1946.

Peters, Charles. *Five Days in Philadelphia: The Amazing "We Want Willkie!" Convention of 1940 and How It Freed FDR to Save the Western World*. New York: Public Affairs, 2005.

Pogue, Forrest C. *George C. Marshall: Education of a General, 1880–1939*, vol. 2, *Ordeal and Hope, 1939–1942*. New York: Viking, 1963.

Reynolds, David. *The Creation of the Anglo-American Alliance, 1937–41: A Study in Competitive Co-operation*. Chapel Hill: University of North Carolina Press, 1982.

Richardson, James D., ed. *A Compilation of the Messages and Papers of the President, 1789–1897*. Washington, DC: Bureau of National Literature, 1889.

Robertson, David. *Sly and Able: A Political Biography of James F. Byrnes*. New York: Norton, 1994.

Roll, David L. *The Hopkins Touch: Harry Hopkins and the Forging of the Alliance to Defeat Hitler*. New York: Oxford University Press, 2013.

Roosevelt, Eleanor. *The Autobiography of Eleanor Roosevelt*. Boston: Harper, 1961.

——. *This I Remember*. New York: Harper, 1949.

Roosevelt, Elliott, ed. *F.D.R.: His Personal Letters, 1928–1945*, vol. 2. New York: Duell, Sloan and Pearce, 1950.

Roosevelt, James. *Affectionately, F.D.R.: A Son's Story of a Courageous Man*. With Sidney Shalett. London: George G. Harrap, 1960.

——. *My Parents: A Differing View*. With Bill Libby. Chicago: Playboy Press, 1976.

Rosenman, Samuel I. *Working with Roosevelt*. New York: Harper and Brothers, 1952.

Schewe, Donald B., ed. *Franklin D. Roosevelt and Foreign Affairs, January 1937–August 1939*. New York: Garland, 1979.

Schlesinger, Arthur Jr. *The Coming of the New Deal*. Boston: Houghton Mifflin, 1959.

——. "Introduction to the FDR Tapes." *American Heritage*, February/March 1982.

Scroop, David. *Mr. Democrat: Jim Farley, the New Deal, and the Making of Modern American Politics*. Ann Arbor: University of Michigan Press, 2009.

Sherwood, Robert E. *Roosevelt and Hopkins: An Intimate History*. New York: Harper and Brothers, 1948.

Shesol, Jeff. *Supreme Power: Franklin Roosevelt vs. the Supreme Court*. New York: W. W. Norton, 2010.

Shirer, William. *Berlin Diary: The Journal of a Foreign Correspondent, 1934–1941*. New York: Knopf, 1941.

——. *Rise and Fall of the Third Reich*. New York: Simon and Schuster, 1960.

Shogan, Robert. *Hard Bargain: How FDR Twisted Churchill's Arm, Evaded the Law, and Changed the Role of the Presidency*. New York: Scribner, 1995.

Slocum, William J. *Reilly of the White House*. New York: Simon and Schuster, 1941.

Smith, Jean Edward. *FDR*. New York: Random House, 2007.

Stein, Charles W. *The Third Term Tradition: Its Rise and Collapse in American Politics*. New York: Columbia University Press, 1943.

Stimson, Henry L., and McGeorge Bundy. *On Active Service in Peace and War*. New York: Harper and Brothers, 1947.

Timons, Bascom M. *Garner of Texas: A Personal History*. New York: Harper and Brothers, 1948.

Tugwell, Rexford G. *The Art of Politics*. Garden City, NY: Doubleday, 1958.

———. *The Democratic Roosevelt: A Biography of Franklin D. Roosevelt*. Garden City, NY: Doubleday, 1957.

———. *In Search of Roosevelt*. Cambridge, MA: Harvard University Press, 1972.

Tully, Grace. *F.D.R., My Boss*. New York: Charles Scribner's Sons, 1949.

Waller, Douglas. *Wild Bill Donovan: The Spymaster Who Created the OSS and Modern American Espionage*. New York: Free Press, 2011.

Ward, Geoffrey C. *Before the Trumpet: Young Franklin Roosevelt, 1882–1905*. New York: Perennial Library, 1986.

———. *A First Class Temperament: The Emergence of Franklin Roosevelt*. New York: Harper and Row, 1989.

Weintraub, Stanley. *Final Victory: FDR's Extraordinary World War II Presidential Campaign*. Boston: Da Capo, 2012.

Welles, Sumner. *The Time for Decision*. New York: Harper, 1944.

White, William Allen. *The Autobiography of William Allen White*. New York: Macmillan, 1946.

Willkie, Wendell. "We the People." *Fortune*, May 1940.

Woolner, David B., and Richard G. Kurial, eds. *FDR, the Vatican, and the Roman Catholic Church in America, 1933–1945*. New York: Palgrave Macmillan, 2003.

INDEX